Banff, Jasper & Glacier

NATIONAL PARKS

D0199794

Jasper National Park
p130

Banff National Park
p46

Around Banff National Park
p114

Waterton Lakes National Park
p216

Glacier National Park
p172

Around Glacier National Park
p206

Gregor Clark, Michael Grosberg, Craig McLachlan

Contents

BANFF SUMMER ARTS
FESTIVAL (P25)

PIKA (P249), JASPER
NATIONAL PARK

Contents

UNDERSTAND

SURVIVAL GUIDE

SPIRIT ISLAND, MALIGNE LAKE (P159)

SPECIAL FEATURES

Welcome to Banff, Jasper & Glacier

Sit atop a mountain, hike through the forest, feel the spray of a waterfall: Banff, Jasper and Glacier offer outdoor experiences at their simplest and best.

Historical Heritage

While other countries protect ancient ruins and medieval castles, the Rocky Mountains offer up Banff, Jasper and Glacier, legendary natural wonders replete with crenelated peaks, majestic meadows and scenery-shaping glaciers that together make up an important part of North America's historical jigsaw. Of the hundreds of national parks scattered around the world today, Banff, created in 1885, is the third oldest. Associated with the development of America's cross-continental railroads, which lured wealthy visitors, these protected areas practically invented modern tourism, and their hold on the popular imagination has not diminished.

Wilderness Walks

There are bucketloads of things to do in Banff, Jasper and Glacier, from an easy round of golf to heart-in-your-mouth whitewater rafting. But arguably the most rewarding activity in the parks is the simplest – hiking. Walking along a well-maintained trail amid classic mountain splendor is one of life's great spiritual diversions. You won't be the first convert: hiking, by default, was the primary means of transportation for the indigenous peoples of the Rockies and the early European explorers who followed.

Protected Environments

Acting as a litmus test for the tricky balance between ecological integrity and a rip-roaring visitor experience, the Rocky Mountain national parks have long played a key role in safeguarding North America's natural environment. Glacier protects an ecosystem largely free from human meddling. Banff exhibits some of the finest wildlife-watching in North America, and Jasper is a dark-sky preserve devoid of unnecessary light pollution; underneath the myriad adventure opportunities lies savvy park management paving the way to a greener future.

Outdoor Accessibility

One of the advantages of the Rocky Mountain parks is their accessibility. Banff, in particular, embodies the fragile, sometimes controversial, juxtaposition between the tamed and the untamed. While some frown at the commercialization of Banff Ave, the home comforts have their merits. Outfitters and guides add safety to potentially complicated trip planning, while speedy gondolas allow people who might otherwise not have the opportunity to get up above the timberline to experience flower-carpeted alpine meadows and wild animals roaming through their natural habitats.

Why I Love Banff, Jasper & Glacier

By Gregor Clark, Writer

I first visited Banff and Jasper in a May blizzard, on an unplanned detour while hitchhiking from California to France at age 20 (really!). Totally smitten, I made a point of visiting Glacier a year later, and I've been returning regularly ever since. No place on earth awes me like the northern Rockies' vast unbroken sweeps of evergreen forest, the snow-covered stratification of the Icefields Pkwy's chiseled crags, the unparalleled thrill of crossing paths with a perfectly camouflaged bighorn in Waterton's high country or watching a grizzly from afar on the Mt Assiniboine trail. Primeval nature at its finest.

For more about our writers, see p288

Above: Plain of Six Glaciers hike (p60), Banff National Park

Banff, Jasper & Glacier National Parks

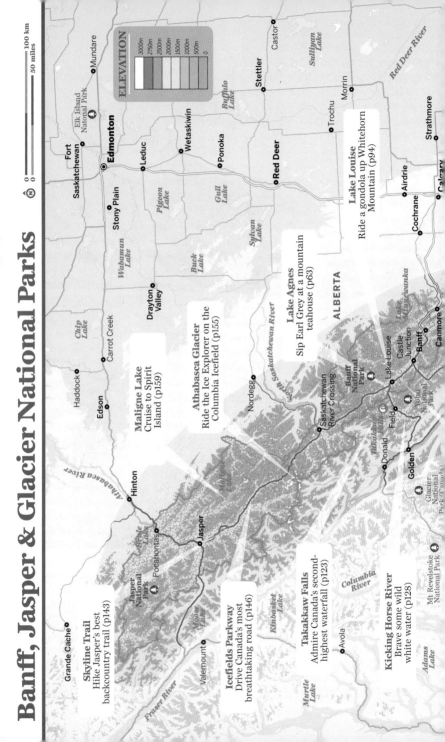

ELEVATION

3000m
2750m
2500m
2000m
1500m
1000m
500m
0

50 miles
100 km

Skyline Trail
Hike Jasper's best backcountry trail (p143)

Maligne Lake
Cruise to Spirit Island (p159)

Athabasca Glacier
Ride the Ice Explorer on the Columbia Icefield (p155)

Lake Agnes
Sip Earl Grey at a mountain teahouse (p63)

Lake Louise
Ride a gondola up Whitehorn Mountain (p94)

Icefields Parkway
Drive Canada's most breathtaking road (p146)

Takakkaw Falls
Admire Canada's second-highest waterfall (p123)

Kicking Horse River
Brave some wild white water (p128)

ALBERTA

Canmore Nordic Centre
Enjoy world-class skiing and mountain biking (p115)

Mt Assiniboine
Hike to the Canadian Matterhorn (p69)

Crypt Lake Trail
Climb Waterton's adventurous cliffside trail (p219)

Moraine Lake
Paddle across an azure lake (p94)

Radium Hot Springs
Soak in a volcanic spring (p127)

Going-to-the-Sun Road
Experience Glacier's classic road trip (p188)

Two Medicine Valley
Spot bears in a mountain valley (p194)

BRITISH COLUMBIA

ALBERTA

MONTANA

IDAHO

WASHINGTON

CANADA

USA

Glacier National Park

Waterton Lakes National Park

Kootenay National Park

▲ Mt Assiniboine (3618m)

McGregor Lake
Flathead Lake
Columbia Lake
Upper Arrow Lake
Lower Arrow Lake
Kootenay Lake
Mabel Lake
Shuswap Lake
Okanagan Lake
Priest Lake
Pend Oreille Lake
Lake Roosevelt

Kootenay River

Bassano
Taber
Lethbridge
Vulcan
Nanton
Claresholm
Cardston
Browning
St Mary
Babb
Essex
Fort Macleod
Pincher Creek
Waterton Townsite
Whitefish
Kallspell
Fernie
Sparwood
Elko
Fort Steele
Cranbrook
Crawford Bay
Yahk
Sandpoint
Brisco
Radium Hot Springs
Fairmont Hot Springs
Canal Flats
Balfour
Nelson
Castlegar
Rossland
Creston
Newport
Colville
Greenwood
Penticton
Kelowna
Oyama
Vernon
Cherryville
Nakusp
Sicamous
Salmon Arm
Two Medicine Valley

Banff, Jasper & Glacier's
Top 20

1

Icefields Parkway

1 There are amazing road trips, and then there's the Icefields Pkwy (p74, p146). This iconic highway unfurls for 230km (143 miles) between Lake Louise and Jasper, and takes in some of the most mind-blowing mountain panoramas anywhere on the Continental Divide. En route you'll pass cerulean lakes, crashing cascades, gleaming glaciers and the largest area of unbroken ice anywhere in North America, the mighty Columbia Icefield. It's a true trip of a lifetime, so fuel up, sit back, and let one of the world's great scenery shows unfold.

Going-to-the-Sun Road

2 The start is inauspicious enough: a signposted turning off US 2, the blink-and-you'll-miss-it village of West Glacier, followed by a serendipitous plunge into dense forest around Apgar. It's only on the shores of Lake McDonald (pictured) that the views start getting better and better, until you feel as if the Going-to-the-Sun Rd (p188) really is – well – going to the sun. The highpoint is Logan Pass on the Continental Divide. After that it's all downhill to St Mary, amid more jaw-dropping scenery and potent lessons in glacial erosion.

TRIPHOTOS / SHUTTERSTOCK ©

DEAN FIKAR / SHUTTERSTOCK ©

Afternoon Tea at Lake Agnes

3 After slogging all day on the mountain trails around Lake Louise, what could be more civilized than a cup of Earl Grey and a slice of homemade cake? The historic teahouse (p63) at Lake Agnes has been serving refreshments to weary walkers since 1901 when it was built by the Canadian Pacific Railway, and it remains an ideal stop-off for parched hikers tackling the trail to the Big Beehive. For an altogether posher experience, you can enjoy the C$56 tea spread in the Chateau Lake Louise.

Skyline Trail

4 Cross-park views of Jasper are par for the course on the widely celebrated Skyline Trail (p143). It could have had any number of descriptive names conferred upon it – the Homeric path, the celestial walk, the resplendent ramble – but instead its name describes it exactly as it is: a 45.8km (28.7-mile) promenade through Jasper's splendidly glaciated high country that offers kilometer after kilometer of seemingly endless skyline. Is there a more spectacular hike anywhere in North America? Possibly not.

Wildlife Watching

5 Black and grizzly bears may be the holy grail for wildlife spotters, but there are plenty of other animals to seek out, too. The parks support a hugely diverse range of species, from elk and bighorn sheep (pictured) to mountain goats, marmots and moose, not to mention an entire aviary of unusual birds. The best time to see wildlife (p21) is always at dawn or dusk; bring along decent binoculars and a telephoto lens to help with the perfect view.

Mt Assiniboine

6 If it's a taste of the wilds you're yearning for, Mt Assiniboine (p69) is where you'll find it. The mountain's pyramid-shaped peak marks the start of some of the finest backcountry trails anywhere in the Canadian Rockies. With its secret lakes, soaring mountains and remote backcountry campgrounds, Assiniboine feels like another world compared to the busy trails of Banff. It takes some effort and dedication to get here, though – you'll need legs of steel, sturdy boots, proper supplies and, of course, a sense of adventure.

MATTEO COLOMBO / GETTY IMAGES ©

Moraine Lake

7 Canoes have been the preferred method of transport in the Rockies since time immemorial, and they're still the ideal way to explore the region's lakes and rivers. Canoes and kayaks can be hired on many of the region's waterways, but few water journeys can match Moraine Lake (p94) in the scenery stakes. Paddling out across this peacock-blue lake in a traditional canoe, gazing up to the icy summits of Wenkchemna Peak, you'll feel like you've been transported back in time to the days of the early pioneers and voyageurs.

Glacier's Historic Hotels

8 As much museums of park history as evocative places to stay, Glacier's historic hotels date from 1910s, when they were built by the Great Northern Railway to accommodate travelers fresh off busy cross-continental steam trains. Paying homage to Swiss-chalet-style architecture and sited in areas of outstanding natural beauty, these noble structures survive today with their rustic spirit intact. Old-school rooms in places like the Many Glacier Hotel (p198; pictured) lack TVs, air-con and fancy gadgets, but retain bags of gilded-age glamor.

Sunshine Meadows

9 Climb above the tree line in the Rocky Mountains and you're in a different domain, an ethereal world of impressionistic flower meadows, chirping marmots, glassy mountain lakes and jagged peaks above the clouds. The easiest access point to this wild terrain is at Banff's Sunshine Meadows where a summer gondola (p92) whisks hikers up to the Continental Divide for fabulous short and long hikes, some of them guided. Extra bonus: Sunshine Meadows metamorphoses into Banff's finest ski resort in the winter months.

Canmore Nordic Centre

10 The Rockies' rugged landscape of mountains and valleys makes perfect terrain if you're into mountain biking. Many of Banff and Jasper's trails are designated as multiuse, meaning they're open to hikers and horseback riders as well as cyclists, but for the best cycling head for the groomed trails of the Canmore Nordic Centre (p115). There are more than 100km (62 miles) of routes to explore, ranging from easy rolls to epic singletracks, and the regular skills clinics can help you get the most out of your ride.

Bears in Two Medicine Valley

11 Bear sightings inspire the whole gamut of adrenaline-fuelled feelings in humans, from fascination, intrigue and reverence, to shock and blind fear. You can grab a cocktail of all five in the Two Medicine Valley (p194), once one of Glacier National Park's more accessible haunts but, in the days since car traffic diverted to the Going-to-the-Sun Rd, a deliciously quiet corner preferred by hikers, solitary fishers and – er – bears. At last count the park had in the vicinity of 400 grizzlies and substantially more black bears. Do you feel lucky?

Lake Louise

12 No one should leave this mortal coil without first setting eyes upon the robin-egg-blue waters of Lake Louise nestled below the hulking Victoria Glacier and ringed by an impressive amphitheater of mountains. True, the lakeshore crowds can sometimes resemble a giant emporium of selfie sticks, but grab your photos from a more unique angle – high on the slopes of Mt Fairview, for instance, or gazing back down the Plain of Six Glaciers from the Victoria Glacier – and solitude could conceivably be yours.

Tonquin Valley

13 In winter Jasper's visitors drop to a trickle, with most never venturing beyond the comforting skiing hub of Marmot Basin. What they're missing is some of the best icy backcountry in Canada. The Tonquin Valley – already well known to summer hikers and horseback riders – is a snow-blanketed nirvana equipped with an Alpine Club of Canada hut and a rustic backcountry lodge (p165), allowing fit visitors to practice the art of hut-to-hut cross-country skiing. Characterized by manageable elevation and minimal avalanche risk, it's a 'haute route' without the height, or the danger.

12

13

Maligne Lake

14 Beyond its oft-visited northern shore, Maligne Lake (p159) remains a wilderness lake bequeathed with the kind of grandiose scenery that early explorers such as Mary Schäffer would still recognize. The only way to penetrate this watery kingdom's southern reaches is to hike in through backcountry, venture out solo on a kayak, or – for more relaxed day-trippers – enjoy it communally on a daily boat launch. The object of everyone's longing is the calendar-cover view of tiny Spirit Island backed by an amphitheater of appropriately 'rocky' mountains.

Jasper Skytram

15 It probably wouldn't happen today, but back in the 1960s, in an era when mechanical geeks were experimenting with fancy new gimmicks, the Jasper park authorities built this high-speed cable car (p157) to a lofty knoll on 2466m (8088ft) Whistlers Mountain. Hiking purists may disapprove, but the tramway provides an easy way for people of all ages and abilities to enjoy the beautiful alpine tundra. On a clear day, the views up top stretch all the way from the Athabasca River valley to Mt Robson, the highest peak in the Canadian Rockies.

Takakkaw Falls

16 First Nations people had it right when they named this thundering waterfall (p123): Takakkaw translates as 'it is magnificent' in the Cree language, and you'll probably find yourself thinking the same thing when you first set eyes on it. With a main drop of 255m (836ft), Takakkaw is one of Canada's most impressive cascades. A trail leads through pine forest to the base of the falls, affording grand views across the valley toward Cathedral Mountain and the rest of Yoho National Park.

White-Water Rafting

17 There are few activities that induce a more white-knuckle, heart-in-mouth, seat-of-the-pants adrenaline hit than hurtling downriver in an inflatable raft armed with nothing but a paddle and a prayer. Despite the apparent danger, white-water rafting is actually well within the capability of most people. Guided trips are run on many rivers, including the Bow, Kananaskis (pictured) and Kicking Horse (p129). While you're guaranteed to get soaked to the skin, you're also sure to have a huge grin on your face once you're finally back on terra firma.

ADAM HINCHLIFFE / SHUTTERSTOCK ©

PIXELJOY / SHUTTERSTOCK ©

Waterton's Crypt Lake Trail

18 Doable in a day thanks to a water taxi with service to the trailhead, Waterton Lakes' thrilling obstacle-laden hike includes a climb up a ladder, a crawl through a narrow rocky tunnel and another climb up a sheer rock face with a cable for assistance, ending at gorgeous Crypt Lake (p220). The ascent begins quickly, and soon you'll take in up-close views of waterfalls, mountains and lakes below. On your return trip, allow enough time to catch the last boat of the day – it's the only easy way back!

Hot Springs

19 If it weren't for the geothermal springs that bubble up from beneath the mountains, Banff and its neighboring national parks may never have come into existence. The craze for spa bathing was instrumental in attracting early visitors to the park during the late 19th century. While the original site at the Cave & Basin National Historic Site is now off-limits to bathers, you can still take a dip in the giant outdoor pool at Banff's Upper Hot Springs (p85; pictured), as well as its sister springs in Jasper and Kootenay National Parks.

Athabasca Glacier

20 Driving on a glacier: sounds more like the kind of stunt pulled on a car-crazy TV show than something you could actually do, right? Wrong. At Jasper's humungous Columbia Icefield, specially adapted Ice Explorer vehicles crawl and crunch across the Athabasca Glacier (p155), affording amazing views of crevasses, seracs and an endless horizon of ice. You'll even get the chance to disembark briefly and set foot on the 400-year-old snow. Tours leave every 15 to 30 minutes from the Columbia Icefield Centre in summer.

Need to Know

For more information, see Survival Guide (p257)

Entrance Fees
Banff/Jasper: adult day-pass C$9.80; Glacier: single entry/weekly pass US$20/35; Waterton Lakes: adult day-pass C$7.80

Number of Visitors (2018)
Banff: 4,181,854; Jasper: 2,425,878; Glacier: 2,965,030; Waterton Lakes: 568,807

Year Founded
Banff: 1885; Waterton Lakes: 1895; Jasper: 1907; Glacier: 1910

Money
ATMs in Banff, Jasper and Glacier townsites; scarce elsewhere. Credit cards widely accepted.

Cell Phones
Coverage is spotty outside townsites. Phone must be compatible with Canadian/US network.

Driving
Most major roads are sealed; some minor roads are gravel/dirt. Snow tires or chains required in some areas in winter.

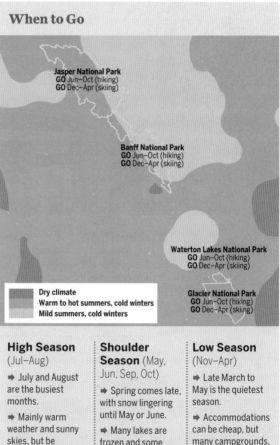

When to Go

Jasper National Park
GO Jun–Oct (hiking)
GO Dec–Apr (skiing)

Banff National Park
GO Jun–Oct (hiking)
GO Dec–Apr (skiing)

Waterton Lakes National Park
GO Jun–Oct (hiking)
GO Dec–Apr (skiing)

Glacier National Park
GO Jun–Oct (hiking)
GO Dec–Apr (skiing)

Dry climate
Warm to hot summers, cold winters
Mild summers, cold winters

High Season (Jul–Aug)

➡ July and August are the busiest months.

➡ Mainly warm weather and sunny skies, but be prepared for sudden thunderstorms.

➡ Trail closures and hiking restrictions during buffalo berry season (mid-July onwards).

Shoulder Season (May, Jun, Sep, Oct)

➡ Spring comes late, with snow lingering until May or June.

➡ Many lakes are frozen and some trails remain closed until early summer.

➡ June is the wettest month in Banff and Jasper.

Low Season (Nov–Apr)

➡ Late March to May is the quietest season.

➡ Accommodations can be cheap, but many campgrounds, trails and activities are closed.

➡ Weather permitting, ski areas usually open from early December to early May.

Useful Websites

Lonely Planet (www.lonely
planet.com/canada/alberta/
banff-and-jasper-national-parks,
www.lonelyplanet.com/usa/
rocky-mountains/glacier
-national-park) Destination
information, hotel bookings,
traveler forum and more.

National Parks Canada (www.
pc.gc.ca) Comprehensive info
for Canada's national parks; for
campground reservations, visit
www.reservation.pc.gc.ca.

US National Parks (www.nps.
gov) US parks, including Glacier;
for campground reservations,
visit www.recreation.gov.

Important
Numbers

Banff Visitor Centre	☏403-762-1550
Jasper Visitor Centre	☏780-852-6176
Glacier National Park HQ	☏406-888-7800
Waterton Visitor Centre	☏403-859-5133
Emergencies (all parks)	☏911

Exchange Rates

AUD	A$1	C$0.90	US$0.68
CAN	C$1	C$1	US$0.76
Euro zone	€1	C$1.50	US$1.13
JPN	¥100	C$1.25	US$0.95
NZ	NZ$1	C$0.86	US$0.65
UK	£1	C$1.59	US$1.20
USA	US$1	C$1.32	US$1

For current exchange rates see
www.xe.com.

Daily Costs
Budget:
Less than C$100

➡ Camping or dorm room in
hostel: C$20–C$50

➡ Self-catering from
supermarkets: C$20

➡ Hiking on local trails using
public transport: free–C$20

Midrange:
C$100–C$400

➡ Double room in a hotel:
C$200–C$300

➡ Lunch and dinner with
drinks in local midrange
restaurants: C$50

➡ Compact car hire: C$50

Top End:
More than C$400

➡ Suite in a luxury hotel or
lodge: from C$350

➡ Three-course meal with
wine: C$80–C$100

➡ Guided minibus tour: C$100

Opening Dates
Banff
Hwy 1 between Banff and Lake
Louise open year-round. High
trails closed until at least June.

Jasper
Icefields Pkwy between Lake
Louise and Jasper closes during
heavy snowfall. Minor roads
snowbound between December
and May. Most trails open by
late June.

Glacier
The only main road (Going-to-
the-Sun Rd) is closed until June.
Minimal services maintained at
Apgar Village in winter.

Waterton
Most facilities open May to
September. Red Rock Pkwy
closes from September to May;
Akamina Pkwy partially closes
November to May.

Park Policies &
Regulations

Hunting Not permitted in any of
the parks. Firearms are banned
in Banff, Jasper and Waterton,
and restricted in Glacier.

Park Passes Anyone intending
on stopping in the national
parks will require a park pass
(these can be purchased at park
entrances).

Pets Must be kept on a leash
at all times and are not allowed
in backcountry shelters. Pets
are prohibited from all trails in
Glacier National Park.

Trail Etiquette and Safety Stay
on the trails and avoid cutting
across switchbacks, which
causes unnecessary erosion and
damages fragile plants.

Wildlife and Cultural Artifacts
It is illegal to remove any natural
or cultural artifacts from the
parks, including rocks, stones,
minerals and fossils, as well as
antlers, nests, bird eggs, plants,
cones and wildflowers.

Getting There
& Around

Most visitors travel by car or
camper van. Getting around the
parks without your own vehicle
can be challenging, but is not
impossible.

Car & Motorcycle All of the
parks are accessible on clearly
signposted, well-maintained
roads.

Train VIA trains serve Jasper.
Amtrak serves Glacier with its
transcontinental *Empire Builder*.

Bus Glacier has an excellent
free park shuttle linking the
trailheads. In Canada, buses
connect Banff with Lake Louise
and Jasper.

For much more on
getting around,
see p275

PLAN YOUR TRIP NEED TO KNOW

What's New

Free Youth Admission at Canada's National Parks

In 2018 Parks Canada began offering free national parks admission to all young people aged 17 and under. This family-friendly policy is expected to remain in place indefinitely.

Expanded Public Transport in Banff National Park

Banff's public transit system, Roam (p111), launched new bus routes to Johnston Canyon and Lake Louise, ushering in hassle-free, low-cost access to two of the national park's most popular attractions.

Jasper's Gleaming New Hostel

HI's already stellar hostel network just added a little sparkle with the May 2019 opening of a modern, amenity-packed 157-bed facility in Jasper Town (p164).

Kananaskis Nordic Spa

Now there's yet another reason to visit Kananaskis Country, the 'local's secret' wilderness just outside Banff's borders. This spiffy new spa (p120) soothes hikers' sore muscles with hot pools, a sauna, a steam cabin, massages and more.

Red Jammer Buses Go Electric

By the time you read this, several of Glacier's vintage 1930s 'Red Jammer' buses (p195) will have been retrofitted to run on electric hybrid motors – reducing pollution while still retaining all the retro design features that have made them a National Park Service icon.

Whistlers Campground Renovation

Jasper's flagship campground, Whistlers (p164), is getting a massive facelift. Look for it to reopen in 2021, with all facilities and campsites rebuilt from the ground up.

New Look for an Icefields Pkwy Icon

Cathedral ceilings and humungous picture windows offer front-row views of the Athabasca Glacier at the newly renovated Glacier View Lodge (p163), smack at the heart of the Icefields Pkwy.

Expanding the Whitefish Trail

Extended to include the brand new Haskill Lake boardwalk and viewing platform in 2018, Whitefish's beloved rec trail (p213) is a haven for hikers, cyclists, horseback riders, cross-country skiers and bikers.

Rebirth of Glacier's Historic Backcountry Chalet

Originally built by the Great Northern Railway in 1914, then devastated by a 2017 forest fire, Sperry Chalet (p200) will rise phoenix-like from the ashes when reconstruction work completes in 2020.

New Hostel and Gastropub in Canmore

Sip a microbrew or two while savoring killer mountain views at Grizzly Paw Brewery's brand-new Tank 310 gastropub (p119), then retire to the cool confines of the recently opened Canmore Downtown Hostel (p117).

For more recommendations and reviews, see **lonely planet.com**

If You Like...

Wildlife Watching

Vermilion Lakes Tranquil lakes within easy reach of Banff Town where you can often spot beavers and grazing elk. (p88)

Bow Valley Pkwy Running parallel to the Trans-Canada Hwy, this old forest road is an ideal place to see wildlife from your car. (p72)

Lake Louise Gondola Look out for grizzly bears foraging on surrounding avalanche slopes as you glide upwards. (p94)

Many Glacier One of the best places in Glacier to see bears, mountain goats, bighorn sheep and moose. (p194)

Icefields Pkwy Rocky Mountain wildlife flourishes in the virgin wilderness bordering this remarkable 230km highway. (p146)

Logan Pass A favorite high-altitude hangout for bighorn sheep, mountain goats and hoary marmots. (p191)

Lake Minnewanka Whole herds of bighorns often congregate near this lake just north of Banff. (p91)

Lookouts & Views

Sulphur Mountain Banff's most famous mountaintop vista is reached by an 11km trail or the Banff Gondola. (p89)

Skyline Trail Views stretch from the Colin Range to the Athabasca Valley on this epic backcountry trek. (p143)

Fairview Build leg strength climbing to one of the best (and highest) viewpoints of Lake Louise. (p63)

Whistler's Summit Hike or catch a cable car up to Jasper's best-loved viewpoint amid a backdrop of high alpine tundra. (p140)

Parker Ridge Gaze across the Saskatchewan Glacier from this windy ridge halfway along the Icefields Pkwy. (p65)

Going-to-the-Sun Rd This amazing roller-coaster road boasts 85km (53 miles) of nonstop views. (p188)

Glaciers

Athabasca Glacier This grand glacier is but a fragment of the enormous Columbia Icefield. (p155)

Grinnell Glacier See Glacier's most accessible ice river from atop the Continental Divide, or down below from Many Glacier. (p194)

Saskatchewan Glacier Another spur tongue from the Columbia Icefield; this one is best seen from Parker Ridge. (p65)

Jackson Glacier One of 25 fast-disappearing icefields in Glacier National Park. Don't miss the lookout on Going-to-the-Sun Rd. (p191)

Adventure Activities

White-water rafting Ride the Kicking Horse River's wild class IV rapids – and prepare to get wet! (p81)

Caving Explore a subterranean world of stalactites and underground pools in the Rat's Nest Cave near Canmore. (p116)

Mountain biking Jasper National Park has, arguably, the best and most varied off-road biking network in Canada, while Canmore and Whitefish also offer superb trails. (p147)

Via Ferratas Try out these adrenaline-packed, fixed-protection climbing routes at the top of Banff's Mt Norquay. (p82)

Lakes & Waterfalls

Lake Louise Without doubt one of the most iconic vistas in Canada, drawing omnipresent crowds. (p93)

Johnston Canyon See three waterfalls in a single canyon on cleverly adapted boardwalks crammed with day-trippers. (p58)

Lake McDonald Take a trip or paddle a canoe across the waters of Glacier's stateliest lake. (p191)

Maligne Lake Jasper's most famous lake is the ideal place to launch a backcountry kayaking trip. (p159)

Takakkaw Falls This enormous waterfall in Yoho National Park makes a dramatic main plunge of 255m (836ft). (p123)

Waterton Lake Cross the 49th parallel on a boat cruise with the opportunity to hike back into Canada afterwards. (p227)

Moraine Lake Brave the predawn crowds to view a sublime sunrise from the Rockpile. (p94)

Amethyst Lake Experience true wilderness at this remote lake backed by the rugged Ramparts. (p32)

Hiking

Highline Trail A sometimes vertiginous, always spectacular, trail that traverses Glacier's unique geological formations. (p179)

Cory Pass Loop A knuckle-whitening adventure hike a stone's throw from the urban comfort of Banff Town. (p57)

Lake Agnes & the Beehives Moderate trek to a wonderful backcountry teahouse perched above the scenic splendor of Lake Louise. (p62)

Skyline Trail Rated by many as one of Canada's best multiday hikes, with fantastic long-distance views and a pleasant lodge for overnighting. (p143)

Dawson-Pitamakin Loop A Glacier ranger favorite, this spectacular hike along exposed ridges crosses the Continental Divide twice. (p182)

Top: Ice-climbing, Maligne Canyon, Jasper National Park (p154)

Bottom: Mountain biking, Whitefish (p33)

Winter Activities

Downhill skiing Hit the family-friendly slopes at Montana's Whitefish Mountain Resort, or tackle heart-stopping off-piste action at Banff's Big Three. (p213)

Ice-climbing The raging torrent of Maligne Canyon transforms into an eerie ice domain when the temperature dips below zero. (p138)

Skating Summer boating lakes become winter skating rinks with a good selection in Jasper, including Pyramid Lake. (p158)

Cross-country skiing Canmore's Nordic Centre hosted the 1988 Winter Olympics and its cross-country ski facilities remain top-notch. (p115)

Fat Biking Zip through the snowy forest on the groomed trails at Whitefish Bike Retreat. (p33)

Dog-sledding Travel in the manner of Canada's early explorers pulled by a team of huskies in Canmore. (p116)

History & Heritage

Banff Park Museum A wild menagerie of stuffed beasts and animal heads adorn the walls of Banff's oldest museum. (p88)

Whyte Museum of the Canadian Rockies Mountain art takes centre stage at this excellent museum in Banff. (p85)

Native American Speaks Regularly held at the St Mary Visitor Center in Glacier. (p202)

Spiral Tunnels Train enthusiasts will find plenty to pique their interest in Yoho's ingenious railway route across the Rockies. (p123)

Buffalo Nations Luxton Museum This Banff museum also has some intriguing examples of First Nations costume, art and craftwork. (p89)

Many Glacier Hotel Classic example of Glacier's woody 'parkitecture' building style dating from 1915. (p198)

Prince of Wales Hotel This gabled Swiss-style architectural beauty set on a promontory overlooking Upper Waterton Lake evokes the Empire spirit. (p230)

Museum of the Plains Indian Exceptional collection of costumes, art, craftwork and artifacts honoring the culture of the Blackfeet and other indigenous groups. (p211)

Off-the-Grid Accommodations

Skoki Lodge A 1930s backcountry lodge with afternoon tea, great food and comfortable but rustic rooms. (p104)

Sperry Chalet Historic Glacier landmark with memorable dinners; built in 1913, burnt in 2017, restored in 2020. (p200)

Assiniboine Lodge Cozy backcountry lodge offering helicopter transfers, warm showers and a sauna! (p126)

Granite Park Chalet Historic cook-your-own-meals lodge on Glacier's spectacular Highline Trail, built by Great Northern Railway in 1914. (p200)

Shovel Pass Lodge Jasper's oldest backcountry lodge sits halfway along its finest trail – the Skyline. (p165)

Tonquin Valley Backcountry Lodge Ski in, hike in or ride a horse: this rustic heaven sits 24km from the nearest road. (p165)

Shadow Lake Lodge Wake up to an alpine meadow in a little visited corner of Banff's backcountry. (p104)

Quiet Spots

Tonquin Valley No road access means guaranteed tranquillity in this remote Jasper valley. (p165)

Sunshine Meadows Take the gondola up to these peaceful mountain meadows criss-crossed by high-altitude trails. (p59)

Consolation Lakes Just an hour's walk from Moraine Lake, yet a world away from the tourist bustle. (p60)

Two Medicine Valley No hotels, no restaurants, but plenty of wildlife and practically zero crowds. (p194)

Peter Lougheed Provincial Park Locals will be your main companions at this gorgeous, less visited Kananaskis Country park. (p120)

Exploring Beyond the Parks

Whitefish Bike Retreat Spend the night and explore the trails at this cyclist-friendly hostel outside Whitefish, Montana. (p33)

Folding Mountain Taproom Join the locals at this hopping new microbrewery en route to or from Jasper. (p170)

King Creek Ridge This Kananaskis Country trail is unsignposted and insanely steep, but the views are unbelievable! (p120)

Elevation Place Give your kids their best rainy day *ever* at Canmore's Olympic-sized pool and climbing wall. (p115)

Month by Month

January

Chilly temperatures and crisp snow transform the mountains into an eerily quiet white wilderness, except for the slopes around Banff and Jasper, which are crammed with skiers and snowboarders.

Ice Magic

During this annual competition (www.banfflakelouise.com/ice-magic-festival), held in January at the Fairmont Lake Louise, teams of ice carvers battle it out to create sculptures fashioned from 136kg (300lb) blocks of ice.

Snow Days

Snow sculptures, block parties, snow-sliding events, big-name bands and a huge game of street hockey characterize Banff's celebration of all things snowy (www.banfflakelouise.com/snow days).

Jasper in January

Jasper's atmospheric winter festival (http://january.jasper.travel) hosts plenty of family-friendly events, including cross-country skiing, sleigh rides, skating and a chili cook-off.

February

Winter holds the mountains in an icy grip, with frequent snowfalls and subzero temperatures. Backcountry skiing, snowshoeing and other snow sports are in full swing.

Canmore Winter Carnival

This boisterous festival (www.canmore.ca/residents/town-events/canmore-winter-carnival) attempts to raise the winter spirits with log-sawing, ice-carving and beard-growing contests, but the Trapper's Ball is the highlight.

March

Little has changed in the mountains by March: snow and ice still cloak the landscape, with the spring thaw still months away.

April

Late April sees the first hints of spring – snowmelt at lower elevations and the odd warm sunny day – but don't put away the balaclava just yet.

Jasper Pride Festival

Wrap yourself in a rainbow flag and hit the ski slopes for this four-day LGBT–themed party (www.jasperpride.ca). Save time and energy to hit the town afterwards for special outdoor events, film screenings and – to cap it all off – a drag show.

Big Mountain Dummy Derby & Brewfest

Free-flowing beer from around the region accompanies an action-packed demolition derby on skis at Montana's Whitefish Mountain Resort.

May

The snows finally begin to thaw and spring creeps into the Rockies in mid-to late May. It's still cold though; most lakes stay frozen until June.

June

The summer season is usually underway by mid-June, with ski areas reopening to host warm-weather activities such as climbing, hiking and cycling. Alpine flower meadows unfurl their first blooms in late June.

🏃 Waterton Wildflower Festival

This nine-day event (www.watertonwildflowers.com) in Alberta's 'hidden secret' park is over a decade old and offers photography workshops and guided walks through the freshly carpeted flower meadows, with accompanying experts identifying the species.

July

Summer settles in by July, and everyone starts to look forward to long days of hiking, cycling and other outdoor activities. Colorful blooms blanket mountain meadows.

⭐ Canada Day

Food booths, fireworks and outdoor concerts take place beneath the maple-leaf flag in a hot flush of patriotic pride. Look out for ebullient street processions in Banff and Jasper on July 1.

⭐ North American Indian Days

The largest of several celebrations held on the Blackfeet Indian Reservation through the year, this event in Browning, MT has displays of traditional drumming and dancing (www.facebook.com/ndndays).

August

The warmest month of the year coincides with a host of special events, as well as the Rockies' busiest tourist season. The weather is mostly hot and dry, but watch out for thunderstorms.

☆ Canmore Folk Festival

Top folk acts descend on Canmore for this lively music festival (www.canmorefolkfestival.com), held every year since 1978 over the Heritage Weekend. The main stage is in Centennial Park, but there are extra gigs at many cafes and bars around town, too.

☆ Banff Summer Arts Festival

Culture takes center stage for this month-long showcase of artistic activity at the Banff Centre, hosting everything from opera, theater and street performance to art exhibitions. It kicks off in late July and runs through August.

⭐ Jasper Heritage Rodeo

Since 1926 bull-riders and steer-wrestlers have been congregating in Jasper for this annual hoedown and rodeo, held in mid-August (www.facebook.com/jasperheritagerodeo).

September

Fall brings a blaze of color to the mountain parks, making it one of the most spectacular seasons for hiking – especially now the summer crowds have left.

Days remain warm, but the nights are getting chilly.

⭐ Canmore Highland Games

Canmore celebrates its Scottish roots with a day of caber tossing, piping, drumming, sheepdog trials and a traditional ceilidh to round things off (www.canmorehighlandgames.ca).

October

The seasonal interval between the end of summer and the start of the ski season means less crowds and lower hotel rates.

☆ Jasper Dark Sky Festival

Introduced in 2011, this annual event (www.jasperdarksky.travel) celebrates Jasper's status as a Dark Sky Preserve with classical concerts under the stars and talks at the planetarium from visiting astronomers and astronauts.

November

Winter is knocking on the door in November, which usually sees the first snowfall of the season and the opening of some of the area's higher ski resorts.

☆ Banff Mountain Film & Book Festival

Since the mid-1970s, this seven-day film and literature festival (www.banffcentre.ca/mountainfestival) has celebrated the spirit of mountain adventure through films, videos, readings and lectures.

Itineraries

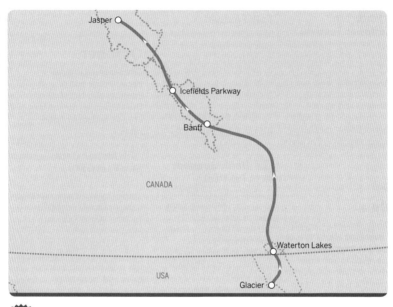

Jasper

Icefields Parkway

Banff

CANADA

Waterton Lakes

USA

Glacier

2 WEEKS Rocky Mountain Road Trip

This once-in-a-lifetime trip takes in four parks and covers pretty much everything the Rocky Mountains have to offer.

Start out with three days exploring **Glacier** and the magnificent mountain scenery around Going-to-the-Sun Rd and warming up with some short hikes around Many Glacier. On day four, head north across the Canadian border for more hiking in **Waterton Lakes**, followed by afternoon tea and spectacular vistas at the Prince of Wales Hotel. Spend the next day driving north to **Banff**, your base for the next four days. How you divide the time is up to you, but make sure you factor in the gondola ride up Sulphur Mountain, wildlife spotting around Vermilion Lakes and the Bow Valley Pkwy, a boat trip across Lake Minnewanka and at least one day hike. Day 10 is set aside for more mind-blowing scenery around Lake Louise and Moraine Lake, followed on day 11 by a drive up the **Icefields Pkwy** – it won't take long for you to realize why it's often dubbed the world's most spectacular road. Round the trip off with three days in **Jasper**, including a cruise on Maligne Lake, a day hike, a ride on the Jasper Skytram and a dip in Miette Hot Springs.

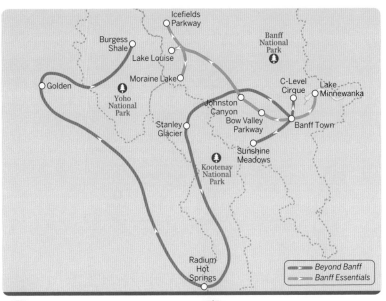

Legend:
- ▬▬ *Beyond Banff*
- ▬▬ *Banff Essentials*

 **Beyond Banff**
(1 WEEK)

This itinerary combines day hiking around Banff with a side trip into the neighboring national parks in British Columbia.

For the first few days, base yourself in **Banff Town** and spend the time breaking in those boots. Start with a gorgeous afternoon stroll to see Bow Falls and the fantastically shaped hoodoos just east of downtown along the Bow River. Later in the week, hike up to an icefield at **C-Level Cirque** or trek through the colorful wildflowers of **Sunshine Meadows**.

From Banff, head west across the Alberta–British Columbia border into **Kootenay National Park**. Take the time to hike up to **Stanley Glacier** before chilling in the 'hot' and 'cool' pools of **Radium Hot Springs**, both fed from a volcanic spring hidden deep beneath the mountainside.

From Radium, the route loops north via **Golden**, a lively little town. From here, the road heads east along the Kicking Horse Valley into **Yoho National Park**, where you can spend the remaining few days admiring the sights: don't miss Emerald Lake, Takakkaw Falls and a guided walk to the fossil fields of the **Burgess Shale**.

 **Banff Essentials**
(5 DAYS)

This five-day itinerary squeezes in Banff's key sights, with the emphasis on sightseeing rather than hiking.

Kick off with a day exploring **Banff Town**, a lively mini-metropolis with a cosmopolitan mix of shops, bistros, pubs and museums. Check in for some chateau luxury at the historic Fairmont Banff Springs Hotel, followed by a day exploring **Lake Minnewanka**, canoeing on the Bow River and relaxing in the Upper Hot Springs Pool.

On day three, drive out of Banff and detour off the Trans-Canada Hwy and onto the **Bow Valley Pkwy**. Keep your eyes peeled for wildlife, and don't miss the famous waterfalls of **Johnston Canyon**. By mid-afternoon, you'll reach the iconic sight of **Lake Louise** and nearby **Moraine Lake**, both renowned for their sapphire-blue waters and stunning mountain settings. Spend day four stretching your legs, either on the dramatic trail along the Plain of Six Glaciers, or on the steep climb to Lake Agnes and the Beehives.

On day five, drive along the breathtaking **Icefields Pkwy**, passing jagged peaks, mighty glaciers and sparkling lakes.

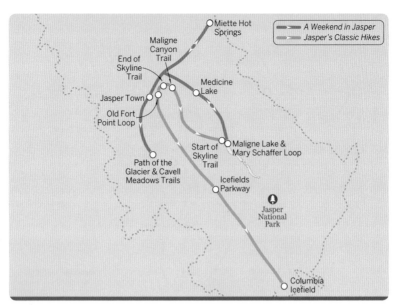

3 DAYS
A Weekend in Jasper

Even with only a long weekend at your disposal, it's still possible to get a taste of what makes Jasper special. Base yourself in Jasper Town, and take three little day excursions.

On the first day, tick off **Jasper Town**: get an early morning ticket for the Jasper Skytram, visit the museum, pick up lunch from the Bear's Paw Bakery, then spend an afternoon at Patricia and Pyramid Lakes. Stroll along the Discovery Trail as the sun sets, with a smart dinner at Evil Dave's.

On day two, pack a picnic from Patricia St Deli and drive along Maligne Lake Rd – a hot spot for wildlife. Watch for bear and moose as you wind through the wildlife corridor towards **Medicine Lake**, then head for nearby **Maligne Lake** for a guided cruise to tiny Spirit Island and an early evening walk on the **Mary Schäffer Loop**.

On your last day, it's time to hit the trail. Jasper has lots of day hikes, but it's hard to top the spectacular **Path of the Glacier and Cavell Meadows Trails**. Reward yourself with an evening soak at **Miette Hot Springs**, followed by farewell drinks and dinner at Jasper Brewing Company.

1 WEEK
Jasper's Classic Hikes

You've seen Jasper's must-see sights, so now's the time for something a bit more challenging with this hike-centric itinerary.

Warm up with some easy hikes around town. The steep but short **Old Fort Point loop** takes you to a vantage point high above the Athabasca River, while the **Maligne Canyon** trail leads you past spectacular canyon views without ever straying too far from civilization.

Now you're ready for the wilder stuff. The two- to three-day **Skyline Trail** is without doubt one of North America's premier overnight hikes, taking in everything from snowy peaks and glacial lakes to lofty passes with mind-boggling views. You don't even have to rough it, thanks to the cozy Shovel Pass Lodge.

After the exertion, it's time to sit back and let the views come to you. Spend a day driving south along the Jasper section of the **Icefields Pkwy**, and finish up with a visit to the **Columbia Icefield**, the largest area of ice this side of the North Pole. Most people trundle up in an Ice Explorer, but a guided walk will give you an even more memorable perspective.

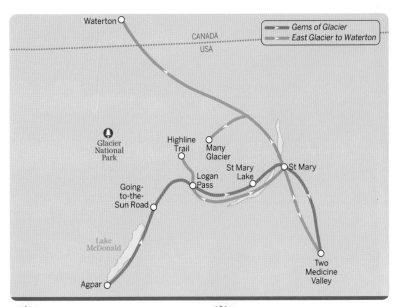

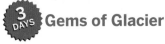 **Gems of Glacier**
3 DAYS

Three days in Glacier will bag you the highlights if you don't stray too far from the Going-to-the-Sun Rd. Use one of the hotels or motels around Apgar as your launchpad and then employ the park's handy free shuttle to get you from west side to east with various stop-offs en route.

On day one, explore around **Apgar**, West Glacier and nearby Lake McDonald, perhaps taking a walk among ancient rainforest on the Trail of the Cedars, or admiring mountain scenery on the Avalanche Lake Trail.

On day two, travel east along the **Going-to-the-Sun Rd**, one of America's most stunning stretches of asphalt. You can take your own vehicle or climb aboard one of the vintage Red Jammer buses, which have been trundling along the road since 1936. Stop to see the sights: the tumbling cascades of Bird Woman Falls and the Weeping Wall, the dramatic stretch of highway over **Logan Pass**, and the Jackson Glacier Overlook, which affords a knockout view of one of the park's namesake glaciers.

Stay overnight at **St Mary Lake**, and spend your last day hiking trails and spotting wildlife in **Two Medicine Valley**.

1 WEEK **East Glacier to Waterton**

This trip focuses on the eastern side of the Rockies in Glacier National Park, using the small settlement of **St Mary** as a base. Afterwards, you'll be within striking distance of Waterton Lakes just across the border in Canada.

Spend the first couple of days exploring **Going-to-the-Sun Rd**. **Two Medicine Valley** is a short drive south of St Mary, while **Logan Pass** lies to the west: both are fantastic areas for walking and wildlife watching. To get underneath Glacier's skin, a hike is essential – the Sun Point to Virginia Falls Trail starts near St Mary Lake, while the **Highline Trail** starting at Logan Pass is one of the park's most popular – and spectacular. Frequent buses on Going-to-the-Sun Rd mean you don't even need to worry about transport.

Then it's north for a couple of days in **Many Glacier**, arguably the national park's most beautiful valley. Reward yourself with a stay in the Many Glacier Hotel, overlooking Swiftcurrent Lake.

Finish up with some more hiking and sightseeing in **Waterton**: don't miss the classic Carthew–Alderson Trail.

Lake O'Hara hike (p125), Yoho National Park

Plan Your Trip
Activities

If you want to sample a full gamut of spine-tingling outdoor activities in a well-equipped but refreshingly pure wilderness, you've come to the right place. All the parks excel in backcountry hiking, Banff and Jasper up the ante with ski resorts, while Canmore and Golden are two of Canada's adrenalin-sports capitals.

Hike Grades

For ease of use and to help you decide which one to take, we've graded our favourite hikes into three difficulty levels.

Easy

Mostly flat, simple walking on clearly defined trails, suitable for families and inexperienced hikers. Some may be paved and suitable for wheelchair users or people with reduced mobility.

Moderate

May feature significant elevation gain, steep sections and/or ungroomed areas of trail (such as rubble, stones or moraines). Suitable for any hiker with an average level of fitness.

Difficult

Expect very steep climbs, sections of exposed and unmaintained trail, challenging terrain and occasional route-finding. These hikes are for experienced hikers, and will entail long days and significant distances. Pack appropriate equipment.

Planning Your Trip

Whatever outdoor pursuit you prefer, the Rockies present a wealth of ways to immerse yourself in spectacular scenery.

When to Go

When you choose to visit the mountain parks depends on what you want to do. Winter is long in the Rockies, with snow often covering the landscape from November into May. Most summer activities take place between June and September, although the exact periods vary according to seasonal conditions.

Summer Activities

June–September Peak activity season, with the most reliable weather. Most trails are open by late June or early July. It's worth waiting to do longer overnight hikes for the warmer temperatures of late July and August.

July–August By far the busiest times on the trails, so if you prefer solitude, the shoulder months are a better bet.

September–October Fall brings autumnal colors, and most trails are comparatively quiet and dry; watch for early snow at higher elevations.

Winter Activities

➡ The ski season runs roughly from late November until April, depending on conditions.

➡ Some hiking trails stay open in winter for snowshoeing and/or cross-country skiing.

Outdoor Activities
Hiking & Backpacking

If there's one activity that sums up the spirit of the Rockies, it's hiking. No matter where you travel in the parks, there's a trail nearby that'll whisk you up spectacular mountains, into picturesque forests or down a dramatic gorge.

The Rockies are a destination *par excellence* for experienced hikers, but have plenty to offer novice walkers, too. Some trails have interpretive signs that are ideal for families, while others feature paved sections designed for people with limited mobility.

Day Hikes

The term 'day hike' covers everything from an hour-long woodland stroll to an eight-hour haul to a mountain pass. Any route that takes less than eight hours to complete, or covers a round-trip of less than 24km (15 miles), is generally practical for a day hike.

You might not quite reach the edge of the true wilderness in a single day, but you can still experience an astonishing variety of terrain and enjoy plenty of wonderful views.

Read up on your chosen route before setting out to make sure it suits your ability level and that you know what to expect. Latest trail reports and wildlife warnings are available from visitor centers and websites.

Overnight Hikes

There are hundreds of backcountry routes scattered around the Rockies, offering hikers opportunities for wilderness immersion in some of the parks' most distant and little-visited corners.

➡ Trips can last anywhere from a couple of days to a couple of weeks.

➡ Overnight hikes require a wilderness pass and backcountry campground reservations.

➡ The majority of overnight hikes are within the capabilities of most hikers, as long as you're properly equipped and reasonably fit.

➡ You'll need to pack in food, a tent and sleeping bag, first-aid supplies, bear spray and all other equipment, and pack out all your rubbish.

Responsible Backcountry Hiking

The general rule in the backcountry is to leave everything as you find it – the Leave No Trace (www.leavenotrace.ca) website has some excellent advice on ways to reduce your environmental impact.

➡ Pitch on sites previously used by other campers to avoid unnecessary damage to the landscape.

➡ Keep your campsite clean to avoid attracting animals.

➡ Store food, toiletries and cooking equipment in bear-proof lockers if available, or suspend them between two trees at least 4m (13ft) above the ground and 1.3m (4ft) from each trunk.

➡ Use biodegradable soap and wash dishes well away from rivers and streams.

➡ A portable stove is more ecofriendly than a campfire, as it prevents unnecessary scorching of the ground.

➡ Check current fire restrictions before setting out and adhere to them on the trail. If you do have a fire, don't cut anything down to burn as fuel – dead wood is OK, green wood certainly isn't.

➡ If you get caught short on the trail, move well away from the path and at least 70m (230ft) from any water source, dig a hole, do the deed and cover it with dirt. Pack out toilet paper in a sealed bag.

Rules & Permits

No matter where you're hiking, you'll need a valid park pass and, if you're exploring the backcountry, backcountry campground reservations and a wilderness permit for each night of your stay. The Canadian parks also require a permit for fishing or building a campfire.

Further information is available at park visitor centers or the following websites:

Banff www.pc.gc.ca/en/pn-np/ab/banff/visit/tarifs-fees

Jasper www.pc.gc.ca/en/pn-np/ab/jasper/visit/tarifs-fees

Glacier www.nps.gov/glac/planyourvisit/permitsandreservations.htm

It's best to leave a full trip itinerary with park staff if you're traveling in remote country or doing any hazardous activities (such as mountaineering or rock climbing) – but remember to sign in once you're back; otherwise a search party may be sent after you!

It's extremely important to stay on the trails – cutting across switchbacks, avoiding muddy patches and tramping trail fringes causes unnecessary 'braiding' of the path and damages the fragile alpine environment.

Trail Guides

A standalone hiking guide can be a useful purchase, as they have extra space to detail precise trail distances, marker points, full elevations and compass bearings for specific routes. There are lots of different guides to choose from.

Standard hiking textbook *The Canadian Rockies Trail Guide* by Brian Patton and Bart Robinson, first published in 1971, is still many people's preferred guide. Simple layout, no-nonsense text and trail descriptions for 229 hikes are all user-friendly, although the format looks dated.

TOP AREAS FOR OVERNIGHT HIKES

➡ Skoki Valley (p71), Banff

➡ Egypt Lake (p68), Banff

➡ Mt Assiniboine (p69), Banff

➡ Kananaskis Country (p119)

➡ Tonquin Valley, Jasper

➡ Skyline Trail (p143), Jasper

➡ Gunsight Pass (p180), Glacier

➡ Lake O'Hara (p125), Yoho

➡ Northern Highline-Waterton Valley (p186), Glacier

Cycling along the Bow River near Banff Town (p76)

The Falcon Guide to Hiking Glacier & Waterton by Erik Molvar is a useful all-around guide for these two parks.

Best Maps

Gem Trek Publishing (www.gemtrek.com) Excellent maps covering the Canadian Rockies, with scales ranging from 1:35,000 to 1:100,000.

National Geographic Trails Illustrated (www.natgeomaps.com) Useful 1:100,000 map of Glacier/Waterton Lakes.

Going Solo

Walking alone (especially in the backcountry) is inherently more risky – your chance of encountering wildlife is greater, there's no one to go for help if you get into trouble or sprain an ankle, and no one to blame if you get lost due to bad navigation skills! If you do decide to hike alone, take the following precautions:

➡ Pack a compass and a good trail map, and make sure you're familiar with basic navigation techniques.

➡ Look out for recent wildlife warnings at trailheads, which will also be posted in park visitor centers.

➡ Pay attention to group access restrictions and seasonal trail closures around Lake Louise in summer.

➡ Let someone know where you're planning on hiking and what time you expect to be back.

➡ Sing loudly on the trail, shout and clap your hands to warn animals of your approach.

➡ Be particularly wary about wildlife around noisy streams or dense forest.

➡ Carry bear spray in an easily accessible place, and make sure you know how to use it. Also check expiry dates on the canister.

Cycling

There are plenty of routes open to mountain bikers in Banff, Lake Louise, Kananaskis and Jasper. Waterton Lakes also has a small selection of routes, but mountain biking is banned on all trails in Glacier.

You'll find excellent bike trail networks outside the parks at the Canmore Nordic Centre (p115), **Whitefish Bike Retreat** (☏406-260-0274; www.whitefishbikeretreat. com; 855 Beaver Lake Rd; tent sites/dm/r $40/50/110; ❄️🐾) and Golden's Kicking Horse Mountain Resort (p128), which has its own cyclist-friendly gondola.

Canoeing on Moraine Lake (p80), Banff National Park

Road riding is most popular along the Bow Valley Pkwy, Minnewanka Loop and the Icefields Pkwy, but you won't get away without tackling a few hills.

Preparation, Equipment & Safety

➡ Rent bikes and equipment in Banff, Canmore, Lake Louise, Golden, Jasper, Kananaskis, Whitefish and Waterton.

➡ Always wear a helmet, take a puncture repair kit and/or spare inner tubes, and a basic trail tool kit including hex keys, screwdrivers and chain tool.

➡ Trail conditions vary widely, from flat, paved trails to technical single tracks with hazards such as branches, rocks and knotted roots. Do your research before you set out.

➡ Cyclists are particularly prone to surprise bear encounters due to the speed and silence with which they travel. Make plenty of noise, slow down in dense forests, and take extra care near rivers and on windy days.

Fishing

With hundreds of waterways and lakes open for angling, the mountain parks are, unsurprisingly, a paradise for aspiring anglers. Arctic grayling, rainbow trout, brown trout, brook trout, lake trout, northern pike, mountain whitefish and lake whitefish are all abundant, although some species (such as bull trout, cutthroat trout and kokanee salmon) have suffered a major decline in recent years and are protected by law.

The most popular angling areas include the Bow River and Lake Minnewanka in Banff; Maligne Lake, Pyramid Lake, Amethyst Lake and Princess Lakes in Jasper; and Lake McDonald and St Mary Lake in Glacier.

Rules, Regulations & Seasons

To fish anywhere in Banff and Jasper, you will need to buy a fishing permit, available from park visitor centers. It's important to be sure about your catch, as you'll be fined if you're caught in possession of one of the species protected by park authorities. If in doubt, catch-and-release is the way to go.

No fishing permit is required across the border in Glacier. Casting on the park's boundaries may require a Montana state fishing license, and waters on Blackfeet Indian Reservation land (such as part of

Lower Two Medicine Lake) require permits from the reservation.

➡ The season in Canada generally runs from June to September, with a slightly longer season in Glacier.

➡ It's illegal to fish with natural bait, chemical attractants or lead tackle.

➡ You cannot have more than one line at a time in the water and may not fish from two hours after sunset to one hour before sunrise.

➡ Some waters are catch-and-release zones only, while most others have catch limits for particular species.

➡ Consider employing a local guide, who can provide gear and tackle, help you find the choicest waters and make sure you stay within the rules.

Horseback Riding

People have been taking pack trips around these parts since the days of the earliest settlers, and the horseback tradition remains strong to this day. Many trails in Banff, Jasper and Glacier are open to horseback riders as well as hikers, and horses are also welcome at many backcountry campgrounds and lodges.

Most people choose to saddle up with a local guiding company, but it's possible to bring along your own steed. If you're trotting off into the Canadian backcountry, you'll need a grazing permit in addition to your wilderness pass. Comprehensive listings of pack-trip companies and outfitters are available from Alberta Outfitters Association (www.albertaoutfitters.com) and **Montana Outfitters & Guides Association** (☑406-449-3578; www.montanaoutfitters. org; 5 Microwave Hill Rd, Montana City).

White-Water Rafting & Float Trips

The Rockies have some of the best white water in Canada. Most local activity companies tackle rapids rated between I (easy) and III (moderate). Equipment, safety gear and trained guides are all supplied – but you'll need to know how to swim, and be prepared to get very wet.

More sedate float trips on rivers are ideal for families and often provide a good way of spotting water birds and wildlife. The rafting season is May through September, with highest river levels (and therefore the most rapids) in spring.

Two of the best Canadian rivers for rafting are the Kicking Horse and Kananaskis; Banff, Canmore and Golden all have plenty of operators who run trips. Jasper also has its own network of white-water rivers, while in Glacier, the Middle and North Forks of the Flathead River offer the best stretches of white water for rafting.

Canoeing & Kayaking

The region's indigenous peoples have been using canoes for thousands of years (an example followed by the early European settlers and voyageurs), and canoeing and kayaking are still the best ways to get out on the water.

Nonmotorized boats (including canoes, dinghies and kayaks) are allowed on nearly all waterways in the Canadian parks, but motorboats are banned, except on Lake Minnewanka. The rules are less strict in Glacier, with most waterways open to boats.

➡ Canoes and kayaks are readily available for hire at many lakes.

➡ Banff's best places for canoeing are Lake Louise, Moraine Lake, Bow River and Vermilion Lakes. Cruises are offered on Lake Minnewanka. You can also paddle on Emerald Lake in Yoho.

➡ In Jasper, Maligne Lake offers superb canoeing and commentated cruises to Spirit Island. Pyramid Lake is another good spot.

➡ In Glacier, hire boats and cruises are offered on Lake McDonald, St Mary, Swiftcurrent Lake and Josephine Lake.

➡ In Waterton, Cameron Lake is the best lake for boating, with rowboats and canoes for rent.

EXTREME PURSUITS

Looking for extra adrenaline? No problem! The mountain parks have plenty of ways to get your blood pumping.

➡ Live out your Jack London fantasies on a dogsledding expedition

➡ Plumb the depths of the Rat's Nest cave system

➡ Challenge the rapids on the Kicking Horse and Kananaskis Rivers

➡ Soar through the skies on a heli-hiking expedition

➡ Scramble around the peaks of Mt Edith Cavell or Canmore

Wildlife Watching

With a rich and varied animal population ranging from bighorn sheep to wolverines, elk and grizzly bears, the parks offer plenty of opportunities for wildlife spotting. The best times for wildlife watching are dawn and dusk. Animals tend to go wherever humans don't, so less-frequented areas of Kananaskis and Kootenay are excellent places for wildlife seekers, as are the more remote areas of Jasper and Glacier. Even on the fringes of busy Banff Town you're bound to cross paths with at least a few wild animals.

Wildlife can be highly unpredictable and often perceive humans as a threat, so be careful not to get too close (even more docile-looking animals such as elk can be dangerous, especially during calving season). A good pair of binoculars or a telephoto lens will help you see the show from a distance.

Rock Climbing & Mountaineering

Banff and Jasper are both well-known destinations for rock climbers, but the mountainous terrain is generally challenging and technical and mostly more suited to experienced alpinists, rather than novices.

An exception are the Via Ferratas (fixed-protection climbing routes) in Banff's Mt Norquay and Kicking Horse Mountain Resort; they offer a safe, guided climbing experience on some truly incredible crags.

The **Alpine Club of Canada** (www. alpineclubofcanada.ca) and the **Association of Canadian Mountain Guides** (www.acmg.ca), both based in Canmore, provide general advice on climbing in the Rockies and can help put you in touch with local mountain guides.

Skiing & Snowboarding

While perhaps not quite on a par with Whistler, Banff and Jasper have a growing reputation for winter sports – and with more than five months of snow every year, it's hardly surprising.

Banff & Jasper

Banff's three main resorts are Mt Norquay, Lake Louise and Sunshine Village, collectively known as the **Big Three** (www. skibig3.com). Lift passes covering all three resorts are available, or you can buy individual resort passes if your time is limited.

Jasper's skiing hotspot is Marmot Basin (p153), just off the Icefields Pkwy. The slopes and facilities are generally a little quieter than in Banff, making Marmot a good destination for first-time skiers.

The facilities at all four resorts are excellent, with ski and snowboarding schools, childcare facilities, terrain parks and half-pipes for snowboarders, as well as public transportation to the slopes and lots of groomed and powder runs.

Bars and restaurants in the townsites of Banff and Jasper are within easy reach, making for a lively après-ski culture.

TOP SPOTS FOR WILDLIFE

Bow Valley Pkwy, Banff (p72) Elk, moose, occasionally black bears

Emerald Lake Area, Yoho (p123) Moose, black and grizzly bears

Icefields Pkwy, Jasper (p146) Elk, moose, mountain goats, bighorn sheep, bears

Kananaskis Country (p119) Golden eagles

Lake Louise Gondola, Banff (p94) Grizzly bears on the avalanche slopes

Lake Minnewanka, Banff (p91) Bighorn sheep, mountain goats, pika, ground squirrels

Maligne Lake Rd, Jasper (p148) Moose, mountain goats, occasionally wolves

Many Glacier, Glacier (p194) Mountain goats, black and grizzly bears

Smith–Dorrien/Spray Trail Rd, Banff (p121) Mountain goats, bighorn sheep

Tonquin Valley, Jasper (p145) Moose, bighorn sheep, marmots, caribou, bears

Two Medicine Valley, Glacier (p194) Grizzly bears

Vermilion Lakes, Banff (p88) Elk

Elk, Bow Valley Pkwy (p93), Banff National Park

Other Resorts

There are a few other winter sports resorts just outside the park boundaries. Nakiska (p121) in Kananaskis Country, about an hour's drive south of Canmore, was originally developed for the 1988 Winter Olympics, and still has a good reputation among skiers and snowboarders. It's usually a lot quieter than Banff, but has fewer runs and simpler facilities. Shuttle buses run throughout the ski season from Banff and Canmore.

The Kicking Horse Mountain Resort (p128), near Golden, is the Rocky Mountains' newest ski resort (and one of the only ones to be granted development permission in the last 20 years). With more than 1120 skiable hectares, over 120 runs and a vertical drop of 1260m (4133ft), it's also fast becoming one of the best.

Whitefish Mountain Resort (p213), 11km (7 miles) south of Whitefish, is another prime ski destination, with the excellent Fishbowl Terrain Parks, a vertical drop of 717m (2353ft) and 105 marked trails spread over a massive 3000 acres (1214 hectares).

Cross-Country Skiing

Cross-country skiing offers a chance to explore the national parks' gloriously empty backcountry deep into midwinter; many trails around Banff, Lake Louise, Kananaskis, Jasper and Whitefish are specifically kept open for cross-country skiers from December through March, with a more limited range of trails also open in Glacier, Waterton and Yoho.

➡ Park authorities supply trail maps of open routes, and you'll find lessons and equipment rental from most outdoor activity operators and some ski schools.

➡ Trails aren't always signposted and can be difficult to make out under heavy snow cover. Check conditions before you set out.

➡ Remain alert to avalanche danger, especially in remote areas.

➡ Backcountry skiers should carry emergency supplies, including an avalanche beacon, a full repair kit, a compass and a detailed topographical map.

Plan Your Trip
Family Travel

The Rocky Mountain parks are the perfect places to entertain and educate children: light on gimmicks, but heavy on inspiration. Listen to fascinating tales from indigenous storytellers, feel the thrill of your first-ever bear sighting, or enjoy the good old-fashioned simplicity of a game of cards or charades around the campfire.

Best Activities for Kids

Ice Explorer Tour
Trundle up the Athabasca Glacier in an ATV.

Elevation Place
Canmore's world-class climbing wall and Olympic-size pool are rainy-day nirvana.

Canoeing on Moraine Lake
Paddle across this idyllic mountain lake.

Gondola Rides
Zip up the mountainside in Banff, Jasper and Lake Louise.

Horseback Riding
Trot through the Rockies and enjoy a trailside cookout.

Wildlife Watching
From marmots to moose, the Rockies are a paradise for wildlife spotters.

White-Water Rafting
Get wet and wild on the Bow, Kicking Horse, Flathead and Kananaskis Rivers.

Ranger-Led Programs
Join rangers for hikes and evening campfire talks, or earn your junior ranger badge.

Banff, Jasper & Glacier for Kids

Sights & Attractions

Compared to the true wilderness parks in Alaska and the Yukon with next-to-zero infrastructure, the Rocky Mountain parks are positively family friendly, laying on many activities specifically for children.

Inevitably, it's the outdoor pursuits that are going to be the main attraction. Wildlife walks, white-water rafting, canoeing and horseback riding are all popular family pastimes, and most activity providers are well set up for dealing with kids.

Children qualify for discounted entry to nearly all sights (generally around half-price for ages five to 15, while under-fives often go free). Family tickets, which usually include entry for two adults and two children, are also available for many tours and sights.

Hiking

Hiking is one of the best all-round family activities. Many of the trails around the parks are well maintained and easily within the scope of active kids. Older kids should be capable of tackling some of the shorter overnight hikes, including staying out in the backcountry.

Trails that encompass a variety of sights are usually more fun for inquiring young minds, and there are many examples of walks that take in a mix of forest, mountain, river and canyon, or those that wind their way through well-known wildlife habitats. Several trails have interpretive panels to help you understand the geographical features, flora and fauna.

If the kids are interested in nature, it might be a good idea to join an organized hike. Many local guides are accredited by organizations such as the Interpretive Guides Association (www.interpretive guides.org) and can help children really engage with the natural world they're walking through. The main tour operators in Banff run morning and evening wildlife tours, on which you'll have a good chance of spotting elk, moose and other animals.

Remember to take along all the necessary supplies, including plenty of water, hats, sunscreen and, most importantly, trail snacks. Good-quality rain gear will also come in handy in case of sudden rainstorms.

Cycling

Jasper, Banff and Banff's neighboring community of Canmore have excellent on- and off-road cycling networks with plenty of easy grades for kids. Most bike-rental companies offer children's bikes, child helmets and protective pads, as well as trailers and 'tag-a-longs' for younger children. Top areas for biking include the self-contained Canmore Nordic Centre (p115), which has a huge system of trails catering for all ages and abilities, and Golden, BC's Kicking Horse Mountain Resort (p128).

Canoeing & Rafting

Canoes and kayaks are readily available for hire on Lake Louise, Moraine Lake, Maligne Lake, Lake McDonald, Emerald Lake and many others throughout the summer months. For more thrills, white-water rafting on the Kicking Horse, Flathead and Kananaskis Rivers is a guaranteed knuckle-whitener, although – depending on the class of rapids – there are sometimes minimum age stipulations. More popular with families are relatively sedate 'float trips', such as those offered on the Bow and Athabasca Rivers. All canoeing and rafting companies provide suitable boats for kids, or spaces in adult boats, along with child-sized life vests.

If you prefer to let someone else do the steering, there are scenic boat cruises on Lake Minnewanka, Maligne Lake, Waterton Lake and others.

Horseback Riding

Horse travel is part of Rocky Mountain folklore and requires minimal skills if you're a first-timer. Most horse-trip companies provide small ponies and child-friendly saddles, and cater as much for novices as for experienced riders.

Banff Trail Riders (p82) has lots of easy rides in Banff (from one hour in duration) and also offers a great evening trail cookout, complete with BBQ steak and home-made baked beans.

You can usually visit the horses at Spray River Corral and the Warner stables, near the Cave and Basin in Banff; phone ahead to check the stables are open for visitors.

In the hills outside Jasper, Jasper Riding Stables (p153) also offers plenty of family-friendly horseback riding, including two-hour trips around nearby Patricia Lake.

Skiing, Snowboarding & Other Winter Activities

In winter, skiing and snowboarding are the main outdoor pastimes. All of the ski resorts in Banff, Jasper and Kananaskis, as well as Whitefish Mountain Resort near Glacier, have runs that are specially tailored for younger users. Child-size skis, snowboards, goggles and gear are all available for hire. Banff's Mt Norquay is deemed particularly family friendly.

Most resorts offer ski lessons and snowboard schools, as well as day care and baby-sitting services. For more info, the website for Banff's Big Three (www.skibig3.com) ski resorts will give you some idea of what's on offer.

Cross-country skiing and snowshoeing are also fun ways to explore the winter

---

TOP HIKES FOR KIDS

- ➡ Johnston Canyon (p58)
- ➡ Sundance Canyon (p54)
- ➡ Maligne Canyon (p138)
- ➡ Garden Path Trail (p59)
- ➡ Mary Schäffer Loop (p140)
- ➡ Moose Lake Loop (p141)
- ➡ Crypt Lake Trail (p220)
- ➡ Avalanche Lake Trail (p177)
- ➡ Swiftcurrent Lake Nature Trail (p183)

landscape: The trails around Jasper townsite and the Lake Louise area are good places to start. Ice-skating is equally popular on the parks' frozen lakes, including Lake Louise in Banff and Lake Mildred in Jasper.

Ranger Programs

Glacier operates the US National Park Service's excellent Junior Ranger Program (www.nps.gov/kids/jrrangers.cfm), in which kids pick up a free ranger booklet from park visitor centers. The booklet contains activities, questionnaires, quizzes and games to complete during their stay; they'll earn a Junior Ranger badge and a certificate when the book is completed. Before you even set out for the national park, kids can sign up to become a WebRanger at www.nps.gov/webrangers, where there are plenty of online games, puzzles and activities to pique their interest.

The Canadian Rocky Mountain parks – Banff, Jasper, Yoho, Kootenay and Waterton Lakes – all run an Xplorers Program (www.pc.gc.ca/en/serapprocher-connect/xplorateurs-xplorers) aimed at kids aged six to 11. Kids are given a paperback *Xplorer* booklet full of interesting facts and tasks. They must complete a given number of tasks in order to claim a special souvenir. Booklets are available at any park information center.

Hands-on interpretive activities are often run at day-use areas or on trails in Banff. Activities range from stories about legendary park characters to field studies of bugs. Upcoming activities are displayed on the park website.

Parks Canada also provides regular educational programs at main campgrounds in Banff, Jasper, Waterton Lakes and Kootenay, with slide shows, talks, films and activities exploring many aspects of the parks, including wildlife, natural history and geology. Campgrounds with regular programs include Tunnel Mountain, Johnston Canyon and Lake Louise in Banff, Waterfowl Lakes on the Icefields Pkwy, and The Whistlers and Wapiti in Jasper. You don't have to be a campground guest to attend.

In West Glacier in the US, the Glacier National Park Visitor Center holds similarly entertaining ranger talks and presentations throughout summer, and the Apgar Nature Center in Apgar Village holds Junior Ranger programs in July and August.

Children's Highlights

Banff & Around

Banff Gondola (p89) Ride the sky-skimming cable car to the top of Sulphur Mountain.

Bow River (p80) Float the low-grade rapids below Bow Falls or hire a canoe and paddle over to Vermilion Lakes for some beaver spotting.

Lake Agnes Teahouse (p63) Hike up for afternoon tea above Lake Louise.

Canmore Cave Tours (p116) The Rat's Nest cave system has over 65km (40 miles) of underground tunnels to explore.

Boo the Grizzly Bear (p128) The Rocky Mountains' only captive grizzly bear lives in a refuge on Kicking Horse Mountain Resort, meaning sightings are practically guaranteed.

Old School Bus Ice Cream (p118) Grab a cone or a cup at Canmore's beloved yellow school bus.

Jasper

Maligne Lake (p159) Jump aboard a cruise boat to Spirit Island.

Jasper Skytram (p157) More gravity-defying cable cars.

Columbia Icefield Adventure (p155) Go for an Ice Explorer ride on the Athabasca glacier.

Moose Lake Loop (p141) Prowl in search of giant ungulates on this easy loop walk.

Jasper Town Trails (p147) Hike or pedal the scenic trails that fan out directly from Jasper's townsite.

Miette Hot Springs (p160) Splash around in geothermally heated waters.

Glacier & Waterton

Going-to-the-Sun Road (p195) Ride this spectacular road in a vintage 'Jammer' bus.

Native America Speaks (p202) Watch First Nations culture in action at the St Mary Visitor Center.

Many Glacier Valley (p194) Top spot for wildlife and glacier spotting.

Lake McDonald (p191) Dip a canoe oar into the frigid but beautiful water of this picture-perfect lake.

Planning

For all-round information and advice, check out Lonely Planet's *Travel with Children*.

Accommodations

Most hotels will happily accept kids, and many places allow children under a certain age to stay in their parents' room for no extra charge (the exact age varies according to the hotel). Extra pull-out beds are often available; otherwise ask for a triple or family room.

➡ Many hotels have facilities such as games rooms, saunas and swimming pools with water slides to help fend off boredom once the day's activities are done.

➡ For larger families, booking out a whole hostel dorm can be cheaper than an equivalent hotel room, especially when you factor in free use of the guest kitchen. The big HI hostel in Banff has private self-catering cabins ideal for families.

➡ Many cabin complexes and some hotels have self-catering suites with fully equipped kitchens.

➡ Larger campgrounds host regular interpretive programs and activity sessions for children. Some also have playgrounds.

Dining

Most restaurants in the parks are kid friendly, with the exception of some of the more upmarket establishments. Kids' menus are widespread, especially in hotels and the main town restaurants. Some Canadian drinking establishments will serve kids food at sit-down tables in the early evening, but are legally prohibited from doing so after 10pm.

Driving

➡ In Alberta and BC, it's a legal requirement that children under six and weighing less than 18kg (40lb) are secured in a properly fitted child-safety seat. In BC kids over 18kg but under 1.45m (4ft 9in) must use a booster seat (this is also recommended in Alberta).

➡ In Montana, US, kids under six years of age or under 27kg (60lb) must use a child-safety seat.

➡ Drivers are responsible for ensuring that other passengers are safely secured and wearing seat belts. Safety seats for toddlers and children are available from all the major

---

RAINY-DAY ACTIVITIES

Bad weather can put a dent in even the best-laid plans, so here are a few ideas on what to do when the sun won't play ball.

Banff Park Museum (p88) Get spooked out by stuffed beasts.

Lux Cinema in Banff (p108) Top place for catching the latest flicks.

Elevation Place (p115) Indoor climbing walls and a huge indoor pool beckon at Canmore's state-of-the-art recreation centre.

Hot Springs in Banff, Jasper and Radium (p127) Get wet and stay warm.

Museum of the Plains Indian (p211) Learn about First Nations culture on the Blackfeet Indian Reservation.

---

rental companies for a small daily fee; it's best to reserve them at the time of booking.

What to Pack

For Babies & Toddlers

Back sling or child-carrier rucksack Perfect for hiking the trails and keeping your hands free.

Portable changing mat Plus hand-wash gel and other essentials; trail toilets are very basic.

Child's car seat Avoid the extra expense and hassle of renting onsite.

Stroller with rain cover Essential in case of bad weather.

For Five- to 12-Year-Olds

Rain gear A good raincoat and plenty of warm layers will be indispensable.

Proper footwear A pair of boots or decent trail shoes will help avoid sprained ankles and keep feet dry. Sneakers are not a good idea.

Nature guides Essential for trailside identification of wildflowers, birds and animals.

Binoculars For long-distance wildlife watching.

First-aid kit Including disinfectant, antibiotic cream, Band-Aids, blister cream and moleskin patches for hot spots in boots.

Spare batteries For flashlights, games etc.

Plan Your Trip

Travel with Pets

The four main national parks in this book have varying rules regarding pets (which primarily means dogs). The Canadian parks have a reasonable cache of pet-friendly facilities, while Glacier is much more limited. For horse owners, decent trail-riding options abound. Pet snakes, iguanas and guinea pigs are probably best left at home.

Best Spots for Dogs

Sundance Trail, Banff
A flat, paved trail near Banff Town, shared with walkers, cyclists and horseback riders.

Marsh Loop, Banff
This pleasant dirt trail is usually peaceful and offers lovely views of the Bow River.

Lake Minnewanka, Banff
The lakeshore makes a perfect place for a family picnic.

Johnson Lake, Banff
A quiet lakeside trail that's often shared with summer sunbathers.

Mary Schäffer Loop, Jasper
Part-wooded walk on the eastern shoreline of Maligne Lake.

Lake Annette, Jasper
You can follow a paved trail around Lake Annette, but be on the lookout for elk and deer.

Moose Lake Loop, Jasper
Offers a quick escape from the Maligne Lake crowds.

Rules & Regulations

➡ In Banff and Jasper, dogs are allowed on most trails and at most campgrounds (both frontcountry and backcountry), but you're required to keep them securely leashed at all times.

➡ In Glacier, dogs are banned from *all* park trails, but are allowed in drive-in campgrounds, along park roads open to vehicles and in most picnic areas.

➡ You are required by law to clean up after your dog, so remember to bring along plastic bags or a pooper-scooper.

➡ Bring along all necessary supplies, including food and any medications, as they'll be almost impossible to buy outside the townsites.

➡ Guide and service dogs should wear reflective vests to indicate their working status.

Border Crossings

For many people, visiting the national parks is very much a family affair and often that doesn't just mean mom, dad and the kids. Plenty of people also decide to bring their pets along on their park adventure, but you definitely need to be prepared for the added complications that come with having your furry companion in tow.

The same rules and regulations apply to dogs of all sizes, regardless of whether they're a dachshund or a Doberman. If you're crossing the US–Canada border, you may be asked for a pet-health certificate and/or rabies certificate issued by an accredited veterinarian.

For exact rules, consult the relevant government agency. If bringing an animal into Canada, this generally means the Canadian Food Inspection Agency (www.inspection.gc.ca); if crossing into the US, relevant agencies may include the Centers for Disease Control (www.cdc.gov), the US Department of Agriculture (www.usda.gov), and/or the health agency of the state you're traveling into.

Health & Safety

In addition to the official rules, it's also worth considering how dogs will be perceived by any wild animals you might meet out on the trail. To elk, caribou and moose, dogs will probably be perceived as a threat, while to other beasts (such as cougar and bears) they might resemble prey. Either way, bringing your dog along puts you at increased risk in the evnt of an animal encounter – previously placid bears have been known to become enraged due to the noise of a barking dog.

➡ Ticks are a common parasite in the Rockies, especially in spring. Check your dog's coat carefully for ticks after any long walk, and remove any you find.

➡ Make sure you keep your dog leashed at all times, and discourage them from eating berries, fungi or other unknown plants.

➡ Urinating near streams and water sources is a major cause of giardia and other water-borne parasites, so discourage your dog from doing so.

Choosing Accommodations

It's important to think about two things before you bring your pet along to the parks: what they'll do while you're out on the trail or exploring the sights, and where they'll stay overnight. Leaving your dog leashed up isn't much of a holiday for them – so it's best to decide beforehand what

BEST PET-FRIENDLY HOTELS

➡ Tekarra Lodge (p164)
➡ Juniper (p100)
➡ Moose Hotel & Suites (p98)
➡ Fairmont Chateau Lake Louise (p103)
➡ Pocahontas Cabins (p166)

kind of trip you're planning on, and how bringing a pet will fit into those plans.

Several hotels in Banff and Jasper accept dogs, including all hotels operated by the Banff Lodging Company (www.bestofbanff.com) and Jasper's Mountain Park Lodges (www.mpljasper.com). Pet fees in addition to the standard room rate generally range between C$15 and C$25 per night per pet. Most campgrounds accept dogs, but unless they're very obedient, they should always be securely tethered. In Glacier, no hotels within the park accept pets, though some outside its borders will. Campgrounds will accept them (as long as they're kept on a lead).

There's also a useful online directory of animal-friendly accommodations in Canada at **Pet Friendly** (www.petfriendly.ca).

Hotels listed in this book that welcome pets have been given a dog's paw symbol.

Veterinarians

Veterinary services are limited to the main town areas.

The **Alberta Veterinary Medical Association** (www.abvma.ca) has online listings of veterinary services throughout the province, including locations in Jasper, Banff, Canmore and Pincher Creek.

Near Glacier, **Whitefish Animal Hospital** (www.whitefishanimalhospital.com) is a full-service vet for dogs, cats and other small animals.

Kennels

The **Canmore Veterinary Hospital** (www.canmorevet.com) has limited boarding facilities for pets.

DOG DOS & DON'TS

➡ Do keep dogs leashed at all times

➡ Do keep them quiet and under control in campgrounds

➡ Do check them regularly for ticks, fleas and other parasites

➡ Do bring extra water, food and supplies

➡ Don't let them eat berries and plants on the trail

➡ Don't let them run off into the undergrowth, especially in grassy meadows or wooded areas

➡ Don't leave them locked up in hot cars or RVs

➡ Don't let them bark at horses

➡ Don't assume everyone likes dogs

Three Dog Ranch (☑406-862-3913; www. threedogranchmontana.com; 5395 Hwy 93, Whitefish; ⊘7.30-11am & 2:30-5.30pm Mon-Fri, 8:30-11am & 2:30-5pm Sat, 8-8:30am & 3-3:30pm Sun) Grooming, day and overnight care, and pet store 2 miles south of Whitefish, Montana.

Lost & Found

If you have lost or found an animal, contact the relevant authorities as soon as possible. In Canada, the **Royal Canadian Mounted Police** (www.rcmp-grc.gc.ca) is your best point of contact. In the Glacier area, **Lost Pet Flathead** (www.lostpet flathead.com) maintains regularly updated listings of lost and found pets.

Horse Trails & Equestrian Facilities

Horse owners are permitted to bring their own animals to the national parks for recreational use. Many trails in Banff, Jasper and Glacier are open to horses, but seasonal conditions such as mud, swollen rivers, snow cover, plus wildlife activity can change that at short notice. Some areas are also permanently closed to horse use and in the backcountry there are strict quotas to prevent overuse and to protect wilderness areas. Contact park authorities for the latest advice on which routes are open or closed to horses, or consult the websites detailed here.

If you just fancy a quick day ride, or you don't want the hassle of transporting your own horse to the park, contact one of the commercial horse-guiding companies, some of which will let you bring your own animal on organized trips and provide stabling facilities.

For more information and advice, pick up the free *Horse User's Guide* from park offices, or consult the following webpages for each park: Banff (www.pc.gc.ca/en/ pn-np/ab/banff/activ/cheval-horse); Jasper (www.pc.gc.ca/en/pn-np/ab/jasper); Glacier (www.nps.gov/glac/planyourvisit/private stockuse.htm).

Permits & Corrals

➡ If you're trekking into the Canadian backcountry, you'll need a wilderness pass (C$9.80), as well as a grazing permit (C$1.90) for each night.

➡ In Glacier, backcountry permits are free, but advance reservations incur a US$40 fee.

➡ Most backcountry campgrounds in Canada accept horses, but some in Glacier are closed to horse use. Discuss your route and make advance reservations with park staff.

➡ In Banff, public corrals are available at Pipestone River, Mosquito Creek and 2km (1.2 miles) east of Saskatchewan Crossing along Hwy 11.

➡ In Jasper, there are corrals at the trailheads at Portal Creek, Poboktan, Nigel Creek, Athabasca Pass trail, Miette Lake trail and Fiddle Pass trail.

➡ In Glacier the corrals are not for public use, though there is one small exception. The Many Glacier corral can be used as an overnight stop for riders undertaking the Continental Divide Trail.

➡ Depending on the corral, maximum stays are usually between 48 and 72 hours.

On the Road

Banff National Park

Best Hikes

➡ Healy Pass (p59)

➡ Plain of Six Glaciers (p60)

➡ Larch Valley (p62)

➡ Cory Pass Loop (p57)

Best Places to Stay

➡ Skoki Lodge (p104)

➡ Fairmont Banff Springs (p97)

➡ Paradise Lodge & Bungalows (p102)

➡ Buffaloberry (p97)

Why Go?

In the hit parade of top sights in Canada, Banff justifiably ranks as many people's number one. As much a piece of Canadian history as a natural wonder, the nation's oldest national park, founded in 1885, is what Canada is all about: a feral, but largely accessible, wilderness that attempts to cater for everyone – and largely succeeds – from bus-tour seniors to hard-core mountaineers.

Indeed, one of the great beauties of Banff is its juxtaposition of the untamed and the civilized. Grizzly bears roam within growling distance of diners clinking cocktails at the romantic Banff Springs Hotel, while weary hikers fresh from summit attempts queue up for ice cream with golfers clutching nine irons. Striking a clever balance between yin and yang, Banff is a park with two distinct personalities. Popcorn on Banff Ave or rehydrated soup at a backcountry campground in the middle of nowhere? Take your pick – or enjoy both!

Road Distance (KM)

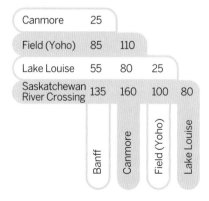

	Banff	Canmore	Field (Yoho)	Lake Louise
Canmore	25			
Field (Yoho)	85	110		
Lake Louise	55	80	25	
Saskatchewan River Crossing	135	160	100	80

Note: Distances are approximate

Entrances

There are four main road entrances into Banff National Park. All are open year-round, weather permitting. The main East Gate is on Trans-Canada Hwy 1, 7km (4.3 miles) west of Canmore, and has manned tollbooths where you can purchase park passes (they all accept cash, cards and check). If you already have a pass, you can use the right-hand lane to avoid queuing at the tollbooths. The other park entrances are on Trans-Canada Hwy 1 eastbound from Yoho National Park, Hwy 93 northbound from Kootenay National Park, and Hwy 93 southbound from the Icefields Pkwy. If you're driving, remember to hang your pass from your rearview mirror so that park staff know you've already paid.

DON'T MISS

A major lure of the Lake Louise area is its two hike-in tea-houses built in the first half of the 20th century by some of the park's early pioneers. Moderate but well-trodden trails to each establishment help hikers get away from the intense clamor of the lakeside and into a calmer, more serendipitous realm.

The Lake Agnes Teahouse (p63) sits 3.5km up a steep-ish trail in a hanging valley beside a beautiful lake. It was built in 1901 by the Canadian Pacific Railway and has been serving tea and other snacks (including scones) since 1905. The Plain of Six Glaciers Teahouse (p61) is within viewing distance of the Victoria Glacier (behold the thunderous avalanches) at the head of Lake Louise. It was constructed by Swiss guides in 1927 and has been in the tea business since 1959. The 5.5km trail to reach it is slightly gentler than the Lake Agnes trek.

Both teahouses sit at 2100m above sea level. Neither has electricity nor road access; supplies are brought in by foot, horse or helicopter.

When You Arrive

➡ Buy your park pass from the tollbooths at Banff's East Gate or from a park visitor center. Daily passes cost C$9.80/8.30/19.60 per adult/senior/family. Children 17 years and under get free admission.

➡ Check the latest trail reports at the Banff Information Centre or online at www.pc.gc.ca/apps/tcond/cond_e.asp?opark=100092.

➡ Some campgrounds operate on a first-come, first-served system: arrive early at your chosen site (ideally by 11am) for the best chance of securing a pitch.

PLANNING TIPS

Accommodations in Banff and Lake Louise are expensive and scarce in summer, so book early. To cut costs, avoid peak months or stay outside the park.

Fast Facts

Area 6641 sq km (2564 sq miles)

Highest elevation 3618m (11,870ft)

Lowest elevation 1310m (4297ft)

Reservations

Accommodations bookings are handled by the Banff Tourism Bureau (p110). For advance reservations at Tunnel Mountain, Two Jack, Johnston Canyon and Lake Louise campgrounds, contact the **Parks Canada campground reservation service** (☎877-737-3783; www.reservation.pc.gc.ca; ⊙7am-7pm). For backcountry campground reservations and wilderness passes, contact the Banff Visitor Centre (p110).

Resources

Parks Canada (www.pc.gc.ca/eng/pn-np/ab/banff/index.aspx)

Banff & Lake Louise Tourism (www.banfflakelouise.com)

Banff Town website (www.banff.ca)

Banff National Park

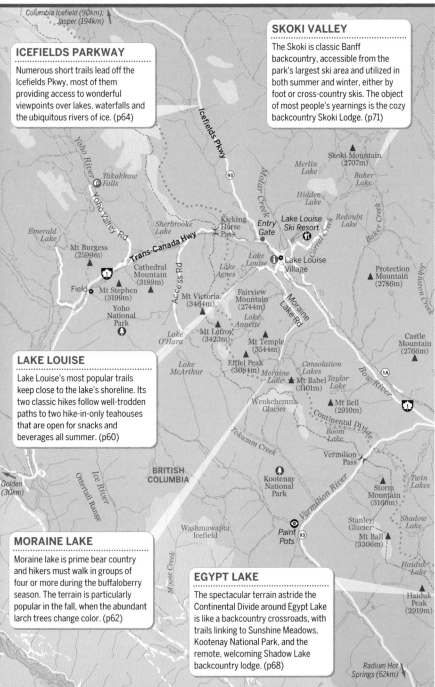

ICEFIELDS PARKWAY

Numerous short trails lead off the Icefields Pkwy, most of them providing access to wonderful viewpoints over lakes, waterfalls and the ubiquitous rivers of ice. (p64)

SKOKI VALLEY

The Skoki is classic Banff backcountry, accessible from the park's largest ski area and utilized in both summer and winter, either by foot or cross-country skis. The object of most people's yearnings is the cozy backcountry Skoki Lodge. (p71)

LAKE LOUISE

Lake Louise's most popular trails keep close to the lake's shoreline. Its two classic hikes follow well-trodden paths to two hike-in-only teahouses that are open for snacks and beverages all summer. (p60)

MORAINE LAKE

Moraine lake is prime bear country and hikers must walk in groups of four or more during the buffaloberry season. The terrain is particularly popular in the fall, when the abundant larch trees change color. (p62)

EGYPT LAKE

The spectacular terrain astride the Continental Divide around Egypt Lake is like a backcountry crossroads, with trails linking to Sunshine Meadows, Kootenay National Park, and the remote, welcoming Shadow Lake backcountry lodge. (p68)

Columbia Icefield (90km); Jasper (194km)

Yoho River

Takakkaw Falls

Yoho Valley Rd

Emerald Lake

Mt Burgess (2599m)

Cathedral Mountain (3189m)

Field

Mt Stephen (3199m)

Yoho National Park

Sherbrooke Lake

Trans-Canada Hwy

Kicking Horse Pass

Icefields Pkwy

Molar Creek

Merlin Lake

Skoki Mountain (2707m)

Baker Lake

Hidden Lake

Redoubt Lake

Lake Louise Ski Resort

Entry Gate

Lake Louise

Lake Louise Village

Corral Creek

Baker Creek

Johnston Creek

Protection Mountain (2786m)

Access Rd

Lake Agnes

Fairview Mountain (2744m)

Mt Victoria (3464m)

Lake Annette

Moraine Lake Rd

Castle Mountain (2766m)

Lake O'Hara

Lake McArthur

Mt Lefroy (3423m)

Mt Temple (3544m)

Eiffel Peak (3084m)

Moraine Lake

Consolation Lakes

Mt Babel (3101m)

Taylor Lake

Mt Bell (2910m)

Bow River

Wenkchemna Glacier

Continental Divide

Boom Lake

Tokumm Creek

Golden (30km)

Ice River

Ottertail Range

BRITISH COLUMBIA

Kootenay National Park

Vermilion River

Vermilion Pass

Storm Mountain (3160m)

Twin Lakes

Washmawapta Icefield

Moose Creek

Paint Pots

Stanley Glacier

Mt Ball (3306m)

Shadow Lake

Haiduk Lake

Haiduk Peak (2919m)

Radium Hot Springs (62km)

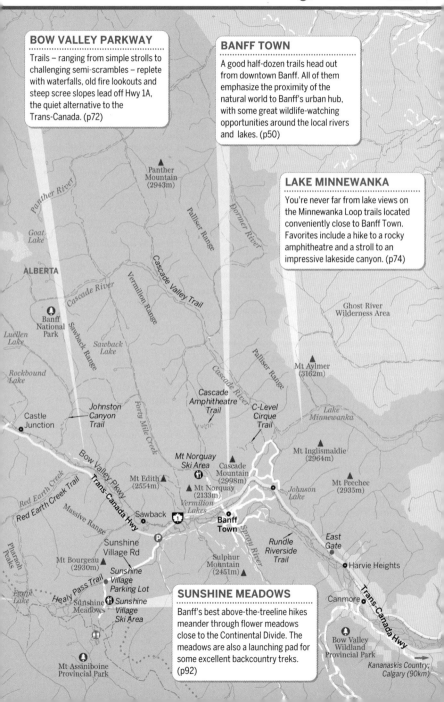

BOW VALLEY PARKWAY

Trails – ranging from simple strolls to challenging semi-scrambles – replete with waterfalls, old fire lookouts and steep scree slopes lead off Hwy 1A, the quiet alternative to the Trans-Canada. (p72)

BANFF TOWN

A good half-dozen trails head out from downtown Banff. All of them emphasize the proximity of the natural world to Banff's urban hub, with some great wildlife-watching opportunities around the local rivers and lakes. (p50)

LAKE MINNEWANKA

You're never far from lake views on the Minnewanka Loop trails located conveniently close to Banff Town. Favorites include a hike to a rocky amphitheatre and a stroll to an impressive lakeside canyon. (p74)

SUNSHINE MEADOWS

Banff's best above-the-treeline hikes meander through flower meadows close to the Continental Divide. The meadows are also a launching pad for some excellent backcountry treks. (p92)

0 — 10 km
0 — 5 miles

Panther River

Panther Mountain (2943m)

Palliser Range

Dormer River

Goat Lake

ALBERTA

Cascade River

Vermilion Range

Cascade Valley Trail

Ghost River Wilderness Area

Banff National Park

Luellen Lake

Sawback Range

Sawback Lake

Palliser Range

Mt Aylmer (3162m)

Rockbound Lake

Forty Mile Creek

Cascade River

Lake Minnewanka

Castle Junction

Johnston Canyon Trail

Cascade Amphitheatre Trail

C-Level Cirque Trail

Red Earth Creek

Bow Valley Pkwy

Red Earth Creek Trail

Trans-Canada Hwy

Massive Range

Mt Edith (2554m)

Mt Norquay Ski Area

Mt Norquay (2133m)

Cascade Mountain (2998m)

Mt Inglismaldie (2964m)

Johnson Lake

Mt Peechee (2935m)

Sawback

Vermilion Lakes

Banff Town

Pharaoh Peaks

Mt Bourgeau (2930m)

Sunshine Village Rd

Sunshine Village Parking Lot

Healy Pass Trail

Sunshine Meadows

Sunshine Village Ski Area

Sulphur Mountain (2451m)

Spray River

Rundle Riverside Trail

East Gate

Harvie Heights

Egypt Lake

Canmore

Trans-Canada Hwy

Mt Assiniboine Provincial Park

Bow Valley Wildland Provincial Park

Kananaskis Country; Calgary (90km)

🥾 DAY HIKES

Does hiking get any better than this? Banff's astounding 1600km (1000-mile) network of marked trails – regularly checked and meticulously signposted – is a highlight of Canada and a credit to the Parks Service who lay out and maintain them. You'll rarely get lost in this walkers' paradise. Trails are graded between easy (green), moderate (blue) and difficult (black), and fastidiously logged for weather closures and wildlife warnings. Always check the 'trail conditions' tab on the Parks Canada website (www.pc.gc.ca/en/pn-np/ab/banff) before starting off.

Many trails lead out directly from Banff Town. Others start within easy driving or cycling distance. Some undulate through thick forest populated by black bears. Others penetrate vast ethereal wildernesses above the tree line. You can set out for hours, days, even weeks – anything is possible, from the kid-friendly interpretive Fenland Trail to the adrenaline-loaded Cory Pass Loop.

Successful hiking requires basic common sense. Wear comfortable footwear, take plenty of water and trail snacks, and pack warm, layered clothing and waterproofs for the famously fickle mountain weather.

Banff Town & Around

🥾 Bow Falls & the Hoodoos

Duration Three-hour round-trip

Distance 10.2km (6.4 miles)

Difficulty Easy

Elevation Change 60m (197ft)

Start/Finish Banff Park Museum, Banff Town

Nearest Town Banff

Transportation Bus, bike, foot

Summary A scenic stroll from Banff, tracking the Bow River through woodland all the way to the Hoodoos.

Despite its proximity to downtown Banff, this easy ramble quickly leaves both traffic noise and tourists behind and delves into the forests and rivers east of the main town, ending at the otherwordly landscape of rocky pillars known as the Hoodoos.

Start out from the parking lot beside the Banff Park Museum at the south end of town and head for the river, where you'll find the Bow River Trail, a popular jaunt for Banff cyclists and joggers. The flat trail (Map p88) tracks the river east for about 1.2km (0.7 miles), where it reaches a set of two staircases and climbs to Buffalo St.

Continue briefly east on Buffalo St, following the pedestrian lane up to the **Surprise Corner Viewpoint** (Map p87; Buffalo St) and parking lot, where you can gaze out over the rushing white water of Bow Falls (p86). You could turn around here and retrace your steps, but it's worth carrying on to the Hoodoos.

From the parking lot, the trail descends through larch and pine woodland and again runs parallel to the river, passing several inlets and small beaches en route to a wide, open grass meadow at around the 3km (1.9-mile) mark, from where there are fine southerly views to Mt Rundle on the opposite side of the river.

From here the trail climbs gently up onto the canyon wall above the river, with great views across the Bow Valley – make sure you stick to the main trail, as several faint subtrails veer off along the riverbank and are much tougher going. After 5.1km (3.2 miles) you'll reach the **Hoodoos interpretive trail**, from where you can look out over the Hoodoos rising above the snaking course of the Bow River. The Hoodoos themselves are predominantly made of limestone, with a hard cap of magnesium-rich rock at the top; eons of wind and rain have carved them into a complex topography of twisted towers and weird spires.

Return along the same route, or if your legs are feeling the strain, catch a bus back to Banff from Tunnel Mountain Dr.

🥾 Fenland Trail & Vermilion Lakes

Duration 30-minute round-trip

Distance 2.1km (1.3 miles)

Difficulty Easy

Elevation Change Negligible

Start/Finish Forty Mile picnic area, Banff Town

Nearest Town Banff

Transportation Car, bike, foot

Summary Quiet forest walk that follows the green Echo and Forty Mile Creeks through the fenlands.

Popular with Banff cyclists and joggers, this short trail travels through a variety of natural habitats: woodland, marsh, fen, riverbed

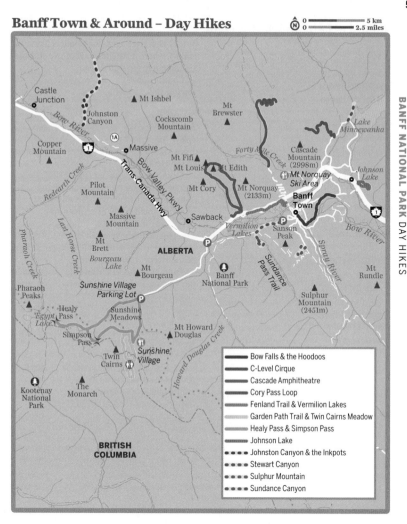

▬▬▬	Bow Falls & the Hoodoos
▬▬▬	C-Level Cirque
▬▬▬	Cascade Amphitheatre
▬▬▬	Cory Pass Loop
▬▬▬	Fenland Trail & Vermilion Lakes
▬▬▬	Garden Path Trail & Twin Cairns Meadow
▬▬▬	Healy Pass & Simpson Pass
▬▬▬	Johnson Lake
●●●●	Johnston Canyon & the Inkpots
●●●●	Stewart Canyon
●●●●	Sulphur Mountain
●●●●	Sundance Canyon

and wetland. Begin the trail at the Forty Mile Creek Picnic Area, just north of the 'Welcome to Banff' sign on Lynx St. If you're coming from downtown, there's a connecting trail on the left side of Lynx St, just over the rail tracks. Bring along some mosquito repellent as the biting bugs can be rampant along here, and pick up one of the free trail leaflets from the start of the trailhead.

The flat dirt trail (Map p87) travels through the trees and crosses several wooden bridges where you can view the river and the rich **fenland**; look out for wooden posts that match points of interest on the trail leaflet. It's a rich habitat for **wildlife** – listen for

tapping woodpeckers, whistling chickadees, honking Canada geese and, in autumn, bugling elk. Try also to spot the many flowers and plants that thrive in the fenland – sedges, grasses, willows, poplars and dogwoods all flourish in the nutrient-rich groundwater. The only drawback is the constant thrum of traffic traveling along the Trans-Canada Hwy/Hwy 1 nearby, but it does at least give you a sense of how the local wildlife must feel about the racket on the main road.

If you want a longer hike, you can extend the walk by crossing the large bridge about halfway around the loop and heading left down the road to the **Vermilion Lakes**, a

HIKING IN BANFF NATIONAL PARK

NAME	REGION	DESCRIPTION	DIFFICULTY
Fenland Trail & Vermilion Lakes	Banff Town	Flat woodland trail leading to network of lakes where you'll often spot grazing elk	easy
Sundance Canyon	Banff Town	Wild canyon walk reached via paved riverside trail from Banff	easy
Bow Falls & the Hoodoos	Banff Town	Riverside walk to Banff's most famous waterfall and a landscape of weird rock towers	easy
Sulphur Mountain	Banff Town	Steep hike up flank of Sulphur Mountain with wraparound views	moderate
Cascade Amphitheatre	Banff Town	High-level trail across ski fields to classic glacial cirque hidden among mountains	moderate-difficult
Johnston Canyon & the Inkpots	Bow Valley Pkwy	Visits Bow Valley's best-known waterfalls and continues to colorful mountain tarns	moderate
Cory Pass Loop	Bow Valley Pkwy	Tough climb to a rugged pass followed by a scree descent	difficult
Bow Glacier Falls	Icefields Pkwy	Start at Num-Ti-Jah Lodge and walk across boulders and moraines to impressive glacial cascade	easy-moderate
Parker Ridge	Icefields Pkwy	Switchbacking climb to stunning knife-edge ridge above Saskatchewan Glacier	moderate
Peyto Lake & Bow Summit Lookout	Icefields Pkwy	Busy trail to lookout above Peyto Lake, leading to quieter climb to old fire lookout	moderate
Sunset Lookout	Icefields Pkwy	Little-used trail to superb fire lookout with views of rivers, glaciers and peaks	moderate
Helen Lake	Icefields Pkwy	Often-overlooked route up to lake-filled mountain meadow with vistas of Icefields Pkwy	moderate
Plain of Six Glaciers	Lake Louise	Superb walk to glacier viewpoint, with option to stop at historic teahouse	moderate
Lake Agnes & the Beehives	Lake Louise	Steep walk to Lake Louise's most famous teahouse and lofty summit high above	moderate-difficult
Saddleback & Fairview	Lake Louise	Double summit trail from shores of Lake Louise to above-the-clouds viewpoint at top of Fairview	moderate-difficult
Skoki Valley	Lake Louise	True classic of the Rockies, exploring one of the most beautiful backcountry valleys near Lake Louise	moderate-difficult
Paradise Valley & the Giant's Steps	Lake Louise	Difficult Lake Louise trail, hiking through wild valley frequented by goats, marmots and grizzly bears	moderate-difficult
Johnson Lake	Lake Minnewanka	Short ramble around a small placid lake	easy
Stewart Canyon	Lake Minnewanka	Flat lakeshore trail to hidden forest canyon; canoeing possible	easy
C-Level Cirque	Lake Minnewanka	Hike past old mine workings to ice amphitheater high above Lake Minnewanka	moderate
Consolation Lakes Trail	Moraine Lake	Escape Moraine Lake crowds into wild mountains past glassy lakes	easy

 Wildlife Watching   View   Great for Families   Rock Climbing

DURATION	ROUND-TRIP DISTANCE	ELEVATION CHANGE	FEATURES	FACILITIES	PAGE
30min	2.1km (1.3 miles)	negligible			p50
2½-3hr	8km (5 miles)	145m (476ft)			p54
3hr	10.2km (6.4 miles)	60m (197ft)			p50
4hr	11km (6.8 miles)	655m (2149ft)			p55
6hr	15.4km (9.6 miles)	640m (2100ft)			p57
4hr	10.8km (6.7 miles)	215m (705ft)			p58
5-6hr	13km (8.1 miles)	920m (3018fft)			p57
3hr	7.2km (4.4 miles)	155m (509ft)			p64
2hr	4km (2.5 miles)	250m (820ft)			p65
2hr	6.2km (3.8 miles)	245m (803ft)			p66
3hr	9.4km (5.8 miles)	250m (820ft)			p67
4hr	12km (7.5 miles)	455m (1493ft)			p66
4-5hr	13.5km (8.4 miles)	365m (1198ft)			p60
4hr	10.8km (6.6 miles)	495m (1624ft)			p62
5-6hr	10.2km (6.4 miles)	1013m (3323ft)			p63
4 days	50.4km (31.3 miles)	up to 1136m (3727ft)			p71
6-7hr	20.3km (12.6 miles)	385m (1263ft)			p63
45min	3km (1.9 miles)	negligible			p54
1½-2hr	5.6km (3.5 miles)	negligible			p56
4hr	8.8km (5.4 miles)	455m (1493ft)			p56
2hr	6km (3.8 miles)	65m (213ft)			p60

Fishing   Waterfalls   Restrooms   Drinking Water

HIKING IN BANFF NATIONAL PARK (CONTINUED)

NAME	REGION	DESCRIPTION	DIFFICULTY
Larch Valley & Sentinel Pass	Moraine Lake	Wildflowers and native larches in mountain meadow overlooking Ten Peaks, with add-on to high-level pass	moderate
Garden Path Trail & Twin Cairns Meadow	Sunshine Meadows	Wonderful walk through high mountain meadows and past lakes	easy
Healy Pass & Simpson Pass	Sunshine Meadows	Rewarding walk that affords fantastic glimpses over Continental Divide	moderate-difficult
Egypt Lake & Gibbon Pass	Sunshine Meadows	Great option for first-timers in backcountry, taking in lakes and moderately demanding mountains	moderate-difficult
Mt Assiniboine	Sunshine Meadows	Unforgettable journey into wild backcountry around shining pinnacle of Mt Assiniboine	difficult

🚌	*Public Transport to Trailhead*	👫	*Ranger Station Nearby*
🔺	*Backcountry Campsite*	⛐	*Picnic Sites*

wetland that's popular with wildlife spotters. The lakes area 4km (2.5-mile) round-trip from the bridge turnoff. In late May and early June the trail is often closed due to aggressive female elk, which use the area for calving.

🥾 Sundance Canyon

Duration 2½- to three-hour round-trip

Distance 8km (5 miles)

Difficulty Easy

Elevation Change 145m (476ft)

Start/Finish Cave & Basin National Historic Site

Nearest Town Banff

Transportation Bike, foot

Summary A delightful route around a river canyon, with views of a gushing waterfall, rugged mountains and the Bow Valley.

The tarmacked Sundance Trail begins just beyond the Cave & Basin National Historic Site, 1km from downtown Banff. The first part is flat and easy with views of the Bow River to your right and Sulphur Mountain to your left, passing through a few sections of marsh and wetland, where you'll often spy wading birds and dragonflies.

There's a dirt track on the left side of the trail that is reserved for horses, which is handy as it keeps the main trail free of horse manure. If you fancy taking a break, you'll find riverside benches dotted along the trail.

After around 2km (1.2 miles) you'll reach a junction. Fork left on the tarmacked trail veering away from the river and climb gently uphill. The canyon hike proper starts at the end of the tarmacked trail, where there is a bike rack, and passes steeply up the left side of a tumbling waterfall. After crossing the wooden bridge and scrambling up a section of rocks and boulders, you'll come out on the mainly flat, sun-dappled trail, which tracks a bubbling stream through the wooded **canyon**. In summer it's always filled with birdsong and butterflies, and the shady forest makes a rich habitat for lichen, mosses and wildflowers; take along a nature guide to help you spot the species.

After crossing a couple more wooden bridges the trail loops back on itself; after about 1.6km (1 mile), it reaches a **lookout point**, from where there are tree-framed views across the Bow Valley to the distant mountain peaks – look closely and you can even see the twisting outline of Trans-Canada Hwy/Hwy 1. From here the trail descends through switchbacks to the bike lock-up. Retrace your steps back to the start.

🥾 Johnson Lake

Duration 45-minute round-trip

Distance 3km (1.9 miles)

Difficulty Easy

Elevation Change Negligible

Start/Finish Johnson Lake parking lot

Nearest Town Banff

Transportation Car, bike

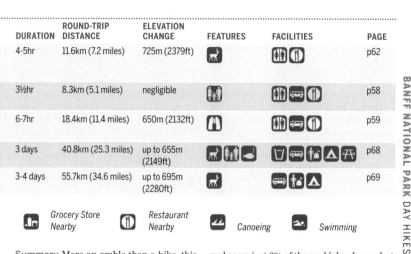

DURATION	ROUND-TRIP DISTANCE	ELEVATION CHANGE	FEATURES	FACILITIES	PAGE
4–5hr	11.6km (7.2 miles)	725m (2379ft)			p62
3½hr	8.3km (5.1 miles)	negligible			p58
6–7hr	18.4km (11.4 miles)	650m (2132ft)			p59
3 days	40.8km (25.3 miles)	up to 655m (2149ft)			p68
3–4 days	55.7km (34.6 miles)	up to 695m (2280ft)			p69

Grocery Store Nearby   Restaurant Nearby   Canoeing   Swimming

Summary More an amble than a hike, this walk circles around the shore of a popular recreational lake, mixing wooded and open-air sections, with the option of a paddle in the water when the weather's warm.

Ringed by fir forest and encircled by an easy trail with views of Cascade Mountain, Johnson Lake makes a lovely place to combine a lakeside picnic with a leisurely stroll. Compared to nearby Lake Minnewanka, it's little more than a pond, but on warm summer days it's the nearest thing Banff has to a seaside getaway: sun-worshippers and beach bums throng to the lake to lounge around in the sunshine. The waters are also ideal for gentle kayaking and paddleboarding, although, with no lakeside boat concession, you'll need to bring your own craft (or rent one in Banff).

To reach the lake, follow Lake Minnewanka Rd north of Trans-Canada Hwy/Hwy 1 and take the first right. The next junction is signposted right to Johnson Lake. From the parking lot, follow the trail past a few picnic tables down to the lakeshore, and pick up the trail on the lake's right (southern side). Initially you'll pass through a grassy section overlooked by power lines from the nearby hydroelectric dam, but the dirt trail soon passes into the fir and spruce woods by the lakeshore.

The trail emerges at an earthen dike on the eastern edge of the lake after about 1.6km (1 mile). The forest to the east is one of the few areas of unmanaged woodland left in Banff National Park, with many old Douglas fir trees. **Johnson Lake** itself sits in the montane zone, a subalpine area that makes up just 3% of the park's landscape but provides a crucial, vegetation-rich habitat for wildlife. Look out for birds and insects as you walk, and see if you can spot any trout or spotted frogs in the water.

On the northern side of the lake the trail sticks close to the water and passes a small **marsh** formed by a tributary off the main lake. Nearby is a shady area under the trees that makes an excellent **picnic spot**. From here it's a short walk back to the parking lot.

Sulphur Mountain

Duration Four-hour round-trip

Distance 11km (6.8 miles)

Difficulty Moderate

Elevation Change 655m (2149ft)

Start/Finish Between Banff Gondola & Upper Hot Springs Pool

Nearest Town Banff

Transportation Bus, bike

Summary Savor your superiority over the gondola-goers after climbing this challenging mountain.

If you want to test your calf muscles, this leg-sapping route up the side of Sulphur Mountain is just the ticket. While mere mortals ride to the top on the gondola (which you'll glimpse occasionally as you ascend the mountain), the sense of achievement you'll get by arriving on foot is worth the climb.

The trail starts at the northwest end of the gondola parking lot, near the Upper

Hot Springs Pool. You start climbing almost immediately on the well-marked trail (a daily workout for some of Banff's fitter residents), with **viewpoints** of Mt Rundle and Banff as you ascend. Most of the trail is along well-graded switchbacks and becomes increasingly steep the further you go; the last section, where the trail arrows straight up the mountainside, is really tough going.

Once at the top, grab an ice cream at the gondola station as a reward and stroll along to **Sanson Peak**, where you'll find Norman Bethune Sanson's old weather station and great views over the whole valley.

Hikers used to get a free trip back down on the gondola, but now you'll have to pay half the standard fare, so you might as well just make the downhill trudge instead.

🚶 C-Level Cirque

Duration Four-hour round-trip

Distance 8.8km (5.4 miles)

Difficulty Moderate

Elevation Change 455m (1493ft)

Start/Finish Upper Bankhead parking lot

Nearest Town Banff

Transportation Car, bike

Summary Throw your own echo into the silent peaks around a natural amphitheater.

This popular trail starts out from the Upper Bankhead parking lot, 3.5km (2.2 miles) from Trans-Canada Hwy/Hwy 1 along Lake Minnewanka Rd. It's relatively short, but steep, and the cirque itself – a deep glacial bowl carved out by a long-gone glacier and surrounded by jagged mountaintops – makes a worthy reward for the climb. Snow lingers in the cirque well into summer; if you're hiking here in early spring, there is a danger of avalanches, so it's worth checking at the park office on trail conditions before you set out.

The route starts from the west side of the parking lot and climbs for about 20 minutes through green forest, often sprinkled with violets, calypso orchids and clematis in summer, before reaching the first remains of the **old anthracite coal mine** of Lower Bankhead; the C-Level in the hike's name refers to the level where the miners once worked.

You'll pass more abandoned mine workings and capped-off shafts as the route climbs. After around 45 minutes of climbing, the forest thins out and you'll begin to catch glimpses back toward Banff Town, Mt Rundle and the nearby lakes, and you'll pass through a few sections with steep drop-offs. A little over an hour into the hike, you'll emerge into the **C-Level Cirque** itself.

Pikas, golden-mantled ground squirrels and the occasional hoary marmot can often be seen scurrying beside the path as you continue along the rough trail skirting the right edge of the cirque. Soon you'll join up with the last steep, rubbly section and climb to a high **lookout knoll**. Rest here and admire the fabulous views stretching back down the valley toward Lake Minnewanka, Banff and the Bow River, before retracing your steps.

🚶 Stewart Canyon

Duration 1½- to two-hour round-trip

Distance 5.6km (3.5 miles)

Difficulty Easy

Elevation Change Negligible

Start/Finish Lake Minnewanka parking lot

Nearest Town Banff

Transportation Car, bike

Summary A level hike that takes in the north shore of Lake Minnewanka plus an impressive river canyon.

With several of the trails around Lake Minnewanka closed during buffalo-berry season due to grizzly-bear activity – including the hike to Aylmer Lookout – this easy walk up to Stewart Canyon is the area's best option for a summer hike.

The trail starts from the recreational area near the boat ramp on the west side of the lake, and travels for a few hundred meters along a flat, paved section past picnic tables and BBQ shelters. The trailhead proper is marked by an information panel, where you'll find notices about trail closures during the buffalo-berry season.

From here the trail passes onto a wooded dirt track offering views of the **turquoise lake**; initially it's just about passable for sturdy wheelchairs, but it becomes increasingly rooty and rocky the further you travel. The trail tracks into pleasant forest, heading over a wooden bridge above the **Cascade River** at the 1.6km (1-mile) mark. On the far side of the river, there's a fork in the trail: the right-hand branch leads up to Aylmer Pass, so take the left fork.

The trail follows the canyon side for another 1.2km (0.7 miles), eventually bringing you to the edge of a river gully. Follow the trail down into the gully, then bear left and clamber across the boulders and rocks to the bottom of the **canyon** and the edge of the Cascade River. The canyon itself is named after George Stewart, first superintendent of Canada's first national park. The water level here has risen by about 25m (80ft) since Lake Minnewanka was last dammed in 1941.

Retrace your steps to the parking lot.

🕅 Cascade Amphitheatre

Duration Six-hour round-trip

Distance 15.4km (9.6 miles)

Difficulty Moderate–difficult

Elevation Change 640m (2100ft)

Start/Finish Mt Norquay parking lot

Nearest Town Banff

Transportation Car

Summary Huge views and a technical hike make this trail a good option if you're after something challenging.

You'll start out high and keep on getting higher on this mountain trail into a hanging valley beneath **Cascade Mountain**, carved out by glaciers that melted away long ago. It's a favored hangout for marmots and pikas, and a well-known spot for appreciating alpine wildflowers in late July and early August, but it's tough going and largely through forest, so you won't get too many views until the end.

Head up Mt Norquay Rd from Banff Town all the way to the ski-lodge parking lot. The trail starts as a service road at the far end of the lot and passes the Mystic chair lift before descending into lodgepole pine forest. Continue straight ahead at the Mystic Pass–Forty Mile Summit junction. After 3km, you'll reach the banks of **Forty Mile Creek**; keep to the right and cross over the bridge.

From here the real climb begins as the trail continues through the forest to a junction with the Elk Lake Summit Trail at the 4.3km (2.7-mile) mark. Keep right and catch your breath ahead of a series of brutal switchbacks that carry you 2.3km (1.4 miles) up the pine-forested western slope of the mountain.

Just before arriving at the valley, the trail levels off and a number of faint paths head to the right. These lead to the summit ridge, which is suitable for mountaineers only, so stick to the main path until you emerge at a lovely **alpine meadow**, which is dotted with white anemone and yellow lilies in summer.

The trail becomes indistinct but continues for about 1km (0.6 miles) to the upper end of the amphitheater, where the vegetation thins out and boulders litter the ground. Rest here for a while before you head back and you'll be able to watch **marmots** and **pikas** scurrying between the rocks.

🕅 Cory Pass Loop

Duration Five to six hours

Distance 13km (8.1 miles)

Difficulty Difficult

Elevation Change 920m (3018ft)

Start/Finish Fireside picnic area

Nearest Town Banff

Transportation Car, bike

Summary Banff's black-diamond hike incorporates mega-steep climbs, some rock scrambling and a scree descent; it's a thrilling white-knuckle ride for those fit enough to tackle it.

The trailhead for Cory Pass is at the Fireside picnic area at the southern end of the Bow Valley Pkwy just off Trans-Canada Hwy/Hwy 1. Although only 8km (5 miles) from Banff town centre, the trail's black (difficult) rating puts off many hikers, meaning splendid isolation is practically guaranteed.

The first part of the trail is deceptively flat, with Trans-Canada Hwy/Hwy 1 traffic noise reminding you of its presence below. After 1km (0.6 miles), the trail divides. Take the left fork and proceed steeply uphill. The next 1.5km (it'll seem more like 4km!) climbs mercilessly upwards with almost no respite. When you reach the top of the crag, the path briefly flattens out, undulating along the ridge line, but after another 30 minutes or so you'll arrive at a new challenge: a steep rocky face where you'll have to undertake a 15m (50ft) downhill rock scramble to reach a dip below. Take extreme care in wet weather.

Re-entering the forest briefly, the path flattens out, traversing a steep slope and climbing gradually toward **Cory Pass**. As the trees thin out, the path becomes increasingly narrow and a little exposed, requiring care and concentration. Cory Pass is visible long before you reach it. Stop briefly at the summit and admire your conquest. **Rock pillars** near the summit of Mt Edith tower above you and the Bow Valley sparkles below.

Snow cover and weather permitting, continue the loop by dropping over the other side of the pass into an awe-inspiringly barren landscape of cliffs and rocky pinnacles. The path descends a loose scree slope steeply and then begins to traverse around the back of **Mt Edith**. It's tough going, but the sight of monolithic **Mt Louis** opposite will stoke your enthusiasm.

You'll eventually trade scree for a rock fall scattered with larger boulders. The path is less distinct here. A short ascent up a muddy slope brings you back into a dwarf forest bisected by avalanche chutes. Make plenty of noise – this is prime bear country. As the forest thickens and descends, you'll reach a junction with the 40 Mile Creek trail. Carry on down Edith Pass for 2.9km (1.8 miles) to the initial trail junction. From here, it's 1km (0.6 miles) back to the Fireside picnic area.

🚶 Johnston Canyon & the Inkpots

Duration Four-hour round-trip

Distance 10.8km (6.7 miles)

Difficulty Moderate

Elevation Change 215m (705ft) to Inkpots

Start/Finish Johnston Canyon parking lot

Nearest Town Banff

Transportation Car/bus

Summary A classic canyon hike past two of the park's most impressive waterfalls.

The paved path through Johnston Canyon to its twin waterfalls is one of Banff's highlights, which means it's nearly always jammed with people – but don't let its popularity put you off. It's a must-see destination, and you can usually beat the worst of the crowds by turning up early – if you arrive before 9am you'll usually have the canyon practically to yourself.

The asphalt trail cuts through the center of the lush canyon, traversing several suspended catwalks high above the surging waters of **Johnston Creek**, which has carved out the canyon from the surrounding limestone rock. Shaded by trees, the towering **canyon walls** are covered with mosses, lichen and ferns, and black swifts can often be seen darting around the treetops during their nesting season from late June to September. It's also a great walk to do in the rain, as a downpour only adds to the spectacular force of the falls.

The first paved section (suitable for wheelchairs) leads to the **Lower Falls** after 30 minutes. Here you can duck through a natural cave right into the spray of the falls – be prepared to get wet, and bring a waterproof bag to protect your camera. The route to the Upper Falls (about 45 minutes from the Lower Falls) is steeper and crosses a few staircases, passing the mineral and algae-encrusted wall known as the **Travertine Drape**. You can descend to another platform viewpoint at the bottom of the **Upper Falls**, but it's worth continuing on up the trail for a reverse view of the falls as they plunge over the cliff edge into the canyon below.

Most people turn back at this point, but they're missing out on another nearby natural marvel: the colorful ponds known as the **Inkpots**. From the Upper Falls, the trail climbs fairly steeply through the forest for 3km (1.9 miles) and then descends into a vast mountain meadow. Here you'll find the six Inkpots, encircled by snowcapped mountains; the pools get their name from the bright blue-green water that bubbles up from natural springs deep inside the mountain.

From the Inkpots, trails lead deep into the backcountry: northeast along Mystic Pass and Forty Mile Creek, and northwest along Johnston Creek (often used by bears as a drinking hole). Both are overnight trips, so you'll need proper supplies and a wilderness pass to tackle either trail. Otherwise, return the way you came to the Johnston Canyon parking lot.

🚶 Garden Path Trail & Twin Cairns Meadow

Duration 3½-hour round-trip

Distance 8.3km (5.1 miles)

Difficulty Easy

Elevation Change Negligible from ski area, 655m (2148ft) from parking lot

Start/Finish Sunshine Village ski area

Nearest Town Banff

Transportation Car or shuttle bus, gondola

Summary The easiest of the hikes from Sunshine Village takes in lakes, flowers and a viewpoint of Simpson Pass.

This might be the easiest option in Sunshine Meadows, but it's certainly not short on views. The flat, well-marked trail meanders past three glimmering alpine lakes and through lush meadows filled with summer wildflowers, leading to a grandstand lookout above the Continental Divide. Watch out for ground squirrels bounding around the pathway and take along a field guide to help you check off the summer blossoms.

Catch the **gondola** from its base station at the parking lot up to the Sunshine Village ski area. The trailhead starts on the southern side of the ski area, passing under the line of the main gondola up to Standish Ridge.

From here it's a gentle 10-minute climb up to the first fork, where you should stay right. At the top of the hill, you enter the **alpine meadows**, sprinkled with mountain flowers and larch trees; you'll soon reach the summit of the **Great Divide** and cross over into British Columbia. At the next junction, keep right; the left fork leads to Quartz Hill and the soaring Citadel Pass.

Over the crest of the hill, the terrain rolls downward to **Rock Isle Lake**, so called for the distinctive wooded islet that juts out from the middle of the water. Above the lake there's a good **lookout** with views of Standish Ridge to the right and Quartz Hill to the left, with a distant glimpse of the snowy pinnacle of Mt Assiniboine.

Rejoin the trail and head left at the next junction. The path winds through larch trees and past pebble-filled streams en route to the Grizzly and Larix Lakes Loop. Continue over the next junction for **Grizzly Lake**, and follow the lakeshore to the **Simpson Valley Lookout**. The pass is named after George Simpson, governor of the Hudson's Bay Company, who made the first foray along the valley in 1841. From the viewpoint, the trail loops around green-blue **Larix Lake** and rejoins the main Garden Path Trail.

You could return to Sunshine Village the way you came, but for better views head back via Twin Cairns Meadow. Turn left at the first junction after Rock Isle Lake, signposted to Standish Viewpoint. It's worth detouring 500m (0.3 miles) off the main trail to reach the **Standish Ridge Viewpoint**, which offers a 360-degree panorama encompassing Citadel Pass, Simpson Valley and Healy Pass.

Descend back to the main trail and turn right (north) across **Twin Cairns Meadow**. After 2km (1.2 miles) you reach a T-junction; take a detour left to **Monarch Viewpoint** (100m), which has excellent views of Mt Assiniboine on a clear day. Turn back from the viewpoint and follow the path back down to Sunshine Village, 1.6km (1 mile) away, via a winding trail through the woods.

Note that the last gondola returns downhill at 6pm; if you miss it, you'll need to walk downhill an extra 5km to the parking lot.

🥾 Healy Pass & Simpson Pass

Duration Six- to seven-hour round-trip

Distance 18.4km (11.4 miles)

Difficulty Moderate–difficult

Elevation Change 650m (2132ft)

Start/Finish Sunshine Village parking lot

Nearest Town Banff

Transportation Bus, Car

Summary Wildflowers, forest and lofty mountain ramparts combine on this varied hike, which ascends from the valley floor right to the rooftop of Sunshine Meadows.

For an above-the-tree-line Sunshine Meadows adventure, this challenging route up Healy Pass traverses lush meadows with an uninterrupted vista of peaks and lakes. It's ideally undertaken late in the season, when the weather's best.

The trailhead begins at the Sunshine Village parking lot, near the gondola base station. It leads up a rocky service road, passing into forest after 800m (0.5 miles). From here the trail crosses Sunshine Creek and ascends steadily along Healy Valley, canopied by spruce and fir trees. Look out for red squirrels, woodpeckers, chickadees and Clark's nutcrackers in the trees. The trail then leads along Healy Creek, reaching the Healy Creek Campground after 5.7km (3.5 miles).

From here the forest opens up and the trail levels off into a more gradual climb as it enters **Healy Meadows** by a gurgling stream. The meadows are alive with wildflowers throughout July and August. You'll pass the junction for Simpson Pass Trail on the left at the 7.7km (4.8-mile) mark, but press on to Healy Pass first, another 1.5km (0.9 miles) further on through beautiful alpine terrain.

Perched at 2330m (7644ft) atop the escarpment of Monarch Ramparts, **Healy Pass** offers one of the Rockies' great views. It's only 1km (0.6 miles) from the Great Divide, and looks over some of the region's most dramatic sights, including the witch's-hat peak of Mt Assiniboine far to the southeast. To the west are Egypt, Mummy and Scarab Lakes, shining brightly beneath the Pharaoh Peaks, and to the north, the aptly named Massive Range broods along the horizon. You might even spy grizzlies and black bears on the open meadows around the pass.

Descend the way you came back to the Healy Meadows junction and take the trail toward Simpson Pass. Interspersing marshy meadows with stands of forest, the path passes a junction for Eohippus Lake before dropping down to **Simpson Pass** at 2135m (7004ft), a narrow meadow furnished with a couple of red bollards that mark the border between Alberta and British Columbia.

The path reenters forest and traverses beneath a low escarpment before crossing a creek and climbing to Wawa Ridge. Views over meadows flecked with cotton grass and small ponds open out and you'll soon be delivered to the dramatic **Monarch Viewpoint** at the edge of Sunshine Meadows. From here it's a 1.6km (1 mile) descent down to Sunshine Village where you can grab a snack in the **Mad Trapper's Saloon** (www.skibanff.com/eat-shop/eat/village; mains C$14-20; ⏱10:30am-11pm), then catch the gondola or walk 5km back down to the parking lot.

Lake Louise & Around

🥾 Consolation Lakes Trail

Duration Two-hour round-trip

Distance 6km (3.8 miles)

Difficulty Easy

Elevation Change 65m (213ft)

Start/Finish Moraine Lake

Nearest Town Lake Louise

Transportation Car

Summary It's only a short uphill stroll from Moraine Lake, but this trail still offers a taste of the wild Rockies.

Most people never get much further than the Moraine Lake shoreline, but to reach the real scenery you really do have to stretch your legs. This short trail winds through rocks and boulders to a duo of sparkling mountain lakes backed by brooding cliffs. The walk is straightforward, although you will need proper hiking boots – the trail gets very muddy in spring and autumn, and traverses an area of rough, rocky boulders en route to the lakeshore. Note also that the Consolation Lakes are prime bear habitat, and fall under group-access restrictions in summer.

Heading east from the parking lot, follow signs for the **Consolation Lakes**. You'll pass a small bridge and skirt the back of the **Lake Moraine Rockpile**, crossing over a rocky moraine before ascending into pine forest. This section of the trail offers great views

up the side of Mt Babel and back over the shoreline peaks of Moraine Lake.

For the next 1.6km (1 mile), the trail winds by the trees along the shores of the clattering **Babel Creek**. Some sections get very muddy after snowmelt and heavy rain, but try not to take any shortcuts off the main path, as it damages the fragile forest habitat.

You'll reach the **Consolation Lakes** after 3km (1.9 miles), tucked into the base of a distinctive U-shaped glacial valley dotted with rough boulders, scree and smashed rocks, which make for difficult walking. Take extra care as you cross the rocks toward the shore of the **Lower Lake**. The valley is trammeled by Panorama Ridge to the east, Mt Bell to the southeast and the sharp peaks of Mt Quadra and Bident Mountain at the northern side of the lake. The icy monsters to the west are Mt Fay and Mt Babel.

The trail to the **Upper Lake** crosses some treacherous areas of boulders and scree, so unless you're an experienced scrambler, it's best to settle for the views from the Lower Lake before heading for home.

🥾 Plain of Six Glaciers

Duration Four- to five-hour round-trip

Distance 13.5km (8.4 miles)

Difficulty Moderate

Elevation Change 365m (1198ft)

Start/Finish Fairmont Chateau Lake Louise

Nearest Town Lake Louise

Transportation Car

Summary One of the Lake Louise classics, ending at a historic teahouse with views across the Victoria and Lefroy Glaciers.

This perennially popular hike from Lake Louise punches up the rubble-strewn glacial valley to the foot of Victoria and Lefroy Glaciers, twin tongues of glittering ice jammed between regal peaks. It's a jaw-dropper of a hike that'll leave you breathless in more ways than one. You'll need sturdy boots, warm layers and a good rain shell; walking poles are useful for keeping yourself upright on the shifting moraines. The trail is often one of the last to open after spring due to snow and avalanche danger; check trail conditions at the park office before you start out.

Follow the paved shoreline walk from the Fairmont Chateau Lake Louise for 2km (1.3 miles) to the lake's southwestern end, then

Lake Louise & Around – Day Hikes

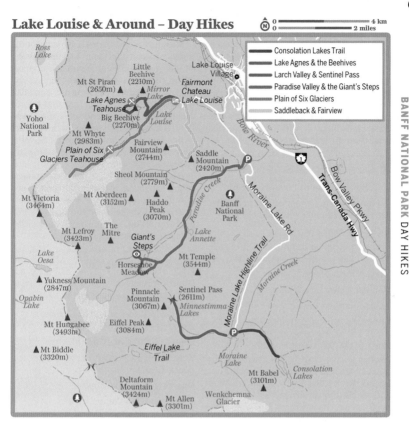

BANFF NATIONAL PARK DAY HIKES

head along the edge of the river flats, watching as the glacial creek feeding the lake becomes a torrent. The trail climbs steadily through forest, emerging occasionally to give you views of the glacial ravine. At the 3.3km (2-mile) mark and again at the 4km (2.5-mile) mark, you'll meet trails branching off to the right, leading to the highline trail to the Big Beehive and Lake Agnes. Ignore these and press on up the valley, as the tree cover gradually thins out and you emerge onto switchbacks. You'll have plenty of opportunity to stop and catch your breath, as well as to gaze at the rapidly approaching glaciers to the southwest and the ice-strewn slopes of Mts Lefroy and Victoria. Keep your ears open for the rumble of avalanches crashing off the distant Victoria Glacier, especially late in the morning.

After two hours and 5.5km (3.4 miles) of climbing, you'll reach the Plain of Six Glaciers Teahouse (snacks & meals C$9.50-25; 9am-5pm mid-Jun–early Oct), constructed in 1927 as a way station for Swiss mountaineering guides leading clients up to the summit of Mt Victoria. Nestled in a quiet glade, the twin-level stone and log chalet looks like something out of the pages of Heidi, and dishes up homemade sandwiches, cakes, gourmet teas and hot chocolates to a steady stream of puffed-out hikers.

Despite its allure, sensible walkers leave the treats of the teahouse for the return walk, as the main hike isn't over yet. From the clearing, the trail leads a further 1.6km (1 mile) uphill to the Plain of Six Glaciers itself, tracking a rubbly ridge that can be slippery in wet weather and is exposed to vicious winds funneled up the valley.

Although there's nothing to mark it, you'll know you've reached the lookout when you have a grandstand view of the front edge of the Victoria Glacier and can see back down the valley to Lake Louise and the chateau. In the 1800s the glacier covered most of the surrounding area. From the lookout, a path leads up the face of the moraine to the cliff edge and a small waterfall; it's very slippery, so only tackle it if you're a competent scrambler. You should see the cleft of Abbot Pass from the top. Once you've admired the views, retrace your steps down the moraine and visit the teahouse before heading back down the valley. If your legs are up to it, you could detour along the signposted highline trail, which links up with the route to Lake Agnes and the Big Beehive.

🏃 Larch Valley & Sentinel Pass

Duration Four- to five-hour round-trip

Distance 8.6km (5.3 miles) to Larch Valley, 11.6km (7.2 miles) to Sentinel Pass

Difficulty Moderate

Elevation Change 535m (1755ft) to Larch Valley, 725m (2379ft) to Sentinel Pass

Start/Finish Moraine Lake

Nearest Town Lake Louise

Transportation Car

Summary A popular trail through larch forest and alpine meadows with wonderful views of the Wenkchemna Peaks.

Another of the Lake Louise area's quintessential hikes, this route offers one of the best perspectives on the Valley of the Ten Peaks and travels through some of the park's finest larch forests. Snow lingers at higher elevations well into spring, so it's best visited in fall when the valley turns into a sea of autumnal colors. Strong hikers can extend the walk for an impressive mountain panorama at Sentinel Pass.

Start on the Moraine Lake Trail and veer right at the signpost for Larch Valley into dense forest, traveling up a set of switchbacks that gain over 350m (1148ft) in 2.5km (1.6m miles).

At the first junction, the left trail leads to Eiffel Lake (another great destination that's often quieter than the Larch Valley trail). Follow the right-hand turn and climb further into the fragrant forest, emerging after about 3.5km (2.2 miles) into the wide-open spaces of **Larch Valley**. The meadows are famous for their wildflowers, but the high-alpine habitat is extremely fragile, so don't step off the main trail if you can possibly help it.

From here, the path breaks above the tree line and continues to the little **Minnestimma Lakes** at about the 4.5km (2.8-mile) mark. From here, there's an amazing view of

eight of the 10 Wenkchemna Peaks, as well as the white mass of the **Fay Glacier**.

Most hikers end the walk here, but if the weather's good and your legs are feeling strong, you could continue up and over the 2611m (8566ft) **Sentinel Pass**, one of the highest maintained passes in the Canadian Rockies. It's a hard, tiring trail that crosses slippery areas of talus and scree; don't even think about tackling it in snow or heavy rain, as the weather can turn suddenly. Check the forecasts before you set out, and bring extra layers and rain gear.

From the top of the pass, experienced hikers can make a truly epic circle down into the adjacent Paradise Valley, but you'll be stranded at the other end unless you've got two vehicles. Note this route falls under group-access restrictions.

🏃 Lake Agnes & the Beehives

Duration Four-hour round-trip

Distance 10.8km (6.6 miles)

Difficulty Moderate to Lake Agnes, moderate–difficult to Big Beehive

Elevation Change 495m (1624ft)

Start/Finish Fairmont Chateau Lake Louise (p103)

Nearest Town Lake Louise

Transportation Car

Summary The walk that practically everyone who visits Lake Louise wants to do. It's crowded, but the sights are unmissable.

This is one of the most popular walks in the Lake Louise area, so it's worth doing early or late in the day to beat the crowds. It's a fine, well-marked route taking in forest trails, hidden lakes and scenic viewpoints, as well as a famous teahouse – but it is formidably steep (especially around the Big Beehive), so bring plenty of water and take regular rests. You can either make it a stand-alone hike or combine it with the Plain of Six Glaciers hike.

Begin on the Lake Louise shoreline trail, and take the fork on the right after about 800m (0.5 miles) as it ascends into forest. The path zigzags through the trees for about 45 minutes, with occasional views back over the lake to Fairview Mountain, before emerging at the glassy surface of **Mirror Lake**, famous for its photogenic reflection of the Big Beehive. The lake makes a good place to refuel before continuing on the steep climb to Lake Agnes itself.

The trail divides at Mirror Lake. You can reach Lake Agnes via the right-hand trail, but the most straightforward route is to take a left from the lake and then an immediate right after about 100m for the direct climb to the teahouse (left here leads on to the Plain of Six Glaciers hike). It's a steep slog through the forest for a further 15 minutes, but you'll have good views of the mountains as the trees begin to thin out. The final section passes a waterfall and traverses a near-vertical set of wooden stairs before emerging at the lake and the teahouse.

Lake Agnes is named after Lady Susan Agnes Macdonald (wife of former prime minister Sir John Macdonald), who made the climb to the lake in 1890. There's been a **teahouse** (www.lakeagnesteahouse.com; lunch C$7.50-15; ⊗ 8am-5pm early Jun–early Oct) here since 1901, but the present building is actually a replica built in 1981. It serves a huge selection of exotic teas ranging from golden monkey to 'Imperial Keernun' sacred blend, but tables can be scarce at peak times. Soups, cakes and sandwich platters are also available if you're after something more substantial.

Once you've fueled up at the teahouse, you can take an optional detour to the top of the **Little Beehive** (105m/344ft elevation gain) before heading around the right side of the lake en route to its bigger brother, the **Big Beehive** (135m/442ft elevation gain), which you'll reach after 1.6km (1 mile) of relentless, leg-shredding switchbacks. Needless to say, the summit rewards the effort: you'll enjoy a sky-topping vantage over the entire Lake Louise area, with the Slate Range to the northeast, the Bow Valley southeast and Lake Louise and its surrounding peaks way below. It's a truly unforgettable lookout, but you'll need a head for heights.

From the top, you can either retrace your steps to Lake Agnes, or descend south toward the Plain of Six Glaciers trail.

🥾 Saddleback & Fairview

Duration Five- to six-hour round-trip

Distance 7.4km (4.6 miles) to Saddleback, 10.2km (6.4 miles) to Fairview

Difficulty Moderate–difficult

Elevation Change 600m (1970ft) to Saddleback, 1013m (3323ft) to Fairview

Start/Finish Lake Louise

Nearest Town Lake Louise

Transportation Car

Summary Big vistas from two of Lake Louise's most famous viewpoints, but tough going all the way to the top.

This hike starts out steep and just keeps getting steeper, climbing to a famous pass between Fairview and Saddle Mountain, and an even more famous summit lookout. There's no getting around the elevation gain, but at least you'll feel like you've earned the view.

Start at the viewpoint in front of the Fairmont Chateau Lake Louise, and follow signs pointing to Saddleback. After around 300m, you'll reach a junction: the left fork joins up with the Moraine Lake Highline Trail, while the right fork emerges at a viewpoint above the lake. The main trail lies dead ahead.

Climb sharply along the snaking trail, ascending relentlessly through spruce and larch forest. To the north, ever grander views of the Trans-Canada Hwy/Hwy 1 and the mountains beyond unfold as you continue upward all the way to **Saddleback** at the 3.7km (2.3-mile) mark.

The landscape of Lake Louise opens up like a panoramic picture book once you finally reach the top of the pass. It's a superb place to tick off some of the main peaks around Lake Louise: south is Mt Temple, while southwest are Sheol Mountain and Haddo Peak. A compass and a topo map are useful to help identify each mountain.

Directly north of the pass is the trail to the top of **Fairview**, the craggy peak that dominates the southern side of Lake Louise. You don't necessarily have to tackle the path to the top, but it's worth the toil if you're up to it. Basic scrambling skills and sturdy boots with plenty of grip will come in handy, as some sections can be rocky and slippery. Once you reach the top, you'll realize exactly how the mountain got its name.

🥾 Paradise Valley & the Giant's Steps

Duration Six- to seven-hour round-trip

Distance 20.3km (12.6 miles)

Difficulty Moderate-difficult

Elevation Change 385m (1263ft)

Start/Finish Paradise Valley parking area, Moraine Lake Rd

Nearest Town Lake Louise

Transportation Car

Summary An unforgettable route along a remote mountain valley, rated by many seasoned hikers as one of their favorite destinations in the Canadian Rockies.

Paradise Valley goes head to head with Larch Valley in the scenic stakes. It's a showstopper, tracing a route past ice-crowned summits, delicate cornices, scree slopes and a natural rock cascade called the Giant's Steps. This is prime grizzly habitat, so group-access restrictions may be in force – take care and make extra noise. Trails were rerouted in 2007 to reduce the risk of bear encounters.

The trailhead is located at a small parking lot about 2.5km (1.6 miles) along Moraine Lake Rd. The first section travels gently through forest, tracking the course of Paradise Creek. At 1.1km (0.7 miles) from the trailhead, you'll cross the Moraine Lake Highline Trail between Lake Louise and Moraine Lake; turn right (north), then almost immediately left (west) for Paradise Valley.

The trail then crosses the creek a couple of times before passing the right-hand fork to Saddleback at the 4.2km (2.6-mile) mark. Ignore the junction and continue south toward Lake Annette, which you'll reach after a brief but stiff climb at around the 5.8km (3.6-mile) mark. This peaceful lake feels thrillingly remote, surrounded by lonely mountains and silent forest that remain snow clad until well into July. It also offers soaring views of nearby Mt Temple, the highest peak around Lake Louise, and the third highest in Banff National Park.

From the lake, the trail rolls southwest toward the head of the valley, dominated by the dramatic Horseshoe Glacier and a cluster of impressive peaks. The tallest of all is Mt Hungabee, which means 'chieftain' in the Stoney language. As you continue southwest, the specter of Pinnacle Mountain appears to the south, while to the northwest across the valley, the glacier-flanked slopes of Mt Lefroy loom above a sparkling blue glacial lake. This section is one of the most dramatic in the entire national park; take your time and don't forget to take plenty of pictures.

After 8.5km (5.2 miles), you'll reach a right-hand fork leading to the northwest. Take the turnoff and follow the path down toward a bridge over Paradise Creek. Soon afterwards, you'll reach another junction: straight ahead takes you to the little Paradise Valley Campground, while the right-hand fork leads to the tumble of rock slabs known as the Giant's Steps after about 300m. Check ahead at the park office if camping, as the campground can close when there's bear activity.

From the Giant's Steps, you can either retrace your steps or make an optional loop around the edge of Horseshoe Meadow (keep an extra eye out for bears here). On the south side of the meadow, you'll pass the connector trail south to Sentinel Pass, while the main trail leads northeast back toward Lake Annette.

Icefields Parkway

🚶 Bow Glacier Falls

Duration Three-hour round-trip

Distance 7.2km (4.4 miles)

Difficulty Easy–moderate

Elevation Change 155m (509ft)

Start/Finish Num-Ti-Jah Lodge

Nearest Town Lake Louise

Transportation Car

Summary Cross river flats and moraine fields to reach a glacier-fed waterfall.

When Jimmy Simpson used to lead his guests along this well-worn walk in the early 1900s, the Bow Glacier still filled much of the basin at the end of the trail. These days it has shrunk into the mountains, leaving a boulder-filled valley and the clattering Bow Glacier Falls in its wake. It's an easy and rewarding jaunt, with just one steep section and a fine finish as you cross the moraine moonscape up to the face of the falls. It's a good one to consider on rainy days, when the cascade is at its most powerful.

The trailhead starts just behind Jimmy Simpson's former hotel, Num-Ti-Jah Lodge, 37km (23 miles) from the southern end of the Icefields Pkwy. The first section winds along the lakeshore, with views of Crowfoot Mountain and the Wapta Icefield. After 2km (1.2 miles) you reach the edge of the lake, and follow the path southwest across a rock bed. Follow the cairns across the rocky terrain, heading for a distant staircase and the canyon mouth.

After 3.5km (2.2 miles) the steep staircase leads you up a forested ridge alongside the canyon; watch your step if it has been raining, as there are no handholds and there's a long drop to your left. About halfway up you'll pass a massive boulder jammed into the valley, which climbers have to cross in order to follow the route to the high-altitude Bow Hut, the starting point for many ascents.

Icefields Parkway – Day Hikes

After 10 minutes or so the staircase ends and the trail leads onto the edge of the huge moraine field, sprinkled with boulders, rocks and stones and backed by the distant crash of the **Bow Glacier Falls** plunging 100m (328ft) over the edge of the valley. Cairns mark the route across the valley to the falls themselves; walking poles will come in handy here, as it's usually slippery underfoot. Finish up with a drink and a picnic beside the cascade before retracing your steps back to the lodge.

🥾 Parker Ridge

Duration Two-hour round-trip

Distance 4km (2.5 miles)

Difficulty Moderate

Elevation Change 250m (820ft)

Start/Finish Parker Ridge parking lot

Nearest Town Saskatchewan River Crossing

Transportation Car

Summary If you want to see a glacier in all its glory, you can't beat this steep ascent onto the crest of an impossibly scenic ridge near the Banff–Jasper border.

If you only do one hike along the Icefields Pkwy, make it Parker Ridge. It's short enough to crack in an afternoon, but leads to one of the most impressive lookouts of any of Banff's day hikes, with a grandstand view of Mt Saskatchewan, Mt Athabasca and the gargantuan Saskatchewan Glacier. Bring warm clothing and a decent coat, as the wind on the ridge can be punishing.

The first part of the walk is pretty uneventful. From the parking lot the trail runs through a narrow wood before emerging on the hillside and entering a long series of switchbacks. As you climb, you look down onto the main road as it recedes into the distance, and every step improves the panorama of mountains across the valley. Near the top, the trail briefly turns nasty, ascending sharply before you finally stumble over the crest of the ridge at the 2km (1.2-mile) mark, puffed out and panting, to be greeted by an arctic blast of wind and an explosive panorama of peaks and glaciers.

To the west loom Mts Athabasca and Andromeda, and just to their south is the gleaming bulk of the Saskatchewan Glacier, which lurks at the end of a deep valley. At almost 13km (8-miles) long, the glacier is one of the longest in the Rockies, but it's actually just a spur from the massive 230-sq-km (88-sq-mile) Columbia Icefield that lies to the north. For the best views, turn left and follow the trail southeast along the edge of the ridge, stopping at one or more of the unmarked viewpoints along the way.

On the way back down the trail, you can swing left onto a narrow spur trail, which climbs for 15 minutes to another ridge crest, marked by rough cairn shelters where you can escape the wind and look down over the parkway. Retrace your steps and rejoin the main trail for the descent to the parking lot.

🚶 Peyto Lake & Bow Summit Lookout

Duration Two-hour round-trip

Distance 6.2km (3.8 miles)

Difficulty Moderate

Elevation Change 245m (803ft)

Start/Finish Peyto Lake parking lot

Nearest Town Saskatchewan River Crossing

Transportation Car

Summary An old fire road passing the famous Peyto Lake viewpoint up to an abandoned fire lookout high above the Bow and Mistaya Valleys.

You'll have plenty of company along the first part of this trail to the Peyto Lake Lookout, where practically every Icefields Pkwy visitor stops to snap a photo or two of this stunning blue-green glacial lake. The panoramas just keep getting grander as you leave the crowds behind and continue ascending to the Bow Summit Lookout, a high-country perch with long views north and south along the Icefields Pkwy.

You reach the initial Peyto Lake Lookout after an easy 15 minutes through the forest from the main parking lot. Leave behind the crowds on the main wooden lookout and continue to a three-way junction; the left

trail leads to the upper parking lot, while the right and middle trails continue on a forested loop with interpretive signs detailing various aspects of the alpine environment.

Continue along the middle trail (the left side of the loop), looking out for a dirt road on your left signposted for 'Bow Summit Lookout.' Branch left here and follow the dirt road as it traces a zigzag course uphill, bending abruptly to the right at one point, then crossing through a dirt- and pebble-strewn clearing and doubling back to the left.

From here the trail continues to climb, with wildflowers replacing the increasingly scarce trees. At the 2.5km (1.5-mile) mark the road dips into a rocky bowl, often frequented by sunbathing marmots and bisected by a tinkling stream. Cross the bowl and set out on the last ascent of 500m (0.3 miles), crossing two hills to the Bow Summit Lookout. North is Mistaya Valley rising southwards up to Bow Pass, east is Cirque Peak, and southeast across the Bow Valley is the great sweep of Crowfoot Glacier.

🚶 Helen Lake

Duration Four-hour round-trip

Distance 12km (7.5 miles)

Difficulty Moderate

Elevation Change 455m (1493ft)

Start/Finish Helen Lake parking lot

Nearest Town Lake Louise

Transportation Car

Summary Steep route leading up to a hidden valley renowned for its glorious display of summer wildflowers.

This is one of the most beautiful high-altitude valleys along the Icefields Pkwy, and in summer it's also one of the top places to see a Technicolor display of Canadian wildflowers. You'll have a real sense of solitude at the top, and the mountain panoramas of Cirque Peak and Dolomite Peak are outstanding. It's best done in good weather; you're quite exposed on the trail and at the top, and the views are disappointing if it's sheeting with rain. The high mountain meadows also remain snowbound until well into July. Bears are fairly common visitors to the area, so hike in a group and make plenty of noise on the trail.

The trailhead is 33km (20.5 miles) along the parkway, near the turnoff to the Crowfoot Glacier viewpoint. From the Helen Lake parking lot, follow the dirt trail through

WORTH A TRIP

MISTAYA CANYON

Looking for a scenic place to stretch your legs along the Icefields Pkwy, without the exertion of a full-fledged hike? Just 5km south of Saskatchewan River Crossing, the 15-minute trail to Mistaya Canyon makes an easy, worthwhile detour. The dirt track leads gently downhill through forest for around 500m (0.3 miles) before emerging high above the pounding swirl of the Mistaya River, which rises in Peyto Lake far to the south.

From the bridge you can watch the river plunge impressively down into the curves and curls of the potholed limestone ravine, and watch how the action of the water has carved out the canyon's tortuous shape. From the far side of the bridge the path leads on to two much more challenging trails, including the long slog up to the disused Sarbach fire lookout, a 10.6km (6.6-mile) round-trip, and the historic route to Howse Pass, the first fur-trading route established through the Canadian Rockies. It's 4.3km (2.7 miles) to the Howse River.

spruce and fir for a 3km (1.9-mile) ascent. As the forest thins, you'll be treated to fine views of Crowfoot Glacier and Bow Lake across the valley.

Near the top of the ascent, an area of old burned forest slowly levels out into an ancient glacial valley, spotted with stands of pine and larch, and carpeted with vivid displays of wildflowers between July and August. The trail winds across a couple of creeks and leads past a massive rockslide, where you'll often be able to spot marmots squeaking among the rocks, before rising up and over a flat plateau of heather and alpine grass all the way to Helen Lake at the 6km (3.7-mile) mark.

The lake offers a superb viewpoint back down the valley. To the north is the lumpy prominence of Cirque Peak, and to the east are the chimneylike stacks of Dolomite Peak along the horizon, named by early explorers for its resemblance to the Dolomite Mountains of northern Italy. Break the hike here and savor the solitude; few hikes give you such a sense of the age and silent power of the country.

For a longer walk, strong hikers could continue northeast from the lake for the lonely lookout of Dolomite Pass, reached after another 2.9km.

🏃 Sunset Lookout

Duration Three-hour round-trip

Distance 9.4km (5.8 miles)

Difficulty Moderate

Elevation Change 250m (820ft)

Start/Finish Sunset Lookout parking lot

Nearest Town Saskatchewan River Crossing

Transportation Car

Summary An abandoned fire lookout

commanding unbroken views of the North Saskatchewan Valley.

This remote trail is just a few kilometers inside the northern border of Banff National Park, and it feels a long way from anywhere. It's mainly used as an access route for backpackers on the way to Pinto Lake and the wilderness area beyond, but the first section gives you a sense of adventure without actually having to camp out overnight.

From the parking lot on the east side of the parkway, 16.5km north of Saskatchewan River Crossing, the trail climbs sharply through lodgepole pine forest, roughly following the course of Norman Creek. In late July the forest is thick with buffalo-berry bushes, so it's a favorite feeding ground for hungry grizzlies – check for trail closures before you start out, and make noise to avoid surprise encounters. The path leads past a dramatic canyon carved out by Norman Creek, before zigzagging back into forest and reaching the left-hand junction for the lookout after around 2.9km (1.8 miles).

From here, it's another 1.8km (1.1 miles) to the lookout site, dangling high above the forest. Far below are the Graveyard Flats, crisscrossed by the neighboring Alexandra and North Saskatchewan Rivers. A roll call of remote mountains looms on each horizon, including Mt Saskatchewan to the west and faraway Bow Peak to the south. The fire lookout itself operated between 1943 and 1978; you can still make out its foundations and the remains of cables that were once connected to the lookout's lightning conductor.

Back at the main trail, you can either turn right back to the parking lot, or turn left and strike out for Sunset Pass, 7.6km (4.7 miles) from the trailhead. Beyond lies some of Banff's wildest backcountry, including Pinto Lake and the White Goat Wilderness Area.

🚶 OVERNIGHT HIKES

Banff's day hikes offer ample adventure for most people, but for a real appreciation of the park's wild side you've got to head into the backcountry. With a network of trails crisscrossing the high mountains, and a selection of routes ranging anywhere from two days to several weeks, there are enough backcountry trips here to satisfy the most mile-hungry hiker; the real challenge lies in choosing which one to do.

You don't necessarily have to submit a full trip itinerary when you purchase your wilderness pass, but it's often a good idea; if you're not back by the specified date, a search party will set out to look for you, so it's vital that you report back to park authorities once your trip is finished to avoid triggering a false alarm.

Wild camping is only permitted in certain remote areas – contact the Banff Visitor Centre (p110) for details. In the backcountry, you have to pack out all your garbage by law.

🚶 Egypt Lake & Gibbon Pass

Duration Three days one-way to Vista Lake/Twin Lakes trailhead

Distance 40.8km (25.3 miles) one-way to Vista Lake/Twin Lakes trailhead

Difficulty Moderate–difficult

Elevation Change Up to 655m (2149ft)

Start Sunshine Village parking lot

Finish Vista Lake/Twin Lakes trailhead, Hwy 93

Nearest Town Banff

Transportation Bus/car

Summary An ideal introduction to the world of the backcountry, crossing meadows and a mountain pass en route to a network of glittering lakes.

This backcountry classic starts out as a standard day hike to Healy Pass and just keeps on going. Rather than turning back

Egypt Lake & Gibbon Pass

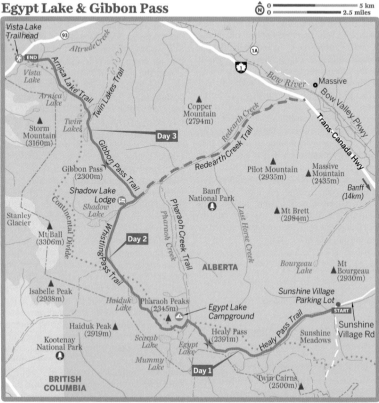

once you've crossed the Continental Divide, you'll continue on for another 3km (1.9 miles) to reach the high mountain tarns around Egypt Lake. Time it right and you'll be greeted with a profusion of wonderful summer wildflowers or autumnal trees. Whenever you choose to come, you'll have a sweeping panorama of the Monarch Ramparts, the Ball Range and the Alberta–British Columbia border. Best of all, it's relatively straightforward for a backcountry hike, which unfortunately also means it can get crowded in season.

DAY 1: SUNSHINE VILLAGE PARKING LOT TO EGYPT LAKE CAMPGROUND
4 HOURS / 12.4KM (7.7 MILES)

Start out on the Healy Pass hike from the Sunshine Village parking lot, and once you crest **Healy Pass**, continue northwest into forest, passing Pharaoh Creek after 3km (1.9 miles). A little further on, you pass a trail on the right to Egypt Lake Warden Cabin, then cross a bridged creek into a meadow, where you'll find your overnight spot of Egypt Lake Campground and Shelter. Book well ahead for both in season.

Several spur trails radiate out from the campground and provide excellent day-hike options, including the 4.2km (2.6 miles) to Natalko (Talc) Lake and the 2.8km (1.7-mile) trail to Pharaoh and Black Rock Lakes.

DAY 2: EGYPT LAKE CAMPGROUND TO SHADOW LAKE
5-6 HOURS / 14.4KM (8.9 MILES)

Ringed by forest and the Pharaoh Peaks, **Egypt Lake** is one of the loveliest high-altitude lakes in the park. It shimmers a short 15-minute stroll from the Egypt Lake Campground. A couple of good side-trips in the vicinity beckon to **Scarab Lake** and **Mummy Lake**. To continue on the main hike, ascend **Whistling Pass**, supposedly named for the hooting hoary marmots that live there, although it could equally be named for the whistling wind that often whips across the top of the pass. From here, it's another 9km (5.6 miles) paralleling the Continental Divide to **Shadow Lake**, where you can overnight at the campground or backcountry lodge.

DAY 3: SHADOW LAKE TO VISTA LAKE TRAILHEAD
5-6 HOURS / 14KM (8.7 MILES)

From Shadow Lake, you have a choice of routes back to civilization. You could head northeast for 13.9km (8.6 miles) along Redearth Creek, but the more scenic option is

the 14km (8.7-mile) route over **Gibbon Pass** via **Twin Lakes** and **Arnica Lake**, which ends at the Vista Lake/Twin Lakes trailhead on Hwy 93 in Kootenay National Park. Note that regardless of which route you choose, you'll need to arrange for someone to pick you up or have a second vehicle parked at trail's end.

🏃 Mt Assiniboine

Duration Three to four days

Distance 55.7km (34.6 miles)

Difficulty Difficult

Elevation Change Up to 695m (2280ft)

Start Sunshine Village ski area

Finish Mt Shark trailhead

Nearest Town Banff

Transportation Car/gondola/shuttle

Summary An unforgettable journey to the iconic peak of Mt Assiniboine, passing through high-altitude meadows, pristine lake country and wild river valleys.

This multiday hike ventures into the heart of Mt Assiniboine Provincial Park, an area famous not just for its pyramidal mountain (Canada's Matterhorn), but also for its meadows, lakes and seemingly endless hiking options.

There are several routes into the park, including from Sunshine Village, from Kootenay National Park along the Simpson River Trail, and from Kananaskis Country along Bryant Creek (accessed near Mt Shark, about a 43km drive from Canmore along the gravel Smith-Dorrien/Spray Trail Rd).

The best option is to combine the Sunshine Village and Bryant Creek trails, creating a stunning 55.7km (34.6-mile) route tracking the ridge of the Great Divide. You'll need a car at either end of the trail to avoid getting stranded; alternatively, leave your car at Mt Shark, catch a lift back to the Sunshine Village parking lot, then take the gondola or hike up to Sunshine Meadows from the parking lot. If you're feeling really flush, you could even catch a helicopter into the park from Canmore, but that really would be cheating.

The following trip includes two days of hiking into the park and a one- or two-day hike back out to Mt Shark. There are possibilities for at least three days of sidetrips at Lake Magog. Though popular, it's still real backcountry: bear precautions and proper supplies are essential.

Mt Assiniboine

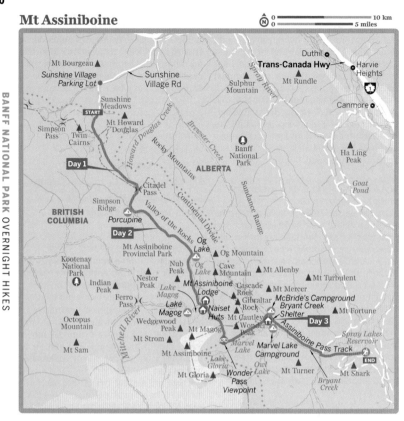

DAY 1: SUNSHINE VILLAGE SKI AREA TO PORCUPINE CAMPGROUND

5 HOURS / 13.6KM (8.4 MILES)

The hike officially starts at Sunshine Village ski area, accessible from the Sunshine Village parking lot by a summer gondola. Begin day one with the hike for the Garden Path Trail. At the junction at the 1.3km (0.8-mile) mark, instead of continuing west toward Rock Isle and Grizzly Lake, turn south toward Citadel Pass. The trail crosses briefly into British Columbia, passing the Howard Douglas Lake and Campground en route to Citadel Pass at the 9.3km (5.8-mile) mark. If the weather's clear, from here you should have a great view of Mt Assiniboine spiking skywards, way off to the southeast.

After 12.6km (7.8 miles) the trail meets the junction to Porcupine Campground (where most hikers spend their first night). To reach the campground, head right (south and steeply downhill) for another kilometer (0.6 miles).

DAY 2: PORCUPINE CAMPGROUND TO LAKE MAGOG

6 HOURS / 15.9KM (9.9 MILES)

On day two, climb southeast from the campground for 4.7km (2.9 miles) to rejoin the main trail, which heads into the aptly named Valley of the Rocks. The enormous boulders that crowd this lengthy valley are left over from a long-ago rockslide, the largest anywhere in the Rockies; it feels wild and desolate at the best of times, but in bad weather seems positively unearthly. The valley runs southeast for 5.7km (3.6 miles), but the rocky path makes it tough going. Also note that there is no water in the Valley of the Rocks, so make sure you're stocked up before you start out.

If the rocky traverse has worn you out, you could break overnight at Og Lake Campground, but if you feel up to it, it's worth continuing across Og Meadows for another 5.5km (3.4 miles) to reach Lake Magog, the main base for explorations around Mt Assiniboine.

There is a superb campground perched above the lakeshore, offering a grandstand viewpoint up the snowy slopes of Mt Assiniboine. There are also several rustic Naiset Huts and the wonderful Assiniboine Lodge (dating from 1928) situated near the lake; all are heavily oversubscribed in season, so book as early as possible to be sure of a place. Hikers (even those who are camping) are welcome at the lodge for afternoon tea, cake, beer and wine from 4pm to 5pm daily.

DAY 3: LAKE MAGOG TO MT SHARK TRAILHEAD
9 HOURS / 26.2KM (16.3 MILES)

If you've managed to sort out transportation at the Mt Shark end, the best option for day 3 is to head out of the park via spectacular **Wonder Pass** (a hike of just over 25km/15 miles from Lake Magog). It's a wonderfully scenic walk in its own right, passing the shining expanse of **Marvel Lake**, the 6th-largest lake in Banff National Park, and **Bryant Creek**, site of an eponymous trail, warden's office and shelter.

It's a long route to do in one day, so you might feel like breaking the walk in two. With prior reservations you can stay at the Bryant Creek shelter; otherwise, there are a couple of campgrounds near Marvel Lake's eastern end (McBride's and Marvel Lake, both reservable via the Parks Canada website), which you'll reach around 12km (7.4 miles) from Lake Magog.

Alternatively, you could just visit Wonder Pass and Marvel Lake as a day hike, camping another night at Magog Lake before retracing your route back to the trailhead across Sunshine Meadows.

🥾 Skoki Valley

Duration Four-day round-trip

Distance 50.4km (31.3 miles) round-trip

Difficulty Moderate–difficult

Elevation Change Up to 1136m (3727ft)

Start/Finish Fish Creek trailhead

Nearest Town Lake Louise

Transportation Bus/car

Summary A dreamy landscape of high mountains and lakes awaits around the Skoki Valley.

It might not have the lush greenery of some of Banff's other backcountry destinations, but for the desolate beauty of its high mountains and truly unparalleled views,

Skoki Valley is a gem. The Skoki area has been a popular skiers' hangout since the 1930s, but these days it has also become a regular haunt of summer hikers, especially for those visitors itching to try out a night at Skoki Lodge, one of Banff's most historic ski lodges.

You can expect a mix of mountain landscapes en route – meadows, peaks, lakes and barren rock – and a massive sense of achievement once you're done.

DAY 1: FISH CREEK TRAILHEAD TO MERLIN MEADOWS
8 HOURS / 17.6KM (10.9 MILES)

The first day is a full-blown, hard mountain hike, so start as early as possible to be sure of camping in daylight. The trip starts out at an elevation of 1690m (5545ft), with the first wooded section following Temple Fire Rd steeply uphill for 3.9km (2.4 miles). Overnight guests at Skoki Lodge (p104) can avoid this fire-road section thanks to a free shuttle bus operated by the lodge.

The fire road reaches Temple Lodge and crosses a ski slope before ascending to a meadowy area with great views of the Slate Range after around 6.5km (4 miles). At the 7.1km (4.4-mile) mark you'll pass **Halfway Hut**, a day shelter once used by skiers heading for Skoki Lodge, and the Hidden Lake Campground, where you can take an overnight break if you wish.

Most people push on to **Boulder Pass**, situated above Ptarmigan Lake with a view of Ptarmigan Peak, Redoubt Mountain and Mt Temple to the southwest. Take a break here and admire the vista, then continue north via **Deception Pass**, looking out for the **Skoki Lakes** on your left before reaching Skoki Lodge after 16.4km (10.2 miles). Base yourself at the lodge or the nearby **Merlin Meadows Campground**, another 1.2km northwest.

DAY 2: MERLIN MEADOWS TO RED DEER LAKES
6 HOURS / 11.4KM (7.1 MILES)

On the second day, backtrack the 1.2km (0.7-mile) trail and explore the high mountain scenery around Skoki Lodge, including the 6.2km (3.8-mile) round-trip to **Merlin Lake**. Back at the lodge, head south and take the left-hand (east) fork along the 'Jones Pass' Trail, which skirts past the southern flanks of Skoki Mountain.

Spend the night at Red Deer Lakes Campground, a walk of 4km (2.5 miles) from the lodge.

Skoki Valley

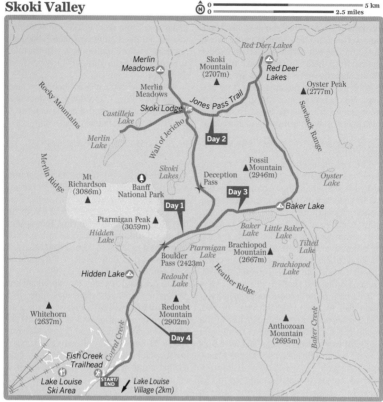

DAY 3: RED DEER LAKES TO HIDDEN LAKE CAMPGROUND

6-7 HOURS / 11.7KM (7.3 MILES)

On day three, head south through the alpine meadows around Oyster Creek and Cotton Grass Pass, before veering westwards along the northern shore of Baker Lake and rejoining the main Skoki trail just south of Deception Pass. On the way back down the valley, you'll have a fine outlook of Ptarmigan Peak (3059m/10,035ft) to the west and Redoubt Mountain (2902m/9520ft) to the south. Camp at the Hidden Lake Campground, near the Halfway Hut.

DAY 4: HIDDEN LAKE CAMPGROUND TO FISH CREEK TRAILHEAD

2-3 HOURS / 9.7KM (6 MILES)

On the final day, take an early-morning jaunt up to Hidden Lake itself (2.6km/1.6-mile round-trip), a classic glacial tarn nestled among craggy peaks. Rejoin the main trail and hike back to the start point at Fish Creek.

🚗 DRIVING

🚗 Bow Valley Parkway

Duration Two to 2½ hours

Distance 52km (32.2 miles)

Speed Limit 60km/h (37mph)

Start Banff Town

Finish Lake Louise

Summary If you prefer scenery to speed, this leisurely drive between Banff Town and Lake Louise is a must-do.

The Bow Valley Pkwy (also known as Hwy 1A) runs parallel to the Trans-Canada Hwy/Hwy 1 practically all the way to Lake Louise, but it's an altogether more tranquil drive. It's particularly well known for its wildlife; you'll have a great chance of spotting elk and bighorn sheep, especially early and late in the day, and if you're really lucky, you might even spot an elusive moose or black bear.

Needless to say, this also makes the Bow Valley Pkwy a hotspot for collisions with animals, so keep your speed well down and keep your eyes peeled for wildlife on the edge of the road. The parkway's eastern end between the Fireside Picnic Area and Johnston Canyon is closed from 6pm to 9am during spring mating season (March to late June). The speed limit on the parkway is 60km/h (37mph) dropping to 30km/h (19mph) at certain points.

From Banff Town, head west on Trans-Canada Hwy toward Lake Louise, taking the exit for Bow Valley Pkwy at the 5km (3.1-mile) mark. Soon after passing underneath the picturesque wooden archway that marks the parkway's start point, the road curves into forest, passing the Muleshoe Wetlands and the Sawback Range, which underwent a prescribed burn in 1993. Interpretive panels along the route explain the science behind forest fires.

After around 15km (9.3 miles) the road divides briefly before passing Johnston Canyon at the 18km (11.2-mile) mark. The smooth-sided limestone gorge through which Johnston Creek flows has been carved out by the river over the last 8000 years. You can walk upstream past two major waterfalls on walkways that occasionally dip beneath overhanging cliffs. Trees and moss cling to the canyon edges providing an ideal habitat for birds. Just west of the canyon is a viewpoint overlooking the grassy Moose Meadows, once a favorite moose hangout, but now more often frequented by elk.

Around 5km (3.1 miles) further west, look out for a panel marking the site of Silver City, one of several boom towns that briefly flourished around the Bow Valley during a series of mineral rushes in the 1880s and '90s. Silver City lasted barely two years – 3000 prospectors flocked to the site in 1883 after silver was said to have been found here, but the town collapsed in 1885 when it transpired that the discovery was nothing more than a moneymaking ruse propagated by unscrupulous entrepreneurs.

At the 24.5km (15.2-mile) mark you'll pass Castle Junction, where a branch road heads over the Trans-Canada Hwy toward Kootenay National Park. There's a small gas station and general store at the junction, which makes a good place to pick up drinks, snacks and ice cream. You'll also find cabins, a campground and a wilderness hostel here.

North of the junction at the Castle Cliffs Viewpoint, you can spy the craggy profile of Castle Mountain, so named for its castellated, fortress-like appearance, created by a combination of geological forces and natural erosion. After WWII the mountain was

Bow Valley Parkway

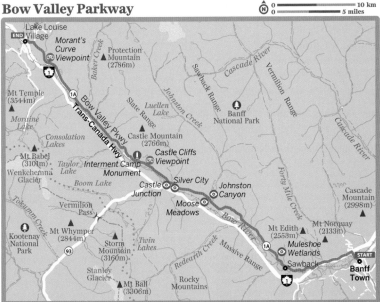

briefly renamed Mt Eisenhower in honor of the US general, but locals were far from keen on the change and it was restored to Castle Mountain in 1979, although the stand-alone pillar at the southern end is still known as Eisenhower Peak.

Another 6km (3.7 miles) on, you'll pass a small **Internment Camp Monument** that marks the site of a former prison camp that housed Ukrainian immigrants during WWI. Nearby is another pullout with grand views of Mt Whymper and the important wildlife corridor across the Vermilion Pass.

Continuing northwest toward Lake Louise, look out for a viewpoint looking southwest to-ward Storm Mountain, before crossing Baker Creek en route to the viewpoint at **Morant's Curve**, a site much favored by the Canadi-an Pacific Railway and National Geographic photographer Nicholas Morant (1910–99), whose images helped publicize Banff during its early days as a national park.

The Bow Valley Pkwy ends after 47km (29.1 miles) at a T-junction. The right turn heads toward the Lake Louise Gondola, while the left turn heads toward Lake Louise and Trans-Canada Hwy.

🚗 Minnewanka Loop

Duration 1-1½ hours round-trip

Distance 16.5km (10.2 miles)

Speed Limit 50km/h (31mph)

Start/Finish Banff

Nearest Town Banff

Summary A circular route taking in a trio of the park's loveliest lakes.

This loop makes a good morning or after-noon drive. There are great views of Cas-cade Mountain, the Palliser Range and the Fairholme Range, and trailheads for several hikes along the way. Note that this route is closed due to snow cover between Novem-ber and mid-April or May.

Take Banff Ave northeast from Banff Town, following signs for Lake Minnewan-ka. Cross under Trans-Canada Hwy/Hwy 1 and begin climbing along the lower flanks of Cascade Mountain. On the right is **Cascade Ponds**, a picnic area around small pools of water.

Drive past the right-hand turn for John-son Lake and continue north toward the stacked-up spires of the Palliser Range. At roughly the 3km (1.9-mile) mark, look out for the right-hand turn to **Lower Bankhead**,

🚗 Driving Tour
Into the Icefields

START LAKE LOUISE VILLAGE
END SUNWAPTA PASS
LENGTH 125KM (78 MILES); TWO HOURS

This once-in-a-lifetime road trip starts in Lake Louise village and follows the southern section of the Icefields Pkwy to Sunwapta Pass, at the border with Jasper National Park. It's a long route, so set out early and leave yourself plenty of time to enjoy the drive. Make sure you start out with a full tank, as the only gas stations en route are at Lake Louise and Saskatche-wan River Crossing. The road is officially open year-round, but is often closed due to snow between November and April. Note that the speed limit on this road is 90km/h (56mph). Large trucks are also banned, making for a quieter, more pleasant jour-ney. See p146 for the Jasper National Park section of the Icefields Pkwy drive.

Start at Lake Louise and head north along Trans-Canada Hwy/Hwy 1 to the signed turnoff to Jasper. You'll reach a Parks Canada entrance gate 2km (1.2 miles) north of the junction; assuming you already have your parks pass, you can zip through without stopping.

To the west rises the Waputik Range, dominated by the 2755m (9039ft) Waputik Peak, overlooking the winding Bow River. Around 16.1km (10 miles) from the start of the parkway you'll reach ❶ **Hector Lake**, named after James Hector, a geologist and naturalist who accompanied the historic Palliser Expedition to chart unexplored areas of western Canada between 1857 and 1860.

After 33km (20.5 miles), stop at the ❷ **Crowfoot Glacier lookout**, to see the icy behemoth nestled on the rocky flanks of Crowfoot Mountain above ice-blue Bow Lake. The glacier was named for its three clawlike 'toes,' but unfortunately its lowest toe had melted by the 1940s.

At the northern end of Bow Lake is ❸ **Num-Ti-Jah Lodge**, built by the fa-mous trailsman Jimmy Simpson, who was born in England in 1895, but went on to become one of the Rockies' best-known explorers, adventurers and guides. The lodge makes an ideal stop for lunch, and you can always burn off the calories by following the trail to Bow Falls.

From Bow Lake, the road climbs toward **4 Bow Pass**, which at 2069m (6788ft) is the highest point on the parkway. Nearby you'll find the turnoff to the busy **5 Peyto Lake & Bow Summit Lookout**, named after the park warden Bill Peyto. A 400m (0.2-mile) wooded trail leads from the parking lot to a decked viewpoint that looks out over the sapphire-blue lake. It's usually packed, but there's a quieter viewpoint further on, near the path to Bow Summit Lookout.

Back in the car, head 6km (3.7 miles) further north to a pullout overlooking Snowbird Glacier, which clings to the edge of Patterson Mountain like an avalanche frozen in midmotion. Further north is the parking lot for **6 Mistaya Canyon**, reached by a 500m (0.3-mile) walk from the pullout. Carved out by the Mistaya River, the curving limestone canyon is spanned by a wooden bridge from where you can look right down into the pounding white water.

A short drive northwest brings you to the **7 Saskatchewan River Crossing**, established by 19th-century fur trappers who crossed the North Saskatchewan River here on their way through the Rockies to British Columbia. Today, it marks the junction of Hwy 93 (the Icefields Pkwy) and Hwy 11 (the David Thompson Hwy). It is home to the only facilities between Lake Louise and the Columbia Icefield – a basic motel, cafeteria-style restaurant and gas station.

From the Crossing, the road traverses river flats (often frequented by elk and birdlife) en route to Cirrus Mountain, where snowmelt streams down the mountainside, creating a sheet of waterfalls known as the **8 Weeping Wall**, which freeze solid in winter. From here the road sweeps around a huge hairpin known as the **9 Big Bend** and climbs up the aptly named Big Hill; at the top there's a fantastic viewpoint that looks back down the North Saskatchewan Valley and to Mt Saskatchewan. Nearby are the aptly named Bridal Veil Falls, named for the interlaced pattern of their cascade.

At 125km (78 miles) into the trip, you'll reach the barren treeless **10 Sunwapta Pass**, 2023m (6637ft) above sea level and the most avalanche-prone section of the road in winter. The pass marks the boundary with Jasper National Park; you can either retrace your route back to Lake Louise, or continue on the Icefields Pkwy into Jasper Town.

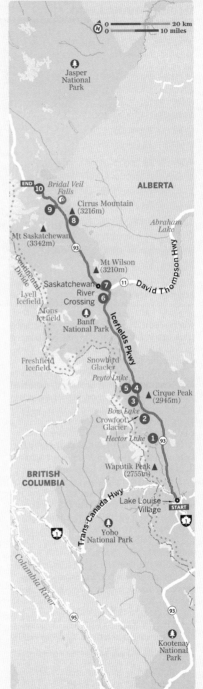

Minnewanka Loop

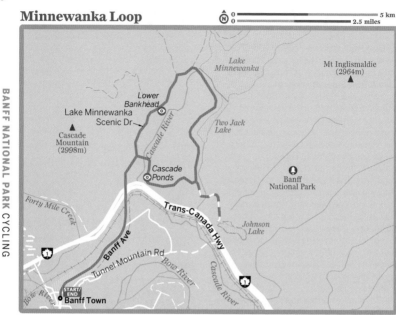

where you can follow a self-guided trail around the ruins of an abandoned coal-mining town constructed by the Canadian Pacific Railway (CPR).

After 6km (3.7 miles) you'll arrive at Lake Minnewanka. Time your arrival right and you'll be able to jump on a boat for a trip around the lake; otherwise, just wander along the shoreline or stop for something cold from the lakeside snack shack.

From Lake Minnewanka, watch for bighorn sheep as you follow the road across a dam toward Two Jack Lake, another popular spot with picnickers and sunbathers. The jagged mountain that looms up behind the lake is Mt Rundle, a crinkled ridge that runs for 12km south all the way to Canmore.

A little further on, 11km (6.8 miles) along the route, is the junction for Johnson Lake, another lakeside getaway for locals looking to escape the Banff bustle. If it's sunny, you can join people sunbathing around the lakeshore, or wander around the lake trail on cloudier days. Brave souls sometimes take the plunge into the lake's chilly waters, but you'll need a steely constitution (and preferably a wetsuit) to join them, as it stays chilly well into high summer.

From the junction the road trundles downhill and rejoins the main loop road. Turn left to head back to Banff.

CYCLING

Road cyclists will love Banff's paved surfaces. The Bow Valley Pkwy (p93) makes for a bracing, but flattish ride, as does the mega-popular Legacy Trail (p78) into Canmore. More challenging is the undulating Lake Minnewanka Loop (p74) and the short but tough grunt up to the Sunshine Village base station. Another gradual but unrelenting climb is the 11km-long Moraine Lake Rd near Lake Louise.

Mountain bikers fresh from sojourns in Jasper or Kananaskis Country may find Banff's trails a little more constricting. Many of the park's paths are designated 'hiking only,' but with a protected area this large, there are still plenty of options to flick through your gears on a multifarious mixture of fire roads and daring singletrack.

Two excellent off-road options are the Goat Creek Trail (p79), a double-tracked former fire road that's good for families (with confident kids aged eight and up) and the Rundle Riverside, a root-infested singletrack that will test more experienced mountain bikers. Both trails run between Canmore and Banff. Backcountry cyclists can follow the 29.2km (18.1-mile) out-and-back Cascade Trail, an undulating old fire road that'll quickly get you away from civilization. The trail starts from the Upper Bankhead car park, 3.5km (2.2 miles) from Banff Town on the Lake Minnewanka Loop.

The free *Mountain Biking and Cycling Guide*, available at park offices, details the most popular routes, which are often shared-use trails with horseback riders and hikers.

Rentals

Gear Up CYCLING
(Map p116; ☑403-678-1636; www.gearupsport.com; 1302 Bow Valley Trail; bike rental/ski rental per day from C$50/20; ☺9am-6pm; 🛈) This easy-to-navigate Canmore rental shop is handy on account of its position within free-wheeling distance of the start of the Legacy Trail (p78). As well as trail bikes, they've got junior, full-suspension and trailers, climbing gear, paddleboards and both alpine and Nordic skis. Bikes come with a handy repair kit, plus helmet and lock.

Snowtips/Bactrax CYCLING, SKIING
(Map p88; ☑403-762-8177; www.snowtips-bactrax.com; 225 Bear St; bike rental per hour/day from C$10/35, cross-country/alpine ski rental per day from C$20/40; ☺8am-8pm Jun–mid-Oct, 7am-9pm rest of year) Family-owned for 40 years, Banff's best-value rental outlet can have you kitted out in a matter of minutes, with oodles of choices including town, road and kids' bikes. Other useful rental gear includes hiking boots, day packs, coolers and tents. In winter, you'll find ski packages with cross-country, backcountry and snowboard options, plus snowshoes, ice skates and more.

Banff Soul CYCLING, SKIING
(Map p88; ☑403-760-1650; www.banffsoul.com; 203a Bear St; bike rental per hour/day from C$10/35, ski rental per day from C$75; ☺8am-8pm Nov-Apr, 9am-7pm May-Oct) This is a good ski and cycling crossover outfitter. Hire bikes are mostly road bikes and town cruisers.

Banff Cycle CYCLING
(Map p88; ☑403-985-4848; www.banffcycle.com; 203 Bear St; per day hybrid/e-bike/road bike C$49/89/99) Sharing space with the Banff Soul bike shop, this outfit rents out high-quality Cannondale hybrids, De Rosa road bikes and Specialized e-bikes.

Trail Sports CYCLING, SKIING
(☑403-678-6764; www.trailsports.ab.ca; Canmore Nordic Centre, 2003 Olympic Way; bike per 2hr/day from C$40/60, ski package per 2hr/day C$25/30; ☺9am-6pm) If you're visiting Canmore Nordic Centre (p115), you don't even need to bring your own equipment. Bike rentals are available from Trail Sports, directly opposite the visitor office. The center also offers 90-minute guided rides and skills clinics with certified instructors (C$90 for one person, C$135 for a group of up to five). In winter you can rent cross-country skis here.

Moraine Lake via Tramline

Duration Three to five hours round-trip

Distance 30km (17 miles)

Difficulty Difficult

Start/Finish Lake Louise Village

Nearest Town Lake Louise

Transportation Car

Summary Technically challenging, but rewarding; experienced mountain bikers rate this as the best trail in the Lake Louise area.

Technically challenging but rewarding, this trail is rated the best in the Lake Louise area by many experienced mountain bikers.

The trail to Moraine Lake begins outside the old Laggan station (now the Lake Louise Station Restaurant), and the first section follows the course of the old tramline that once ferried visitors up to Lake Louise in the early 1900s. If you want to avoid the uphill

Moraine Lake via Tramline

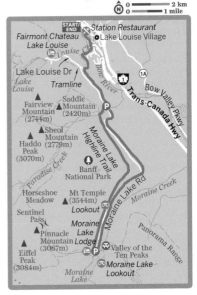

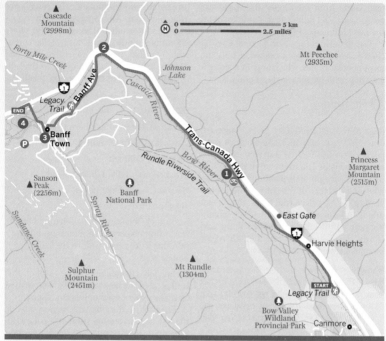

Cycling Tour
Legacy Trail

START ALBERTA VISITOR INFORMATION
CENTRE, CANMORE
END VERMILION LAKES, BANFF TOWN
LENGTH 26.8KM (16.7 MILES); TWO HOURS

This massively popular paved trail that parallels the Trans-Canada Hwy/Hwy 1 into Banff is good for a gentle meander or a brisk commute.

Though mainly flat, the Legacy trail alongside Hwy 1 is best tackled starting out from Canmore, due to more favorable tailwinds and its slight overall descent into Banff. The trail is paved throughout and split into two lanes; always cycle on the right. Although pedestrian traffic is light, there are cyclists aplenty.

The official starting point is on the Bow Valley Trail (Canmore's main through road) on the northwest side of town opposite the Alberta Visitor Information Centre. An urban bike lane heads safely out here from the center of Canmore. The starting point is marked by a multicolored guidepost equipped with a count-o-meter detailing how many people have used the trail on any particular day/week/month.

The paved path parallels Hwy 1 and the railway line for most of its duration, dipping occasionally into small stands of trees. About 8km (5 miles) northwest of Canmore you'll come to the ❶ **Valleyview picnic area**, where it is possible to stop and enjoy an unimpeded view of Mt Rundle.

As you approach Banff, another trail forks right under the highway. This leads to ❷ **Cascade Ponds**, a popular picnic area. Continue straight ahead for Banff. Soon after the fork, the trail curves west, veering away from Hwy 1 and joining the top end of Banff Ave. Here you'll encounter the only road crossing (Tunnel Mountain Rd) and pass the Banff Mountain Resort. Continue 3.5km (2.2 miles) along the paved path into ❸ **Banff Town**.

You can end the ride here, but it's well worth continuing along the lovely final section of trail, which follows the north shore of the ❹ **Vermilion Lakes** for a few kilometers before eventually reaching a junction with the Bow Valley Pkwy. From here, retrace your steps to return to Banff Town or Canmore.

section, you could drive to the Paradise Valley parking lot and start the ride there.

If you're tackling the tramline, park opposite the Station Restaurant. Cross the bridge and set out along the broad trail, climbing steeply to Louise Creek and eventually linking up with busy Lake Louise Dr – take care crossing here, as traffic is fast and heavy.

Turn down Moraine Lake Rd. Look for the Paradise Valley parking lot on the right, which also marks the start of the Moraine Lake Highline Trail. There's a junction about 1km (0.7 miles) from the Paradise Valley parking lot; turn left (south) to get onto the Highline.

Here's where the fun really starts: the trail zips into rocky, rooty **singletrack** that's tough and technical. Note this section is a grizzly favorite and is sometimes closed during the peak buffalo-berry season from mid- to late summer – check with a park office before setting out, and make lots of noise at all times to avoid any bear-shaped surprises.

From here the views and the riding are fantastic as you follow the eastern flank of **Mt Temple** and encounter wonderful perspectives over the Valley of the Ten Peaks, Moraine Lake and Consolation Valley. The route is rough, narrow and exposed in places – take it easy and admire the views. After around 10km (6.2 miles) you'll roll down to the shore of **Moraine Lake**.

You can retrace the same route or head back along the paved (and steep) Moraine Lake Rd to complete the loop.

🚴 Goat Creek Trail

Duration Two to three hours one way

Distance 19.1km (11.9 miles)

Difficulty Moderate

Start Whiteman's Gap, Canmore

Finish Banff Town

Nearest Towns Canmore & Banff

Transportation Car/minibus

Summary A great doubletrack between Banff and Canmore along an old fire road that's good for fit families or off-road cycling novices.

Goat Creek Trail is a great doubletrack between Banff and Canmore, along an old fire road that's a good fit for families or off-road cycling novices.

This much-recommended one-way route is best done starting from Canmore due to the favorable overall descent (1000m or 3280ft) into Banff. You can organize it with two vehicles, or use Roam bus No 3 (every 30 to 60 minutes) to ferry you back to Canmore. Alternatively, the energetic might consider cycling back along the easier Legacy

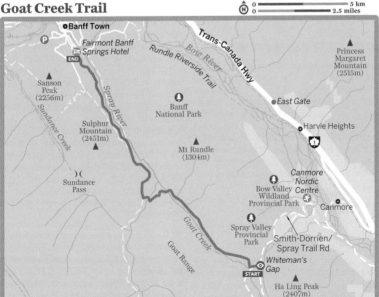

Goat Creek Trail

Trail to make a challenging loop. Some bike shops offer a shuttle service to the trailhead.

It's a pretty easy ride along dirt and gravel doubletrack, with a few climbs and steep sections, as well as a fiddly bridge crossing and a few blind corners – watch out for other trail users, especially cyclists coming in the opposite direction.

The trailhead is high above Canmore at Whiteman's Gap, up the dirt Smith-Dorrien/Spray Trail Rd past Canmore Nordic Centre (a steep 5km climb out of town if you're not using a car or shuttle). The first section travels through pine and spruce forest along the course of Goat Creek, with the Goat Range to the south and Mt Rundle to the north. It feels wild and rewardingly remote and you can either roll along at a leisurely pace or pin back your ears and pick up the speed.

After 9.3km (5.8 miles) you'll reach a bridge over the Spray River. Turn right at the junction to begin the second section, which follows an old fire road all the way to Banff. About 4.1km (2.5 miles) along this road, you'll pass another bridge on your right, which leads to the Mt Rundle Backcountry Campground. Stay left here and continue another 5.7km (3.6 miles) along the Spray River's western bank for a very scenic re-entry into civilization. You'll know you've reached Banff's southeastern outskirts when you see the Fairmont Banff Springs Hotel rising like a castle opposite beautiful Bow Falls.

🏃 OTHER ACTIVITIES

Although hiking and cycling are Banff's raison d'être and the best (and cheapest) way of experiencing the immense Rocky Mountain scenery, the park has other adventurous allures, from longstanding pursuits like horseback riding and fishing to the recent penchant for via ferratas (fixed-protection climbing routes). Unlike most other North American parks, Banff also has downhill ski areas (three of 'em) meaning it remains popular even in the frigid winter months.

ℹ️ Activity Companies

Banff has several agencies that can book a range of activity packages in and around the national park. Most have lots of experience with younger clients and people who are new to the sports, so they offer a great way to try out something different. If you're doing a lot of activities, booking through one agency

can be very convenient, but you'll often get better deals by going direct to the provider.

Banff Adventures ADVENTURE
(Map p88; 📞403-762-4554; www.banffadventures.com; 211 Bear St, Bison Courtyard; ⊘7:30am-9pm Jun-early Oct, 9am-5pm rest of yr) Banff's main activity-booking company can organize a huge range of activities with experienced local operators, ranging from ATV tours to heli-hikes and rafting trips, and puts together its own combo packages (such as the Raft, Ride & Relax tour). Its winter packages are equally comprehensive.

White Mountain Adventures ADVENTURE
(📞403-760-4403; www.whitemountainadventures.com; 137 Eagle Cres; excursions from C$79; ⊘8am-5pm Mon-Fri) From easy strolls to snowshoeing and heli-hiking to exploring the frozen waterfalls of Johnston Canyon, this well-regarded adventure tour service offers guided trips along popular Banff trails, covering nature spotting, local history and points of interest. It also runs the helpful Mt Assiniboine shuttle (p111) in the summer. Rates vary according to activity; see the website for details.

🛶 Canoeing & Kayaking

Canoes and kayaks have played a pivotal role in Canada's history, particularly among the First Nations tribes. With numerous rivers and lakes (most of which are closed to motor boats) speckling the park, small human-powered boats remain popular with generations of tourists. You can hire (expensive) canoes from boathouses at Lake Louise (p94) and Moraine Lake (www.morainelake.com/day-visits; boat rental per hour C$120; ⊘9am-5pm mid-Jun–mid-Sep, weather permitting), although the water is generally frozen from October to mid-May.

Stand-up paddleboarding has recently become popular on Banff's more sheltered lakes. Paddleboards (including more easily transported inflatable varieties) can be hired at the Adventure Hub on Banff Ave (www.skibig3.com/adventure-hub) and at the Banff Canoe Club for between C$59 and C$125 a day.

★ **Banff Canoe Club** CANOEING, KAYAKING
(Map p88; 📞403-762-5005; www.banffcanoeclub.com; cnr Wolf St & Bow Ave; canoe & kayak rental per 1st/additional hour C$45/25, SUP/bike rental per hour C$30/12; ⊘9am-9pm mid-Jun–Aug, reduced hours mid-May–mid-Jun & Sep) Rent a

canoe or kayak and slide up the Bow River or the narrower, lazier Forty Mile Creek to Vermilion Lakes. Both routes will take you past gorgeous scenery with lots of opportunities for wildlife spotting (such as beavers). Stand-up paddleboards and cruiser bikes are also available for rent. Note that you cannot leave your belongings in the office cabin.

☘ White-Water Rafting

The best rafting is outside the park (and province) on the Kicking Horse River in Yoho National Park, BC. There are class IV rapids here, meaning big waves, swirling pools and a guaranteed soaking. Lesser rapids are found on the Kananaskis River and the Horseshoe Canyon section of the Bow River. The Bow River around Banff is better for mellower float trips.

There are many companies to choose from, but it's always wise to go with an established operator, as white-water rafting is potentially a highly dangerous sport. Banff companies run trips to all of the above rivers.

Rapids are classed from I (easy) to V (expert) – the extreme class VI is for rapids that have rarely been completed successfully.

Hydra River Guides   RAFTING
(Map p88; ☑ 403-762-4554; www.raftbanff.com; 211 Bear St; ⊙ 7:30am-9pm) This well-regarded company has been running rafting trips for over three decades. The most popular is the 20km Kicking Horse Classic (C$149), with varied rapids (up to class IV) and a BBQ lunch; novices and families will appreciate the sedate Mild float trip (adult/child C$79/59); for late risers there's the midafternoon Last Waltz (C$115).

Chinook Rafting   RAFTING
(☑ 866-330-7238; www.chinookrafting.com; Hwy 1A; rafting adult/child from C$97/62; ⊙ mid-May–mid-Sep) A great company for families, Chinook runs four-hour trips on Class II and III sections of the beautiful Kananaskis River. Kids must be five years or older to participate.

Rocky Mountain Raft Tours   RAFTING
(☑ 403-762-3632; www.banffrafttours.com; Golf Course Loop Rd; ⊙ mid-May–late Sep; 🚹) Banff's oldest rafting company sticks to what it knows best: easy floats down the Bow River from its put-in point just below Bow Falls. Tours feature an hour on the water as you drift 7km downstream past the Hoodoos to the base of Mt Rundle. Attractively priced youth tickets encourage family participation; kids aged two years and older are welcome.

☘ Fishing

The fish in Banff might not be as plentiful as they were in the days of Bill Peyto and co, but angling is still a quintessential way to experience Banff's sedate side.

A fishing permit (per day/year C$9.80/ 34.30) is required for angling anywhere in the national parks, and can be purchased at visitor centers. Due to an outbreak of whirling disease in 2016, strict catch-and-release regulations have been in effect for all species except lake trout in recent years. See Banff's Fishing Regulations webpage (www.pc.gc. ca/en/pn-np/ab/banff/activ/peche-fishing #Banff) for current catch allowances and other up-to-the-minute info.

The most popular area to fish is the Bow River, which is open year-round (although ice fishing is always banned). Ghost Lake, Lake Minnewanka, Two Jack Lake and the Vermilion Lakes are usually open mid-May to early September.

Banff Fishing Unlimited   FISHING
(☑ 403-762-4936; www.banff-fishing.com) Year-round fly-fishing, spin casting and lake fishing with experienced local guides. The full-day 'Walk and Wade' trip (from C$189 per person) takes you to some of the finest trout-fishing spots on the upper Bow River.

Tightline Adventures   FISHING
(☑ 403-763-9669; www.tightlineadventures.com; 2-person fishing trip C$600-650; ⊙ May-Oct) Specializes in dry fly-fishing for rainbow and brook trout on the Upper and Lower Bow River.

Lake Minnewanka Guided Fishing   FISHING
(☑ 866-606-6700; www.banffjaspercollection.com/ attractions/lake-minnewanka-cruise/fishing; Minnewanka Loop Dr; half-day trip for 2 adults from C$575; ⊙ mid-May–early Sep) Offers guided boat trips on Lake Minnewanka fishing for lake trout and whitefish.

☘ Climbing

Climbers have been flocking to Banff's sky-piercing peaks and finger-numbing rock faces since the sport first took off in the late 1800s. Yamnuska, Mt Rundle and Ha Ling Peak are just some of the best-known ascents, but there are hundreds more to discover. Unless you're an experienced climber, it's worth employing the services of a local guide to make sure you get the most out of your experience on the mountain and stay safe at the same time.

VIA FERRATAS

Banff's newest adventure activity was invented by the Italian military in WWI and has been popular in Italy for nearly a century. Engaged in a terrifying conflict with the Austrians in the Dolomites during the Great War, the Italians adapted ways of using ladders and ropes to build fixed-protection climbing paths known as via ferratas (iron roads) in order to ease the movement of troops and supplies across the rugged Alpine peaks. Upgraded with steel steps, narrow suspension bridges and heavy-duty wire after the war, the via ferratas became popular with tourists and were promoted as a cross between strenuous hiking and full-blown rock-climbing. Suddenly, non-mountaineers were able to experience the kind of thrills normally reserved for skilled alpinists and given access to terrain that would have otherwise remained out of bounds.

Via ferratas in North America are a relatively new phenomenon. Banff's operation – which offers guided-only trips – opened with two routes in 2014, and has expanded to four routes as of 2019. It is the first and – so far – only 'iron road' in a Canadian national park.

You don't need any mountaineering experience to use a via ferrata, just a reasonable level of fitness, a head for heights and a healthy sense of adventure. Safety is assured by using a standard via ferrata harness equipped with two carabiner clips. One carabiner clip is always attached to a ladder or cable ensuring you don't fall off.

Canmore can validly claim to be the climbing capital of Canada and is the HQ of the legendary **Alpine Club of Canada** (☑ 403-678-3200; www.alpineclubofcanada.ca; Indian Flats Rd), founded by AO Wheeler in 1906. The organization can put you in touch with qualified guides across the Canadian Rockies.

Via Ferrata   OUTDOORS
(☑ 844-667-7829; www.banffnorquay.com/summer/via-ferrata; Mt Norquay; ⊙ mid-Jun–mid-Oct) These fixed-protection climbing routes on Mt Norquay let your test your head for heights. Choose from the Explorer (C$169, 2½ hours), the Ridgewalker (C$219, four hours), the Skyline (C$279, five hours) and the Summiteer (C$349, six hours), which includes a three-wire suspension bridge to the top of Mt Norquay. Prices include full safety kit, accompanying guide and passage up the Norquay chairlift to the start point.

Yamnuska Mountain Adventures   CLIMBING
(☑ 403-678-4164; www.yamnuska.com; 50 Lincoln Park, Suite 200; ⊙ 8:30am-5pm Mon-Sat) This well-regarded company offers instruction in rock climbing, ice climbing, backcountry skiing, avalanche skills and mountaineering for participants of all levels, along with overnight excursions, camps and comprehensive mountain skills training programs lasting from one month to an entire academic semester.

On Top Mountaineering   CLIMBING
(☑ 403-678-2717; www.ontopmountaineering.com; 340 Canyon Close) This long-established, locally run outfit organizes outstanding outdoor adventures in the Rockies, including ice climbing, backpacking, classic peak ascents and five-day climbing courses. Other trips include trekking across glaciers from Bow Lake to Peyto Lake in summer and backcountry hutto-hut skiing in winter. Alternatively, devise your own custom route with a private guide (from C$520 per day for two people).

🏌 Golf

Banff Springs Golf Course   GOLF
(Map p87; ☑ 403-762-6801; www.fairmont.com/banff-springs/golf/; Golf Course Rd; green fees 9/18 holes C$105/249; ⊙ May-Oct) Laid out in 1928 and impressively located in the shadow of Mt Rundle and Sulphur Mountain, this is one of the Rockies' most famous courses, with a total of 27 holes. You'll need to dress up for the occasion: no denim or sweats allowed; dress shorts only and collared shirts required for men. Shoe and club rentals are available.

🏇 Horseback Riding

Banff's first European explorers – fur traders and railway engineers – penetrated the region primarily on horseback. You can recreate their pioneering spirit on guided rides with a handful of well-established operators.

Banff Trail Riders   HORSEBACK RIDING
(Map p88; ☑ 403-762-4551; www.horseback.com; 138 Banff Ave; guided rides per person C$64-196) Trail Riders' two stables in Banff and Spray Creek run lots of horseback-riding tours. Easy one- to three-hour trips run regularly along the Bow River, Sundance Loop, Bow Valley and the Spray River. For an authentic frontier

experience, it also offers an afternoon cook-out (C$152 to C$162); there are also pony rides for kids aged three to five (C$24).

For something more challenging, multi-day expeditions to Trail Riders' backcountry lodges start at $679 per person for a two-day trip. It also offers special trips geared toward photographers and wildlife enthusiasts.

Timberline Tours   HORSEBACK RIDING
(☑403-522-3743; www.timberlinetours.ca; St Piran Rd; ☺8am-9pm late May-early Oct) This outfitter has its corral near Lake Louise. It offers 1½-hour trips along the lake (C$95); half-day rides up to Lake Agnes Teahouse (C$159) or the Plain of Six Glaciers (C$199 to C$239); and full-day rides to Paradise Valley, Skoki Lodge, Baker Lake or the Moraine Lake High-line Trail (C$279). Overnight trips (C$650 to C$2275, two to seven days) are also available.

🎿 Skiing & Snowboarding

Strange though it may seem, there are three ski areas in the national park (something almost unheard of in a US national park), two of them in the vicinity of Banff Town and a third near Lake Louise. Lofty, snowy Sunshine Village (p84) is considered world-class; Lake Louise (p84) has more skiable terrain than practically anywhere else in Canada; while Mt Norquay, 5km (3.1 miles) from downtown Banff, is your half-day family-friendly option.

You can get a collective ticket for all the Banff resorts with a Big Three ski pass (www.skibig3.com), which allows you access to a combined area of 31.4 sq km (12.1 sq miles) and 356 runs.

Passes include gondolas, lifts and free shuttles to the ski domains, but as always you'll usually get better value if you buy them as part of an organized package tour, which includes accommodations at local hotels. The peak months are December and January, especially during the school holidays around Christmas and New Year. For the best deals, aim to ski early or late in the season; snow lingers at many of the highest runs until late April and even early May, and discounts are often substantial for off-season packages.

All the resorts have ski schools where you can pick up the basics or graduate to more advanced skills, as well as day-care facilities for younger kids. The websites for each resort have regular snow reports and piste webcams so you can check the snow before you go.

Mt Norquay   SKIING
(☑403-762-4421; www.banffnorquay.com; Mt Norquay Rd; day ski pass adult/youth/child C$89/68/35; ☺9am-4pm; 🚡) Mt Norquay is the nearest ski area to downtown Banff and the park's smallest, covering 77 hectares with 74 runs. The resort's limited size and sometimes iffy snow keeps away the serious powder hounds and provides a non-intimidating scene for families and beginners. However, Norquay also offers a few steep, little-known double-black-diamond runs.

It also has snow tubing, night-skiing at weekends and spectacular scenery.

SCRAMBLING

Rock-climbers tired of strapping on ropes and crampons or hikers in search of a more knuckle-whitening challenge will find common ground in the edgy if sometimes hard-to-define sport of 'scrambling.' Often described as a cross between rock-climbing and hiking, scrambling is the practice of hiking across wild and rugged mountain terrain on indistinct trails usually with the aim of bagging a peak. Although no specific equipment is required, scrambling calls upon certain basic skills including using hands for support, descending scree slopes, crossing snowfields and small streams, and employing rudimentary route-finding skills.

To engage in the activity, you'll need to be relatively fit, sure-footed, adventurous and adept with a map and compass. You'll also need to be well prepared for any unscripted outdoor eventualities.

Some of Banff's best scrambles tackle mountains close to Banff Town. Parks Canada publishes scrambling guides for Mt Rundle (http://www.publications.gc.ca/site/eng/428703/publication.html) and Cascade Mountain (www.publications.gc.ca/site/eng/415260/publication.html). Another popular route is Mt Temple near Lake Louise.

A good (and safe) way of preparing yourself for scrambling is to undertake a special skills and safety course run by mountaineering experts Yamnuska Mountain Adventures. Two-day courses cost C$425 and include a guided scramble on a local mountain.

WILDLIFE CROSSINGS

As you drive north from Banff Town toward Lake Louise along the Trans-Canada Hwy/ Hwy 1, look out for the six arched, tree-covered overpasses spanning the road. They're not for humans, but are actually wildlife crossings, which have been specially designed to allow Banff's animals to cross the road without fear of getting mowed down by a passing truck or recreational vehicle (RV).

Trans-Canada Hwy sits slap bang in the middle of several key 'wildlife corridors' (migratory routes between seasonal habitats) that crisscross the Bow Valley. Thousands of animals have been killed while trying to cross the highway over the years, especially since the road was widened to four lanes in 1981, and collisions with vehicles remain the number one cause of wildlife fatalities in the national park.

In order to reduce the risk of accidents and protect the park's increasingly fragile animal population, the wildlife crossings were built at a cost of around C$1 million each starting in 1988, alongside 38 other underpasses that tunnel beneath the road at various points.

They seem to be working: according to recent Parks Canada studies, medium and large mammal fatalities dropped from 41 in 2006 to only 19 in 2015, and through 2016 more than a dozen animal species have used the crossings in excess of 165,000 times. Intriguingly, animals seem to have adapted to the crossings at different speeds: elk and deer began using them almost straight away, while it took as long as five years for warier species such as bears and wolves to adapt to them.

Different species also appear to have preferences for the types of bridges they like to use: elk, deer, moose, wolves and grizzly bears seem to like crossings that are high, wide and short, while black bears and cougars prefer them long, low and narrow.

A new project is currently underway to monitor exactly which animals are using the crossings and how often, using DNA from barbed-wire fur traps positioned at the crossing entrances. Once the data has been collected and analyzed, additional crossings may be built near Lake Louise in coming years. Watch this space – or rather, watch this road.

Sunshine Village SKIING
(www.skibanff.com; day ski pass adult/youth C$114/ 89) If restricted time or funds mean that you can only ski one resort in Banff, choose Sunshine. Its 13.6-sq-km ski area is divided between 137 runs and the 6-hectare Rogers Terrain Park. With such a huge area, the resort can comfortably handle several thousand skiers and still feel relatively uncrowded. It boasts the country's first heated chairlifts, too.

All the runs are at high elevations (over 2133m), so snow conditions are nearly always reliable on the three mountains (Lookout, Standish and Goat's Eye). It's also unusual in that it only needs to manufacture a small amount of snow every year: snow pack in good years can be up to 9m. The downside: it can be windy and cold.

Sunshine is only around 15km from downtown Banff, so many ski packages use off-mountain accommodations and employ shuttle buses to get you up to the resort.

Lake Louise Ski Resort SKIING
(☏ 403-522-3555; www.skilouise.com; 1 Whitehorn Rd; day pass adult/youth C$114/98; ◈) Lake Louise is the largest of Banff's 'Big Three' resorts (the other two being Sunshine and Norquay). It offers a humongous 1700 hectares of skiable land divided between 145 runs. It's great for families, with a good spread of beginner-rated (25%) runs on the Front Side/South Face (especially around the base area), along with plenty of intermediate-rated (45%) runs.

Lake Louise has plenty of powder and off-piste skiing for advanced skiers, too, as well as a snowboard park and tube rides. However, its average snowfall is only around half that of Sunshine Village, meaning that snow machines are often used to supplement the natural snowpack.

The lodge is well equipped; take a break on the patio of the Bear's Den Smokehouse and enjoy a view of the runs.

🏃 Cross-Country Skiing

It might not offer the adrenaline surge of downhilling, but cross-country skiing has a long mountain heritage and is one of the few ways to explore the national park's trails in winter. It's one of Canada's fastest-growing sports, and you'll even see people practicing their skills in the summer months (using rollerblades rather than skis).

Over 80km (50 miles) of trails are groomed by park authorities specifically for the use of cross-country skiers, including the Spray River Loop, Cave and Basin Trail, Cascade Fire Rd and the Golf Loop near Banff, and the Moraine Lake Rd and Lake Louise Shoreline Trail near Lake Louise village.

Check with Parks Canada (www.parkscanada.gc.ca/banff) to see which trails are open before you set out, as heavy snowfall can mean that trails are closed at short notice.

Cross-country gear can be rented at any of the ski stores in Banff or Lake Louise, and most local activity agencies can help book taster sessions if you're a first-timer.

🎿 Other Winter Sports

Skiing isn't Banff's only winter activity. Ice-skating is often possible at various spots, depending on seasonal conditions. The Fairmont hotels in Lake Louise (p103) and Banff (p97) both maintain small skating areas, as does the Banff Recreation Centre. Vermilion Lakes, Johnson Lake and Lake Minnewanka often have skateable ice, but check with a park office first.

Another way to get out into the backcountry in winter is on snowshoes, which are thought to have been used by First Nations people in the Rockies for hundreds of years. Most local mountaineering and activity companies offer taster sessions in both snowshoeing and ice-skating, and can also arrange guided ice-climbing trips for intermediate and advanced climbers.

Fat biking has also taken off around Banff in recent years, and shops around town offer quality rentals for around C$60 per day. There are some excellent places to ride, including the unplowed Moraine Lake Rd, Goat Creek Trail between Banff and Canmore, and the trails leading up to Tunnel Mountain and Lake Minnewanka. Note that cross-country skiers share some of these same trails; fat bikers should steer clear of all track-set areas.

👁 SIGHTS

Banff is a piece of history in itself. Founded in 1885, it is the world's third-oldest national park (and Canada's oldest). Cataloguing past triumphs and tribulations, Banff Town supports a healthy cache of four museums, virtually unparalleled for a 'natural' national park.

👁 Banff Town

It seems hard to believe when you first lay eyes on Banff Town, but this overgrown village of less than 10,000 souls is the largest metropolis in the entire national park. Thankfully, Banff has largely avoided North America's notorious penchant for sprawl – though its few city blocks *do* manage to squeeze in a surprising amount of commercial hustle and bustle.

A resort town with boutique shops, nightclubs, museums and fancy restaurants may seem incongruous in this wild setting. But Banff is no ordinary town. It developed as a service center for the park that surrounds it. Today it brings in busloads of tourists keen to commune with shops as much as with nature; artists and writers are also drawn to the Rockies' unparalleled majesty. Whether you love or loathe Banff's cosmopolitan edge, wander 15 minutes in any direction and you're back in wild country, a primeval world of bears, elk and wolves.

⭐ Whyte Museum of the Canadian Rockies   MUSEUM
(Map p88; 📞 403-762-2291; www.whyte.org; 111 Bear St; adult/student/child C$10/5/free; ⊙ 10am-5pm) Founded by local artists Catharine and Peter Whyte, the century-old Whyte Museum is more than just a rainy-day option. It boasts a beautiful, ever-changing gallery displaying art from 1800 to the present, by regional, Canadian and international artists, many with a focus on the Rockies. Watch for work by the Group of Seven (aka the Algonquin School). There's also a permanent collection telling the story of Banff and the hardy men and women who forged a home among the mountains.

Attached to the museum is an archive with thousands of photographs spanning the history of the town and park; these are available for reprint. The museum also organizes guided walking tours focused on Banff's history (C$20) and heritage homes (C$10).

Upper Hot Springs Pool   HOT SPRINGS
(www.hotsprings.ca; Mountain Ave; adult/child/family C$8.30/6.30/24.50; ⊙ 9am-11pm mid-May–mid-Oct, 10am-10pm Sun-Thu, to 11pm Fri & Sat rest of year) Banff quite literally wouldn't be Banff if it weren't for its hot springs, which gush out from 2.5km beneath **Sulphur Mountain** at a constant temperature of between 32°C (90°F) and 46°C (116°F) – it was the springs that drew the first tourists to Banff. You can

still sample the soothing mineral waters at the Upper Hot Springs Pool.

Several hotels once occupied the site where the present-day Upper Hot Springs Pool stands – Dr RG Brett's Grand View Villa, built in 1886, was joined by the Hydro Hotel in 1890, but both establishments burnt down and were replaced in the 1930s by a new bathhouse in the fashionable art-deco style.

Renovations have since masked some of the bathhouse's period elegance, but the hot springs still rank as one of the not-to-be-missed Banff experiences – there aren't many places in the world where you can take a hot bath with a mountain view as spectacular as this.

The pools get busy in season, so aim for an early or late dip if you prefer smaller crowds (alternatively, with three weeks' advance notice you can hire the whole place for C$270 per hour). Towels and swimsuits are available for hire.

Bow Falls   WATERFALL
(Map p87) About 500m south of town, just before the junction with Spray River, the Bow River plunges into a churning melee of white water at Bow Falls. Though the drop is relatively small – just 9m at its highest point – Bow Falls is a dramatic sight, especially in spring following heavy snowmelt.

Paved trails run along both sides of the river and make a lovely leisurely afternoon stroll from Banff; in summer go early or late in the day to avoid the endless procession of coach tours. The west-bank viewpoint is the best place to watch the waterfall in full thundering flow, while the east-bank trail leads to another famous viewpoint at Surprise Corner (p50), with a view across the falls toward the Fairmont Banff Springs hotel. It also marks the start of the Hoodoos Trail, which leads along the Bow River to a landscape of bizarre rock pillars shaped by eons of natural erosion.

The river itself begins 100km upstream as meltwater from the Bow Glacier, flowing south through Banff en route to the prairies and Hudson Bay far beyond. The river has been known to First Nations people for well over 10,000 years; to the Cree Nation, it was known as *manachaban sipi* (literally 'the place from which bows are taken').

Fairmont Banff Springs   HISTORIC BUILDING
(www.fairmont.com/banffsprings; 405 Spray Ave) Looming up beside the Bow River, the Banff Springs is a local landmark in more ways than one. Originally built in 1888, and remodeled in 1928 to resemble a cross between a Scottish baronial castle and a European château, the turret-topped exterior conceals an eye-poppingly extravagant selection of ballrooms, lounges, dining rooms and balustraded staircases that would make William Randolph Hearst green with envy.

Highlights include an Arthurian great hall; an elegant, wood-paneled bar; and the gorgeous hot-springs spa. Even if you're not staying here, you're welcome to wander around, and it's worth splashing out on a coffee, a meal or a cocktail in one of the hotel's dozen or so restaurants, lounges and bars.

Banff Avenue   STREET
(Map p88) A little over a century ago, Banff Ave *was* Banff. Initially, the central street was home to little more than a handful of hotels, homesteads and trail outfitters, but the town slowly began to develop following the arrival of the Canadian Pacific Railway (CPR) in 1885 and the opening of the landmark Banff Springs Hotel on the banks of the Bow River in 1888.

Though much of the original architecture of Banff Ave is modern, it's still possible to make out a few of the historic buildings that would have greeted early visitors. The most obvious is the timber-framed Banff Park Museum (p88), which has hardly changed since its construction in 1903. Further along the street, look out for the Cascade Dance Hall at No 120 (built in 1920), the original Brewster Transportation Building at No 202 (built in 1939; now occupied by the Rose & Crown pub), the Banff School Auditorium (built in 1939; now occupied by the Banff Visitor Centre) and St Paul's Presbyterian Church at No 230 (built in 1930).

There are several more historic houses around town that are worth seeking out, best seen on one of the guided tours offered by the Whyte Museum (p85).

Cave & Basin National
Historic Site   HISTORIC SITE
(☏ 403-762-1566; www.pc.gc.ca/en/lhn-nhs/ab/caveandbasin; 311 Cave Ave; adult/child C$3.90/free; ☉ 9:30am-5pm mid-May–mid-Oct, 11am-5pm Wed-Sun rest of year) The Canadian National Park system was effectively born at these hot springs, discovered accidentally by three Canadian Pacific Railway employees on their day off in 1883 (though known to indigenous peoples for 10,000 years). The springs

Banff Town

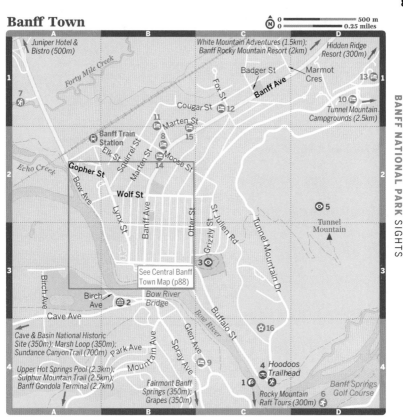

Banff Town

quickly spurred a flurry of private businesses offering facilities for bathers to enjoy the
then-trendy thermal treatments. To avert an
environmental catastrophe, the government
stepped in, declaring Banff Canada's first national park in order to preserve the springs.

There's no swimming here anymore, but
the site has an impressive museum. Visitors

can see the original cave, then stroll out onto
a terrace that covers the former lower mineral springs pool. From here, a boardwalk
with interpretive signage leads uphill to additional springs and the cave's upper vent.

Signposted just behind the complex are
two more walking trails: the 2.3km **Marsh
Loop Trail** across the park's only natural

Central Banff Town

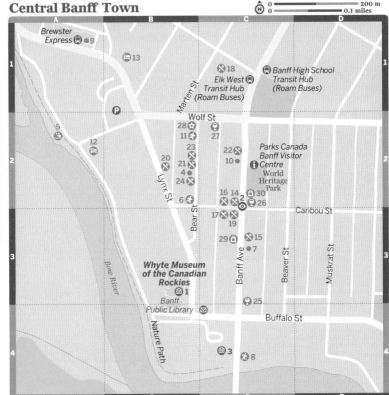

river marsh, and the **Sundance Canyon Trail**, leading along the Bow River to a beautiful side canyon.

Marsh Loop   NATURE RESERVE

This 2.3km loop trail begins near the Cave & Basin National Historic Site (p86) and meanders through one of Banff's most important areas of natural marshland. It's an excellent spot for **bird-watching**: keep your eyes peeled for red-winged blackbirds, green-winged teals and yellowthroats, as well as colorful butterflies and dragonflies. Part of the route follows a wooden boardwalk and leads to a **fish-viewing platform** and a **bird hide**. For a longer walk, you can continue on the trail to **Sundance Canyon**.

South of the Marsh Loop, a band of forest on the flanks of Sulphur Mountain has been designated as the **Middle Springs Wildlife Corridor** to allow large mammals (including bears, wolves and cougars) to migrate across the valley without having to enter the town. The area is permanently off-limits to people, but animals don't always respect the boundaries, so look out for wildlife warnings and trail closures around Marsh Loop and Sundance Canyon.

Banff Park Museum   MUSEUM

(Map p88; ☑ 403-762-1558; www.pc.gc.ca/en/lhn -nhs/ab/banff; 91 Banff Ave; adult/child C$3.90/ free; ⊙ 9:30am-5pm Wed-Sun) Occupying the oldest surviving federal building in a Canadian National Park and dating from 1903, this museum is a national historic site. Its exhibits – a taxidermic collection of local animals, including grizzly and black bears, plus a tree carved with graffiti dating from 1841 – were curated by Norman Sanson, who ran the museum and Banff weather station until 1932.

Vermilion Lakes   NATURE RESERVE

West of town, this trio of tranquil lakes is a great place for **wildlife spotting**: elk, bea-

Central Banff Town

BANFF NATIONAL PARK SIGHTS

vers, owls, bald eagles and ospreys can often be seen around the lakeshore, especially at dawn and dusk. A paved path – part of the Legacy bike trail – parallels the lakes' northern edge for 5.9km, but the proximity of the Trans-Canada Hwy/Hwy 1 means that it's not as peaceful as it could be.

Banff Gondola CABLE CAR
(✆ 403-762-2523; www.banffjaspercollection.com/attractions/banff-gondola; Mountain Ave, Banff Town; adult C$58-74, child C$29-37, after 6pm adult $46-62, child C$23-31; ⊗ 8am-10:30pm late Jun-Aug, to 9:30pm Sep–mid-Oct, reduced hours rest of year) In summer or winter, you can summit a peak near Banff thanks to the Banff Gondola, with four-person enclosed cars that glide up to the top of Sulphur Mountain in less than 10 minutes. Named for the thermal springs that emanate from its base, this peak is a perfect viewing point and a tick-box Banff attraction. There are a couple of restaurants on top, plus an extended hike on boardwalks to Sanson Peak, the site of an old weather station.

Pursuit, the corporation that owns the gondola, has recently moved to a system of 'dynamic pricing' where rates fluctuate according to demand; prices can get quite steep during peak summer season. Some people prefer to hike up the mountain in-

stead on a zigzagging 5.6km trail. You can travel back down on the gondola for half price and recover in the hot springs.

The gondola is 4km south of central Banff. The easiest way to get there is to catch Roam bus No 1; alternatively, you can hunt for a spot in the enormous car park.

Buffalo Nations
Luxton Museum MUSEUM
(Map p87; ✆ 403-762-2388; www.buffalonationsmuseum.com; 1 Birch Ave; adult/senior/child C$10/9/5; ⊗ 10am-7pm May-Sep, 11am-5pm Oct-Apr) The Luxton Museum recounts the story of Alberta's indigenous people, with a strong emphasis on the Cree, Blackfoot, Blood and Stoney nations. The displays are short on informative text, but you'll see some impressive eagle-feather headdresses and exquisite beadwork, including a gorgeous collection of horse bridles and sled-dog harnesses. There are also dioramas and life-size replicas representing traditional activities and events, among them a rather macabre Sun Dance ceremony.

Old Banff Cemetery CEMETERY
(Map p87; Buffalo St) Banff's shaded cemetery is worth a visit, especially if you're interested in the town's history. Some of the gravestones date back to the 1890s; among the famous folk buried here are the pioneering

Banff National Park Region

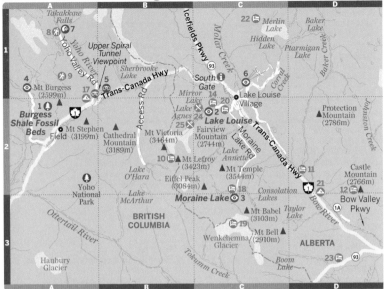

Banff National Park Region

trail guides Tom Wilson (who discovered Lake Louise), Jim Brewster (the founder of Brewster Transportation) and Bill Pey- to; the artists Peter and Catharine Whyte; and the frontierswoman, naturalist and writer Mary Schäffer Warren, whose house

◉ Around Banff Town

Lake Minnewanka

Cradled high above town between the Palliser and Fairholme ranges, Lake Minnewanka is the largest body of water in the national park – 24km (15 miles) long, 142m (465ft) deep and barely a few degrees above freezing. Known to Stoney people as *minn-waki* ('the lake of the spirits'), the lake was believed to be haunted by the spirits of the dead, perhaps explaining why early Europeans referred to it as Devil's Lake.

The lake has been dammed three times at its western end: in 1895, 1912 and finally in 1941, when the water level was raised by around 30m, completely submerging the lively summer settlement of Minnewanka Landing, which had four avenues and three streets lined with hotels, shops and saloon bars. Today the drowned town is off-limits to everyone except scuba divers, so you'll have to content yourself with a picnic or a stroll along the lakeshore. There's a small seasonal cafe next to the car park that serves sandwiches, drinks, ice cream and other snacks. Bighorn sheep can often be seen grazing along the lakeshore.

Minnewanka is the only lake in Banff that allows motorboats. You can rent motor launches from the boathouse, or head out with Lake Minnewanka Cruises (☑866-606-6700; www.banffjaspercollection.com/attractions/lake-minnewanka-cruise; Minnewanka Loop Dr; adult/child classic cruise C$58/29, explorer cruise C$81/41; ◷classic cruise hourly 10am-6pm late Jun–mid-Sep, noon-5pm mid-Sep–mid-Oct; explorer cruise 10am late Jun-early Sep), whose one-hour boat trips include a commentary on the history, geology and mythology of the lake, plus an optional visit to the glacial pass known as the Devil's Gap.

Minnewanka also marks the start of several hikes. The gentle trail to Stewart Canyon is a great family option, while hardier walkers might want to tackle Aylmer Lookout (11.8km/7.3 miles one way, 560m/1837ft elevation gain) or continue on to Aylmer Pass (13km/8 miles one way, 810m/2657ft elevation gain). Note that the Aylmer trails are closed during the buffalo-berry season between mid-July and September, as the area is a frequent hangout for grizzly bears.

can be seen just across the street from the cemetery.

Tunnel Mountain MOUNTAIN
(Map p87) It might be Banff's smallest mountain at 1692m, but Tunnel Mountain is still one of the town's most recognizable landmarks. The mountain's distinctive rippled profile, which looms over the east side of town, was known to the Stoney people as *tatanga* (buffalo), as it resembles a sleeping buffalo when seen from the north and east.

From the north side of St Julien Rd, a short trail (4.3km) switchbacks up the mountainside to the summit, offering an airy view over Banff Town.

The mountain gets its modern name courtesy of the CPR surveyor Major AB Rogers who, while laying the groundwork for the arrival of the railway in Banff in 1882, devised a harebrained plan to blast a 275m-long tunnel through the base of the mountain to avoid the twists and turns of the Bow River. Incensed at the projected cost, Rogers' superiors ordered him to find an alternative, and the railway was subsequently rerouted north of the mountain at a fraction of the original price.

Mt Norquay

One of Banff's 'Big Three' ski resorts in the winter, Mt Norquay is named after John Norquay (premier of Manitoba from 1878 to 1887), who supposedly made the first summit ascent at the end of his premiership in 1887.

Norquay and its chairlift remain open year-round. When the snow melts, people come up here to hike, visit the Cliffhouse Bistro at the top of the chairlift or engage in Banff's newest activity – the via ferrata (p82).

A free shuttle replaces the ski shuttle in the summer, allowing easy access from Banff Town. It stops just above the ski-area parking lot at the base of the chairlift, where you'll also find a small cafeteria-style eating joint. The ski-area parking lot marks the start of two hikes: the long slog to Cascade Amphitheatre (p57), and the shorter trail to the wooded summit of Stoney Squaw Mountain (4.2km/2.6 miles round-trip, 190m/623ft elevation gain).

Sunshine Meadows

Straddling the Continental Divide and the border between Alberta and British Columbia, Sunshine Meadows is Banff's metaphoric rooftop, an expanse of high alpine meadowland stretching for 15km (9.3 miles) between Citadel Pass and Healy Pass.

In winter it's one of Banff's three ski areas, but come summertime, it becomes one of the easiest places in the Rockies for hikers to get above the tree line to experience exuberant wildflowers, mirror-like lakes and huge mountain views without the use of a helicopter or several pints of sweat. Once the snows thaw, Sunshine marks the start of several fabulous trails.

Summer passage up to the meadows is handled, between late June and early September, by the Sunshine Sightseeing Gondola (403-705-4000; www.banffsunshine meadows.com/sightseeing; Sunshine Ski Area; adult/child/family C$45/23/109; 8am-6pm late

---

THE BIRTH OF A NATIONAL PARK

Canada's present-day national-park system can trace its origins back to the discovery of three geothermally heated springs near Banff in the autumn of 1883. Although First Nations people had known about the hot springs around Banff for well over 10,000 years, the first white man to set eyes on them was James Hector, who recorded the springs on the Palliser expedition of 1859, probably following the advice of local Stoneys. Two surveyors working for the Canadian Pacific Railway revisited the springs in 1874, but it was brothers Tom and William McCardell, and their partner Frank McCabe, who changed the history of the springs for good.

In the autumn of 1883, they crossed the marshy area to the west of present-day Banff and stumbled across a series of deep chambers filled with naturally hot water. When William was lowered by his companions into one of the caves, he's reported to have described it as being 'like some fantastic dream from a tale of *The Arabian Nights*.' The three companions smelled much more than just the odor of the sulfurous water – with the fashion for spa bathing still in full swing in Europe, and hot water on tap still an undreamt-of luxury, there was the whiff of money around the hot springs. Together they staked a claim on the area, though ownership soon degenerated into legal wranglings over mineral rights and land claims, forcing the government to step in and declare the springs the property of Canada – sowing the seeds for the birth of Banff National Park and the National Park Act, eventually enacted in 1930.

The springs themselves proved to be just the money-spinner the three men had hoped, although none of them saw any of the proceeds. Victorians and First Nations peoples alike believed the waters had healing properties (supposedly good for everything from arthritis to stinky feet), and within a few short years, resort spas had sprung up all across the foot of Sulphur Mountain.

By the early 1900s, the precious water was being pumped to a health sanatorium on the site of present-day Canada Pl, while companies were bottling the water for export to the distant corners of Canada. There were even bars along Banff Ave where customers could take a tot of gin or rum along with a splash of mineral water. And though the medicinal properties of the waters have never quite been proven, there's no doubt that sinking into the hot waters with a view of the surrounding mountains is a fantastically soothing experience.

Jun–early Sep), which whisks hikers from Sunshine's base station – located in a car park at the end of the Sunshine road, 15km from Banff town – up to the ski 'village,' cutting out 6.5km (4 miles) of dull uphill hiking.

At the top of the gondola, Sunshine Village consists of a high-altitude hotel, the Sunshine Mountain Lodge, along with several cafes and restaurants, two or three of which remain open in the summer. The village, at an altitude of about 2300m (7545ft), is on the cusp of several short alpine trails – including the Garden Path Trail (p59) – and a couple of longer ones, most notably the backcountry excursions to Egypt Lake (p68) and Mt Assiniboine Provincial Park (p69).

The gondola departs on a continuous basis between 8am and 6pm. For overnight hikers to Mt Assiniboine (or anybody else who wants it), a one-way gondola ticket is available for C$38. If that's not you, then don't miss the last ride down, or you're in for a long, unwelcome end-of-day trek!

Back down at the base station, you'll find a year-round cafeteria, plus the trailhead for the summer-only hike to Healy Pass (p59); this is the best trail for purists who prefer to reach the high country under their own steam.

To get to the gondola's base station without your own wheels, take one of Sunshine's free hiker shuttles. These depart from Banff's historic train station hourly between 7:10am and 3:10pm, returning from Sunshine at 60-minute intervals between 8:30am and 6:30pm. (For full schedule details, see www.banffsunshinemeadows.com/hours-directions).

Bow Valley Parkway

While most people zoom along busy Trans-Canada Hwy/Hwy 1 with nothing but views of truck tailgates and passing automobiles, wiser souls swing over onto the quieter and much more scenic Hwy 1A, otherwise known as the Bow Valley Pkwy, which runs for 51km (31.6 miles) nearly all the way north to Lake Louise. The route is hemmed in by thick fir forest and mountains, with regular viewpoints looking out across the Bow Valley. It's a great place to look out for wildlife, especially elk, bighorn sheep and even the occasional moose, but take things slow: the regular speed limit is 60km/h (37mph), dropping down to 30km/h (19mph) at certain sections to avoid wildlife collisions.

If you're short on time, at the very least make sure to visit the thundering waterfalls of Johnston Canyon, where a suspended catwalk tracks along the canyon wall to a series of viewpoints overlooking the Lower and Upper Falls. It's one of Banff's most popular sights, and the car park is often full by midmorning; save it for an early morning or late-evening visit. A little further along the parkway is the lookout point at Castle Mountain, one of Banff's most recognizable mountain peaks.

The eastern section of the road between Fireside Picnic Area and Johnston Canyon is closed from 6pm to 9am during spring mating season (March to late June).

⊙ Lake Louise & Around

Considered by many to be the crown jewel of Banff National Park, Lake Louise is nearly impossible to describe without resorting to shameless clichés. Standing next to the serene, implausibly turquoise lake, Banff's wild grandeur feels (and is) tantalizingly close, with a surrounding amphitheater of finely chiseled mountains that hoist Victoria Glacier audaciously toward the heavens.

Famous for its teahouses, grizzly bears and hiking trails, Lake Louise is also renowned for its much-commented-on 'crowds,' plus the incongruous lump of towering concrete known as Chateau Lake Louise. But frankly, who cares? You don't come to Lake Louise to dodge other tourists. You come to share in one of the Rockies' most spectacular sights, one that has captured the imaginations of mountaineers, artists and visitors for more than a century.

Lake Louise 'village,' just off Trans-Canada Hwy/Hwy 1, is little more than an outdoor shopping mall, a gas station and a handful of hotels.

Lake Louise

Stoney people knew about Lake Louise long before the first European settlers arrived, but the first white man to 'discover' it was the railway surveyor and pack guide Tom Wilson, who was taken to the 'Lake of Little Fishes' by indigenous guides in 1882. Originally known as Emerald Lake, it was later renamed in honor of Princess Louise Caroline Alberta, Queen Victoria's fourth daughter and wife of the then Canadian governor-general.

Roughly 2km (1.2 miles) end to end and 70m (230ft) deep, the lake is famous for its

LAKE LOUISE GONDOLA

For a bird's-eye view of the Lake Louise area – and a good chance of spotting grizzly bears on the avalanche slopes – climb aboard the Lake Louise Summer Gondola (☑ 403-522-3555; www.lakelouisegondola.com; 1 Whitehorn Rd; adult/child $38/17; ☺ 9am-4pm mid-May–mid-Jun, 8am-5:30pm mid-Jun–Jul, to 6pm Aug, to 5pm Sep–mid-Oct; ⊕), which crawls up the side of Whitehorn Mountain to a dizzying viewpoint 2088m above the valley floor. Look out for the imposing fang of 3544m-high Mt Temple piercing the skyline on the opposite side of the valley. At the top of the mountain, if you're feeling ambitious, hike the 1.7km loop trail to Kicking Horse Pass Viewpoint or the 3.4km round-trip to Ptarmigan Valley Viewpoint.

Take the gondola up for 360-degree views, and the chairlift down for an open-air thrill. Back at the bottom, snacks and light meals are available at the Lodge of the Ten Peaks (www.lakelouisegondola.com/dining.php; 1 Whitehorn Rd; fast food $7-16; ☺ 8am-4pm May-Sep).

The gondola is about 2km east of Lake Louise village. Complimentary shuttle buses run several times daily from the Fairmont Chateau Lake Louise and Samson Mall. For information on bus departure times, see www.lakelouisegondola.com/shuttle.php.

searingly blue water, caused by light reflecting off tiny particles of 'rock flour' (glacial silt) carried down from the mountain glaciers. On still days the lake becomes a shimmering mirror for the surrounding scenery; it's best seen early or late in the day, when the vibrant colors of the lake are strongest. In winter the scene is transformed into a wonderland of powder-white ice and snow-cloaked peaks. The surface of the lake often freezes over and skaters glide across it, wrapped up tight against the biting mountain cold.

Since Tom's time, the lake has become one of Banff National Park's most famous (and busiest) attractions, and the lakeshore inevitably gets crushingly crowded on summer days. Visit as early as possible to avoid the squash, and spend the rest of the day exploring nearby attractions such as Moraine Lake or the Lake Louise Gondola.

You can usually escape the coachloads of sightseers milling around in front of the Fairmont Chateau Lake Louise by following the lakeshore trail, which tracks through forest along the northern side of the lake, offering fabulous vistas of Fairview Mountain and the Victoria Glacier. A spur trail leads steeply up the mountainside to the famous Lake Agnes Teahouse (p63) and the Big Beehive lookout, but it's a long slog, so you'll need good shoes and plenty of water. Further along the lakeshore trail, you can continue up the valley on the Plain of Six Glaciers walk. There are several more classic hikes leading off around Lake Louise, including the steep climbs up Saddleback (2330m/7644ft) and Fairview Mountain

(2744m/9003ft), which both brood along the lake's southern shore.

For something more sedentary, you can hire canoes from the Lake Louise Boathouse (☑ 403-522-3511; www.fairmont.com/lake-louise/promotions/canoeing; canoe rental per 30min/1hr C$115/125; ☺ 8am-8:30pm Jun-Sep, weather permitting). Once you've got over the shock of the price, you'll be rewarded with a sense of the silence and natural majesty that must have greeted Tom Wilson when he first laid eyes on the lake.

Moraine Lake

Reached by a twisting 13km (8-mile) road that's only open from June to October, the mountainous panoramas around Moraine Lake are arguably even more stunning than those at Lake Louise (p93). Backed by the dagger-point peaks of the Wenkchemna Range, all of which top out over 3000m (10,000ft), Moraine is another sparkling bluer-than-blue lake that's fed by glacial runoff from the surrounding mountains. It's one of the best-known views in the Rockies, and it graced the back of the C$20 bill from 1969 to 1986.

The mountains were originally named in 1894 by the explorer Samuel Allen, using the numbers one to 10 in the Stoney language (*wenkchemna* means 10). All but two of the mountains have since been renamed, but you'll still see some guidebooks and maps using the original Stoney names.

At the eastern end of the lake is the Moraine Lake Rockpile, a massive heap of boulders of somewhat uncertain origin: some geologists think it was created by an ancient avalanche, while others believe it was formed by the long-gone glacier that carved out the rest of the valley. A paved trail leads up to a series of viewpoints at the top of the rockpile, offering a panoramic vista across the lake and the Wenkchemna Peaks beyond. On his first climb up the rockpile in 1899, early adventurer Walter Wilcox wrote: 'No scene has ever given me an equal impression of inspiring solitude and rugged grandeur.' It's hard to argue.

A part-paved trail leads off around the lake's northern shore, linking up with the branch trail to Larch Valley and Eiffel Lake. Another trail leads southeast from the rockpile to Consolation Lakes. Alternatively, you can explore the lake in the manner of the old voyageurs by hiring a canoe from the boathouse next to Moraine Lake Lodge.

⊙ Icefields Parkway

The Icefields Pkwy (p74), the 'road to the clouds,' the Promenade des Glaciers...apply whichever sobriquet you wish; Canada's Hwy 93 is one of the most incredible roads in North America. Paralleling the Continental Divide for 230km (142.6 miles) between Lake Louise and Jasper Town, 122km (77 miles) of this precious parkway lies inside Banff National Park and is replete with fanning glaciers, teeming wildlife and gothic mountains. Miss it at your peril.

The Banff section of the parkway offers a variety of accommodations: campgrounds at Rampart Creek, Mosquito Creek, Silverhorn Creek and Waterfowl Lakes; rustic wilderness hostels with wood-fired saunas at Mosquito Creek and Rampart Creek; hotel rooms at the historic Num-Ti-Jah Lodge, established in the 1920s by the famous Rockies character Jimmy Simpson; and a rather dull and over-priced motel at Saskatchewan River Crossing.

The speed limit on the parkway is 90km/h (56mph), with reduced speeds around Saskatchewan River Crossing and the Columbia Icefield. The road often becomes impassable in winter due to heavy snow, and chains or all-season tires are advisable between October and May. Regardless of the time of year, you'll also need a valid National Park Pass for everyone in your vehicle in order to drive on the parkway. Sights on the parkway are covered in more detail in the 'Into the Icefields' driving tour (p74).

☞ TOURS

Unless you're really short on time or are traveling without your own vehicle, there's no real need to splash out on a guided tour – but if you prefer to let someone else do the organizing (and the driving), a bus trip can be a good way of packing in the sights. Most companies offer pick-up and drop-off from your hotel, and include lunch in their full-day tours.

THE SWISS GUIDES IN CANADA

Following the death of Philip Abbot on Mt Lefroy in 1896, the Canadian Pacific Railway (CPR) knew it had to do something to keep mountaineering enthusiasts boarding its trains for the Rockies.

In order to reassure investors' nerves and ensure the safety of their clients in the mountains, the CPR decided to hire the services of some of Switzerland's top alpine guides, shipping them over at considerable expense with the promise of accommodations, attractive pay and – most importantly – the opportunity to be the first to claim some of the Rockies' numerous unclimbed peaks.

First to arrive in 1899 were Edward Feuz Sr and Christian Haesler, two of Switzerland's most renowned guides, followed a few seasons later by another handful of skilled alpinists, including Edward's trio of mountain-climbing sons, Ernest, Edward Feuz Jr and Walter. In order to help their new employees feel more at home, in 1911 the CPR constructed a small settlement of Swiss-style timber chalets just outside Golden, which became known to locals as the 'Swiss Village' or 'Edelweiss.' Many of the original buildings are still standing.

The Swiss guides played an important role in the development of Canadian mountaineering, and were instrumental in the formation of the Alpine Club of Canada, which was based in Golden during its early years.

Though Feuz Sr never permanently settled in Canada, he continued to visit most summers until his death in 1965, leading over 100 new routes and becoming the first man to climb 78 Canadian peaks. During his 50-year career, he never lost a client.

Founded way back in 1892 by the entrepreneurial Brewster brothers Bill and Jim, **Brewster Sightseeing** (Map p88; ☑ 403-760-6934; www.banffjaspercollection.com/brewster-sightseeing; 100 Gopher St; ⊙ 7am-9pm) is one of Banff's oldest guiding firms and is still one of the town's busiest tour operators. Today it also operates several of the park's most lucrative sights, including the Banff Gondola, Lake Minnewanka Cruises and the Columbia Icefield Skywalk.

In the early days visitors were ferried around by packhorse and mule train, but these days the transportation is rather plusher: Brewster's tours are run in large motor coaches, complete with air-con and guided commentary. The big buses feel a bit impersonal compared to smaller operators, and stopovers at sights along the way (especially on the full-day tours) can be whistle-stop brief.

Brewster offers a variety of combo packages to a cocktail of sights, which can save you money; see the website for details.

Discover Banff Tours (Map p88; ☑ 403-760-5007; www.banfftours.com; Sundance Mall, 215 Banff Ave; ⊙ 7:30am-9pm), another of Banff's big tour operators, runs smaller buses than Brewster, so things feel a bit less regimented – you can even hire your own personal guide.

🛏 SLEEPING

Despite having enough hotel rooms to rival a town three times its size, finding a place to sleep in Banff Town can be tricky. Demand is huge, and rates are notoriously expensive, especially in peak season. Many visitors choose to cut costs by camping, hosteling, hiring recreation vehicles or staying in nearby Canmore. Regardless of where you stay, book well ahead, especially if you're coming in June, July or August.

🛏 Banff

Camping

Tunnel Mountain CAMPGROUND **$**
(Tunnel Mountain Dr; tent sites C$27.40, RV sites C$32.30-38.20) Banff's massive campground is split over three separate 'villages' halfway up the slope of Tunnel Mountain, offering 1149 reservable sites. It fills to capacity in summer thanks to its convenient location just minutes from downtown Banff. With its many trees, it's not as grim as it sounds, but if you're truly after tranquility, you might want to look elsewhere.

BANFF CAMPGROUNDS

Banff has 14 frontcountry campgrounds catering for tents, recreational vehicles (RVs) and camper vans. Most are open from around June to mid-September, although Tunnel Mountain Village Two and Lake Louise Trailer campgrounds open year-round.

Advance reservations are available for Tunnel Mountain, Two Jack, Johnston Canyon, Lake Louise and some sites at Rampart Creek. The Parks Canada website (www.reservation.pc.gc.ca) starts taking reservations in January each year for a fee of C$11 in addition to regular camping fees. Book as far ahead as possible, as sites fill up fast.

Sites at all other campgrounds are allocated on a first-come, first-served basis, so the best way to claim a spot is to turn up early (around the official 11am checkout time is best) or check with parks staff about which campgrounds currently have availability. Banff Park Radio (101.1FM) also releases regular bulletins on campgrounds with available sites. It's a good idea to stay in one place over weekends; sites are generally easier to come by midweek.

There's a maximum stay of 14 nights and a maximum occupancy of six people per site. At larger campgrounds you can pay fees at the entry kiosk, but at smaller campgrounds, you'll have to self-register: find a vacant site first, then go to the self-registration shelter, remembering to enter your name, site number, license plate and duration of stay on the envelope along with the relevant fees. If it's late when you arrive, you can do this in the morning, or sometimes staff will come around and collect your fees in person in the morning.

Fires are usually allowed at campsites where there's a fire pit – you'll need to buy a fire permit (C$8.80, including wood) from the campground entrance. Watch for fire restrictions during dry periods.

All three areas – Tunnel Mountain I with its 618 tent sites, Tunnel Mountain II with 21 oTENTiks (platform tents sleeping up to six people) and 188 RV sites offering electrical hookups, and the full-service Tunnel Mountain Trailer court with 322 sites – have flush toilets, proper showers and wheelchair-accessible sites. Part of it is open during winter, too, so if you're keen to sleep under canvas at -20°C, you can do it here. Free shuttle-bus service into Banff is available to all campers.

Lodging

Accommodations in Banff Town are generally expensive, especially in summer. There's a long lineup of hotels on Banff Ave, many owned by the gargantuan Banff Lodging Company (www.bestofbanff.com). Booking ahead is strongly recommended. For listings of available accommodations, check the Banff Tourism Bureau (p110) and the Parks Canada Visitor Centre (p110).

★Samesun Banff HOSTEL $
(Map p87; ☑403-762-4499; www.banffhostel.com; 433 Banff Ave; dm incl breakfast from C$65; P@🛜) Catering to a youthful international backpacker crowd, the welcoming Samesun offers a central Banff Ave location, a full lineup of daily activities (hiking, cycling, canoeing, hot springs) and 112 dorm beds spread across modern, compact six- to 14-person rooms (some with fireplaces). A DIY breakfast is included, and the bustling on-site Beaver resto-bar keeps everyone happy with nightly drink specials.

HI Banff Alpine Centre HOSTEL $
(Map p87; ☑403-762-4123; www.hihostels.ca; 801 Hidden Ridge Way; dm from C$55, d with shared/private bath from C$177/214, private cabins from C$238; P@🛜) Near the top of Tunnel Mountain, Banff's HI hostel is well away from the madness of Banff Ave. The classic mountain-lodge style buildings offer spick-and-span accommodations ranging from dorms to private doubles to cabins. Common areas are open and comfortable, with fireplaces, views and an on-site bar and restaurant. Public buses run by the front door, and passes are complimentary.

★Fairmont Banff Springs HOTEL $$$
(☑403-762-2211; www.fairmont.com/banff-springs; 405 Spray Ave; r from C$599; P❄@🛜⛷) Rising like a Gaelic Balmoral above the trees at the base of Sulphur Mountain and visible from miles away, the Banff Springs is a won-

der of early 1920s revivalist architecture and one of Canada's most iconic buildings. Wandering through its grand lobby and elegant lounge, wine bar and restaurant, it's easy to forget that it's also a hotel.

Rooms vary in size and style; some don't feel much different than a standard hotel room, while others have plush modern or old-world decor. Many have incredible views. Service and prices are fit for royalty.

★Buffaloberry B&B $$$
(Map p87; ☑403-762-3750; www.buffaloberry.com; 417 Marten St; r C$465; P❄🛜) Centrally located and surrounded by colorful flowering plants, this purpose-built B&B makes a cheerful, comfortable home base. The four individually decorated bedrooms are heavy on homey charm, and the underfloor heating and nightly turn-down treats keep the pamper factor high. With an ever-changing menu (think baked Camembert egg custard or 'triple B' – blueberry, buttermilk and buckwheat – pancakes), breakfasts are divine.

Banff Log Cabin B&B B&B $$$
(Map p87; ☑403-762-3516; www.banfflogcabin.ca; 222 Glen Cres; cabin incl breakfast C$425; P🛜) If having your own cozy cabin only steps from the rush of Bow River Falls sounds appealing, you'll love this B&B. Wedding planner/photographer owners Sharon and Malcolm ply guests with a comfy bed, prosecco and handmade local chocolates, tea kettles, an outdoor fire pit for roasting marshmallows and loaner bikes for the short ride across the pedestrian bridge into town.

A delicious breakfast is served each morning on your sunny front deck, where you can watch for deer and fawns on the adjacent lawn. Free parking (a rare luxury in Banff) is provided right out front. There's a minimum two-night stay, so you actually have time to settle in and appreciate the place.

Oh, and in case you're wondering why the B&B is so close to the iconic Fairmont Banff Springs hotel, this was once the site of the hotel's private dairy farm!

Banff Aspen Lodge HOTEL $$$
(Map p87; ☑403-762-4401; www.banffaspenlodge.com; 401 Banff Ave; r C$369-459; P🛜) Among the rare Banff hotels that are not part of a corporate chain, the Aspen offers friendly service and tastefully decorated modern rooms finished in earthy tones and sharp pine. Upstairs units, all with

BANFF NATIONAL PARK CAMPGROUNDS

CAMPGROUND	LOCATION	DESCRIPTION	NO OF SITES
Tunnel Mountain Trailer Court	Banff Town	Dedicated RV and trailer site with full hookups	322
Tunnel Mountain Village I	Banff Town	Large, forested, tent-only campground, popular with families, but can get crowded	618
Tunnel Mountain Village II	Banff Town	Mixed-use campground that's handy for Banff Town, but feels a little exposed to the elements	188
Castle Mountain	Bow Valley Parkway	Small woodland campground that's handily located near a grocery store	43
Johnston Canyon	Bow Valley Parkway	One of the park's most scenic and best-equipped campgrounds, with lots of day hikes on its doorstep	132
Protection Mountain	Bow Valley Parkway	Popular with hikers thanks to its proximity to trailheads; recycling and kitchen shelters	72
Mosquito Creek	Icefields Parkway	Very basic, tree-lined campground in the shadow of Mt Hector; southern end of Icefields Pkwy	32
Rampart Creek	Icefields Parkway	The last frontcountry campground south of the Jasper border; rudimentary, but peaceful	51
Silverhorn Creek	Icefields Parkway	Basic sites with no shade surrounding a parking loop	45
Waterfowl Lakes	Icefields Parkway	The best equipped of the Icefields Pkwy campgrounds, with recycling bins, piped water and food storage	116
Lake Louise Tent	Lake Louise	Tent campground next door to the RV campground, protected by a bear-proof fence	206
Lake Louise RV	Lake Louise	RV-friendly campground that keeps 30 sites open in winter	189
Two Jack Lakeside	Lake Minnewanka	Beautiful and very popular lakeside campground with private, secluded sites	74
Two Jack Main	Lake Minnewanka	Scattered pleasantly under the trees, but the lack of shower facilities is a drawback	380

▼	Drinking Water	🚻	Flush Toilets	👪	Great for Families	🏪	Grocery Store Nearby

balconies, are far more appealing than the cramped economy rooms downstairs. The sleek attached Whitebark Cafe (p108) is an excellent spot for coffee or breakfast.

Moose Hotel & Suites HOTEL $$$
(Map p87; ☏ 403-760-8570; www.moosehotel andsuites.com; 345 Banff Ave; r/ste from C$519/699; 🅿✳🛜🏊🐾) Like a mountain lodge pumped up on steroids, the Moose is the biggest new hotel to hit Banff Ave in recent years. The rooftop pools, hot tubs and sauna looking out at the mountains are instantly seductive, while the 174 comfy rooms and suites – each with a patio or balcony – are spacious and agreeably done up in natural wood.

Environmentally friendly touches throughout the hotel include LED lighting, low-flush toilets, refillable water bottles for guests and electric-car charging stations in the free underground parking garage. Other on-site amenities include the full-service Meadows Spa and the Pacini Italian restaurant. At the heart of the complex is the Corner House, a cute 1920s-vintage clapboard home, refurbished as a private suite.

ELEVATION	OPEN	RESERVATION REQUIRED?	DAILY FEE	FACILITIES	PAGE
1440m (4725ft)	May-Oct	yes	C$39		p96
1440m (4725ft)	Jun-Oct	yes	C$28		p96
1450m (4760ft)	year-round	yes	C$33		p96
1450m (4760ft)	May-Sep	no	C$22		p101
1430m (4700ft)	May-Sep	yes	C$28		p101
1450m (4760ft)	Jun-Sep	no	C$22		p101
1850m (6070ft)	Jun-Oct	no	C$18		p103
1450m (4760ft)	Jun-Oct	some sites reservable	C$18		p103
1650m (5410ft)	Jun-Sep	no	C$16		p103
1650m (5410ft)	Jun-Sep	no	C$22		p103
1540m (5050ft)	Jun-Sep	yes	C$28		p102
1540m (5050ft)	year-round	yes	C$33		p102
1460m (4790ft)	May-Oct	yes	C$28		p101
1460m (4790ft)	Jun-Sep	yes	C$22		p101

	Restaurant Nearby		Payphone		Summertime Campfire Program		RV Dump Station

Fox Hotel & Suites   HOTEL $$$
(Map p87; ☏ 403-760-8500; www.foxhoteland
suites.com; 461 Banff Ave; r C$399-489, ste C$469-
599; P❄❅@🛜🐾🐕) Aesthetically, the Fox
is a step above its neighbors. Its forest-like
lobby is instantly calming, while the 116
rooms, centered on a courtyard, feature at-
tractive animal-themed wallpaper and lots
of natural wood accents. The highlight is
the Cave & Basin–inspired hot tub, with an
opening in the roof that gives out to the sky.
Service is attentive.

Poplar Inn   B&B $$$
(Map p88; ☏ 403-760-8688; www.thepoplarinn.ca;
316 Lynx St; d incl breakfast C$275, apt C$550; P🛜)
Two lovely guest rooms and a brand-new
self-catering two-bedroom apartment grace
this heritage home just steps from Banff Ave.
Luxury touches throughout include Egyptian
cotton sheets; the apartment comes with
kitchen and laundry facilities and a sunny
upstairs deck. Breakfasts feature treats like
Grand Marnier French toast or blueberry
pancakes, while homemade muffins, granola,
fruit and yogurt greet early risers.

STAYING IN THE BACKCOUNTRY

Camping

There are over 50 campgrounds dotted around the Banff backcountry, but they're generally a lot more basic than the national park's other camping areas. Cleared sites, tent pads and pit toilets pretty much sum up the facilities; some also have bear-proof bins or food storage cables. You'll need to pack in everything else (including food, fuel, water-treatment equipment and other supplies). You'll also need to pack everything out again once your trip is finished (including all your rubbish).

All overnight stays in the backcountry require a wilderness pass (per day C$9.80), available from park visitor centers. You'll need to indicate which campgrounds you intend to use when you purchase your pass; advance reservations can be made via the Parks Canada website (www.reservation.pc.gc.ca) for a C$11 fee, and you must stick to these campgrounds once you've booked them. Trail and campground numbers are strictly limited, so you might well find your route is booked out unless you plan ahead, especially in July and August. The maximum stay at any one site is three days.

Beyond the backcountry, wild camping is permitted in some areas. Make sure your campsite is 5km (3.1 miles) from any trailhead, 50m (164ft) off the trail and 70m (229ft) from any water source, and take the usual precautions against bears and forest fires.

Shelters

Parks Canada operates two backcountry trail shelters, one at Egypt Lake and another at Bryant Creek. Both are extremely rustic and offer little more than a roof over your head, a wood stove and an outhouse. You'll need to be completely self-sufficient, with your own bedding, food, cooking equipment and toilet paper. You can book spaces at the shelters for an extra fee of C$6.80 per night when you purchase your wilderness pass.

Alpine Club of Canada Huts

The Alpine Club of Canada (p82) operates several remote huts for climbers and moun-taineers that are also open to backcountry walkers. They range from basic cabins to historic log huts. Most have mattresses, cooking stoves and utensils, but you'll need your own sleeping bag, food and other supplies (including toilet paper and matches).

Reservations are required at all huts and can be made through the Alpine Club of Canada (ACC) up to a month in advance. Key ACC huts include **Abbot Pass Hut** (www.alpineclubofcanada.ca; member/non-member C$30/40; ☺ summer), which sleeps 24 and is perched atop a difficult glacier climb at the end of the Plain of Six Glaciers, and **Castle Mountain Hut** (www.alpineclubofcanada.ca; member/non-member C$30/40; ☺ Jun-Sep), which sleeps six, is located halfway up Castle Mountain and is mainly used by rock climbers.

There's also a string of huts along the Wapta Icefield, allowing adventurers to com-plete the so-called Wapta Traverse. These include **Peyto Hut** (www.alpineclubofcanada.ca; member/nonmember C$30/40; ☺ year-round), which sleeps 18 in summer and 16 in winter; **Bow Hut** (www.alpineclubofcanada.ca; member/nonmember C$30/40; ☺ year-round), sleep-ing 30; and **Neil Colgan Hut** (www.alpineclubofcanada.ca; member/non-member C$30/40; ☺ Jun-Sep), the highest habitable structure in Canada, sleeping up to 18 in summer.

Lodges

For a bit of rustic 'luxury' in the backcountry, there are two historic mountain lodges at Skoki (p104) and Shadow Lake (p104). Both welcome hikers with comfortable beds, cozy fireplace-equipped lounges, afternoon tea and three delicious meals a day.

Juniper　　　　　　　　HOTEL **$$$**
(☎ 403-762-2281; www.thejuniper.com; 1 Juniper Way; r/ste from C$339/404; P❄☎❄) Perched beneath Mt Norquay, the modern, pet-friendly Juniper has comfortable rooms, and suites with Jacuzzis and fireplaces, all surrounded by landscaped native-plant gar-dens. The staff is friendly and welcomes hik-ers, skiers and cyclists. The glassed-in bistro has a creative menu, awesome views and a big patio. With the Trans-Canada Hwy just below, the hotel gets a bit of traffic noise.

Buffalo Mountain Lodge   HOTEL **$$$**
(Map p87; ☎ 800-661-1367; www.crmr.com/buffalo;
700 Tunnel Mountain Dr; r from C$379; ☎) Three
hectares of private forested grounds make
this lodge on Tunnel Mountain one of Banff's
most pleasant mountain retreats. Rooms
have plush rustic charm, with timber beams,
clawfoot tubs, fieldstone log fireplaces and
underfloor heating in the bathrooms. Eat at
the in-house cafe, lounge or dining room or
wander 15 minutes by foot into town.

Bow View Lodge   HOTEL **$$$**
(Map p88; ☎ 403-762-2261; www.bowview.com;
228 Bow Ave; r C$299-399; P✳🖘☎) The
1960s-vintage Bow View is older than most
of the log inns lining Banff Ave, but neat and
tidy all the same. The location is great, steps
from downtown and the river (though river
views from the rooms are obstructed by the
parking lot). Guests get free use of the gym
and pool in the Banff Park Lodge next door.

🛏 Lake Minnewanka

The twin campgrounds around Lake Minnewanka are perennially popular thanks to
their peaceful wooded setting.

Two Jack Lakeside   CAMPGROUND **$**
(Minnewanka Loop Dr; tent & RV sites C$27.40;
☺May-Oct; P) Right on Two Jack Lake, 11km
northeast of town, Two Jack Lakeside is the
most scenic of the Banff-area campgrounds,
usually filling its 74 reservable sites months in
advance. You can now also 'glamp' at Two Jack
in one of 10 'oTENTiks' fully serviced A-frame
'tents' with hot showers and electricity, sleeping up to six people for C$120 per night.

Two Jack Main   CAMPGROUND **$**
(Minnewanka Loop Dr; tent & RV sites C$21.50;
☺Jun-Sep) If the adjacent Two Jack Lakeside campground is full, Two Jack's main
campground 11km northeast of town is a
very pleasant fallback. The 380 pitches, all
reservable on the Parks Canada website
(www.reservation.pc.gc.ca), are spread out
spaciously under the trees just up the road
from the lakeside campground, but the lack
of showers is a big drawback.

🛏 Bow Valley

Set midway between Banff Town and Lake
Louise Village, the Bow Valley gives you a
chance to experience the wilderness and is
also handy for an early start on day hikes.

The only negative to staying in the Bow
Valley is the proximity of the CPR train line.
The melancholy blast of a distant train horn
sounds romantic around a campfire at dusk,
but you might not feel quite so charitable
when it wakes you up at 3am.

Camping

Johnston Canyon
Campground   CAMPGROUND **$**
(Bow Valley Pkwy; tent & RV sites C$27.40; ☺May-
Sep) This lovely creekside campground
opposite the Johnston Canyon parking is
tough to top. It strikes just the right balance
between facilities and camper freedom. The
132 sites are spacious and fairly private, and
you won't feel nearly as hemmed in as at
some of Banff's bigger campgrounds. Flush
toilets and showers are available.

Castle Mountain
Campground   CAMPGROUND **$**
(Bow Valley Pkwy; tent & RV sites C$21.50; ☺late
May–mid-Sep) This small campground has
only 43 first-come, first-served sites, handily placed among pine forest near the Castle
Mountain store. It's beautifully secluded,
with sites arranged around one long woodland loop. Downsides? There's only one wash
block and no showers. Nevertheless, the lovely surroundings means it fills up fast.

Protection Mountain
Campground   CAMPGROUND **$**
(Bow Valley Pkwy; tent & RV sites C$21.50; ☺late
Jun-early Sep) This basic campground along
the Bow Valley Pkwy between Castle Mountain and Lake Louise has 72 first-come,
first-served sites, but with no hookups or
showers, and a rather dreary landscape of
wind-downed trees, it's often quieter than
the other Bow Valley campgrounds.

Lodging

Castle Mountain
Wilderness Hostel   HOSTEL **$**
(☎ 403-762-2367; www.hihostels.ca; Castle Junction; dm C$38; ☺reception 5-9pm, hostel open
yr-round, closed Mon Oct-Apr) With solar electricity, showers and flush toilets, this backcountry cabin has more amenities than your
average 'wilderness hostel.' It offers a simple
kitchen, a couple of gender-sorted 14-bed
dorms and a snug common room set around
a wood-burning stove. Don't be surprised if
you spy an elk or two grazing outside – it's
all part of the backwoods vibe.

Castle Mountain Chalets
CABIN $$

(☎ 403-762-3868; www.castlemountain.com; Castle Junction; chalets C$299-459; 🛜) Right next door to the Castle Mountain store, these log chalets are plain inside but offer a surprising number of mod-cons, including DVD players, dishwashers, wood-burning stoves and even iPod clock-radios. At C$459, the top double-room chalets are decent value for families or two couples, but work out to be expensive for one or two travelers.

Johnston Canyon Lodge & Bungalows
CABIN $$$

(☎ 403-762-2971; www.johnstoncanyon.com; Bow Valley Pkwy; cabins C$310-550; ☉ May–mid-Oct) Built in the late 1920s to accompany the nearby teahouse (now a restaurant), the 42 log cabins at this family-owned resort trade heavily on their proximity to Johnston Canyon. Despite their heritage appearance (complete with porch and smoking chimneys), the interior decor wouldn't look out of place in a modern motel.

Baker Creek Chalets
CABIN $$$

(☎ 403-522-3761; www.bakercreek.com; Bow Valley Pkwy; ste from C$515, 1-/2-bedroom cabin from C$695/800) Set in a quiet glade near Baker Creek, this cabin complex has a choice of single-story chalets, deluxe twin-level loft cabins, or suites inside the main lodge. The style is deliberately old country – wood panels, porches, stoves – but the rates are quite pricey for what you get. Still, kids will absolutely love the wooden ladders up to the loft beds in the twin-level cabins.

📍 Lake Louise

Beautiful as it is, staying around Lake Louise will make a hefty dent in your wallet. The premium location means local hotels can charge ludicrously inflated prices – and they do, especially in summer. Unless there's a really good reason to stay here, you're better off basing yourself in Banff or Yoho and visiting on a day trip.

Camping

Lake Louise Tent & RV Campground
CAMPGROUND $

(www.reservation.pc.gc.ca; Lake Louise village; tent/RV sites C$27.40/32.30; ☉ tent park Jun-Sep, RV park year-round) Near the village, this efficient, wooded 395-site campground accommodates RVs on one side of the river and tents and soft-sided vehicles on the other, protected from bears behind an electric fence. Choose a site away from the railway tracks to enjoy views of Mt Temple in relative peace. Book online through the Parks Canada website.

Lodging

HI Lake Louise Alpine Centre
HOSTEL $

(☎ 403-522-2201; www.hihostels.ca; 203 Village Rd, Lake Louise village; dm/d C$64/192; 🅿) This is what a hostel should be – clean, friendly and full of interesting travelers – and the rustic, comfortable lodge-style buildings, with plenty of raw timber and stone, are fine examples of Canadian Rockies architecture. Dorm rooms are fairly standard and the small private rooms are a bit overpriced, but this is as close as you'll get to budget in Lake Louise. Private rooms with lofts are great for families. Don't miss the on-site Bill Peyto's Café (p107).

★ Moraine Lake Lodge
HOTEL $$$

(☎ 403-522-3733; www.morainelakelodge.com; 1 Moraine Lake Rd; r/cabin from C$717/964; ☉ Jun-Sep; 🅿🛜) 🐾 The experience here is intimate, personal and private, and the service is famously good. While billed as rustic (ie no TVs), the rooms and cabins offer mountain-inspired luxury with big picture windows, wood-burning or antique gas fireplaces, soaking tubs, feather comforters and balconies overlooking the lake. The fine-dining restaurant on-site wins equal plaudits. Canoe use is free for guests.

★ Paradise Lodge & Bungalows
CABIN $$$

(☎ 403-522-3595; www.paradiselodge.com; Lake Louise Dr; cabins C$345-488, r in lodge C$415-475; ☉ mid-May–Sep) These cozy, lovingly restored 1930s log cabins along the Lake Louise road are only moments from the lakeshore. Each is unique, but expect comfy beds, kitchens or kitchenettes and claw-foot soaking tubs. Newer lodge rooms are hotel-style. Cheerful flowery grounds and tree-shaded lawns provide ample lounging opportunities. Kids will love the playground and miniature doghouse cabin for Beau the pooch.

Post Hotel
HOTEL $$$

(☎ 403-522-3989; www.posthotel.com; 200 Pipestone Rd, Lake Louise village; r/cabin from C$445/505; 🅿❄🛜) This stately hotel with old-world charm and tranquil shaded gardens began as a ski lodge in the 1940s. Rooms are generally plush, though the less expensive ones overlook the parking lot.

Better yet, spoil yourself with one of the fireplace-equipped riverside cabins for two, or splurge on the larger Pipestone Cabin or Watson House, suitable for an entire family.

Fairmont Chateau Lake Louise   HOTEL $$$

(☑ 403-522-3511; www.fairmont.com/lake-louise; 111 Lake Louise Dr; d from C$699; P@🛜≋) The opulent Fairmont enjoys one of the world's most enviable locations on the shores of Lake Louise. Originally built in the 1890s and added to in 1925 and 2004, the hotel and its plastered exterior did little to fit in with the surroundings. Nevertheless, the giant interloper's facilities, service and fork-dropping views are undeniably amazing.

Rooms are comfortable, if a little generic. Much of the hotel was destroyed by fire in the 1920s, and the oldest existing wing is from 1913; however, if you're after air-con or don't like cramped quarters, opt for one of the newer rooms. Note that Mountain View rooms may include a view over the parking lot. The spa, dining areas, lobby and shops have unforgettably grandiose decor.

★ Deer Lodge   HOTEL $$$

(☑ 403-410-7417; www.crmr.com; 109 Lake Louise Dr; r from C$329; P🛜) Tucked demurely behind Chateau Lake Louise, historic Deer Lodge dates from the 1920s and has managed to keep its genuine alpine feel intact. The rustic exterior and maze of corridors can't have changed much since the days of bobbed hair and F Scott Fitzgerald. Lodge rooms are fairly small but quaint, while spacious Heritage rooms have smart, boutique-like furnishings.

The beautifully restored lounge and log-cabin sitting room, especially with its stone fireplace ablaze, make time travel feel like a real possibility. Tranquility here is ensured – you won't find a TV anywhere.

🛏 Icefields Parkway

Camping

The campgrounds along the Icefields Pkwy are a lot more basic than many in Banff, but they're ideal if you want to escape the campfire smoke and crowds of the busier sites.

Waterfowl Lakes Campground   CAMPGROUND $

(Icefields Pkwy; tent & RV sites C$21.50; ☉late Jun-early Sep) Tucked between two beautiful lakes about 60km north of Lake Louise, this campground just off the Icefields Pkwy has wooded sites and plenty of hiking opportunities. Facilities for the 116 first-come, first-served sites include flush toilets, hot water, BBQ shelters, food storage and interpretive programs, but no showers. Sites 1, 2, 4, 6 and 10 are all near the lakeshore.

There is no cell coverage here, and there is an alcohol ban on long weekends.

Mosquito Creek Campground   CAMPGROUND $

(Icefields Pkwy; tent & RV sites C$17.60; ☉Jun-mid-Oct) Tucked under Mt Hector in a wooded creekside setting, this primitive 32-site campground has no facilities beyond pit toilets and drinking water – but it's a wonderful spot for those seeking seclusion, especially if you can snag a spot on the creek (sites 1 through 4 are especially nice). Despite the name, mosquitoes aren't usually a problem.

Rampart Creek Campground   CAMPGROUND $

(www.reservation.pc.gc.ca; Icefields Pkwy; tent sites C$17.60; ☉Jun–mid-Oct) With 51 sites (35 reservable), Banff's northernmost campground is primitive, but makes a handy stopover along the Icefields Pkwy. Mountain views are grand and it's not uncommon for an elk or bighorn sheep to putter past your tent. Amenities include well water, dry privies, kitchen shelters and a fire-free loop for fresh-air purists. Reserve ahead via the Parks Canada website.

Silverhorn Creek Campground   CAMPGROUND $

(Icefields Pkwy; sites C$15.70; ☉mid-Jun–Sep) Mainly used by RVs, this rather exposed collection of 45 first-come, first-served sites surrounds a parking loop with no shade. The minimal facilities are limited to pit toilets. For drinking water, you'll have to drive 5km north to Waterfowl Lakes campground.

Lodging

HI Rampart Creek Wilderness Hostel   HOSTEL $

(☑ 403-670-7580; www.hihostels.ca; Icefields Pkwy; dm C$38; ☉reception 5-9pm, closed Thu Oct-Apr) These six-bunk cabins tucked above a remote section of the Icefields Pkwy are much loved by climbers and hikers looking to escape into Banff's backcountry. Facilities include solar electricity, a shared lounge, a lively communal kitchen, and the hostel manager's adorable dog, Miss Cutie – but what *really* sets it apart is the toasty wood-burning sauna steps from icy-cold Rampart Creek.

HI Mosquito Creek
Wilderness Hostel
HOSTEL $

(www.hihostels.ca; dm C$38, private cabin for 2/3/4/5 people C$95/115/135/155; ☺ reception 5-10pm, closed Oct & Tue Nov-Apr) Tucked away under the trees beside a rushing creek, this charming 34-bed backcountry hostel was originally built to house German POWs during WWII. There's a rustic wood-fired sauna, a stove-lit lounge and a pocket-sized (propane-powered) kitchen where you can cook up communal grub. Two 12-bed dorms are supplemented by two private rooms sleeping up to five. No showers or electricity.

Num-Ti-Jah Lodge
INN $$$

(☎ 403-522-2167; www.num-ti-jah.com; d with mountain/lake view C$375/425; ☺ mid-May–mid-Oct; P 🛜) On the edge of Bow Lake, the historic Num-Ti-Jah Lodge is full to the brim with backcountry nostalgia. Built by pioneer Jimmy Simpson in 1923 (12 years before the highway), the carved-wood interior displays animal heads and photos from the golden age. The 16 rooms have big views, but show their age with worn furniture, dated decor and tiny bathrooms.

There are plenty of walking trails straight out the door from the lodge; bears frequent the grounds. The on-site restaurant is grand, and there's a pleasant downstairs sitting area with leather armchairs, stained-glass tabletops and a pool table.

🛏 Backcountry

Traveling in the backcountry doesn't necessarily have to mean roughing it. In the early days of Banff's history, the only people who could afford to explore the national park were wealthy adventurers, and they often expected a bit more comfort than a pup tent and an open campfire. Consequently, a number of backcountry lodges were built by the early trail guides to cater for their guests; a couple of the lodges are still in use today.

★ Skoki Lodge
LODGE $$

(☎ 403-522-3555; www.skoki.com; r per person incl 3 meals & afternoon tea C$240-305) Built in 1931 and overlooking a glorious high mountain valley, Skoki was one of the Canadian Rockies' earliest backcountry lodges and remains one of the most magical places to stay in the whole national park. The rustic but delightfully cozy lodge is only accessible on foot, horseback or skis via an 11km climb over two high mountain passes from Lake Louise.

As you'd expect, the decor is rough and ready – log walls, rustic bunks, kerosene lamps, and water jugs for washing – but that's all part of Skoki's special charm. Rates include two glorious home-cooked meals and a sumptuous afternoon tea prepared by the lodge chef, along with a self-packed box lunch to fuel your daytime exploration of the surrounding mountains, meadows and glacial lakes.

Most people hike in during the summer months, but if you really want an adventure – along with significantly reduced room rates – you can snowshoe or ski to the lodge in midwinter. Regardless of when you visit, there's a two-night minimum stay.

Skoki was briefly managed by Peter and Catharine Whyte (who founded Banff's Whyte Museum).

Shadow Lake Lodge
CABIN $$

(☎ 403-762-0116; www.shadowlakelodge.com; cabin per person incl 3 meals & afternoon tea C$360; ☺ Jun-Sep & Jan-Mar) This lodge offers 12 sweet timber cabins with gorgeous mountain views just a stone's throw from Shadow Lake, 13.2km from the Red Earth Creek trailhead. Though it lacks the heritage kick of Skoki, Banff's other backcountry lodge, the cabins are a little roomier and more private, and come with propane heating, solar-powered lighting and access to hot-water showers.

Afternoon tea and three gourmet meals are included in the price, with beer and wine available for purchase separately. The lodge is open June to September; it reopens January to March for cross-country skiers. There's a two-night minimum stay.

🍴 EATING

Banff Town dining is more than just hiker food. Browse along Bear St, Caribou St and Banff Ave, and you'll find everything from sushi to Cajun to vegan fare. Meanwhile, along the Bow Valley Pkwy and in Lake Louise, historic dining rooms serve authentic Swiss fondue, local wild game and British-style high tea. Even with all this variety, there's plenty of pizza, pub grub and AAA Alberta beef to satisfy traditionalists.

✗ Banff Town

Wild Flour
CAFE **$**

(Map p88; ☑ 403-760-5074; www.wildflourbakery
.ca; 211 Bear St; mains C$5-10; ⊙7am-4pm; 🛜 ✍)

🍴 If you're searching for an inexpensive snack or a relatively guilt-free sugary treat, make a beeline for Banff's best bakery, where you'll find cheesecake, dark-chocolate torte and macaroons – along with breakfasts, delicious fresh-baked focaccia, well-stuffed sandwiches on homemade bread, and soups, all of it organic. Not surprisingly, the place gets busy – but outdoor courtyard seating helps alleviate the crush.

Cows
ICE CREAM **$**

(Map p88; ☑ 403-760-3493; www.cows.ca; 134 Banff Ave; ice cream C$4.95-6.95; ⊙10am-9pm) Banff Ave isn't Banff Ave without an omnipresent queue snaking out the door at Cows, a product of Prince Edward Island. Cows' 30-plus ice-cream flavors are topped by the epic Moo Crunch, an extra-creamy blend of chocolate and peanut-butter cups that may well be physically addictive. Other choices may include Fluff n' Udder, PEI Apple and Moo Maple.

IGA
SUPERMARKET **$**

(Map p88; 318 Marten St; ⊙8am-11pm) Banff's largest supermarket has the best selection for campers and self-caterers.

★ Eddie Burger Bar
BURGERS **$$**

(Map p88; ☑ 403-762-2230; www.eddieburger
bar.ca; 6/137 Banff Ave; burgers C$17-23; ⊙11am-2am, from 11:30am Oct-May) Not your average fast-food joint, Eddie's is devoted to building large, custom-made and crave-worthy burgers, from the usual classics to specialties like the elk burger with blueberry chutney. Add to this a hearty helping of poutine and an Oreo milkshake or a shaken Caesar (cocktail, not salad!) garnished with a chicken wing, and you're set – for the next week.

Thankfully its easy to get comfortable in this diner-style sports bar, and (blessedly!) they keep the kitchen open late (till 1:30am) to satisfy cases of the late-night munchies.

★ Bear Street Tavern
PUB FOOD **$$**

(Map p88; ☑ 403-762-2021; www.bearstreet
tavern.ca; 211 Bear St; mains C$15-25; ⊙11:30am-late) This gastropub hits a double whammy: ingeniously flavored pizzas washed down with locally brewed pints. Banffites head here in droves for a plate of pulled-pork nachos or a bison-and-onion pizza, accompanied by pitchers of hoppy ale. The patio overlooking Bison Courtyard is the best place to linger if the weather cooperates.

Block Kitchen & Bar
TAPAS **$$**

(Map p88; ☑ 403-985-2887; www.banffblock.com; 201 Banff Ave; tapas C$9-28; ⊙11am-11pm; ✍) This casual bar serves up tapas with heavy Asian and Mediterranean influences – or 'Mediterrasian,' as it calls it. The small but creative plates might not satisfy truly ravenous post-hiking appetites, but there are plenty of vegan and gluten-free options. The low-lit interior has a cool and quirky edge, while the breezy sidewalk terrace makes a pleasant perch in summertime.

Nourish
VEGETARIAN **$$**

(Map p88; ☑ 403-760-3933; www.nourishbistro
.com; 211 Bear St; mains C$18-26; ⊙11:30am-10:30pm Mon-Thu, 7:30-10:30am & 11:30am-10:30pm Fri-Sun; ✍) Confronted by a strangely beautiful papier-mâché tree when you walk in the door, you instantly know this vegetarian bistro is not average. With locally sourced dishes like wild-mushroom ravioli, Moroccan cauliflower bites or 27-ingredient nachos with Canadian cheddar or vegan queso, Nourish has carved out a gourmet following in Banff. Dinner is served as shareable tapas and larger plates.

Melissa's Missteak
STEAK **$$**

(Map p88; ☑ 403-762-5511; www.melissasmis
steak.com; 218 Lynx St; mains C$9-50; ⊙7am-10pm; 🍴) Melissa's is a casual, family-friendly, ketchup-on-the-table type of place in a 1928 heritage lodge-style building. One of Banff's favorite places for breakfast, it's equally beloved for its wide-ranging lunch and dinner menu. Steaks and deep-dish pizzas are among its most defining dishes, but with everything from chicken burgers to live Atlantic lobster, you'll definitely find something to suit your mood.

Coyote's Southwestern Grill
FUSION **$$**

(Map p88; ☑ 403-762-3963; www.coyotesbanff.
com; 206 Caribou St; mains C$20-30; ⊙7:30am-10pm) A Banff staple, Coyote's has been serving up satisfying southwestern food since the early '90s. Dishes like flat-iron steak and blue-corn chicken enchiladas will fill the hungriest hiker's belly – or make a preemptive strike with buttermilk pancakes or huevos rancheros in the morning. The atmosphere is home-style, just like the food.

Juniper Bistro   BISTRO $$$

(☑ 403-763-6219; www.thejuniper.com/dining; 1 Juniper Way; breakfast & small plates from C$14, mains C$28-34; ☺ 7am-11pm; ☑) Spectacular mountain views combine with an innovative, locally sourced menu at Juniper's, a surprisingly good hotel restaurant on Banff's northern outskirts. Beyond breakfasts and dinners, the midafternoon 'Graze' menu is also enticing – think small plates of orange and cardamom-poached beets or bison carpaccio with juniper berry and pink peppercorn, all accompanied by fab cocktails and 'mocktails'. Vegetarian, vegan and gluten-free options abound.

Park   AMERICAN $$$

(Map p88; ☑ 403-762-5114; www.parkdistillery. com; 219 Banff Ave; mains C$19-52; ☺ 11am-10pm) Banff gets hip with a microdistillery to complement its microbrewery, plying spirits (gin, vodka and whiskey) and beer made from Alberta's foothills' grain. It all goes down perfectly with a mesquite beef hoagie, fish tacos or anything off the excellent appetizer menu. Cocktails are creative, fun and ever-changing.

Saltlik   STEAK $$$

(Map p88; ☑ 403-762-2467; www.saltlik.com; 221 Bear St; mains C$20-58; ☺ 11:30am-late Mon-Fri, from 11am Sat & Sun) With rib eye in citrus-rosemary butter and peppercorn New York strip loin on the menu, Saltlik is clearly no plain-Jane steakhouse knocking out flavorless T-bones. No, this polished dining room abounds with rustic elegance and a list of steaks the length of many establishments' entire menu. In a town not short on steak providers, this could be number one.

Bison Restaurant & Terrace   CANADIAN $$$

(Map p88; ☑ 403-762-5550; www.thebison.ca; 211 Bear St; mains C$24-66; ☺ 5-10pm Mon-Sat, 10am-2pm & 5-10pm Sun; ☑) Rustically elegant, the Bison is full of trendy, well-off Calgarians dressed in expensive hiking gear, who're drawn by its regionally sourced, meat-heavy menu. Alberta-raised bison naturally takes center stage, in the form of tataki, short ribs, striploin and ribeye steak – but you'll also find outliers like wild-caught British Columbia steelhead trout or small plates of elk poutine, roasted cauliflower and the like.

Maple Leaf Grille   CANADIAN $$$

(Map p88; ☑ 403-760-7680; www.banffmaple leaf.com; 137 Banff Ave; mains C$19-66; ☺ 11am-9pm, to 10pm mid-Jun–Sep 1) With plenty of local and foreign plaudits, the classy Maple Leaf eschews all other pretensions in favor of one defining word: 'Canadian.' The menu is anchored by Albertan beef, along with BC salmon, East Coast cod and Okanagan Wine Country salad. Not surprisingly, the interior is all wood and stone, with local artwork.

Tooloulou's   CAJUN $$$

(Map p88; ☑ 403-762-2633; www.tooloulous.ca; 204 Caribou St; breakfast & lunch mains C$11-25, dinner mains C$25-40; ☺ 7:30am-9:30pm) The bayou meets Banff at Tooloulou's, home to New Orleans classics like catfish po' boys

---

HIKING RESTRICTIONS AROUND LAKE LOUISE

The Lake Louise area is one of three key grizzly-bear habitats in Banff National Park, and supports a number of grizzly sows and their cubs. To avoid bear encounters, park authorities often impose group access restrictions in summer on several trails around Lake Louise, including the Consolation Lakes Trail, Larch Valley, Sentinel Pass, Paradise Valley and Wenkchemna Pass.

Under the rules, hikers are required by law to travel in tight groups of at least four people, and take the usual precautions to avoid bear encounters (make noise on the trail, carry bear spray etc). Other routes (including the Moraine Lake Highline Trail) may also be closed according to bear activity – check ahead with park staff. If you're caught breaching the 'group of four' rule, you'll be up for a hefty fine, so stick to the rules: they're there for your own safety.

The timetable varies every year according to bear activity and the berry season, but usually begins around mid-July and lasts until early September. Restrictions are clearly posted in park offices and at trailheads.

If your group is short, the Lake Louise Visitor Centre keeps a logbook where you can leave your details to get in touch with other hikers to make up the required numbers. Alternatively, leave your details at one of the local hostels or just hang around the trailheads at the start of the day – you're bound to find another group who'll welcome you.

and creole jambalaya. Tooloulou's also doubles as one of the best local spots for breakfast (served till 2pm, but lines start forming as early as 7:45am) – with everything from crab cakes to poached eggs with andouille sausage and hollandaise on a sourdough English muffin.

✕ Bow Valley Parkway

Baker Creek Bistro   EUROPEAN $$$
(☑ 403-522-3761; www.bakercreek.com/baker -creek-bistro; Bow Valley Pkwy; mains C$30-55; ☺ 7am-10pm) This attractive cabin restaurant is located inside the Baker Creek Chalets (p102) complex and is among the few places to eat on the Bow Valley Pkwy. Good thing it's decent, with such exotic lures as wild-caught Vancouver Island salmon and Alberta beef tenderloin with a three-peppercorn demi-glace. It also has a cheaper lounge selling burgers and the like, and a breezy patio.

✕ Lake Louise

Trailhead Café   SANDWICHES $
(☑ 403-522-2006; www.facebook.com/lakelouise AB; Samson Mall, Lake Louise village; sandwiches C$6-10; ☺ 7am-6pm) This is *the* place to come for breakfast or a takeout lunch. Wraps and sandwiches are made to order, the staff are well versed in the espresso machine, and the omelets, buttermilk pancakes and lox cream-cheese bagels will fuel you for the trail without breaking the bank. Expect a queue.

Village Market   SUPERMARKET $
(☑ 403-522-3894; www.facebook.com/LakeLouise VillageMarket; Samson Mall, Lake Louise village; ☺ 8:30am-9pm Jun-Sep, reduced hours Oct-May) A small (and expensive) supermarket where you can stock up on necessities.

Bill Peyto's Café   CAFE $$
(☑ 403-522-2201; www.hihostels.ca/en/about/ hostels/bill-peytos-cafe; HI-Lake Louise Alpine Centre, Village Rd, Lake Louise village; mains breakfast C$11-14, lunch & dinner C$14-19; ☺ 7am-10pm May-Sep, 7:30am-9:30pm Oct-Apr) This hostel-administered resto-pub draws a casual, budget-minded crowd for its reasonably priced food and good draft beer. Fill up on homemade granola or bacon and eggs at breakfast; go for burgers, pasta, battered cod and chips, or mac 'n' cheese at dinner. The patio is nice when the sun (or moon) is shining. Expect queues when the hostel's full.

Mt Fairview Dining Room & Caribou Lounge   INTERNATIONAL $$
(☑ 403-522-4202; www.crmr.com/deer/dining; Deer Lodge, 109 Lake Louise Dr; mains C$15-24; ☺ 7am-9:30pm Sun-Thu, to 10pm Fri & Sat) The Deer Lodge hotel's dining room and its adjacent 1930s log lounge, 500m down the road from Lake Louise, make one of the area's more relaxed spots for breakfast, lunch or dinner. Specialties like elk cranberry sausage, bison pastrami sandwiches, and English-style battered haddock taste all the better while surrounded by honey-colored wooden beams and mountain vistas.

★ Lake Louise Station Restaurant   CANADIAN $$$
(☑ 403-522-2600; www.lakelouisestation.com; 200 Sentinel Rd, Lake Louise village; mains lunch C$16-26, dinner C$20-48; ☺ 11:30am-4pm & 5-9pm Jun-Sep, noon-4pm & 5-8:30pm Wed-Sun Oct-May) Lake Louise's historic train station is the most atmospheric place in town to have a meal. Details like stacks of turn-of-the-century luggage, the stationmaster's desk and the original dining cars out back transport you back to 1910, when the elegant edifice was first built. Dig into maple-glazed salmon, Wiener schnitzel or slow-braised bison ribs and soak up the vintage vibe. Reservations recommended.

Fondue Stübli   SWISS $$$
(☑ 403-522-3989; www.posthotel.com/cuisine/ fondue-stubli; Post Hotel, 200 Pipestone Rd, Lake Louise village; cheese fondue for 2 C$85; ☺ 5:30-10pm) With a bona fide Swiss chef (Hans Sauter) in the kitchen, this cute-as-a-button 24-seat wood-paneled *stübli* is the perfect reward after a chilly day on the slopes or an exhilarating high-country hike. Traditional cheese fondue shares the menu with *fondue bourguignonne* (beef tenderloin cooked in hot oil, C$130) and chocolate fondue (C$29). One order serves two to three people.

Chateau Lake Louise Fairview Dining Room   BRITISH $$$
(☑ 403-522-1817; www.fairmont.com/lake-louise/ dining/fairviewdiningroom; Fairmont Chateau Lake Louise, Lake Louise Dr; tea service C$56; ☺ afternoon tea noon-2:30pm) File it under 'part of the experience.' Rarely will you get afternoon tea served up with these kinds of views. The Chateau Lake Louise's expensive British-style spread includes finger sandwiches, India's best orange pekoe and buttermilk scones with Devonshire-style cream and

BANFF NATIONAL PARK EATING

lemon curd. It's all served up in an atmosphere heavy with Downton Abbey–era nostalgia. Book well in advance.

✕ Icefields Parkway

★ Elkhorn Dining Room CANADIAN $$$

(📞 403-522-2167; www.num-ti-jah.com; Icefields Pkwy; breakfast buffet cold/hot C$14/22, dinner mains C$30-50; ⊙ 8-10am & 6:30-9pm mid-May–mid-Oct) Rustic yet elegant, the Num-Ti-Jah's historic Elkhorn Dining Room lets you step back in time to Jimmy Simpson's original hunting lodge, complete with stone fireplace and majestic views. Dine on elk burgers or crispy steelhead trout beneath the watchful eye of moose, wolverines and other hunting trophies. Guests get seating priority; if you're staying elsewhere be sure to reserve ahead.

🍷 DRINKING & ENTERTAINMENT

Throw a stone in Banff Ave and you're more likely to hit a gap-year Australian than a local. For drinking and entertainment, follow the Sydney accents to local Banff Town watering holes or search the listings at Bow Valley Crag & Canyon (www.thecragandcanyon.ca).

★ Grapes WINE BAR

(📞 403-762-6860; www.fairmont.com/banff-springs/dining/grapeswinebar; Fairmont Banff Springs, 405 Spray Ave; 5-9:30pm Sun-Thu, from 3pm Fri & Sat) Sporting original crown molding and dark wood paneling from its early days as a ladies' writing salon, this intimate wine bar in Banff's Fairmont makes an elegant spot for afternoon aperitifs. British Columbian Meritage and Ontario Riesling share the menu with international vintages, while tapas of house-cured meats, cheeses, pickled veggies and candied steelhead will tempt you to linger for dinner.

Banff Ave Brewing Co MICROBREWERY

(Map p88; 📞 403-762-1003; www.banffave-brewingco.ca; 110 Banff Ave; ⊙ 11am-2am) Banff Ave's sprawling 2nd-floor beer hall bustles day and night, slinging a dozen craft brews created on the premises alongside a wide range of nibbles: buttered soft pretzels, bratwurst, burgers and the like. Late-night half-price pizza specials offer welcome relief to late-returning hikers and help keep things hopping into the wee hours.

Whitebark Cafe COFFEE

(Map p87; 📞 403-760-7298; www.whitebarkcafe.com; 401 Banff Ave; ⊙ 6:30am-7pm) Early risers in need of their java fix should head straight to this sleek corner cafe attached to the Aspen Lodge. It's renowned among locals not only for its superb coffee, but also for its muffins, snacks and sandwiches. For an unconventional (and inexpensive) breakfast, check out its bacon-and-egg breakfast cup, a mini-meal encased in delicious flaky pastry.

St James's Gate Olde Irish Pub PUB

(Map p88; 📞 403-762-9355; www.stjamesgate banff.com; 207 Wolf St; ⊙ 11am-2am) Banff is a Celtic name, so it's hardly surprising to find an Irish pub here, and a rather good one at that. Check out the woodwork, crafted and shipped from the old country. Aside from stout on tap and a healthy selection of malts, there's classic pub grub, including an epic steak-and-Guinness pie.

Rose & Crown PUB

(Map p88; 📞 403-762-2121; www.roseandcrown .ca; 202 Banff Ave; ⊙ 11am-2am) Banff's oldest pub (since 1985!) is a fairly standard British-style boozer with pool tables and a rooftop patio. Among all the town's drinking houses, it's best known for its wide-ranging live-music offerings (from 10pm), which raise the rafters seven nights a week. The soul-satisfying fish and chips also rates a mention.

Banff Centre CONCERT VENUE

(Map p87; 📞 403-762-6301; www.banffcentre.ca; 107 Tunnel Mountain Dr) Perched on the side of Tunnel Mountain, Banff's flagship arts venue hosts a varied program of concerts, lectures, exhibitions and events throughout the year. It's also the main focus for big cultural events, including the Banff Summer Arts Festival in July, the triennial Banff International String Quartet Competition in August and the **Banff Mountain Film & Book Festival** (www.banffcentre.ca/banff-mountain -film-book-festival; ⊙ Oct-Nov) in November.

The Children's Festival in May includes lots of free events.

Lux Cinema CINEMA

(Map p88; 📞 403-762-8595; www.luxbanff.com; 229 Bear St; tickets C$11-13) The local movie house mainly screens first-run films, but also hosts special screenings featuring such fare as recent award winners from the Banff Centre Mountain Film Festival.

🛍 SHOPPING

🛍 Banff Town

★ Monod Sports   SPORTS & OUTDOORS
(Map p88; ☑403-762-4571; www.monodsports.
com; 129 Banff Ave; ☺10am-8pm) Banff's oldest
outdoor-equipment supplier is still the best.
It has women's and men's clothing from
big brands such as Patagonia, Arc'teryx,
Icebreaker, Columbia and North Face, supplemented by dedicated sections for ruck-
sacks, equipment and footwear. The staff is
super-knowledgeable.

Banff Trail Riders Store   CLOTHING
(Map p88; ☑403-762-4551; www.horseback.com;
138 Banff Ave; ☺9am-10pm mid-Jun–Aug, to 6pm
rest of yr) Pick up all the cowboy fashion you'll
ever need for looking the part in the saddle
(or at Wild Bill's Bar), from Stetsons, chaps
and plaid shirts to handmade cowboy boots.

Rocky Mountain Soap Company   COSMETICS
(Map p88; ☑403-762-5999; www.rockymountain
soap.com; 204 Banff Ave; ☺9am-10pm) Banff
branch of the Canmore-based beauty company, selling natural soaps, lotions and creams.

🛍 Lake Louise

Wilson Mountain Sports   SPORTS & OUTDOORS
(☑403-522-3636; www.wmsll.com; Samson Mall,
Lake Louise village; bike/ski rental per day from
C$39/25; ☺8am-7pm) This friendly outdoors
shop sells pretty much *everything* a camper or backcountry adventurer could need. It
also rents a full range of bikes – mountain
bikes, hybrids, electric bikes, kids' bikes,
trail-a-bikes and trailers – along with a
plethora of other gear, from hiking poles
and boots to full-fledged mountaineering
equipment, fishing rods, bear spray, snowshoes and skis, all at reasonable rates.

ℹ Information

DANGERS & ANNOYANCES
The national park is generally a safe place to travel, but as always, you should take the necessary
precautions to avoid unexpected wildlife encounters. Carry bear spray, make noise on the trail and
hike in groups wherever possible. Pay attention
to trail closures and group-access restrictions,
especially around Lake Louise in summer.

It's also important to take extra care on the
road, as road and railway collisions are still the
number one cause of death for wildlife in Banff.

If you're hiking and leaving your vehicle at a
trailhead (especially overnight), make sure you
don't leave any valuables on display. If you're
cycling, use a lock.

EMERGENCY
For fire, mountain rescue and other emergencies, call ☑911.
Park Warden Office (☑emergencies 403-762-
4506, office 403-762-1470) For park-related
matters and to report wildlife sightings (especially bears, cougars, wolverines and lynx).

MEDIA
Bow Valley Crag & Canyon (www.thecrag
andcanyon.ca) Local news and entertainment
listings for Banff and the Bow Valley.
Park Radio 101.1 FM (CFPE) Not-for-profit
radio station with regular trail reports, weather
bulletins and other park news.
Rocky Mountain Outlook (www.rmoutlook.
com) Canmore-based paper that covers general
Banff news. Published Thursday.

MEDICAL SERVICES
Mineral Springs Hospital (☑403-762-2222;
www.covenanthealth.ca/hospitals-care-centres
/banff-mineral-springs-hospital; 305 Lynx
St, Banff Town; ☺24hr) Emergency medical
treatment.

MONEY
Bank of Montreal (107 Banff Ave; ☺10am-
5pm Mon-Fri)
CIBC (98 Banff Ave; ☺10am-5pm Mon-Fri)

POST
Banff Post Office (Map p88; 204 Buffalo St,
Banff Town; ☺9am-5pm Mon-Fri, 11am-3:30pm
Sat)

ℹ USEFUL NUMBERS
The following telephone numbers might
come in useful during your stay:

Avalanche Hazards (☑403-762-1470)
Recorded message detailing areas at
high risk of avalanche.

Banff Weather Office (☑403-762-
2088; www.pc.gc.ca/en/pn-np/ab/banff/
visit/meteo-weather) For the latest weather forecast and warnings.

Road Conditions (☑403-762-1450)
Provided by Rocky Mountain National
Parks.

Trail Conditions (☑403-760-1305;
www.pc.gc.ca/apps/tcond) Trail reports,
wildlife warnings and closures.

ℹ️ GETTING TO LAKE LOUISE & MORAINE LAKE

There's no way to sugarcoat this: with Banff's recent explosion of summer visitors, parking at Lake Louise and Moraine Lake has become a challenge. Even reaching the shoreline at either lake can feel like a Herculean task that requires advance planning during the peak season of mid-June to early September.

The key to success is arriving as early as possible. In the case of Moraine Lake, this generally means no later than 5:30am. Otherwise you'll likely find the lot full of fellow early birds flocking to watch sunrise over the lake. As for Lake Louise, the parking lot here is larger than at Moraine Lake and spread over two levels, so you can often still find a spot anytime until 8am or 9am; after that, be prepared to be waved back down the hill by the army of harried but well-intentioned parking attendants up top.

A more dependable alternative is to walk up from the village to the lake on the pretty Louise Creek Trail. This 3.5km route roughly parallels the main road from Lake Louise village, reaching the lakeshore in less than an hour.

A third possibility is to take public transport. Currently there are three options:

➡ Take Roam bus 8X ($6, 55 minutes) or the slower but more scenic 8S ($6, 80 minutes) from the Banff High School transit hub in Banff to Lake Louise. You can also try catching this same bus from the Lake Louise village bus stop just outside Samson Mall, but if the bus is already crowded with Banff-originating passengers, you may not get on.

➡ Take a shuttle bus from the Lake Louise Park & Ride Overflow Parking Area on Hwy 1, about 5km east of Lake Louise village. These converted yellow schoolbuses run every 20 minutes in peak season and cost $4 round-trip to Lake Louise.

➡ Take a free shuttle operated by the Lake Louise Ski Resort. These shuttles run hourly, originating from the parking lot near the base station of the Lake Louise Summer Gondola.

Once you make it to Lake Louise, you'll find a separate Moraine Lake shuttle ($6) leaving hourly from the Lake Louise lower parking lot.

Sound complicated? Alas, it is. Rest assured that Parks Canada is constantly reassessing the situation, so by the time you read this, there may be new solutions in place. Call or email Parks Canada (☑403-522-3833; pc.lakelouiseinfo@canada.ca) for up-to-the-minute info.

TOURIST INFORMATION

Banff Tourism Bureau (☑403-762-8421; www.banfflakelouise.com; 224 Banff Ave; ⏰8am-8pm mid-May–Sep, 9am-5pm rest of year) Opposite the Parks Canada desks in the Banff Visitor Centre, this info desk provides advice on accommodations, activities and attractions.

Parks Canada Banff Visitor Centre (Map p88; ☑403-762-1550; www.pc.gc.ca/banff; 224 Banff Ave; ⏰8am-8pm mid-May–Sep, 9am-5pm rest of year) The Parks Canada office provides park info and maps. This is where you can find current trail conditions and weather forecasts, and register for backcountry hiking.

Lake Louise Backcountry Trails Office (☑403-522-1264; Lake Louise Visitor Centre, Lake Louise village; ⏰8:30am-7pm Jun-Sep, 9am-5pm Oct-May) Parks Canada desk offering specialist advice on exploring the backcountry area around Lake Louise.

Lake Louise Tourism Bureau (☑403-762-8421; www.banfflakelouise.com; Samson Mall, Lake Louise village; ⏰8:30am-7pm Jun-Sep, 9am-5pm Oct-May) Information on activities and accommodations in Lake Louise Village.

Parks Canada Lake Louise Visitor Centre (☑403-522-3833; www.pc.gc.ca/en/pn-np/ab/banff; Samson Mall, Lake Louise village; ⏰8:30am-7pm Jun-Sep, 9am-5pm Oct-May) Visit Parks Canada's newly renovated digs for national park info and to register for backcountry hikes. You'll also find some good geological displays, a local tourist information desk and a small film theater.

ℹ️ Getting There & Away

Most visitors arrive in the park by car, although regular shuttle services travel to Banff Town and Lake Louise from Calgary airport, and there's a daily bus to Jasper.

BUS

The **Banff Airporter** (☑403-762-3330; www.banffairporter.com; Banff to Calgary Airport adult/child C$68/34) airport shuttle bus runs 11 times daily from Calgary airport to Banff Town. Buses provide door-to-door service to/from almost any address in Banff and also stop in Canmore.

Brewster Express (Map p88; ☑403-221-8242; www.banffjaspercollection.com/

brewster-express; 100 Gopher St; adult/child Banff to Calgary Airport C$72/36, to Jasper C$120/60, to Lake Louise C$37/19) runs a similar shuttle service from Calgary airport to Banff 10 times daily, picking up and dropping off passengers at several Banff hotels or at its main office in downtown Banff. One bus daily continues to Lake Louise and Jasper.

Greyhound buses stopped operating in Alberta in 2018, making it hard to travel any further afield than Calgary, Lake Louise or Jasper without your own wheels.

CAR

If you're arriving by air, the easiest option is to rent a car at either Calgary or Edmonton airports. A few of the major car-hire companies also have offices along Banff Ave in Banff Town.

With the exception of heavy summer traffic often clogging the roads to Lake Louise and Moraine Lake, driving in the Banff area is generally a breeze. There is ample free parking in Banff Town, both on the streets and in several lots.

Note that the speed limit on main highways within the national park (the Trans-Canada Hwy and Icefields Pkwy) is 90km/h, as opposed to the 110km/h limit that prevails outside the park.

TRAIN

Banff's historic train station is at the northwest edge of downtown on Railway Ave. The only passenger train that stops there is the luxurious, but expensive, Rocky Mountaineer (www.rocky mountaineer.com), which is essentially a tourist train selling travel packages for trips between Banff, Lake Louise, Kamloops and Vancouver, BC.

❶ Getting Around

Unlike Glacier in the US, Banff National Park has no free hikers' shuttle. However, newly expanded public bus service and a small collection of private shuttles help fill the void.

BICYCLE

Banff is well geared for cyclists, with a nice network of trails and plenty of bike shops and rental companies dotted around Banff Town. Very few trailheads have cycle racks, but some rental companies offer shuttle services to main trails.

BUS

Roam (☑ 403-762-0606; www.roamtransit. com; adult/child local routes C$2/1, regional routes C$6/3) runs Banff's excellent and expanding network of public buses.

Five local routes serve Banff Town and its immediate surroundings:
➡ route 1 to Banff Hot Springs
➡ route 2 to Tunnel Mountain
➡ route 4 to Cave and Basin
➡ route 6 to Lake Minnewanka

➡ route 7 to the Banff Centre

Slightly more expensive regional buses serve the following destinations:
➡ route 3 to Canmore
➡ route 8X to Lake Louise (express route)
➡ route 8S to Lake Louise (slower but more scenic, follows the Bow Valley Pkwy)
➡ route 9 to Johnston Canyon

All routes pass through Roam's main transit hub at **Banff High School** (Map p88; Banff Ave), with many also stopping at the **Elk West Transit Hub** (Map p88; Banff Ave) on the opposite side of Banff Ave. Schedules and route maps are available online (www.roamtransit.com) and at all bus stops. A day pass costs C$5 for local buses or C$15 for regional buses.

Banff's three ski resorts (Sunshine, Mt Norquay and Lake Louise) run free shuttles to their base gondolas in the winter and summer.

White Mountain Adventures serves hikers returning from Mt Assiniboine with its **Mt Assiniboine Shuttle** (☑ 403-760-4403; www.white mountainadventures.com/mt-assiniboine -shuttle; 1-way Mt Shark trailhead-Canmore C$75, to Banff C$90; ⊙ shuttle 4:30pm Jun-Sep). The service runs from Mt Shark trailhead back to Banff Town every afternoon at 4:30pm; reserve ahead.

CAR

Trans-Canada Hwy/Hwy 1 runs straight through the center of the park via Canmore, Banff Town and Lake Louise village. The single-lane Bow Valley Pkwy (Hwy 1A) runs parallel to Hwy 1, and is closed in spring from 6pm to 9am to protect wildlife.

Within the national park, speed limits are usually 90km/h (56mph) for major roads, and 30km/h to 60km/h (19mph to 37mph) on secondary roads, unless otherwise indicated.

Outside Banff Town and Lake Louise, the only gas stations within the national park are at Castle Junction (32km west of Banff) and Saskatchewan River Crossing (80km north of Lake Louise).

Most parking lots at trailheads and in Lake Louise village and Banff Town are free, but pay careful attention to posted time limits (generally two hours maximum for in-town parking).

TAXI

Due to the distances between sights, taxis aren't a very practical way of getting around, although they can make an economical way of getting to trailheads for families and groups of more than three people. A fare between Banff Town and Canmore is approximately C$50.

Banff Taxi (☑ 403-762-0000; www.banff transportation.com/banff-taxi-service.html) Taxi service for Banff and the surrounding area.

Lake Louise Taxi (☑ 403-522-2700; www. lakelouisetaxi.ca)

I VIEWFINDER / SHUTTERSTOCK ©

1. Johnston Canyon Falls (p93)
Admire two thundering waterfalls from a suspended catwalk at Johnston Canyon.

2. Lake Louise Gondola (p94)
This gondola takes you 2088m (6850ft) above the valley floor to offer a bird's-eye view of the Lake Louise area.

3. Plain of Six Glaciers (p60)
This jaw-dropper of a hike from Lake Louise takes you up the rubble-strewn glacial valley.

4. Peyto Lake (p66)
It's not a trip to the Icefields Pkwy without snapping a photo or two of this stunning blue-green glacial lake.

Around Banff National Park

Best Places to Stay

➡ Canmore Clubhouse (p117)

➡ Mt Engadine Lodge (p122)

➡ Paintbox Lodge (p117)

➡ Canmore Downtown Hostel (p117)

➡ Sundance Lodges (p121)

Best Places to Eat

➡ Crazyweed Kitchen (p118)

➡ Mt Engadine Lodge Dining Room (p122)

➡ Gaucho Brazilian Barbecue (p118)

➡ Communitea (p118)

➡ Grizzly Paw (p118)

Why Go?

Although many visitors never venture much beyond Banff, it's well worth taking the time to explore the area outside the park, which is blessed with the same sky-high scenery, but with fewer visitors and quieter trails.

A stone's throw from the park's eastern boundary, the low-key community of Canmore is popular with outdoors enthusiasts of all stripes. The Alpine Club of Canada, Canada's national organization for climbers founded in 1906, has its home here, as does the Canmore Nordic Centre, whose Olympic-caliber trail network is nirvana for mountain bikers and cross-country skiers.

Further east, the rugged mountains and lakes of Kananaskis Country are Calgary's favorite weekend playground. The twin attractions here are the mountains and lakes of Peter Lougheed Provincial Park and the more civilized pleasures of Kananaskis Village, home to a resort hotel, spa, golf course and equestrian center.

When to Go

Banff National Park

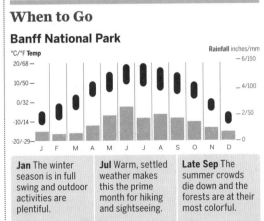

Jan The winter season is in full swing and outdoor activities are plentiful.

Jul Warm, settled weather makes this the prime month for hiking and sightseeing.

Late Sep The summer crowds die down and the forests are at their most colorful.

Canmore

Canmore is Banff for locals, a former coal-mining town that reinvented itself as an outdoorsy hub during the 1988 Winter Olympics, when it hosted the cross-country skiing events. Spend time sitting in a downtown bar or cafe and you'll quickly intuit that most of the population lives here because they love it – and no wonder! The hiking, cycling, skiing and spiky mountain vistas are magnificent, and the rock climbing – Canmore acts as HQ for the Alpine Club of Canada – is world-class. Quieter, cheaper and more relaxed than Banff, Canmore makes a good launching pad for the national park or the more hidden pleasures of Kananaskis Country to the south. Canmore is 24km southeast of Banff Town and 7km from the park's East Gate along Hwy 1.

◎ Sights

Big Head   SCULPTURE

At the end of Main St, half-buried in gravel by the Bow River, sits the impressive sculpture known as the Big Head (for reasons that will quickly become obvious). Created by the artist Al Henderson, the sculpture was inspired by Canmore's name – the original town of Canmore in northwest Scotland was called *ceann mór,* a Gaelic word meaning 'great head' or 'chief.'

Canmore Museum & Geoscience Centre   MUSEUM

(☑403-678-2462; www.canmoremuseum.com; 902b 7th Ave; adult/youth/child C\$12/7/free; ⊙noon-4:30pm Mon-Fri, 11am-4:30pm Sat & Sun Jun-Sep, closed Tue Oct-May) Exhibits at this small museum cover the region's coal-mining past and the community's survival following the mine closure in 1979. Check out the 160-million-year-old petrified cypress stump and the stunning images taken by local photographer Craig Richards.

🏃 Activities

★Canmore Nordic Centre   MOUNTAIN BIKING, SKIING

(☑403-678-2400; www.canmorenordiccentre.ca; Olympic Way; winter day-pass adult/youth/child C\$15/11.25/9, summer trail-use free; ⊙9am-5:30pm) Nestled at the foot of Mt Rundle on the way to the Spray Lakes Reservoir, this huge trail center was originally developed for the Nordic events of the 1988 Winter Olympics. It's now one of western Canada's best mountain-biking and cross-country skiing centers, with over 100km of trails developed by some of the nation's top trail designers.

There are graded routes to suit all abilities, from easy rides on wide dirt roads to technical single tracks and full-on downhills.

In winter, there are over 65km of ski trails – both machine-groomed and natural (ungroomed) – with 6.5km lit for night skiing.

Whatever the time of year, take precautions to avoid wildlife encounters, as you might find that grizzlies, black bears and moose have decided to use the trails, too.

The center is a 4km drive from Canmore, just off Spray Lakes Rd. Cross the Bow River at the west edge of downtown, take Rundle Dr, continue south along Three Sisters Dr and follow signs to the Canmore Nordic Centre.

Elevation Place   HEALTH & FITNESS

(☑403-678-8920; www.elevationplace.ca; 700 Railway Ave; adult/child pool only C\$8/5, full facility C\$16/8; ⊙9am-10pm Mon-Fri, to 9pm Sat & Sun; ☒) Canmore's impressive sports center replicates many of the activities you can do outdoors, so if the weather's not cooperating, this is a fantastic place to escape the elements. The kid-friendly swimming pool is excellent, and the huge indoor climbing wall is an ideal place to get to grips with the basics before you tackle a real crag.

Grassi Lakes Trail   HIKING

The popular 90-minute loop hike (3.8km) to Grassi Lakes is one of Canmore's finest, passing waterfalls and two gem-colored lakes. Soon after leaving the parking lot, you'll reach a fork: to the right is a relatively easy, family-friendly gravel road that winds gradually up to the lakes, while a slightly more challenging wooded path interspersed with staircases climbs to the left.

For the best loop, take the left-hand trail up, which affords the best waterfall views, then descend back to your starting point along the more gradual right-hand path.

Rock climbing is also big here.

Alpine Helicopters   SCENIC FLIGHTS

(☑403-678-4802; www.alpinehelicopters.com; 91 Bow Valley Trail) Hop on a scenic chopper for flights over the peaks of the Three Sisters (C\$150, 12 minutes) or Mt Assiniboine (C\$330, 30 minutes). It also offers heli-hiking, heli-skiing and delivery of supplies to Assiniboine Lodge. Flights are weather-dependent, so it's always best to have a back-up plan in case the clouds roll in. The heliport is south of town on the Bow Valley Trail.

AROUND BANFF NATIONAL PARK CANMORE

Canmore

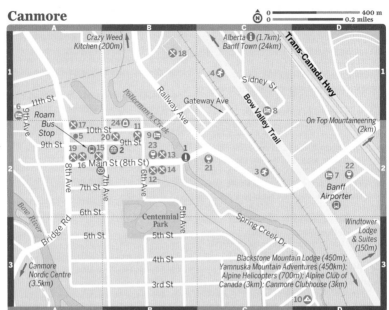

Canmore

Sights

Activities, Courses & Tours

Sleeping

Eating

Drinking & Nightlife

Shopping

Canmore Cave Tours　ADVENTURE
(☑ 403-678-8819;　www.canmorecavetours.com;
129 Bow Meadows Crescent, Unit 202) Buried deep
beneath the Grotto Mountain near Canmore
is a system of deep caves known as the **Rat's
Nest**. Canmore Cave Tours runs guided trips
into the maze of twisting passageways and
claustrophobic caverns. Be prepared to get
very wet and muddy, and brace yourself for
chilly temperatures, as the caves stay at a
constant 5°C (41°F) year-round.

Dogsledding

Following recent controversy over dogsledding and its treatment of animals, it's become doubly important to make sure that
dogsledding companies treat their dogs with
respect and dignity.

Snowy Owl Tours　DOG SLEDDING
(☑ 403-678-4369;　www.snowyowltours.com;　829
10th St; 2hr tour 1-/2-person sled C$425/475, 3- or
4-person sled C$600) Dogsledding has been a

traditional mode of travel in the Canadian Rockies for centuries, and it's a wonderful way to see the wilderness. Snowy Owl offers sled trips ranging from two hours to two days on custom-built sleighs pulled by your own well-cared-for team of Siberian, Canadian and Alaskan huskies. The sledding season is usually from December to April.

Sleeping

Canmore's accommodations generally offer better value than places inside the national park. The **Canmore Bow Valley B&B Association** (www.bbcanmore.com) keeps a list of local B&Bs, and you'll find several motels and hotels along the Bow Valley Trail.

Canmore offers abundant apartment and condo rentals, many advertised online. One good resource is **Rentals in the Rockies** (www.rentalsintherockies.com).

★ Canmore Clubhouse HOSTEL $
(☑ 403-678-3200; www.alpineclubofcanada.ca; Indian Flats Rd; dm C$45, d & tr C$100; P ⓢ) Steeped in climbing history and mountain mystique, the Alpine Club of Canada's beautiful hostel sits on a rise 5km east of town, with stellar views of the Three Sisters through big picture windows. Dorms in the main building have access to a spacious guest kitchen and are supplemented by sweet, well-priced, three-person private rooms in the Boswell Cabin just uphill.

Canmore Downtown Hostel HOSTEL $
(☑ 403-675-1000; www.canmoredowntownhostel.ca; 302 Old Canmore Rd; dm with shared/private bathroom C$50/55, d/tr C$185/216; ⓢ) A welcome addition to Canmore, this bright modern hostel opened in 2019 and has already won a loyal following. It has a spacious 2nd floor common room, teal-walled guest kitchen and clean wood-clad dorms. The microbrewery just across the parking lot doesn't hurt, and it's only a short walk to the shops and restaurants of downtown Canmore.

Three Sisters Campground CAMPGROUND $
(☑ 403-673-2163; www.bowvalleycampgrounds.com; Hwy 1, Dead Man's Flats; tent & RV sites C$26; ⊙ mid-Apr–Oct) For pretty sites and a relatively peaceful atmosphere, head to this campground in the satellite community of Dead Man's Flats, 11km east of Canmore. The tent spaces furthest from the highway are generally the quietest and you're handily positioned near plenty of hiking trails. RVs are welcome but there are no hook-ups.

Bow River Campground CAMPGROUND $
(☑ 403-673-2163; www.bowvalleycampgrounds.com; Hwy 1; tent/RV sites C$28/40; ⊙ May-Oct) The best option for camping close to Canmore is this riverside site 1.6km southeast along Hwy 1. It's sandwiched between the river and the highway, so it's not as peaceful as it could be, but it's pleasant enough if you can bag a spot by the water.

Canadian Artisans B&B $$
(☑ 403-678-4138; www.canadianartisans.ca; 1016 9th Ave; d C$250; P ⓢ) This quirky B&B is tucked away in the forest on the edge of Canmore. Two wooden suites are detached from the main house; they're comfortable, if not plush. The Treehouse Suite has picture windows, stained-glass door panels, a futuristic shower and a lovely vaulted roof. The Foresthouse is somewhat more cramped, with a whirlpool tub next to the queen-sized bed.

Paintbox Lodge B&B $$$
(☑ 403-609-0482; www.paintboxlodge.com; 629 10th St; r C$275-399; P ⓢ) Run by ex-Olympic skiers Thomas Grandi and Sarah Renner, this B&B takes Canadian decor to a new level, right down to the tartan carpet. Its five unique suites offer a mix of country chic and luxury comfort. For maximum space ask for the Loft Suite, which sleeps four and features beamed ceilings, mountain-view balcony and sexy corner tub.

All rooms share use of the mountain kitchen, kitted out with top-of-the-range Miele appliances, including an espresso machine.

Lady Macdonald Country Inn GUESTHOUSE $$$
(☑ 403-678-3665; www.ladymacdonald.com; 1201 Bow Valley Trail; r C$260-335; P ⓢ) This quaint little inn wouldn't look out of place in small-town Connecticut, with its elegant verandas, turrets and wooden siding. Rooms are petite, with wrought-iron beds, cushions and some floral print for good measure. Each is unique so it's worth checking out a few.

The Vermilion Room has a Jacuzzi and views of Ha Ling Peak, the Cascade Room has a gas fireplace, and the Three Sisters Suite has wall-to-wall mountain views. Locally sourced breakfast is included.

Blackstone Mountain Lodge HOTEL $$$
(☑ 888-830-8883; www.blackstonelodge.ca; 170 Kananaskis Way; d/ste from C$255/360; P ✳ ⓢ ≋) The pick of several Clique properties around Canmore, the Blackstone is located east of downtown just off the Bow Valley Trail, in a rather soulless cluster of

similar high-end hotels. Traditional rooms have plush linens, while suites come with their own fully equipped kitchen (complete with oven, dishwasher and washing machine), making them ideal for families.

✖ Eating

Canmore has a surprising number of great places to dine – so many, in fact, that people often drive over from Banff solely for the pleasure of eating here. For self-catering supplies, head for Canmore's large **Safeway supermarket** (1200 Railway Ave; ⊘8am-11pm).

★ Communitea
CAFE $

(✐403-688-2233; www.thecommunitea.com; 1001 6th Ave; mains C$12-15; ⊘8am-7pm Jun-Sep, 9am-5pm Oct-May; ☏) ✐ Ethically aware and all organic, this community cafe exudes a warm, relaxed vibe and colorful modern aesthetic. Food is fresh and local, with noodles, rice bowls, smoked salmon and avocado toast, wraps, salads, and plenty of vegan, veggie and gluten-free options. Sip fresh-pressed juices, well-executed coffee and, of course, every type of tea you can conceive of.

Rocky Mountain Bagel
CAFE $

(✐403-678-9978; www.thebagel.ca; 830 Main St; bagels C$7-12; ⊘6am-6pm; ☏) ✐ Is there anything better in life than sitting by the fireplace or out under the flower baskets at Rocky Mountain Bagel, studying the morning shadows on the Three Sisters peaks while enjoying a toasted maple bagel and a latte? Possibly not. Bagelwiches, pizza bagels, breakfast bagels or a bag of bagels to go. Rocky Mountain Bagels has it covered.

Old School Bus
ICE CREAM $

(621 Main St; 1/2/3 scoops C$4.25/5.75/7.25, kid's scoop C$2.50; ⊘11am-10pm) Permanently parked just off Main St, this converted school bus is *the* place for ice cream in Canmore. The chalkboard hawks a tempting spectrum of flavors, from white chocolate to blackberry to peanut butter, and the milkshakes are heavenly too. Cash only.

Rocky Mountain Flatbread
ITALIAN $$

(✐403-609-5508; www.rockymountainflatbread. ca; 838 10th St; pizza C$14-31; ⊘11:30am-9pm Sun-Thu, to 10pm Fri & Sat; ☏) ✐ In this outdoorsy town where you naturally end up craving pizza, Rocky Mountain Flatbread is a fabulous apparition. The thin-crusted flatbreads start simple, but you can rev things up with additional ingredients like smoked bison, fig and Brie, or lemon chicken and apple.

Grizzly Paw
PUB FOOD $$

(✐403-678-9983; www.thegrizzlypaw.com; 622 Main St; mains C$18-25; ⊘11am-11pm Sun-Thu, to midnight Fri & Sat) ✐ Alberta's best microbrewery (offering seven year-round beers plus seasonal specials) is hiding in the mountains of Canmore. With beer and food pairings, big burgers, hand-crafted sodas and a view-filled patio, it's a popular spot. The purveyors of Beavertail Raspberry Ale and Grumpy Bear Honey Wheat also have a nearby brewery and microdistillery where tours and tasters are available.

PD3 by Blake
CANADIAN $$

(✐403-609-4928; www.blakecanmore.com; 806 8th St; food truck fare C$13-16, tasting menu C$99; ⊘11:30am-late Fri-Tue) When summer rolls around, it's hard to resist PD3's shiny silver double-decker bus parked in a grassy lot and pumping cool tunes. Sit at picnic tables out front and dig into Asian-fusion tacos, burgers, fries, and Saigon slaw with mint-cilantro dressing – all washed down with cold beer and 'boozy slushies' – or enjoy gourmet dining at linen-clad tables inside the bus.

The Wood
STEAK $$$

(✐403-678-3404; www.thewood.ca; 838 8th St; mains C$19-38; ⊘11am-10pm Sun-Thu, to 11pm Fri & Sat) A sunny, spacious front patio and a big indoor fireplace create a relaxed vibe at this log building on a street corner in Canmore's town center. If you need a day off from AAA Alberta steak (not easy here), plump for the excellent salmon burger with sesame-ginger slaw and miso-hoisin aioli. There are over a dozen beers on tap.

★ Crazyweed Kitchen
INTERNATIONAL $$$

(✐403-609-2530; www.crazyweed.ca; 1600 Railway Ave; lunch mains C$16-24, dinner mains C$19-46; ⊘11:30am-10pm Tue-Sun) This flashy bistro on the edge of town feels more big city than small town, with its sharp designer lines, funky artwork and globetrotting menu that takes in everything from wood-fired pizza, Malaysian noodles and Myanmar fish cakes to grass-fed Alberta rib eye. The tropical-themed cocktails lineup is equally inspired, with passion-fruit mojitos, grapefruit margaritas and tamarind whiskey sours.

Gaucho Brazilian Barbecue
BRAZILIAN $$$

(✐403-678-9886; www.brazilianbbq.ca; 629 8th St; all-you-can-eat lunch/dinner C$33/54; ⊘noon-4pm & 5-10pm) Exuding aromas tantalizing enough to lure the local wildlife (a hungry bear nearly wandered through the front door in 2019), this authentic Brazilian barbecue grills scrumptious skewers of chicken, pork, sausages and *picanha* steak. Bring an empty stomach for the all-you-can-eat *rodizio,* or opt for the nightly bar special – four tastes of different meats plus a salad for C$20.

★**Trough**   CANADIAN **$$$**
(📞403-678-2820; www.thetrough.ca; 725 9th St; mains C$34-46; ⊗5:30-9pm Tue-Sun) Canmore's slinkiest bistro is a bit tucked away on 9th St, but worth discovering for a romantic night out. The mother-son team creates amazing dishes like Prince Edward Island (PEI) mussels with house-smoked tomatoes, grilled Alberta lamb chops with rosemary-black pepper marinade, and BC halibut with mango and sweet peppers. With just nine tables, it's wise to book ahead.

🍷 Drinking & Nightlife

★**Tank 310**   MICROBREWERY
(📞403-678-2487; www.thegrizzlypaw.com; 310 Old Canmore Rd; ⊗11am-9pm Thu & Sun, to 9:30pm Fri & Sat) Soaring ceilings and in-your-face views of Mt Rundle and the Three Sisters greet you at this cool gastropub launched by Grizzly Paw Brewing. Views aside, your attention will quickly shift to the beer. A full lineup of Grizzly Paw drafts, from Powder Hound Blonde to Evolution IPA, comes complemented by a solid menu of upscale pub grub.

Where the Buffalo Roam   COCKTAIL BAR
(📞403-675-2222; www.canmoresaloon.ca; 626 Main St; ⊗noon-midnight Mon, 3pm-midnight Tue-Thu, noon-1am Fri & Sat, 10am-midnight Sun) Channeling the aesthetic of a Wild West saloon, this trendy downtown bar specializes in craft cocktails like the Buffalo Sour (bourbon, lemon juice and honey-sage-juniper syrup) and the Misty Mountain Hop (gin, prickly pear vodka, lemon juice, basil and absinthe). Meanwhile, its Wagyu beef burger is hands-down the best bar snack in town.

Rose & Crown   PUB
(📞403-678-5168; www.therosecanmore.com; 749 Railway Ave; ⊗11am-2am) This spit-and-sawdust British pub at the northern end of Main St looks dingy from outside, but things feel a lot more welcoming once you get out onto the riverside patio. Plentiful beers on tap make it a good place to rub shoulders with the locals, and it's also one of Canmore's main venues for live music.

🛍 Shopping

★**Switching Gear**   SPORTS & OUTDOORS
(📞403-678-1992; www.switchinggear.ca; 718 10th St; ⊗11am-6pm) As the name implies, this shop is all about people bringing in their used outdoor gear and selling it consignment-style at bargain prices. This being the Canadian Rockies, there's always an embarrassment of name-brand deals to choose from – jackets, boots, base layers, you name it – supplemented by one of the most impressive displays of brand-new wool socks you'll find anywhere.

ℹ Information

Travel Alberta Canmore Visitor Information Centre (📞403-678-5277; www.travelalberta. com; 2801 Bow Valley Trail; ⊗9am-7pm May-Oct, to 5pm Nov-Apr; 📶) This regional visitor center with a free wi-fi lounge, just off the Trans-Canada Hwy northwest of town, focuses on the Canmore/Banff/Lake Louise area.

Canmore General Hospital (📞403-678-5536; 1100 Hospital Pl; ⊗24hr) Come here for emergency assistance.

Post Office (801 8th St; ⊗9am-5pm Mon-Fri, to noon Sat)

ℹ Getting There & Away

Canmore is easily accessible from Banff Town (20 minutes) and Calgary (1¼ hours) via the Trans-Canada Highway (Hwy 1).

The **Banff Airporter** (📞403-762-3330; www. banffairporter.com; Coast Canmore Hotel, 511 Bow Valley Trail; Canmore to Calgary Airport adult/child C$65/32.50) runs 11 buses daily between the Coast Canmore Hotel and Calgary Airport. Brewster (p110) offers more expensive and less frequent connections to the airport and downtown Calgary (C$72, six to nine daily).

Bus 3, operated by Roam (p278), makes the 25-minute run between Canmore and Banff every 30 to 60 minutes. Buses stop downtown on 9th St near 7th Ave.

Kananaskis Country

The area collectively known as Kananaskis Country (or K-Country to the locals) covers a vast area to the south and east of Banff National Park, comprising several side-by-side provincial parks and protected areas, including Peter Lougheed Provincial Park, Elbow Valley, Sheep Valley, Ghost River Wilderness Area and Don Getty Wildland Provincial Park.

While visitors and tourists make a beeline for Banff's trails, many Albertans prefer to hike in K-Country, where the routes are quieter, the scenery is just as impressive and that all-important sense of wilderness is much easier to come by. It's less well known than Banff, but with a bit of research you'll find some fantastic hikes and trails, as well as plenty of sky-topping peaks, mountain lakes and outdoor pursuits. And with less traffic and no fencing, you are likely to encounter plenty of wildlife here.

🏃 Activities

Horseback riding, white-water rafting and downhill skiing are all popular activities. The best facilities in the area are around Kananaskis Village, which consists primarily of the Pomeroy Kananaskis Mountain Lodge (p122). Numerous walking trails, as well as the paved Bill Milne bike path, lead out from here. The 'village' also has a useful outdoor shop, **Kananaskis Outfitters** (📞403-591-7000; www.kananaskisoutfitters.com; 1 Mt Sparrowhawk Cres, Kananaskis Village; bike/ski rental per day from C$50/30; ⊙9am-7pm Jul & Aug, shorter hours rest of year), which rents bikes.

★ Peter Lougheed Provincial Park   HIKING
(www.albertaparks.ca/peter-lougheed) K-Country's quiet trails and backcountry offer superb hiking, especially around this 304-sq-km park on the west side of Kananaskis Valley, which includes the Upper and Lower Kananaskis lakes and the highest navigable vehicle pass in Canada. It's an excellent area for wildlife spotting: watch for foxes, wolves, bears, lynx and coyotes.

This area is an important wildlife corridor and the valley has been subjected to very little development. Recommended half-day hikes include the 5km loop to the natural bowl of Ptarmigan Cirque (two hours) and the 3km trail to **Boulton Creek** (one hour). Longer day routes include the 7.2km hike to **Mt Indefatigable** (four hours) and the 16km **Upper Kananaskis Lake Circuit** (five hours).

Trail leaflets and information on conditions are available from the park's visitor center near Kananaskis Lakes.

★ King Creek Ridge   HIKING
You have to be something of a masochist to tackle this 6.2km out-and-back trail, but the views up top are beyond belief. Starting from the King Creek picnic area on the east side of Hwy 40, parallel the highway briefly north on a clear but unsignposted footpath to bypass a creek gully, then head northeast straight up into the hills.

Over the next 1.5km you'll gain about 500m as the trail climbs relentlessly up through a mix of forest and steep flowery meadows. After about 90 minutes your efforts are rewarded as you crest King Creek Ridge and wave after wave of knife-edged mountains unfolds to the east, with the entire Kananaskis Valley spread out below you to the north and south. Turn left (north) to continue along the ridgeline as long as you like. You'll reach the ridge's high point (2420m) about 3.1km into the hike. From here, retrace your steps down the mountain.

Ptarmigan Cirque   HIKING
This 5km, two-hour loop hike starts in the high country near Highwood Pass (at 2206m, the highest paved pass in Canada; usually open from June to October) and just keeps getting higher. Park on the west side of Hwy 40 just south of the pass, then walk back north and cross east over the highway, following the signposted trail for Ptarmigan Cirque.

After zigzagging up through forest for about 1km, you'll come to a fork with a 'Do Not Enter' sign on the right side. Bear left and begin your loop into the alpine zone. The trail soon emerges into high meadows with the forbidding mass of Mt Arethusa (2912m) towering overhead. Continue gently climbing to the now-obvious cirque, then loop gently south (right) and cross a creek to begin your descent back to the parking lot. Along the way you'll pass a pretty waterfall as you ford the creek a second time to return to the base of the loop.

Kananaskis Nordic Spa   SPA
(📞403-591-6800; www.knordicspa.com; 1 Centennial Dr, Kananaskis Village; day pass C$85; ⊙9am-9pm Sun-Thu, to 11pm Fri & Sat) K-Country's splashiest new attraction is this full-service spa with oodles of hot and cold pools, saunas, a steam cabin, an on-site bistro and a variety of massage treatments. A single pass grants all-day access to the grounds. It's first-come, first-served and you must be 18 or older to enter; prepare to join the waiting list during busy periods.

Boundary Ranch   HORSEBACK RIDING
(📞403-591-7171; www.boundaryranch.com; Hwy 40; rides from C$60; ⊙May-Sep) This experienced trail-riding ranch offers lots of options for day rides and longer pack trips, some of which also feature white-water rafting. Ride and lunch packages featuring your choice of steak or burgers are also available.

WORTH A TRIP

THE SMITH-DORRIEN/SPRAY TRAIL ROAD

The Smith-Dorrien/Spray Trail Rd (or Hwy 742 to give it its official title) is a dirt-and-gravel highway that runs for around 62km (38.5 miles) from the Kananaskis Lakes to Canmore. Named after a British commander of WWI, Horace Smith-Dorrien, the rough, unpaved road passes through some of the wildest areas of the Peter Lougheed, Spray Valley and Bow Valley Wildland Provincial Parks.

The scenery is stunning, but the road is tough going, especially after heavy rain: be prepared for plenty of ruts and potholes, and go slow unless you want to wreck your rental car's suspension. There are several lakeside picnic areas en route where you can break the journey and drink in the mountain scenery. The northern section of the road into Canmore beyond Goat Creek is extremely steep, so take extra care here.

For much of its length, the road tracks the eastern edge of the Spray Lakes Reservoir, which provides much of Canmore's power through a hydroelectric dam built in 1950. Apart from the dam, the valley is almost entirely unpopulated, so it's a brilliant area for wildlife spotting: Rocky Mountain sheep, mountain goats, elk, moose and even bears can often be seen along the sides of the road, especially early or late in the day (take things slow if you want to have a chance of actually seeing anything). After dark you might even be lucky enough to hear the ghostly howl of a wolf echoing through the mountains, as the Spray Valley is a seasonal hunting ground for one of the Bow Valley's last remaining wild wolf packs.

The road also provides access to some of the K-Country's most remote trails, including the stunning Bryant Creek route (p69) into Mt Assiniboine Provincial Park from the Mt Shark parking lot, the 10km (6.4-mile) Chester Lake Trail, and the arduous 15km (9.3-mile) hike to Burstall Pass (five hours).

Nakiska SKIING
(www.skinakiska.com; Hwy 40; day pass adult/youth C$90/68; ⊙9am-4pm early Nov–mid-Apr) The K-Country's only ski resort was one of the main venues for the 1988 Winter Olympics. It's still a popular place to hit the slopes, though the facilities and runs are much less developed than in nearby Banff. Shuttle buses run throughout winter from Canmore and Banff, making Nakiska a credible (and often quieter) alternative to the Big Three.

🛏 Sleeping & Eating

The best sleeps in this part of the world involve bedding down under the stars at one of K-Country's many campgrounds (see www.kananaskiscountrycampgrounds.com for a full list), parking your backpack at the wilderness hostel near Kananaskis Village, or sinking into comfort at remote Mt Engadine Lodge.

Hotels are thin on the ground beyond the Pomeroy Kananaskis Mountain Lodge (p122). Those not camping often stay in Canmore and visit on day trips.

Dining options are limited. Hit Mt Engadine Lodge for gourmet dining or Kananaskis Village's small cluster of eateries for more mainstream fare.

Self-catering supplies for campers are available from the small stores at Fortress

Junction, Mt Kidd RV Park, Boulton Creek Trading Post and Kananaskis Village.

★ **Sundance Lodges** CAMPGROUND $
(✆403-591-7122; www.sundancelodges.com; Kananaskis Trail/Hwy 40; campsites C$34, small tipis C$70, large tipis or trappers' tents C$94-99; ⊙mid-May–Sep) For that authentic Canadian experience, try the hand-painted tipis and old-timey trappers' tents at this privately run campground. As you'd expect, facilities are basic – sleeping platforms and a kerosene lantern are about all you'll find inside – so you'll need the usual camping gear, but kids are bound to lap up the John Muir vibe.

This is billed as a family place and quiet-time rules (from 10pm to 8am) reflect this.

HI Kananaskis Wilderness Hostel HOSTEL $
(✆403-591-7333; www.hihostels.ca; 1 Ribbon Creek Rd, Kananaskis Village; dm/d C$38/95; ⊙reception 5-9pm, closed late Oct-late Nov & 2 weeks in Apr; [P][✿]) The rustic exterior at this place just north of Kananaskis Village might fool you into thinking you'll be roughing it, but inside you'll find HI's most luxurious wilderness hostel, with indoor plumbing, propane-heated showers, shiny pine floors, plush sofas, a fire-lit lounge and a kingly kitchen. Four private rooms supplement the

14-bed dorms, and the region-savvy manager is very welcoming.

Mt Kidd RV Park
CAMPGROUND $

(☏ 403-591-7700; www.mountkiddrv.com; 1 Mt Kidd Dr; RV sites without/with hookups C$37/54; ☺year-round) Halfway along the Kananaskis Valley and handily placed for the facilities around Kananaskis Village, this place is the best option for trailer and RV campers, with full hookups and over 200 sites, plus comprehensive facilities, including tennis courts, a kids' wading pool, laundry, a basic grocery store and games rooms with ping pong, pool and foosball.

Boulton Creek Campground
CAMPGROUND $

(☏ 403-591-7226; www.albertaparks.ca/peter-lougheed; Kananaskis Lakes Rd; tent sites C$26, RV sites C$40-47; ☺May–mid-Oct) With more than 160 reservable sites, this campground offers privacy, lots of forest cover and good facilities, including a small camp store and an ice-cream shop. Its central location near the park visitor center and the Kananaskis Lakes makes it very popular.

William Watson Lodge
CABIN $

(☏ 403-591-7227; www.williamwatsonlodgesociety.com; Kananaskis Lakes Rd; 1-bedroom cabin C$30, 2- or 3-bedroom cabin C$40, campsites C$16; ☺year-round; P) This subsidized cabin complex is specially designed for visitors with disabilities, with fully accessible one- to three-bedroom cabins and 20km of trails in a quiet wood, as well as organized activities to help guests get out and explore. You'll need your own food and bedding. There are also 13 RV sites with full hookups. Priority is given to Alberta residents.

★ Mt Engadine Lodge
LODGE $$$

(☏ 587-807-0570; www.mountengadine.com; 1 Mt Shark Rd; s/d/q C$199/525/549, glamping tent C$525, d/q cabin C$499/599; P🐾) You can't get much more rural – or more peaceful – than this remote mountain lodge decorated with antler chandeliers and antique skis and snowshoes. Lodge rooms and family suites with balcony and sitting room overlook unspoiled meadows and a natural salt lick frequented by moose. Surrounding the lodge are cozy cabins and glamping tents sleeping two to four.

Lodge rates include four hearty meals, including a build-your-own lunch, afternoon tea and a gourmet dinner whipped up by a five-star chef. Look for the Mt Shark Rd turnoff on the west side of the Smith Dorrien/Spray Trail Rd, about 30km northwest of the Kananaskis Lakes or 40km south of Canmore.

Pomeroy Kananaskis Mountain Lodge
HOTEL $$$

(☏ 403-591-7711; www.lodgeatkananaskis.com; 1 Centennial Dr, Kananaskis Village; r from C$459; P🐾@🐾🐾) Kananaskis 'village' effectively consists of this sprawling lodge and its outbuildings, which include several restaurants and the popular new Kananaskis Nordic Spa (p120). Completely renovated after its purchase by Marriott in 2017, the lodge first garnered international fame in 2008 when it hosted the G8 summit (with Bush, Putin and Blair), an event that helped put K-Country on the map.

Moose Family Kitchen
CAFE $

(☏ 403-591-7979; mains C$5-11; ☺8am-10pm daily) Presided over by its delightful Japanese chef-owner, this no-nonsense cafe in the heart of Kananaskis Village serves an eclectic mix of bagels, sandwiches, panini, milkshakes, ramen, curry and teriyaki bowls. It's not fine dining, but it's all served with a smile, and it's one of the few budget options in K-Country.

★ Mt Engadine Lodge Dining Room
CANADIAN $$

(☏ 587-807-0570; www.mountengadine.com; Smith Dorrien/Spray Trail, Kananaskis; brunch/afternoon tea/dinner C$25/17.50/55; ☺tea 2-5pm, dinner 7pm, brunch 10am-1pm Sun) It's worth detouring off the Smith Dorrien/Spray Trail for a bite at this charming backwoods lodge. Drop-ins are welcome for the daily afternoon tea, which features freshly baked goods, fancy cheeses, local meats and fresh fruit. With 24 hours' notice, day trippers can also enjoy the lodge's renowned multicourse family-style dinners (nightly) or the sumptuous Sunday brunch. As you contemplate the stunning view, a moose may well wander past.

ℹ Information

Kananaskis Information Centre at Barrier Lake
(☏ 403-678-0760; www.albertaparks.ca; Hwy 40; ☺9am-1pm & 1:30-6pm mid-Jun–early Sep, shorter hours rest of year) Located 6.5km south of the junction of Hwys 1 and 40.

Elbow Valley Visitor Centre
(☏ 403-678-0760; www.albertaparks.ca; Hwy 66; ☺9am-12:30pm & 1:30-4:30pm Fri-Sun mid-May–mid-Oct) Just west of Bragg Creek.

Peter Lougheed Discovery & Information Centre
(☏ 403-678-0760; www.albertaparks.ca/peter-lougheed; Kananaskis Lakes Trail; ☺9:30am-4:30pm Mon-Thu, to 5:30pm Fri-Sun Jul & Aug, 9:30am-4:30pm daily rest of year,

closed mid-Mar–early May & mid-Oct–early
Dec) Near the junction of Hwys 40 and 742,
north of Kananaskis Lakes.

❶ Getting There & Away

Brewster Express (p96) runs buses between
the Pomeroy Kananaskis Mountain Lodge in
Kananaskis Village to Calgary's airport (adult/
youth C$72/36). You can also sometimes catch
a shuttle from the lodge to Nakoda Resort on
Hwy 1, where you can meet up with Brewster
buses to Banff or Jasper.

Navigating K-Country is much easier if you
have your own wheels. There are two main roads
through the area, which link up near the Kananaskis Lakes to form a convenient loop. The main
Kananaskis Trail (Hwy 40) travels through the
center of Kananaskis Valley from Barrier Lake,
while the unpaved gravel Spray Lakes Trail (Hwy
742) heads northwest from the junction near Lower Kananaskis Lake all the way back to Canmore.

Be sure to double-check your policy if you're
driving a rental; not all rental insurance will
cover you on Hwy 742. Also be aware that there
is virtually no cell-phone service along the route
and no gas stations.

Yoho National Park

To the west of Lake Louise, the Kicking
Horse River bucks and surges into the wild,
ice-crowned mountains of Yoho National
Park, which is located across the Alberta
border in the neighboring province of British Columbia. Though much smaller than
Banff at around 1313 sq km (506 sq miles),
Yoho (from a Cree word denoting awe or
amazement) is every bit as spectacular as its
neighbor: hulking peaks brood along either
side of the plunging Kicking Horse Valley,
and spur roads twist and turn to the area's
most renowned attractions, including the
crashing cascade of Takakkaw Falls and the
glittering, green-blue pool of Emerald Lake.

Yoho is considered valuable to science for
its Burgess Shale formation, first discovered by Charles Walcott in 1909. Its ancient
rocks contain well-preserved fossils of sea
creatures over 500 million years old.

Away from arterial Hwy 1, which cuts
through the middle of the park, Yoho is still
wild, remote country, and you'll find little
in the way of visitor facilities. The only real
settlement is the old railway service town
of Field, just off Hwy 1, 27km (16.7 miles)
to the west of Lake Louise, a quaint little
town that has retained many of its original
19th-century clapboard buildings.

◉ Sights & Activities

Takakkaw Falls WATERFALL
(Map p90) A thundering torrent of water tum-
bles from its source in the nearby Daly Glacier over a sheer cliff face for 255m (836ft),
making it the second-highest waterfall in
Canada. At the end of the road, a trail leads
for around 800m (0.5 miles) from the Takakkaw parking lot to the base of the falls. The
road is open from late June to early October.

**Kicking Horse Pass
& Spiral Tunnels** VIEWPOINT
(Map p90) The historic Kicking Horse Pass between Banff and Yoho National Parks is one
of the most important passes in the Canadian
Rockies. It was discovered in 1858 by the Palliser Expedition, which was tasked with dis-
covering a possible route across the Rockies
for the Canadian Pacific Railway. Accessible
8km east of Field from the westbound lanes
of Hwy 1, the viewing area is often closed and
the view obscured by vegetation.

Emerald Lake LAKE
(Map p90) For most visitors, this vividly colored lake is Yoho's most unmissable sight.
Ringed by forest and silhouetted by impressive mountains, including the iconic profile
of Mt Burgess to the southeast, it's a truly
beautiful – if incredibly busy – spot. Escape
the mobs in a rental canoe. The lake road
is signed off Hwy 1 just to the southwest of
Field and continues for 10km (6.2 miles) to
the lake shore.

**Burgess Shale
Geoscience Foundation** HIKING
(🎫800-343-3006; www.burgess-shale.bc.ca; 201
Kicking Horse Ave; tours adult/child from
C$94.50/65; ◉9am-4pm Tue-Sat mid-Jun–mid-
Sep) The only way to visit the amazing
515-million-year-old Burgess Shale fossil
beds (Map p90) is on a hike led by the Burgess Shale Geoscience Foundation. Book online and follow instructions for the morning
meeting location. There are two core hikes,
one to Walcott Quarry and another to the
adjacent fossil fields on Mt Stephen.

Both are strenuous full-day trips with
plenty of elevation gain, so you'll need to be
fit and wear proper footwear.

Iceline Trail HIKING
(Map p90) Yoho's infamous Iceline Trail has at-
tained legendary status among hikers. With
truly unbelievable views, it follows an airy
ridgeline for 12.8km (8 miles; elevation gain
710m/2330ft) across barren extraterrestrial

rock that was covered by glacial ice as recently as the turn of the 20th century.

The trail affords a mind-blowing outlook of Takakkaw Falls (p123) and the Yoho Valley peaks, as well as a superb panorama over the glittering **Emerald Glacier**. It's a hard trail and can feel very exposed in bad weather, so save it for a settled day.

The route can be done as a day hike, but many people turn it into an overnight trip by linking up with the Yoho Valley Loop for a 21.1km (13.1-mile) round-trip, overnighting at one of the backcountry campgrounds at Little Yoho, Twin Falls or Laughing Falls.

Yoho Lake & Wapta Highline   HIKING

(Map p90) This strenuous route ranks among the finest (and hardest) day hikes in the Rockies. The route starts at the Whiskey Jack trailhead near Takakkaw Falls, and climbs to Yoho Lake before ascending onto the sky-top flanks of Wapta Mountain.

The route descends through forest and ends on Hwy 1, around 1.3km east of Field. In total it's a route of 18.3km (11.4 miles), with an elevation gain of 1010m (3314ft).

Twin Falls & the Whaleback   HIKING

This moderate 16.4km (10.2-mile) return route from Takakkaw Falls parking lot through pine forest takes in four lovely waterfalls: the **Angel's Staircase**, **Point Lace Falls**, **Laughing Falls** and the double-tiered **Twin Falls**.

It's a round-trip of around seven hours, or you can extend it into an overnight trip by camping at Twin Falls Campground and following the Whaleback ridgeline back down the valley. The Whaleback crosses a seasonal bridge across the upper falls; it's sometimes swamped by snow or snowmelt, so check at the park office before setting out. The Whaleback adds around 5km (3.1 miles) to the Twin Falls hike.

🛏 Sleeping & Eating

The four campgrounds within Yoho all close from mid-October to mid-May. In addition to a couple of lodges in the park, you can find a range of lodgings in Field.

Fireweed Hostel   HOSTEL $

(☑ 250-343-6999; www.fireweedhostel.com; 313 Stephen Ave; dm/r from C$30/80; ➡ 🛜) This four-room hostel in Field is a real find, beautifully finished in rustic pine. Dorms are small but smart; each room has two pine bunk beds and a shared bath off the hallway, and all have full use of a kitchen and sitting room.

Kicking Horse Campground   CAMPGROUND $

(Map p90; www.reservation.pc.gc.ca; Yoho Valley Rd; tent & RV sites C$27.40; ⊙ May 23–Oct 14; 🅿 🛜) This is probably the most popular campground in Yoho. It's in a nice forested location, with plenty of space between the 88 sites, and there are showers. Riverside sites (especially 68 to 74) are the pick of the bunch.

★ Truffle Pigs Lodge   HOTEL $$

(☑ 250-343-6303; www.trufflepigs.com; 100 Centre St; r from C$120; ⊙ Jun-Sep; 🅿 ❄ 🛜) Field's only hotel is a timber building with heritage charm. The 14 rooms are fairly simply decked out, though. Some have small kitchens. The owners run the town's well-known restaurant, **Truffle Pigs bistro** (☑ 250-343-6303; www.trufflepigs.com; 100 Centre St; mains from C$12; ⊙ 8am-9pm; 🛜) 🍴, in the same attractive building.

Canadian Rockies Inn   GUESTHOUSE $$

(☑ 250-343-6046; www.canadianrockiesinn.com; 308 Stephen Ave; r from C$125; 🅿 ➡ 🛜) Spotless rooms and enormous beds are the main attractions. All rooms have microwave, kettle and fridge.

Emerald Lake Lodge   LODGE $$$

(Map p90; ☑ 403-410-7417; www.crmr.com/emerald; Emerald Lake Rd; r from C$250; 🅿 ❄ 🛜) Commanding a picture-perfect five-hectare (13-acre) site accessed by a bridge and situated right beside the tranquil shores of Emerald Lake, this lodge couldn't have a better position. The interiors are beautifully appointed; sit back on the porch and enjoy the view.

Siding Café   CAFE $

(☑ 250-343-6002; www.thesidingcafe.ca; 318 Stephen Ave; snacks from C$5; ⊙ 10am-5pm) In a building dating to 1915, Field's general store has been the hub of the community since the early days of the Canadian Pacific Railway. It has a small cafe on the side that dishes up homemade sandwiches and fresh muffins.

ℹ Information

Yoho National Park Information Centre
(☑ 250-343-6783; www.pc.gc.ca; off Hwy 1; ⊙ 9am-7pm May-Oct) Pick up maps and trail descriptions. Rangers can advise on itineraries and conditions. Alberta Tourism staffs a desk here in summer and Friends of Yoho also maintain a book shop.

ℹ Getting There & Away

You'll need your own vehicle to access most of the features in the park.

Lake O'Hara

Hiking destinations don't get much more exclusive than Lake O'Hara. Hidden away among a glorious amphitheater of mountains in the eastern part of Yoho National Park, the area is home to some of the park's most picturesque wildflower meadows and backcountry trails, but it takes an extra bit of effort to get here.

The only way into the Lake O'Hara area is via the 11km (6.8-mile) access road from the parking lot just off Hwy 1. The road is closed to public vehicles, so you'll either have to hike in on foot or try for a spot on one of the hugely oversubscribed **shuttle buses** (☑reservations 877-737-3783; www.pc.gc.ca; adult/child return C$15/8, reservation fee C$12; ☉mid-Jun–Sep) from Field. The four daily buses have a total of 42 places and are always full, so you'll need to book way in advance; you'll also need to reserve well ahead to be sure of a place at Lake O'Hara's hugely popular 30-pitch **campground** (☑reservations 250-343-6433; www.pc.gc.ca; Yoho National Park; tent sites C$10, reservation fee C$12; ☉mid-Jun–Sep).

Reservations for the shuttle bus and campsites at the campground can be made up to three months in advance for a C$11.70 fee by calling the Lake O'Hara reservation line (☑250-343-6344). Facilities in the area are very limited, although hot snacks and drinks are sold at Le Relais day shelter in season (cash only). You'll also need a valid wilderness pass to visit the Lake O'Hara area; camping fees are included if you already hold an annual wilderness pass.

If you want to stay overnight and can't get a spot at the campground, there are also two **Alpine Club of Canada Huts** (☑reservations 403-678-3200; www.alpineclubofcanada.ca; Lake O'Hara, Yoho National Park; per person per night C$36) in Lake O'Hara: the Abbot and Elizabeth Parker. Reservations are mandatory, and include a seat on one of the inbound buses.

Even better, book into one of the gorgeously old-world cabins at **Lake O'Hara Lodge** (☑250-343-6418; www.lakeohara.com; Yoho National Park; s/d from C$500/665, cabins C$940; ☉Jan-Apr & Jun-Oct; ☻☎) ✐, where you'll be treated to home-cooked meals, afternoon tea and hot tubs, despite the fact that you're kilometers away from the outside world. Prices include bus transportation.

For a really exclusive experience, Lake O'Hara also provides access to the remote and fantastically wild **McArthur Valley**, which is strictly off-limits to people until August 15 to protect grizzly habitat. To visit the valley, you need to be granted one of the limited number of hiking permits that are made available each year. Phone the Yoho National Park Information Centre for more information.

Mt Assiniboine Provincial Park

If it's a real wilderness hit you're craving, Mt Assiniboine Provincial Park is the place. With its ice-encrusted slopes and distinctive skyrocket profile, the pointy pinnacle of Mt Assiniboine is one of the most recognizable landmarks of the Canadian Rockies and at 3618m (11,870ft) is the highest peak in the southern ranges.

Dubbed the Matterhorn of Canada thanks to its distinctive pyramidal shape, the mountain and the surrounding 390-sq-km (150-sq-mile) provincial park can only be reached on foot (or, if you flash the cash, by chartered chopper). But you won't regret the effort it takes to get there: the high-altitude trails around the mountain and nearby Lake Magog are some of the most exquisite in the Canadian Rockies. Civilization has never felt so far away.

Most people make the trip into Assiniboine in three to five days; one in, one out, and between one and three days to explore the trails and mountain country around Lake Magog.

Note that most of Mt Assiniboine Provincial Park is across the British Columbia border, so you'll need a valid British Columbia backcountry permit for every night you intend to stay (C$10). If you're overnighting at a campground across the Alberta border (such as Marvel Lake on Bryant Creek) you'll also need a Banff wilderness pass, plus a reservation at the relevant campground. If in doubt, check with staff at one of the park visitor centers before you set out.

You'll find general information on Assiniboine at www.env.gov.bc.ca/bcparks/explore/parkpgs/mt_assiniboine.

🏃 Activities

Needless to say, it's the trails that draw everyone to Mt Assiniboine. The core area centers on **Lake Magog**, with lots of easy day hikes nearby.

Rock climbing and **mountaineering** are for experienced alpinists only. The routes are challenging and the drops are very, very long, so you need to know what you're doing. The mountain was first climbed in 1901 by a trio of mountaineers including James Outram, Christian Hasler and Christian Bohren, but the first man to conquer it solo was Lawrence Grassi in 1925.

Cross-country skiing is another way to explore the park in winter; telemarkers mostly arrive via Assiniboine Pass and need to be prepared for emergency camping and carry an avalanche beacon.

🛏 Sleeping

There are several backcountry campgrounds in Assiniboine, but most people end up pitching at either Lake Magog or Og Lake. All campsites are allocated on a first-come, first-served basis, and cost C$10 per person. Fires aren't permitted anywhere in the park.

If you're camping in Assiniboine, it's also extremely important to take precautions against bears: grizzlies and black bears often trundle through the area, so make use of the bear-proof bins at Lake Magog, Og Lake and Porcupine.

For a bit more shelter you can book a bunk in one of four Naiset Huts (☑ 403-678-2883; www.assiniboinelodge.com; Mt Assiniboine Provincial Park; per person from C$20), which offer simple wooden beds, mattresses and a woodstove, as well as a cooking shelter with propane lights and a stove. Reservations (C$5 per night) are a good idea in summer and mandatory in winter. There's also a 15-person climbing shelter called the RC Hind Hut nestled near the northern face of Mt Assiniboine. Reservations for all huts are made through Assiniboine Lodge.

Assiniboine Lodge　　　　　LODGE $$$
(☑ 403-678-2883; www.assiniboinelodge.com; Mt Assiniboine Provincial Park; r per person C$350, shared/private cabin per person from C$350; ☉ Feb, Mar & Jun-Oct; 🛜) The only lodge in Assiniboine is also the oldest ski lodge in the Canadian Rockies, surrounded by mountain meadows and gloriously backed by Mt Assiniboine. Rustic rooms sleep one or two people (solo travelers usually must share), plus there are shared (three to five people) or private cabins. Rates include meals and hiking-guide service. Helicopter transport is C$175 each way.

ℹ Getting There & Away

Forget public transportation – your only chance of a lift into Assiniboine is aboard a helicopter from the Mt Shark heliport (C$155) or Canmore (C$175), booked through Assiniboine Lodge.

Kootenay National Park & Radium Hot Springs

Stretching for just 8km (5 miles) on either side of Hwy 93 (sometimes known locally as the Kootenay Hwy or the Banff–Windermere Rd), Kootenay (☑ 250-347-9505; www. pc.gc.ca/kootenay; Hwy 93; adult/child C$9.80/free, tent/RV sites C$21.50/38.20; ☉ camping May-Oct) was founded in 1920 as a by-product of the construction of the first automobile highway across the Canadian Rockies. In exchange for helping out with the financial costs of building the road, the Canadian government claimed the slender sliver of land that now makes up the national park. Hwy 93 is the only road through the park, running for 94km (58.3 miles) from just west of Castle Junction across the Alberta–British Columbia border to Radium Hot Springs.

Due to its unusual geography, Kootenay is one of the most fire-prone areas in the Canadian Rockies; the southern section of the park toward Radium Hot Springs has been dubbed 'lightning alley' thanks to its frequent summer thunderstorms. In 2003, 174.1 sq km (67.2 sq miles) of forest in the northern part of the park were damaged by a huge wildfire sparked by lightning, forcing the closure of several popular areas around Tokumm Creek and Marble Canyon. The scars left by the blaze are still plain to see, and while it looks severe, it's worth remembering that wildfires are an essential part of the forest ecosystem, killing off disease and pests, clearing underbrush and weak trees and stimulating fresh growth.

◎ Sights & Activities

The interpretive Fireweed Trails (500m or 2km) loop through the surrounding forest at the north end of Hwy 93. Panels explain how nature is recovering from a 1968 fire. Some 7km further on, Marble Canyon has a pounding creek flowing through a nascent forest. Another 3km south on the main road you'll find the easy 2km trail through forest to ocher pools known as the Paint Pots. Panels describe both the mining history of this rusty earth and its importance to Aboriginal people.

Learn how the park's appearance has changed over time at the Kootenay Valley Viewpoint, where informative panels vie with the view. Just 3km south, Olive Lake makes a perfect picnic or rest stop. A 500m lakeside interpretive trail describes some of the visitors who've come before you.

DON'T MISS

MARBLE CANYON FOSSIL SITE

One of the most exciting new finds in the Rocky Mountain parks in recent years was the discovery in 2012 of an extensive fossil site near Marble Canyon in Kootenay National Park, an area made more accessible after wild fires cleared the mountain slopes of thick forest in the early 2000s. Located only 45km (28 miles) southeast of Yoho National Park's famous Burgess shale fossils, unearthed by Charles Walcott in 1909, the new site is, arguably, of equal importance; 55 species of soft-bodied marine life from the Cambrian period have so far been identified, 12 of them entirely new to science.

The fossils at Marble Canyon, rather like Yoho's Burgess shale, are estimated to be up to 505 million years old and are remarkably well preserved considering their age. Their unearthing is expected to prove vital in promoting a better understanding of life on earth and its long evolutionary process. The site's discovery was officially announced to the world in February 2014, although its exact location has, so far, been kept secret in order to protect it from prying eyes.

Radium Hot Springs   HOT SPRINGS
(☑ 250-347-9485; www.pc.gc.ca/hotsprings; off Hwy 93; adult/child C$7.30/4.95; ☉ 9am-11pm) The large hot springs pools have just been modernized and can get very busy in summer. The water comes from the ground at 44°C, enters the first pool at 39°C and hits the cooler one at 29°C. It's 3km northeast of the township, inside the park gate, with plenty of parking.

🛏 Sleeping

Kootenay National Park has a few lodges and campgrounds inside its border, and nearby Radium Hot Springs has a huge number of lodgings. Mt Assiniboine Provincial Park is limited to wilderness camping, a few huts and a remote lodge.

The three campgrounds have a communal capacity of 383 sites (far, far less than neighboring Banff). Redstreak is the only one that accepts reservations.

Redstreak Campground   CAMPGROUND $
(☑ 877-737-378; www.reservation.pc.gc.ca; Stanley St E, Kootenay National Park; tent/RV sites from C$27.40/38.20; ☉ May 2–Oct 15; ℗) Kootenay's largest campground has 242 sites and tops the list for its facilities. It's a big, busy site, partially wooded, but crisscrossed by many access roads; it's probably not the best place if you're looking for peace and quiet, but it's only a 30-minute walk from both Radium *and* the hot springs.

McLeod Meadows Campground   CAMPGROUND $
(www.reservation.pc.gc.ca; off Hwy 93, Kootenay National Park; tent & RV sites C$21.50; ☉ Jun 13–Sep 16; ℗) An 88-pitch campground located on the banks of the Kootenay River just a 2.6km walk to the shores of pretty Dog Lake. Flush toilets but no showers. Plentiful trees and spacious, grassy sites.

Marble Canyon Campground   CAMPGROUND $
(www.reservation.pc.gc.ca; off Hwy 93, Kootenay National Park; tent & RV sites C$21.50; ☉ Jun 20–Sep 9; ℗) This high-country 61-pitch campground is situated near the Marble Canyon trail, and has flush toilets but no showers. Most sites have tree cover to shelter from the wind. The eastern side has the best views.

★ Kootenay Park Lodge   CABIN $$
(☑ 403-762-9196; www.kootenayparklodge.com; Hwy 93, Vermilion Crossing, Kootenay National Park; d cabins from C$125; ☉ mid-May–late Sep; ℗◑🛜) The pick of the few places to stay inside the park, this lodge has a range of cute log cabins complete with veranda, fridge and hot plates. Think rustic charm. There is a restaurant open June 1 through mid-September, a general store selling coffee and snacks, and for those who can't do without it, spotty wi-fi.

Inn on Canyon   GUESTHOUSE $$
(☑ 250-347-9392; www.villagecountryinn.bc.ca; 7557 Canyon Ave; r from C$109; ℗◑🛜) A cute gabled house just off the main drag. Its rooms are sparkling clean and decked out in country fashion.

Storm Mountain Lodge   LODGE $$$
(Map p90; ☑ 403-762-4155; www.stormmountain lodge.com; Hwy 93; cabins C$369-495; ℗) Just inside the border of Banff National Park and set amid the forest, these luxury cabins were built in 1922 and have been gorgeously restored right down to the copper piping in the bathroom. They're cozy and romantic,

WORTH A TRIP

KICKING HORSE MOUNTAIN RESORT

Some 60% of the 120 ski runs at **Kicking Horse Mountain Resort** (☑ 250-439-5425; www.kickinghorseresort.com; Kicking Horse Trail; 1-day lift ticket adult/child winter $94/38, summer $42/21) are rated advanced or expert. With a 1260m (4133ft) vertical drop and a snowy position between the Rockies and the Purcells, the resort's popularity grows each year. It's renowned for its summer mountain biking, which includes the longest cycling descent in Canada.

The resort is 14km west of Golden, which can be seen year-round from the Golden Eye Gondola.

with a big wooden bed, a fireplace and a claw-foot bathtub. Meals in the equally enchanting lodge are gourmet.

✖ Eating

Big Horn Cafe　　　　　　　CAFE $
(☑ 403-861-2978; www.bighorncafe.net; 7527 Main St; snacks from C$3; ☺ 6am-4:30pm; ☎) An ideal road-trip breaker where you can refuel with coffee and a cinnamon bun or something more savory.

Horsethief Creek Pub & Eatery　PUB FOOD $$
(☑ 250-347-6400; www.horsethiefpub.ca; 7538 Main St E; mains from C$14; ☺ 11:30am-11pm Sun-Thu, to 1am Thu-Sat) Pub food, craft beer, weekly events and occasional live music at this saloon-style pub on the main drag. Standard fare, but good fun too.

Helna's Stube Restaurant　　AUSTRIAN $$$
(☑ 250-347-0047; www.helnas.com; 7547 Main St W; mains from C$24; ☺ 5-10pm Wed-Sun) For something a tad different in the Canadian west, try Helna's, specializing in Austrian casual gourmet dining. Enjoy the *stube*-style with authentic Austrian homemade dishes such as Jäger Spätzle (C$23), pasta served with ham, bacon, onions and mushrooms in a creamy cheese sauce.

❶ Information

The main **Kootenay National Park visitor center** (☑ 250-347-9331; www.radiumhotsprings.com; 7556 Main St E; ☺ visitor center 9am-5pm year-round, Parks Canada May-Oct,

later in summer; ☎) is in Radium Hot Springs. It has excellent resources for hikers.

❶ Getting There & Away

Kootenay National Park is traversed by Hwy 93. **Mt Assiniboine Provincial Park** (www.env.gov. bc.ca/bcparks) is pure wilderness.

Golden

Golden is well situated for national-park explorations – there are six nearby. Whitewater rafting excitement lies even closer, where the Kicking Horse River converges with the Columbia.

Don't just breeze past the strip of franchised yuck on Hwy 1: you'll miss the tidy town center down by the tumbling Kicking Horse river.

◉ Sights & Activities

Kicking Horse Pedestrian Bridge　　BRIDGE
(near 9th Ave) Originally established as a logging town and supply station for the Canadian Pacific Railway, back when the town was simply known as 'the Cache', Golden is split in two by the Kicking Horse River. Just north of the main shopping thoroughfare of 9th Ave is the town's much-loved landmark, the Kicking Horse Pedestrian Bridge, which locals proudly trumpet as the longest freestanding timber bridge anywhere in Canada.

Northern Lights Wolf Centre　　PARK
(☑ 250-344-6798; www.northernlightswildlife.com; 1745 Short Rd; adult/child C$12/6; ☺ 9am-7pm Jul & Aug, 10am-6pm May, Jun & Sep, noon-5pm Oct-Apr; ℗) This small wildlife center houses a small pack of gray wolves and wolf-husky crosses, all born and bred in captivity. Visits include an introduction to the resident wolves – although most of the viewing is done through wire-frame pens.

The center is about a 14km (8.7-mile) drive north of Golden. Head north on Hwy 1, turn right onto Moberly Branch Rd for 2km (1.2 miles), then left onto Upper Donald Rd and follow the signs.

White-Water Sports

Golden is the center for **white-water rafting** trips on the turbulent and chilly Kicking Horse River. Along with the powerful grade III and IV rapids, the breathtaking scenery along the sheer walls of the Kicking Horse Valley makes this rafting experience one of North America's best.

★**Alpine Rafting**   RAFTING
(☑250-344-6521; www.alpinerafting.com; 1509 Lafontaine Rd; raft trips from C$89; ☺Jun-Sep; ⛟) Offers several good family rafting options, including a white-water run for kids aged four years and over, right up to the more extreme class IV+ 'Kicking Horse Challenge.'

Winter Activities

In addition to the many ski runs at Kicking Horse Mountain Resort, the slopes around Golden provide perfect territory for many other winter sports, including the snowmobile and skidoo tours offered by **Snowpeak Rentals** (☑250-344-8385; www.snowpeakrentals.com; 1416 Golden View Rd; tours from C$299).

🛏 Sleeping

★**Dreamcatcher Hostel**   HOSTEL **$**
(☑250-439-1090; www.dreamcatcherhostel.com; 528 9th Ave N; dm/r from C$32/90; ⓟ☺🛜) Run by two veteran travelers, this centrally located hostel has everything a budget traveler could hope for. There are three dorm rooms, five private rooms, as well as a vast kitchen and a comfy common room with a stone fireplace. Outside there's a garden and a barbecue.

Golden Eco-Adventure Ranch CAMPGROUND **$**
(☑250-344-6825; www.goldenadventurepark.com; 872 MacBeath Rd; tent & RV sites C$35, yurts C$52; ☺early Apr–late Sep; ⓟ🛜) Spread over 160 hectares (395 acres) of mountain meadow, 5km south of Golden on Hwy 95, this great campground and outdoors center feels a world away from the cramped confines of municipal camping. Sites are spacious; there are full RV hookups.

Kicking Horse Canyon B&B GUESTHOUSE **$$**
(☑250-899-0840; www.kickinghorsecanyonbb.com; 644 Lapp Rd; d from C$120; ⓟ☺🛜) Hidden away among the hills to the east of Golden, this endearingly offbeat B&B takes you into the bosom of the family the minute you cross the threshold. Run by genial host Jeannie Cook and her husband, Jerry, it's a real alpine home-away-from-home, surrounded by private grassy grounds with views across the mountains.

🍴 Eating & Drinking

★**Bacchus Books & Cafe**   CAFE **$**
(☑250-344-5600; www.bacchusbooks.ca; 409 9th Ave N; mains from C$8; ☺9am-5:30pm) This bohemian hideaway at the end of 8th St is a favorite haunt for Golden's artsy crowd. Browse for books (new and secondhand) in the downstairs bookstore, then head upstairs to find a table for tea among the higgledy-piggledy shelves. Sandwiches, salads and cakes are made on the premises, and the coffee is as good as you'll find in Golden.

Eleven22   FUSION **$$**
(☑250-344-2443; www.eleven22restaurant.com; 1122 10th Ave S; mains from C$12; ☺5-10pm) A cross between a restaurant and a home dinner party, this appealing option has art on the walls of the small dining rooms and all the stars you can count out on the patio. Watch the kitchen action from the lounge area while sharing small plates. Ingredients are sourced locally.

★**Island Restaurant**   INTERNATIONAL **$$**
(☑250-344-2400; www.islandrestaurant.ca; 101 10th Ave; dinner mains from C$14; ☺9am-9pm) On a small river island in the middle of Kicking Horse River in the center of Golden, this place features a flower-embellished riverside patio and international dishes and drinks. The food wears many hats, from a Jamaican-jerk chicken sandwich to Thai Thursdays and full-on Mexican nights on Mondays and Tuesdays.

★**Whitetooth Brewing Company**   MICROBREWERY
(☑250-344-2838; www.whitetoothbrewing.com; 623 8th Ave N; ☺2-10pm) Golden's microbrewery features tank-to-tap brews and a marvelous sunny patio for those long summer evenings. Whitetooth is a hit with locals who come to fill their growlers and relax on the patio. We like the Icefields Belgian-inspired pale ale.

ⓘ Information

Golden Visitor Information Centre (☑250-439-7290; www.tourismgolden.com; 1000 Hwy 1; ☺9am-7pm Jun-Sep) In a purpose-built building on Hwy 1 & 95 into town from the southeast.

ⓘ Getting There & Away

Riders Express (www.riderexpress.ca) runs buses connecting Vancouver, Kamloops and Calgary, with a bus stopping in Revelstoke and Golden in each direction daily.

Jasper National Park

Best Hikes

➜ Skyline Trail (p143)

➜ Tonquin Valley (p145)

➜ Path of the Glacier Trail (p134)

➜ Bald Hills Loop (p142)

Best Places to Stay

➜ HI Jasper (p164)

➜ Patricia Lake Bungalows (p164)

➜ Mt Edith Cavell Wilderness Hostel (p162)

➜ Alpine Village (p165)

➜ Fairmont Jasper Park Lodge (p165)

Why Go?

In a modern world of clamorous cities and ubiquitous social media, Jasper seems like the perfect antidote. Who needs a shrink when you've got Maligne Lake? What use is Facebook when you're a two-day hike from the nearest road? And how can you possibly describe the Athabasca Glacier in a 140-character tweet?

Filled with the kind of immense scenery that could turn the most monosyllabic hermit into a romantic poet, Jasper is a rugged beauty; it's more raw and less tourist-pampering than its southern cousin Banff, and hence host to a more ambitious, adventurous visitor. Its tour de force is its extensive multipurpose trail network, much of it instantly accessible from the park's compact townsite. Backing it up is abundant wildlife, colossal icefields and – for the brave – the kind of desolate backcountry that makes you feel as though you're a good few kilometers (and centuries) from anything resembling civilization.

Road Distance (KM)

	Columbia Icefield Centre	Jasper	Maligne Lake	Mt Robson (Visitor Centre)
Jasper	105			
Maligne Lake	150	50		
Mt Robson (Visitor Centre)	185	85	135	
Pocahontas	150	45	85	130

Note: Distances are approximate

Entrances

There are three main road entrances to Jasper National Park. The East Park Entrance is on Hwy 16 between Jasper and Hinton, just east of Pocahontas. The West Park Entrance is on the same highway, 24km (15 miles) west of Jasper Town, near Yellowhead Pass and the border with British Columbia and Mt Robson Provincial Park. The Icefields Parkway Entrance is 6km south of Jasper Town on Hwy 93, on the way to Lake Louise. You must either buy or show a park pass at all entry gates.

DON'T MISS

Unlike Banff, most of Jasper's trails are multiuse, open to hikers, horseback riders and cyclists. Thanks to this liberal sharing policy, the park is able to offer the best network of off-road cycling trails in Canada – and they're not just for daredevils. Rated green (easy), blue (moderate) or black (difficult), they cater to pretty much everyone, including kids or parents with trailers in tow.

An added bonus is that many of Jasper's trails start directly from the townsite, meaning you don't need to lug your bike around by car or bus. Using a special cycling trail map (free from the info office), numerous loops can be plotted from your hotel or campground, with time to incorporate hiking, swimming, canoeing or grabbing a cup of coffee along the way.

When You Arrive

➡ All visitors intending to stop off in Jasper National Park must purchase a parks pass (adult/senior/family day pass C$9.80/8.30/19.60), even if you're there just for a picnic or short leg stretch.

➡ Passes can be procured at the Jasper Information Centre or at one of the park's three road entrances.

➡ If you're spending a week, an annual pass (C$67.70) works out cheaper and can be used in all national parks across Canada, including Banff, Kootenay and Yoho.

➡ The park is open year-round, though many activities and services are closed during winter.

PLANNING TIP

Overnight stays in the backcountry require a wilderness pass (per person per night C$9.80); pick it up from the park office within 24 hours of heading out.

Fast Facts

Area 11,228 sq km (4335 sq miles)

Highest elevation 3747m (12,293ft)

Lowest elevation 985m (3232ft)

Reservations

Three of Jasper's 10 campgrounds currently accept advance reservations: Wapiti, Wabasso and Pocahontas. Jasper's largest campground, Whistlers, is currently closed for renovation but will resume accepting reservations when it reopens in 2021. Reservations are also recommended for backcountry camping, as Parks Canada limits the number of hikers on each trail. Both frontcountry and backcountry sites can be reserved via the Parks Canada website (www.reservation.pc.gc.ca) starting in late January each year.

Resources

Jasper National Park www.pc.gc.ca/eng/pn-np/ab/jasper/index.aspx

Tourism Jasper www.jasper.travel

JASPER NATIONAL PARK

Jasper National Park

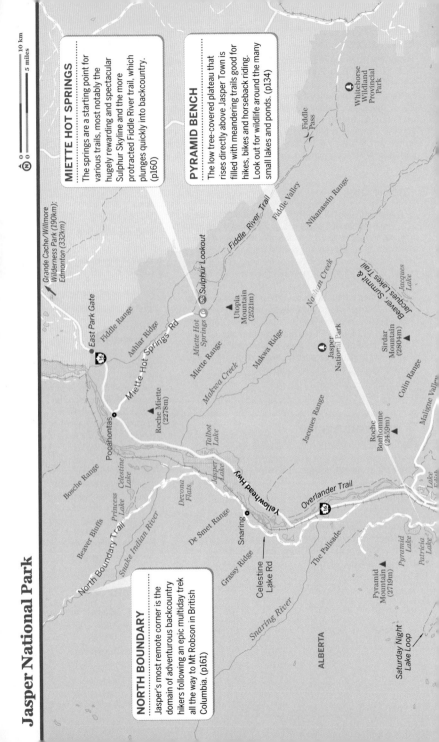

MIETTE HOT SPRINGS

The springs are a starting point for various trails, most notably the hugely rewarding and spectacular Sulphur Skyline and the more protracted Fiddle River trail, which plunges quickly into backcountry. (p160)

PYRAMID BENCH

The low tree-covered plateau that rises directly above Jasper Town is filled with meandering trails good for hikes, bikes and horseback riding. Look out for wildlife around the many small lakes and ponds. (p134)

NORTH BOUNDARY

Jasper's most remote corner is the domain of adventurous backcountry hikers following an epic multiday trek all the way to Mt Robson in British Columbia. (p161)

ATHABASCA RIVER VALLEY

Enjoy flat easy trails, accessible on foot from Jasper Town, beside glacial lakes, rocky knolls and the swirling currents of the Athabasca River. (p149)

MALIGNE LAKE

Short loops on the lake's north shore, steep hikes to viewpoints in the surrounding hills and the start point for the backcountry Skyline trail. (p140)

ICEFIELDS PARKWAY

Long and short hikes lead off Jasper's arterial road, some little more than strolls to waterfalls and lakes, others piercing the remote, glacier-covered backcountry. (p134)

TONQUIN VALLEY

Roadless wilderness, with campgrounds and a backcountry lodge, that is revered by summer hikers and horseback riders, as well as winter cross-country skiers. (p145)

MT EDITH CAVELL

Although the peak itself is best left to mountaineers, you can enjoy its foothills with a walk to a hanging glacier, or a stroll through Jasper's finest alpine meadows. The area is also used as an access point to the wild Tonquin Valley. (p157)

West Park Gate (5km)

Yellowhead Hwy

Jasper

Riley Lakes

Continental Divide

Whistlers Summit (2466m)

Indian Ridge

Trident Range

Tonquin Valley

Amethyst Lake

BRITISH COLUMBIA

Mt Robson Provincial Park

ALBERTA

Astoria River

Cavell Rd

Cavell Lake

Sorrow Peak (3020m)

Mt Edith Cavell (3363m)

Cavell Meadows

Road closed in winter

Moab Lake Rd

Whirlpool River

Geraldine Lakes

Geraldine Fire Rd

Hamber Provincial Park

Icefields Pkwy

Peveril Peak (2679m)

Tekarra Mountain (2693m)

Skyline Trail

Five Lakes Trail

Excelsior Mountain (2791m)

Centre Mountain (2700m)

Curator Mountain (2624m)

The Watchtower (2791m)

Skyline Trail

Medicine Lake

Maligne Lake Rd

Beaver Lake

Lakes

Queen Elizabeth Range

Opal Hills

Little Shovel Pass (2240m)

Evelyn Pass

Maligne Range

Maligne River

Moose Lake

Bald Hills Trail

Maligne Pass Trail

Samson Narrows

Maligne Lake

Mt Unwin (3268m)

Maligne Mountain (3200m)

Helmet Mountain (2890m)

Mt Hardisty (2700m)

Mt Kerkeslin (2909m)

Athabasca River

Athabasca Falls

Brussels Peak (3161m)

Stanwigha Falls

Athabasca River

Icefields Pkwy

Columbia Icefield (74km)

🏃 DAY HIKES

Even when judged against other Canadian national parks, Jasper's trail network is mighty and, with comparatively fewer people than its sister park, Banff, to the south, you'll have a better chance of seeing more wildlife and fewer people.

The park claims to have 1200km (745 miles) of hiking trails, many of which are shared with horseback riders and off-road cyclists. It is rightly famous for the abundance of trails leaving directly from its urban hub, Jasper Town, meaning shuttles or time-consuming drives to trailheads are not always necessary. Many of these trails crisscross the tree-covered plateau situated immediately behind the townsite known as the Pyramid Bench. Others track the Athabasca River Valley and its numerous small lakes.

Icefields Parkway

🏃 Wilcox Ridge

Duration Three hours round-trip

Distance 9km (5.6 miles)

Difficulty Moderate

Elevation Change 400m (1300ft)

Start/Finish Wilcox Trailhead Parking Lot

Nearest Town Jasper

Transportation Private

Summary Straightforward and rewarding hike into the high country near Sunwapta Pass for fine views of Athabasca Glacier.

One of Jasper's most accessible high country walks is this 9km (5.6 miles) out-and-back jaunt on the eastern side of the Icefields Pkwy between Athabasca Glacier and Sunwapta Pass. Turn off the Icefields Pkwy 2km east of the Columbia Icefield Centre; follow signs towards Wilcox Campground but stop in the first parking lot. From the signposted trailhead, the path climbs briefly through forest before emerging above tree line, reaching a pair of red chairs after 30 minutes where you can sit and enjoy Athabasca Glacier views.

If you've already had enough climbing, you can simply return from here to the parking lot. But it's worth pushing on to see the lovely alpine scenery just ahead. As you ascend into open meadows, views open on your left down into a river canyon. Here you're following the route taken in 1896 by Walter Wilcox

and his horseback party, who were headed north from Lake Louise in search of the Athabasca River. Finding their intended route blocked by the Athabasca Glacier, which at the time stretched further across the valley, they detoured into this alpine realm.

At the 3.2km (2-mile) mark you'll reach Wilcox Pass (2370m), marked with a simple green sign. The tempting-looking – but unmaintained – trail directly ahead of you forges onward through a high wildflower-strewn plateau, eventually descending 9km (5.5 miles) to meet Tangle Falls on the Icefields Parkway. Instead you turn left here, following signs for Wilcox Ridge 1.3km (0.8 mile) further along an undulating trail. Up top at the inevitable viewpoint, dramatic near-aerial views of the Athabasca Glacier unfold across the valley. To return to the parking lot simply retrace your steps downhill.

🏃 Path of the Glacier & Cavell Meadows Trails

Duration Three hours round-trip

Distance 9.1km (5.6 miles)

Difficulty Moderate–difficult

Elevation Change 400m (1300ft)

Start/Finish Cavell Meadows parking lot

Nearest Facilities Icefields Parkway

Transportation Private

Summary Angelic glaciers and heavenly scenery give this recently restored mountain trail a distinctly ethereal quality.

With its wings spread celestially between Mt Edith Cavell and Sorrow Peak, Angel Glacier hovers over a small sapphire lake that is afloat with icebergs. The lake's ice-blue sheen is made all the more dramatic for the barren, stony surroundings that were created by the glacier's not-so-long-ago flight across the valley.

The Path of the Glacier Loop is the most popular hike in the area, but, for greater solitude and a brilliant wildflower display (in July), head further up the peak to Cavell Meadows.

To reach the trailhead from Jasper, follow Hwy 93A south to Cavell Rd and then drive 12km (7.4 miles) to a parking lot. Interpretive signs along the route tell the story of both Edith Cavell and the glacier.

Begin by climbing along a newly paved path through an area that was covered by the glacier until the 1950s; small trees and plants are only just beginning to reappear here. You'll pass the Cavell Meadows Trail turnoff on your left after 0.5km (0.3 miles). The Path of the Glacier Trail continues ascending another 0.3km (0.2 miles) to a fantastic viewpoint of **Angel Glacier**, reflected in tiny **Cavell Pond**. Although the trail descends to the water, approaching the famous ice caves here is extremely hazardous. Keep your distance from the caves and beware of falling ice.

From the viewpoint, it's possible to simply retrace your steps to the parking lot. However, a loop around **Cavell Meadows** will treat you to fantastic views and an even better workout. Backtrack to the turnoff for the Cavell Meadows Trail and begin a steep ascent north. The trail soon levels off with clear views of the glacier to the right. This area is strewn with boulders up to 4m (13ft) high, left behind by the glacier. After crossing a stream, switchbacks take you north into the forest; keep right at the junction – 1.5km (0.9 miles) from the start of the Cavell

Meadows Trail – crossing two more streams before entering an open, flowery meadow. About 0.8km (0.5 miles) further on, a side trail branches right to the **Lower Viewpoint**.

Returning to the main trail, a brief climb brings you to another junction. If you've had enough, head left to meet up with the Path of the Glacier Trail; if you've still got some energy and a penchant for climbs, turn right for the Upper Viewpoint.

The way is steep, and the rock-strewn trail becomes fainter and slippery. Continuing uphill to the right brings you to a high subalpine **meadow** with an explosion of flowers. The path runs along a bank of loose shale with a steep drop on the left; then it turns right, where it becomes incredibly steep and rather treacherous.

You'll know you've reached the **Upper Viewpoint** by the yellow marker; the views are also something of a giveaway. Southwest is Mt Edith Cavell; Pyramid Mountain lies to the north and Roche Bonhomme to the

JASPER NATIONAL PARK DAY HIKES

Icefields Parkway – Day Hikes

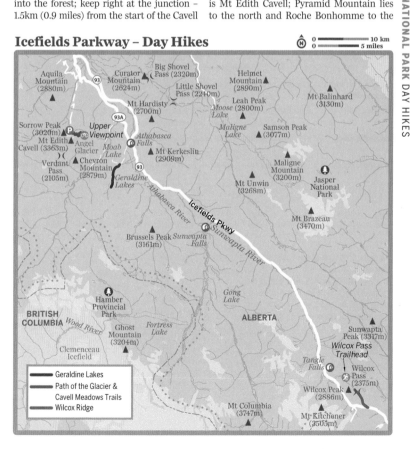

HIKING IN JASPER NATIONAL PARK

NAME	REGION	DESCRIPTION
Wilcox Ridge	Icefields Parkway	Straightforward and rewarding hike into the high country for fine views of Athabasca Glacier
Path of the Glacier & Cavell Meadows Trails	Icefields Parkway	See Angel Glacier resting atop a lake and the finest alpine meadows in Jasper
Geraldine Lakes	Icefields Parkway	A rocky scramble through a staircase-like valley replete with lakes and waterfalls
Tonquin Valley	Icefields Parkway	Wildlife, lush meadows and sparkling lakes, all in the shadow of the Ramparts
Maligne Canyon	Jasper Town & Around	Family-friendly hike through a beautiful river gorge with waterfalls
Mina & Riley Lakes Loop	Jasper Town & Around	Burrow into the woods near town to a couple of placid lakes
Old Fort Point Loop	Jasper Town & Around	A short, steep climb to a stellar view over Jasper Town and surroundings
Whistlers Summit	Jasper Town & Around	A long walk up a steep hill through three different life zones
Mary Schäffer Loop	Maligne Lake Area	Holds the famous Lake Maligne view first seen by Mary Schäffer in the 1900s
Moose Lake Loop	Maligne Lake Area	Offers a peaceful, verdant forest and the chance to spot a moose
Beaver, Summit & Jacques Lakes	Maligne Lake Area	One of the park's simplest 'long' hikes with wide paths and peek-a-boo mountain views
Skyline Trail	Maligne Lake Area	The Rockies' premier backcountry trail, offering infinite views across the mountains
Bald Hills Loop	Maligne Lake Area	A steep grunt up to flower-filled meadows above Maligne Lake
Sulphur Skyline	North of Jasper Town	A short, sharp hike up to a lofty ridge with spectacular views

Wildlife Watching	View	Great for Families	Rest-rooms	Drinking Water	Picnic Sites

northeast. Angel Glacier is suspended to the west; from this height you have an impressive view of its wings and upper half.

Heading back, the descent along the loose shale is tricky. At the junction, turn right to return to the Path of the Glacier Trail.

Geraldine Lakes

Duration Three to four hours round-trip

Distance 10km (6.3 miles)

Difficulty Moderate–difficult

Elevation Change 407m (1335ft)

Start/Finish End of Geraldine Fire Rd

Nearest Town Jasper

Transportation Private

Summary A rocky scramble through a staircase-like valley replete with lakes and waterfalls.

Geraldine Lakes is a hike of two different halves. The first part to Lake No 1 is easy; beyond that you'd better have strong ankles, a head for heights and a penchant for scrambling over bare, sometimes slippery, rock.

The hike starts at a parking lot at the end of Geraldine Fire Rd, an unpaved track that branches off Hwy 93A. Take the obvious trail through the trees and ascend moderately to Geraldine Creek at 1.5km (0.9 miles). In

DIFFICULTY	DURATION	DISTANCE	ELEVATION CHANGE	FEATURES	FACILITIES	PAGE
moderate	3hr	9km (5.6 miles)	400m (1300ft)	🔭	🚻	p134
moderate-difficult	3hr	9.1km (5.6 miles)	400m (1300ft)	🔭	🚻 🪑	p134
moderate-difficult	3-4hr	10km (6.3 miles)	407m (1335ft)	🐟	▲	p136
difficult	2-3 days	53.2km (33 miles)	710m (2329ft)	🦌	▲	p145
easy	1½-2hr	4km (2.5 miles)	100m (328ft)	👪	🚻 🥤 🪑 🍴	p138
easy-moderate	3hr	9km (5.6 miles)	160m (525ft)	🦌 👪	🏪 🍴	p139
easy-moderate	1-2hr	4km (2.5 miles)	130m (427ft)	👪	🪑 🍴	p139
difficult	6½hr	15.8km (9.8 miles)	1280m (4125ft)	🔭	🚻 🥤 🍴	p140
easy	45min	3.2km (2 miles)	negligible	🔭 👪	🚻 🥤 🚌 🍴	p140
easy	45min	2.6km (1.6 miles)	negligible	🦌 👪	🚻 🥤 🚌 🍴	p141
easy-moderate	6-7hr	24km (15 miles)	90m (300ft)	👪 🐟	🚌 🚹 ▲ 🪑	p142
moderate-difficult	2 days	45.8km (28.5 miles)	1400m (4526ft)	🦌 🔭	🚌 🚹 ▲	p143
difficult	4-6hr	10.4km (6.5 miles)	500m (1640ft)	🦌 🔭	🚻 🥤 🚌 🪑 🍴	p142
moderate-difficult	3hr	8km (5 miles)	700m (2297ft)	🔭	🚻 🥤 🪑 🍴	p143

🚌 Transport to Trailhead 🚹 Ranger Station ▲ Backcountry Campsite 🏪 Grocery Store Nearby 🍴 Restaurant Nearby

another 300m (0.2 miles) you'll spy the **first Geraldine Lake** through the trees.

The going gets tougher as you skirt the north shore of the lake on a rougher trail and come up against your first obstacle, a large waterfall at the lake's far end. The trail (no longer obvious) climbs steeply up to the right of the waterfall for 100m (109yd), requiring scrambling skills and a firm footing. The path reappears briefly at the top and then disappears again in another rock field. Watch carefully for small cairns and a yellow marker here that will direct you across the small valley (over the now underground creek), and into some trees on the other side where the trail materializes once again. Coming out of the trees, you'll approach a photogenic second waterfall and another rocky climb and scramble up to **Lake No 2**, which lies a good 400m (0.25-mile) rockhop from the summit. By now you'll have ascertained the unique staircase design of the valley. There are actually two more Geraldine Lakes above Lake No 2, but the trail to reach them is practically nonexistent. Most hikers are satisfied with turning round at the second lake, though a 1.2km (0.7-mile) trail that tracks its southern shore leads to a backcountry campground at the far end.

Jasper Town & Around

🏃 Maligne Canyon

Duration 1½–two hours round-trip

Distance 4km (2.5 miles)

Difficulty Easy

Elevation Change 100m (328ft)

Start/Finish Fifth Bridge parking lot

Nearest Town Jasper

Transportation Car/shuttle bus

Summary This family-friendly hike traces the banks of the Maligne River through a beautiful river gorge, passing a series of waterfalls and historic bridges along the way.

One of Jasper's most rewarding hikes is this amble through a steep, narrow gorge shaped by the torrential waters of the Maligne River. The landscape feels surprisingly wild given its proximity to Jasper Town, yet the easy out-and-back trail involves minimal exertion, making it suitable for all ages and fitness levels.

For a gradual approach to the canyon's most dramatic section, park at the Fifth Bridge parking area just off of Maligne Lake Rd, 8km (5 miles) northeast of Jasper. Begin by crossing **Fifth Bridge**, the newest of six bridges spanning the canyon over its 3.6km (2.2-mile) length, and turn right (upstream) following signs for Canyon Trail (Trail No 7).

The **Maligne River** at this point is already rushing along at a pretty brisk clip, but it's just the beginning. As you follow the gently undulating path upstream through the forest 1.3km to **Fourth Bridge**, the river narrows and the banks steepen. Beyond Fourth Bridge, a series of steps leads uphill into a proper gorge with moss-covered rocky outcroppings. Metal railings provide security for those wanting to take a peek over the edge.

Look carefully and you'll see evidence of small cave openings in the walls of the

Jasper Town & Around – Day Hikes

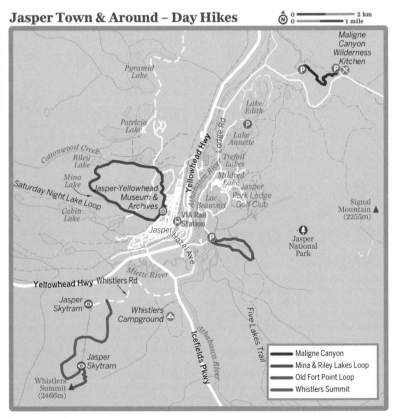

gorge. These are outlets from a system of subterranean limestone channels that carry water beneath the earth's surface all the way from Medicine Lake, 16km (10 miles) upstream, and deposit it here in the canyon.

The bridges get more densely packed as you continue upstream past a series of waterfalls. In wintertime, these freeze solid into sheets of white ice and are popular with ice climbers. **Third and Second Bridges** cross directly above dramatic cascades. Soon thereafter you'll cross **First Bridge**, built in 1914 during Jasper's early tourist heyday. On the far side you can pause for a sandwich or a drink on the riverside deck of Maligne Canyon Wilderness Kitchen (p169) before retracing your steps downstream.

🏃 Mina & Riley Lakes Loop

Duration Three hours round-trip

Distance 9km (5.6 miles)

Difficulty Easy–moderate

Elevation Change 160m (525ft)

Start/Finish Jasper-Yellowhead Museum parking lot

Nearest Town Jasper

Transportation Bus/train

Summary A straightforward tramp to a trio of peaceful lakes that will give you a tantalizing taste of the scope of Jasper's surrounding wilderness.

A whole network of trails (Map p158) heads west from Jasper Town into the forest-covered foothills of the Athabasca Valley. Venture less than 1km (0.6 miles) into this lake-speckled mini-wilderness and you'll quickly leave the hustle and bustle of the townsite behind.

Considered a good first-day orientation hike, the Mina & Riley Lakes Loop leaves from the northwest corner of the Jasper-Yellowhead Museum parking lot. Following trail No 8, climb gently up behind the town before turning rather abruptly into the forest. Keep to the right at the next three junctions, heading west through a mixture of pine, fir and spruce trees until the path widens out into a man-made meadow and firebreak.

After crossing the gravel Cabin Creek Rd, the route plunges quickly back into a thick forest sprinkled with stands of closely packed birch trees. Within minutes, on your left-hand side you'll see swampy **Lower** **Mina Lake**, a large pond guarded by ptarmigan and Barrow's goldeneye ducks. Just beyond is the larger **Upper Mina Lake**, where you'll often spot loons gliding across the green surface.

At the western edge of the lake, turn right and climb up and down some gentle hills through another firebreak to a second junction. Footsore first-timers can shortcut back to town here via trail No 8c. Old stalwarts, meanwhile, can descend the long hill down to **Riley Lake**, which glimmers ethereally with Pyramid Mountain framed behind it. The trail briefly skirts the moss-green edge of the lake before tracking back into the forest. Take a right at the next junction and ascend to **Cottonwood Slough**, which has open views over to the Roche Bonhomme. Continue east to the road, from where trail No 2 returns south to the museum parking lot.

🏃 Old Fort Point Loop

Duration One to two hours round-trip

Distance 4km (2.5 miles)

Difficulty Easy–moderate

Elevation Change 130m (427ft)

Start/Finish Old Fort Point parking lot

Nearest Town Jasper

Transportation Car/walk

Summary For a small effort get big views atop this glacial *roche moutonnée* near Jasper Town, the site of a long-abandoned trading post.

One of Jasper Town's most accessible and instantly rewarding trails is this short, steep climb up to a nearby *roche moutonnée* – a bedrock knob shaped by glaciers – known as Old Fort Point. Unfortunately, you won't find an old fort here. Instead, the name refers to the likely site of a one-time fur-trading post known as Henry House, which was built near here in 1811 by William Henry, a colleague of Canadian-British explorer David Thompson.

The official start point for the Old Fort Point trail (marked trail #1) is at a small parking lot next to a bridge over the Athabasca River. You can reach the parking lot on foot from Jasper Town by following the Wapiti Trail to where it crosses Hwy 16, and then branching left onto the Red Squirrel Trail. The total distance from town to trailhead is 1.6km (1 mile).

From the parking lot, a wooden stairway ascends a tall riverside crag. At the top, next to a monument honoring the natural wonder of the Athabasca River, a short steep slope leads upwards to the hike's summit. You'll need to scramble up another small crag to reach the true summit, but the views of Jasper Town, the Athabasca River Valley and the surrounding peaks are stupendous. On a clear day, count on seeing Mt Edith Cavell, the Whistlers, Pyramid Mountain and the mountains of the Continental Divide bordering British Columbia.

Beyond the summit, the trail dips down with easy gradient into aspen forest. You'll soon come to a four-way junction where the trail becomes open to cyclists, who use it to access the Valley of the Five Lakes (the right-hand fork). Trail No 1a, an easier alternative to trail No 1 used mainly by horses and bikes, goes straight ahead here (take this if you don't like steep slopes). Trail No 1 goes left and descends a steepish gully down to a flat forest path. After 500m (0.3) trail No 1a rejoins on the right. Follow the main trail through a small open meadow and dip back into trees. You'll pass a junction with trail No 7a on the right and then start a short descent back towards the parking lot.

🏃 Whistlers Summit

Duration 6½ hours round-trip

Distance 15.8km (9.8 miles)

Difficulty Difficult

Elevation Change 1280m (4125ft)

Start Trailhead on Whistlers Rd

Finish Summit of Whistlers Mountain

Nearest Town Jasper

Transportation Jasper Skytram Shuttle

Summary A long walk up a steep hill – with a wicked 360-degree view at the top.

If you're a peak bagger, this arduous climb through three different life zones to the top of Jasper's most visited summit – and a handy energy-refueling café – could be the lung-bursting wake-up call you've been waiting for. While most sane people get the Skytram, there are always one or two masochistic maniacs punishing themselves on this 7.9km (4.9 miles) uphill slog.

To get to the trailhead, proceed 2.8km (1.7 miles) west off Hwy 93 along Whistlers Rd to a short, unpaved spur road on the left, which dead-ends in a small parking lot. The hike begins in what is known as the montane life zone of the mountain, consisting of

thick forest and healthy aspen growth but, within 2km (1.2 miles), your uphill endeavors will be rewarded with a rich display of colorful wildflowers. Progressing up toward the tree line, the crippling switchbacks ease momentarily as you pass underneath the midpoint tower of the Jasper Skytram at approximately 1640m (5380ft) of elevation.

Above the tree line the landscape becomes ever more stony and barren, with eagle-eye views of the Athabasca Valley and Jasper Town unfolding like a satellite map beneath you. For the final 1.5km (0.9 miles), from the Skytram's upper terminal to the top, you should have plenty of company, as annoyingly fresh Skytram riders join in for the relatively undemanding dash for the 2466m (8088ft) summit. The stupendous views of lake-speckled valleys and row after row of endless snow-coated peaks are spellbinding. On a very clear day you can see Mt Robson – at 3954m, the highest point in the Canadian Rockies – far off to the northwest.

If you'd prefer a shorter return trip, it's possible to take the Skytram back down the hill – but you'll have to walk another 1.6km downhill from the Skytram's lower station to reach your original starting point.

Maligne Lake Area

🏃 Mary Schäffer Loop

Duration 45 minutes round-trip

Distance 3.2km (2 miles)

Difficulty Easy

Elevation Change Negligible

Start/Finish Maligne Lake parking lot

Nearest Facilities Maligne Lake area

Transportation Maligne Lake Shuttle

Summary View the lake through the eyes of one of Jasper's earliest 'tourists' on this easy waterside ramble.

Following the eastern shoreline of Maligne Lake before dipping into the surrounding forest, this trail gives you a chance to take in the view seen by the first European explorer to cross this body of water. When Mary Schäffer stepped off her raft in 1908, she wrote, 'There burst upon us...the finest view any of us had ever beheld in the Rockies.'

To reach the Mary Schäffer lookout, follow a paved, wheelchair-accessible path past Curly's historic boathouse for about

800m (0.5 miles) to where a quartet of informative signs tell the story of the lake's early 20th-century 'discovery'. Beyond the lookout, the trail continues inland through a spruce, pine and fir forest, with copious roots underfoot barring any further access to wheelchairs and strollers. After passing through a meadow, stay left at two junctions.

Along this path you'll see **kettles**, which are giant depressions left by glacial ice trapped beneath sand and silt. At the third junction, head right to return to the boathouse.

🚶 Moose Lake Loop

Duration 45 minutes

Distance 2.6km (1.6 miles) round-trip

Difficulty Easy

Elevation Change Negligible

Start/Finish Maligne Lake parking lot

Nearest Facilities Maligne Lake area

Transportation Maligne Lake Shuttle

Summary Escape from the crowds on this short but untrampled path, which leads to a tranquil lake renowned for its moose sightings.

Offering a quick escape from the Maligne Lake hordes, this short, easy loop delivers you to a gorgeously placid lake framed by craning trees and embellished by the glacier-chiseled summit of Samson Peak. A moose sighting along the trail is another distinct possibility.

The trail starts in the parking lot at the end of the Maligne Lake Rd and follows the Bald Hills fire road for the first few hundred meters (approximately 300ft). Turn left at the first signpost and you'll quickly enter dense forest, with the lake and its attendant boat cruisers a distant memory.

This new path is the Maligne Pass Trail, but a left at the second junction will divert you in the direction of **Moose Lake** and, if

JASPER NATIONAL PARK DAY HIKES

Maligne Lake Area – Day Hikes

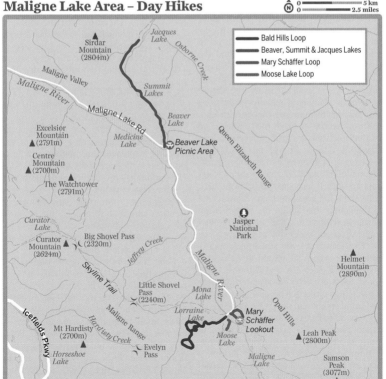

you're extremely lucky, a glimpse of one of those giants of the forest swimming, foraging or hanging out near the shoreline. Moose or no moose, the scenery here is lovely.

With your curiosity satisfied, head north through the woods to the western shore of Maligne Lake and back to the trailhead parking lot.

Beaver, Summit & Jacques Lakes

Duration Six to seven hours

Distance 24km (15 miles) round-trip

Difficulty Easy–moderate

Elevation Change 90m (300ft)

Start/Finish Beaver Lake Picnic Area

Nearest Facilities Maligne Lake area

Transportation Maligne Lake Shuttle

Summary This is one of the simplest 'long' hikes in the park, thanks to its wide paths and minimal elevation gain, but the peek-a-boo views of nearby mountains are immense.

Three lakes and three turnaround options; this popular trail is flat but scenic with decent views of the Colin and Queen Elizabeth mountain ranges opening out around the lakes. The hike is also notable for its accessibility year-round; in winter it becomes a cross-country ski trail and in autumn, thanks to its lower altitude, it remains doable long after other paths have been snowed under.

From the start point at the southern end of Medicine Lake, the trail progresses along a wide dirt track (an old fire road), past some horse stables, to **Beaver Lake** at the 1.6km (1-mile) mark, a small body of water popular with fishermen and bird-watchers. Hike along the lake's west shore with views of the craggy limestone cliffs of the Queen Elizabeth Range to your right. The foot traffic drops off noticeably as you approach the **First Summit Lake** at 4.8km (3 miles). Follow the eastern shore and in 1.2km (0.8 miles) you'll reach **Second Summit Lake**, where the trail can be muddy after rain, due to heavy horse traffic. The valley swings due east at this point and the path enters denser forest on its journey to **Jacques Lake**, 5.2km (3.3 miles) away. This lake is the turnaround point for most day hikers, although there is a campground at its eastern end. Fishing is not permitted. Beyond here, the path continues along the epic Southern Boundary Trail, another 164km (102 miles) of eerie isolation.

Bald Hills Loop

Duration Four to six hours

Distance 10.4km (6.5 miles) round-trip

Difficulty Difficult

Elevation Change 500m (1640ft)

Start/Finish Maligne Lake parking lot

Nearest Facilities Maligne Lake area

Transportation Maligne Lake Shuttle

Summary Get above the tree line on the north shore of Maligne Lake with this steep climb to a bald 360-degree viewpoint.

The road from Jasper dead-ends on the north shore of Maligne Lake, which is home to a chalet, restaurant, boat dock and parking lot. A handful of hikes converge here, all of them well signposted. The Bald Hills trail starts near the parking lot at the northwest corner of the lake on a wide fire road that leads steadily uphill – get used to it; 'uphill' is the central theme of the hike. The more altitude you gain, the more the trees diminish in both density and stature. After 2.5km (1.5 miles), the trail splits. The easier fire road continues following a gradual and circuitous ascent, while a rougher, much steeper trail takes a more direct path. Opting for the steeper route will save you 1.5km (0.9 miles) in distance, but cost a lot more sweat. The paths converge again on the upper cusp of the tree line at the top of the old fire road, close to the site of a demolished fire lookout tower.

Here, the trail flattens out momentarily, traversing the mountain at the top of the tree line, before reaching another path junction. This is the start of the spectacular Bald Hills summit loop. Branch right here and a steep, clearly visible path takes you up a treeless slope to the rocky **summit**, where views unfold in all directions; the perspectives east over **Maligne Lake** and north towards the Skyline Trail and Queen Elizabeth Range are especially dramatic.

Some hikers rest here before descending the way they came but, for the sake of some more fantastic views, it's worth carrying on. Weather permitting, the full loop is clearly visible from the summit. First you track down to an astounding viewpoint over the uninhabited **Evelyn Creek Valley**. From here the path briefly climbs a rocky ridge, before descending and looping through alpine meadows back to the trail junction just below the summit. From here you can retrace your steps to Maligne Lake.

North of Jasper Town – Day Hike

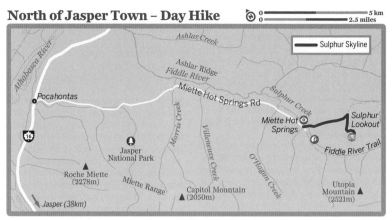

0 _____ 5 km
0 _____ 2.5 miles

Sulphur Skyline

North of Jasper Town

🏃 Sulphur Skyline

Duration Three hours

Distance 8km (5 miles) round-trip

Difficulty Moderate–difficult

Elevation Change 700m (2297ft)

Start/Finish Miette Hot Springs parking lot

Nearest Facilities Miette Hot Springs

Transportation Private

Summary A steep, invigorating hike that delivers spectacular views from a ridge high over one of Jasper's more remote corners.

Two hikes lead out from Miette Hot Springs: a pleasant ramble along the Sulphur River to Sulphur Pass at the start of the backcountry Fiddle River Trail, and this energetic scramble up to the 2050m (6724ft) Sulphur Skyline.

The fickle weather on this hike is notorious and hot sun and thunderstorms can hit in the same afternoon; be prepared for either eventuality. The hike starts innocuously enough at Miette Hot Springs on a wide, paved and sometimes crowded path, which is also the start of a longer hike to Mystery Lake. Ascend gradually and watch as the path narrows to a single track within 1km (0.6 miles). At the 2.2km (1.4-mile) mark at the Shuey Pass Junction, turn right and begin the real climb. Over the next 1.8km (1.1 miles) you'll gain 400m (1312ft) of elevation as the trail switchbacks through scattered forest and grassy slopes. Miraculously, the earlier crowds drop off to just a handful. At

the tree line look out for a giant white boulder left over from an erstwhile glacier. From here it's not far to the **summit** (4km, or 2.5 miles, from the start), where a sea of mountaintops awaits. Look out for Utopia Mountain due west and the distinctive shape of Pyramid Mountain to the northwest. To the south lies the Fiddle River, gradually disappearing off into remote backcountry.

🏃 OVERNIGHT HIKES

Jasper has a huge backcountry, most of it pretty lightly trodden even in peak season, and the most popular multiday hike – the Skyline Trail – is considered one of the best in the nation. If the park has a weakness, it's the lack of overnight trips starting and finishing at the same point. The Saturday Night Lake Loop (described here as a bike trip) is one of the better options on this score and can easily be hiked over two days, overnighting at one of three backcountry campgrounds.

🏃 Skyline Trail

Duration Two to three days

Distance 45.6km (28.5 miles)

Difficulty Moderate–difficult

Elevation Change 1400m (4526ft)

Start Maligne Lake

Finish Maligne Canyon

Summary The crème de la crème of backcountry hiking in the Canadian Rockies, the Skyline Trail is a North American classic that hovers at or above the tree line for roughly 25 of its 45.8km (28.5 miles).

Some hikers spread the expedition over three days, others tackle it in two, while the odd gung-ho trail runner has been known to knock it out in just one. But don't get too ambitious. With a notable lack of trees and little natural shelter en route, the Skyline is notoriously open to the elements, and fickle weather has taken the wind out of many an experienced hiker's sails.

A good, comfortable overnight option for two-day hikes is to reserve a room at the historic Shovel Pass Lodge near the halfway point. Alternatively, there are half a dozen backcountry campgrounds en route (campfires are prohibited), and for a comfortable three-day outing you could camp at Snowbowl and Tekarra Campground, leaving the final descent for the third morning. Transportation to both trailheads is easy, via the Maligne Valley Hiker's Shuttle (p278). Most people leave their car at Maligne Canyon and catch the bus for a 10am start at Maligne Lake.

DAY 1: MALIGNE LAKE TRAILHEAD TO SHOVEL PASS LODGE
7 HOURS, 20.4KM (12.6 MILES)

Starting at the Maligne Lake trailhead (1690m/5545ft), follow the mostly level Lorraine and Mona Lakes Trail through the woods for the first 5km (3.1 miles). Beyond the turnoff for Mona Lake, switchbacks leave the trees behind, passing Evelyn Creek Campground – keep right at the junction – and bringing you into meadows. Up on the slopes of Maligne Range, Little Shovel Pass, at 10.2km (6.3 miles), gives you views back over Maligne Lake and to the gray Queen Elizabeth Range, to the east. The pass was named by Mary Schäffer in 1911, when she and her guides were forced to dig their way through the snow with shovels hastily fashioned out of nearby trees.

From here the trail dips down into the Snowbowl, a lush meadow crisscrossed

Skyline Trail

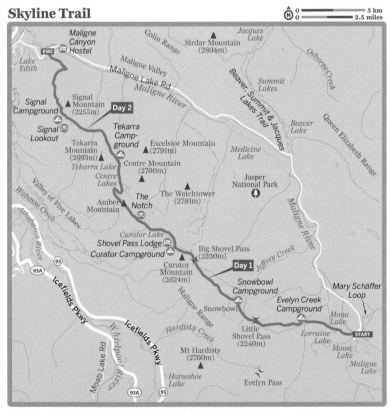

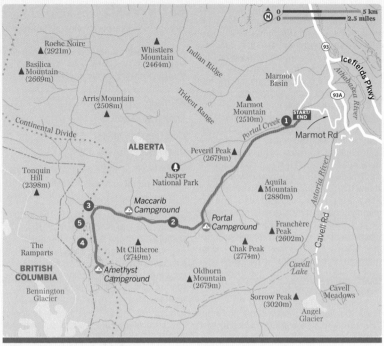

Overnight Hike
Tonquin Valley

START/END MARMOT BASIN RD
LENGTH TWO TO THREE DAYS; 53.2KM
(33 MILES) ROUND-TRIP

Wildlife, lush meadows, sparkling lakes and gorgeous views make roadless Tonquin Valley a mecca for hikers and horseback riders alike. The valley's crowning glory is the Ramparts, a collection of 10 peaks towering like Gothic fortresses over the network of backcountry trails.

The trail begins from the Portal Creek trailhead on Marmot Basin Rd, 6.5km (4 miles) west of Hwy 93A and about 16km (10 miles) south of Jasper Town. The hike to Amethyst Campground is a full day's hike; you can break the journey by staying at one of the two campgrounds en route, or stretch it to a three- or four-day trip by continuing along one of the trails from Amethyst Lake. Campfires are not permitted at any of the campgrounds.

From Marmot Basin Rd, the trail follows ❶ **Portal Creek** southwest and climbs into the Portal, a narrow canyon amid the Trident Range. The path crosses large rockslides beneath Peveril Peak and then descends into a forested valley. A gradual climb takes you past Portal Campground and up toward ❷ **Maccarib Pass** at 11.7km (7.3 miles). As you ascend above the tree line, you can't help but notice Oldhorn Mountain to the south.

Beyond the pass, begin your descent into the meadowland of ❸ **Tonquin Valley** with impressive views of the Ramparts to the west. Maccarib Campground is next to a small creek at 17.8km (11 miles). The trail heads southwest for 6km (3.7 miles) to the northern shore of glistening ❹ **Amethyst Lake**. At the junction, head right if you have reservations at ❺ **Tonquin Valley Backcountry Lodge** (p165), or continue along the shoreline to Amethyst Campground at 26.6km (16.5 miles). On still days, the water reflects the snow-cloaked Ramparts like a mirror.

Either pack up camp the following day and make the return journey along the same route or, if you have time, spend a day exploring around Amethyst Lake before heading back to the trailhead on the third day.

with streams and stretching 7.3km (4.5 miles) along the Maligne Range between Little Shovel Pass and Big Shovel Pass. **Snowbowl Campground** is at 11.8km (7.3 miles).

At the end of the Snowbowl, a short climb brings you up to **Big Shovel Pass** at the 17km/10.5-mile point; here you emerge into rugged, treeless high country with fabulous wide-open views. Soon after, the Skyline passes two main trail intersections. The first is the junction with the Watchtower trail, which branches off to the east where it ultimately connects with the Maligne Lake Rd. The second is the intersection with the Wabasso trail that branches west at the 19km/11.9-mile mark toward the Icefields Pkwy. Descend along this trail if you are overnighting at the **Curator Campground** or the **Shovel Pass Lodge** (p165). Both places are located on the Wabasso trail just over 1km (0.6 miles) west of (and steeply downhill from) the main Skyline Trail.

DAY 2: SHOVEL PASS LODGE TO MALIGNE CANYON HOSTEL

8 HOURS, 25.2KM (15.6 MILES)

Begin the day with a brisk climb up to tiny **Curator Lake**, which is surrounded by vast, windswept terrain. The trail becomes even steeper as it climbs to **the Notch**. At 2510m (8733ft), this is the high point of the trail, with breathtaking views along the Athabasca Valley and, if you're lucky, all the way to Mt Robson in the northeast. Continue on to the summit of **Amber Mountain**, below which the trail switchbacks down to **Centre Lakes**, with the sentinel Centre Mountain to the northeast. The trail heads through a small valley to **Tekarra Lake** and then follows around the north side of Tekarra Mountain, amid the first trees you'll have seen all day. Tekarra Campground lies at 11.3km (7 miles), between the peaks of its namesake and Excelsior Mountain.

Coming back out of the trees, you'll have views of Pyramid Mountain to the northwest and the Roche Bonhomme to the north. It's worth taking the short detour left at 16.2km (10.1 miles) to **Signal Lookout** for even better views. **Signal Campground** is just beyond this junction. From here it's a rather long and uninspiring downhill – 800m (2624ft) of descent over 9km (5.6 miles) – through forest down an old fire road (which is also used by mountain bikers). You'll come in via a small car park on the Maligne Lake Rd close to the Maligne Canyon Hostel.

🚗 DRIVING

Driving along Jasper's well-maintained and uncrowded roads, amid rugged mountains and seemingly endless forests, is one of life's simple pleasures. Keep your eyes peeled for wildlife foraging by the roadside.

🚗 Icefields Parkway Driving Tour

Duration Two hours

Distance 103km (64 miles)

Start Jasper

Finish Columbia Icefield Centre

Nearest Town Jasper

Summary Considered one of the most scenic drives in North America, the Icefields Parkway is a kaleidoscopic mélange of cascading waterfalls and spectacularly carved peaks, whose crowning glory is the glistening Columbia Icefield on the park's southern limits.

It measures 230km (144 miles) from Jasper Town down to Lake Louise, a bejeweled 108km (67-mile) segment of the route traverses Jasper National Park, incorporating some of the region's star attractions.

Driving south out of Jasper, the first highlight is **Mt Edith Cavell** (p157), the town's snowcapped guardian, accessible via a winding spur road off Hwy 93A. Stop here to stroll through flower-filled meadows and catch a glimpse of the peak's wing-shaped Angel Glacier. Rejoin the main parkway for 20km (12.4 miles) and you'll pass **Horseshoe Lake** (p157), with its steep-sided cliffs and clear, bracing waters, followed quickly by the **Athabasca Falls** (p155), the park's most voluminous waterfall, which throws its glacial meltwater over a 23m (75ft) limestone cliff.

Look out for wildlife on the next section of the route as you head south through a wide corridor of mountains that parallels the Continental Divide. Near **Honeymoon Lake** (p162) there's a viewpoint over the Athabasca River, while 2km (1.2 miles) further on, at **Sunwapta Falls** (p155), you can refuel at the homey restaurant or stretch your legs on the short hike to the waterfall.

As the tree cover thins and the river becomes a confusing maze of different channels, you'll start to notice the glaciers. Stop at the **Stutfield Glacier viewpoint**, just past Beauty Creek, to admire this outlying tentacle of the Columbia Icefield; 2km (1.2 miles) further on you'll pass **Tangle Falls** on your left. The drive's apex is the green-roofed **Columbia Icefield Discovery Centre** (Icefields Pkwy) `FREE` and the world-famous **Athabasca Glacier** (p155), which slides like an icy river toward the road. Stop here for interpretive displays, a walk on the Forefield Trail or an excursion onto the glacier aboard a unique Ice Explorer all-terrain vehicle.

See p74 for the Banff National Park section of the Icefields Pkwy drive.

CYCLING

Jasper is well known for its extensive network of multipurpose trails fanning out from the central hub of Jasper Town, including some fantastic singletrack. Cyclists experience few limitations here – in contrast to more rule-ridden US national parks – resulting in some of the most scenic, varied and technically challenging rides in North America. An excellent trail map highlighting cycling routes is available from the Jasper Information Centre and most hotels. Bears are prevalent in the park, so ride with

Icefields Parkway Driving Tour

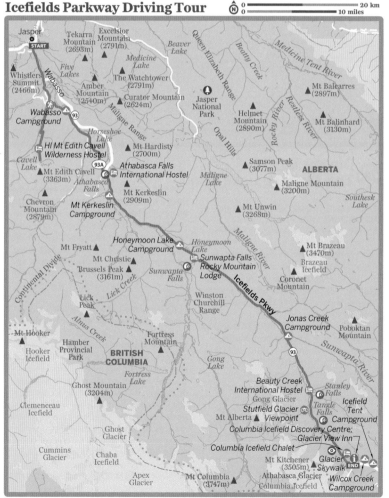

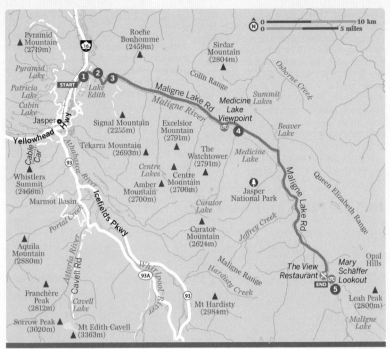

Driving Tour
The Maligne Lake Road

START MALIGNE LAKE RD TURNOFF, HWY 16
END MALIGNE LAKE
LENGTH 46KM (28.5 MILES); 45 MINUTES

The Maligne Lake Rd is as scenic as the destination. Wildlife is rife and with luck you'll spot a wolf, a bear, an eagle or a moose. Obey speed restrictions and watch out for animals.

Begin the tour 2km (1.2 miles) north of Jasper Town; follow Hwy 16 to the turnoff for Maligne Lake Rd, crossing the **1 Athabasca River** and following the road left. Ahead are views of Roche Bonhomme, with its Old Man summit, and to the west lies the rust-colored Pyramid Mountain. At 3km (1.9 miles), the **2 Fifth Bridge** crosses the powerful Maligne River; if you're feeling ambitious, you can head over this suspension bridge and climb the trail into **3 Maligne Canyon** (p138), one of the deepest in the Rockies. An easier way to see this dramatic canyon is via the Upper Canyon Trail; the trailhead is 7km (4.3 miles) along the route.

The road continues east between the Colin Range to the north and the Maligne Range to the south. At 22km (13.6 miles) there's a pull-off for the Maligne River on the right – but you'll see nothing more than a dry creek bed here except on the rare occasions when Medicine Lake floods. The rest of the year, water exits Medicine Lake via an underground cave system. Aboriginals in the area believed the water was whisked away by magic.

The next turnoff, on the northwest corner of **4 Medicine Lake** (p160), offers superb views across the water. Along the north side of the lake, the craggy Colin Range leans flat-faced toward the road, and a delta on the far eastern side of the lake often hosts caribou in early spring and late fall.

When you get to 32km (19.8 miles), look up. Above, you'll see limestone arches cut into the summit of the Queen Elizabeth Range, caused by water that's freezing in the crevices, expanding and shattering the rock. If you've brought a picnic try the rest stop on the left at 40km (24.8 miles), where you can relax beside the river before reaching the more hectic **5 Maligne Lake** (p159), 6km (3.7 miles) up the road.

caution (and bear spray). The season runs from May to October.

If you didn't bring your own bike, you can easily rent a top-notch machine from a number of different outlets. Prices start at C$15/30/50 per hour/three hours/day for front-suspension mountain bikes.

❶ Rentals

If you didn't bring your own bike, you can easily rent a top-notch machine from a number of different outlets. Prices start at C$12/24/32 per hour/three hours/day for front-suspension mountain bikes.

Vicious Cycle CYCLING
(Map p158; ☑780-852-1111; www.viciouscanada.com; 630 Connaught Dr, Jasper Town; bike rental per hour/day from C$8/32; ☺9am-6pm Sun-Thu, to 7pm Fri & Sat) Supercool cycling shop rents bikes in summer by the hour or day, and snowboards in winter. You can also pick up a helmet, trail map and lock. Reserve ahead online.

The Bench Bike Shop CYCLING
(Map p158; ☑780-852-7768; www.thebenchbikeshop.com; 606 Patricia St, Jasper Town; bike rental per hour/day from C$10/30; ☺10am-6pm) A year-round resource for cycling in the Jasper area, the Bench rents out everything from cool European-style city bikes to mountain bikes to winter fat bikes, and offers excellent advice on local trails.

ᯤ Athabasca River Valley Loop

Duration Two to three hours round-trip

Distance 18km (11.2 miles)

Difficulty Easy

Start/Finish Jasper

Nearest Town Jasper

Summary A paved but traffic-light sojourn around the verdant Athabasca River Valley that should whet your appetite for further biking adventures elsewhere.

If you're looking for a safe, flat family bike ride, or just prefer the certainty of a paved road to singletrack, this 18km (11.2-mile) spin around three luminous lakes on the southeast side of the Athabasca River Valley is an ideal option.

Start by tracking south from Jasper Town on the Wapiti Trail alongside Hwy 93A, crossing both the railway line and busy Hwy 16. On the other side of the highway turn left onto the Red Squirrel Trail, which will quickly deposit you on a narrow bridge across the Athabasca River next to the step crags of Old Fort Point. Another 1km (0.6 miles) further on, you'll come to the shores of beautiful **Lac Beauvert** (p159) with the **Fairmont Jasper Park Lodge** (p165) perched on its opposite shoreline. Circumnavigate the lake via the scenic golf course – listening out for shouts of 'fore!' – to the lodge itself, which is well worth closer inspection, before proceeding past the entrance gate and branching off onto the road to **Lake Annette** (p158). With its picnic tables, small beach and paved **lake loop**, this is a great place for lunch and/or a glacier-fed bath (in summer). Almost adjacent to Lake Annette is **Lake Edith** (p159), and an old road, now closed to cars, leads along its south shore. Ultimately this will bring you out onto the busier Maligne Lake Rd. Turn left here and pedal a couple of kilometers to an attractive bridge across the Athabasca River and the junction with Hwy 16. On the west side of the bridge, cross Hwy 16 and pick up the Bighorn Alley Trail on the other side. This smooth singletrack path leads through scattered forest and past the town graveyard back to the north end of Jasper Town.

Athabasca River Valley Loop

᚛ᚏᚐ Saturday Night Lake Loop

Duration Three to four hours round-trip

Distance 27.4km (17 miles)

Difficulty Moderate–difficult

Start/Finish Jasper

Nearest Town Jasper

Summary An interesting technical ride through a root-ridden and sometimes swampy forest, with plenty of nature-watching opportunities and half a dozen quiet, unspoiled lakes.

If Jasper lacks one thing, it is long-distance loop trails, which makes this rollercoaster jaunt all the more satisfying. Even better, it begins and ends in the townsite, yet never feels particularly close to civilization. Sometimes erroneously called the 20-Mile Loop (it's closer to 17 miles), the trail is numbered 3, gains 540m (1771ft) in elevation and never rises above the timberline. There are some tough technical stretches in the middle part of the ride involving mud, roots and short, steep descents.

From the center of Jasper follow Patricia St southwest to Patricia Cres. Turn right at the T-junction and the trailhead is on your left. Proceeding counterclockwise around the loop means you save the best descents till last, so take the right-hand No 3 option and follow the switchbacks out of town up onto the Pyramid Bench. A little over 1km (0.6 miles) of climbing brings you to the end of the dirt Cabin Lake Rd at the eastern end of **Cabin Lake**. From here take the single track along the lake's northeast shore and begin a gradual wooded ascent to smaller **Saturday Night Lake**, 4.3km (2.7 miles) distant (a 400m/437yd spur trail leads off the main trail to the lake and its campground).

The going gets tougher for the next 9km to 10km (5 to 6 miles) with muddy, swampy sections along the base of the Victoria Cross Range, interspersed with some narrow creek crossings and plenty of tree roots. The trail begins to loop back east at the 11.5km (7.2-mile) mark at a log bridge at the bottom of a waterfall. Just beyond here is High Lakes and the second campground (the trail is also a popular two- to three-day hike). You'll be descending now over roots and rocks past Minnow Lake, whereupon things settle down to a smoother pace to **Caledonia Lake**, a peaceful pond amid the trees. Fork left at the trail junction just past the lake and continue for 4km (2.4 miles; passing Marjorie Lake) back to the start point in Jasper Town.

᚛ᚏᚐ Valley of the Five Lakes

Duration Three hours round-trip

Distance 27km (17 miles)

Difficulty Difficult

Start/Finish Jasper

Nearest Town Jasper

Summary The holy grail for Jasper cyclists, this tough but scenic two-wheeled odyssey draws riders from far and wide to test their mettle.

This trail is a hair-raising but gloriously scenic spin through the attractive Athabasca Valley to five turquoise mountain lakes. It has it all, including sweeping singletrack, bone-rattling rocks and roots, sudden downhills and tough, technical inclines. No wonder serious cycling junkies rate it as one of the best off-road rides in North America.

Accessible via trail No 1, which cuts around the back of **Old Fort Point** (p139), Valley of the Five Lakes is popularly tackled as an out-and-back trip from Jasper Town. Linking up with trail No 9 after 2km (1.2 miles), the ride gathers pace with a narrow but nontechnical path meandering seamlessly through quiet tracts of sun-dappled forest to the lakes themselves, approximately 10km (6.2 miles) to the south. With **Lake 1** in sight, things start to get hairy and, if you can make it around all five of these bejeweled watery havens without getting off to push (at least once), consider yourself an aficionado.

After looping around **Lake 4** with its resident loons and shimmering emerald coloration, the trail winds up at a crossroads that offers bikers three distinct options. The first is to double back on the opposite side of the lakes and link up again with trail No 9 for a return ride to Jasper. The second is to cross the plank bridge over the **Wabasso Creek Wetlands** and make for the trailhead and parking lot on Hwy 93. The third is to head south toward **Wabasso Lake** and a second Hwy 93 trailhead, 9km (5.6 miles) away. Look out for wildlife if you elect to follow this last trail, particularly bears and deer.

⚓ OTHER ACTIVITIES

Got any energy left, tired hiker/biker/driver? Thought so! Read on...

⚓ White-Water Rafting & Float Trips

Charging rivers course their way through Jasper National Park. The Athabasca and Sunwapta Rivers are the two most utilized by rafters, who travel mainly on organized trips. The Athabasca has class II rapids, meaning it's considered family friendly and will give you more enjoyment than stress. The word *Sunwapta* means 'turbulent river' in the Stoney language, hinting at tougher challenges. The rapids are rated class III here (on a scale of I to VI), meaning some previous experience is recommended. The rafting season is from mid-May to the end of September. Prices are pretty generic, costing around C$69/99 for the Athabasca/Sunwapta Rivers for three- to four-hour trips, transportation included.

Maligne Adventures   RAFTING
(Map p158; ☑ 780-852-3331; www.maligne adventures.com; 632 Connaught Dr, Jasper Town; adult/child rafting tours from C$99/49.50, wildlife tours from C$69/49) From family-friendly rafting trips to jaunts over class III+ rapids,

this crew will get you on the river. They also organize morning and evening wildlife spotting tours, and run a helpful shuttle for hikers tackling the Skyline Trail.

Jasper Raft Tours   RAFTING
(☑ 780-852-2665; www.jasperrafttours.com; adult/ youth/child C$75/25/10; ☺ mid-May–early Oct) Specializes in family-oriented 90-minute trips (with favorable rates for kids) on the relatively mild Athabasca River. Children aged 2 to 99 are welcome. Book by phone or via the website; groups usually assemble at the Jasper train station (p159).

⚓ Boating

The Athabasca Valley is speckled with hidden lakes and misty ponds, most of which allow rowboats, kayaks, canoes and – more recently – stand-up paddleboards. Of the bodies of water around Jasper Town, Pyramid Lake is the most popular spot, an oasis of tranquility caught in the distinctive shadow of Pyramid Mountain. As the largest natural lake in the Canadian Rockies, Maligne Lake offers visitors the archetypal Jasper experience.

Pyramid Lake Boat Rentals   BOATING
(Map p156; www.mpljasper.com/hotels/pyramid -lake-resort/activity-rentals; Pyramid Lake Rd;

STARGAZING

Stargazing probably isn't the first activity one associates with the dramatic mountain-scaling scenery of Jasper, but interest in the the night sky and its innumerable galaxies is growing in popularity. It harks back to a tradition long practiced by the First Nations and 19th-century European explorers. David Thompson, one of the Jasper area's earliest pioneers, was an expert surveyor and astronomer nicknamed Koo-Koo-Sint, or 'stargazer' by the indigenous people.

Interest in outer space was reignited in 2011 when Jasper was named a 'Dark Sky Preserve' by the Royal Astronomical Society of Canada, earmarking it as an area where light pollution is measured and controlled in order to enhance Milky Way vistas and promote astronomical study.

Every year since 2011, Jasper has held a **Dark Sky Festival** (www.jasperdarksky.travel; ☺ late Oct) in the traditionally quiet month of October, putting on a multitude of diverse events, including visits from well-known astronauts and astronomers and classical concerts under the stars.

More interest was added in June 2015 when a small but expertly curated planetarium was rigged up at a downtown Jasper hotel. Subsequently moved to the Jasper Park Lodge, the 40-capacity auditorium is encased in an ingenious inflatable structure protected by a tent and runs regularly scheduled audiovisual shows about Jasper's night sky. There's also the opportunity to take a peep through the largest telescope in the Rockies and perhaps see the rings of Saturn.

Other easily accessible places to go star-gazing year-round are the small island on Pyramid Lake, 5km (3 miles) northeast of Jasper Town, the north shore of Maligne Lake, and the Athabasca Glacier.

BACKCOUNTRY KAYAKING

Paddling off into the sunset will never seem as alluring as it does on Maligne Lake where wispy clouds share watery reflections with sugar-colored glaciers. Serviced by Curly Phillips' historic Maligne Lake Boathouse, the lake has long been popular with kayakers and canoeists, though few paddlers venture beyond shouting distance of the tourist-heavy north shore. However, for more solitude and a full-on backcountry kayaking adventure, it's possible to explore Maligne Lake's uninhabited shorelines by taking advantage of three paddle-in campgrounds. Hidden Cove is 5km (3.1 miles) south of the north shore bustle on the lake's west side; Fisherman's Bay is 8km (5 miles) further south on the east shore; while Coronet Creek is a kilometer shy of the 22km-long (13.7 miles) lake's southern tip. True to Jasper's backcountry ethos, all the lakeside campgrounds are basic, with boat docks, tent pads, firepits and picnic tables. As space is limited (up to 10 tents per campground), you must book ahead. There's a two-night maximum stay in peak season.

Tour boats ply the lake daily between 9am and 6pm as far south as Spirit Island (14km/8.7 miles from the boathouse). To avoid their foamy wake and other fickle weather conditions, it is best to set out early. Beyond the north shore, Maligne is a wilderness lake with no access roads or services. Be prepared for wildlife encounters, bad weather and backcountry emergencies, but be equally prepared to have a stunningly good time!

---

boat rental per hour C$40, bike rental per hour/day C$20/45) Canoes, rowboats, kayaks and paddleboats for hire on Pyramid Lake, plus mountain bikes for exploring the network of trails between the lake and Jasper Town. In the winter you can get out there with snowshoes, ice skates or fat bikes (all C$30 per half day).

Maligne Lake Boathouse   BOATING
(Map p156; ☑780-852-3370; www.banffjasper collection.com/canadian-rockies/jasper/maligne -lake-boat-rentals; Maligne Lake; rental per hour/day kayak from C$40/165, canoe or rowboat from C$75/200; ⊙9am-4pm Jun–mid-Sep) The historic Curly Phillips Boathouse, dating from 1928, rents canoes, kayaks and rowboats for a paddle around the lake. Not many people paddle all the way to Spirit Island – it would take you all day – but you will have to paddle a ways out to reach where the lake turns its truly spectacular baby-blue color.

🛶 Fishing

Fishing is popular throughout the park, with both locals and visitors. Waters frequented by anglers include Celestine, Princess, Maligne and Pyramid Lakes – though there are many smaller nooks.

Fishing is permitted in these lakes as well as many of the park's other lakes and rivers, including parts of the Athabasca, Maligne and Miette Rivers, as long as you are in possession of a valid permit (day/year

C$9.80/34.30). Most of these waters are only open for short seasons, and many others are closed throughout the year. Visit Parks Canada's fishing regulations website (www. pc.gc.ca/en/pn-np/ab/jasper/activ/activ-ex perience/ete-summer/peche-fishing) or drop into one of its offices for opening dates and fishing restrictions.

On-Line Sport & Tackle   FISHING
(Map p158; ☑780-852-3630; www.fishonline jasper.com; 600 Patricia St, Jasper Town; half/full day trip C$249/369) Rents gear, teaches fly-fishing and runs lots of fishing trips. Prices are based on a minimum of two anglers.

🧗 Climbing

Because of its preponderance of sedimentary rock, Jasper doesn't draw as many ambitious rock climbers as other Rockies hotspots, such as Canmore. The advantage of this is relative solitude. Located up the trail from Fifth Bridge, off Maligne Lake Rd, Rock Gardens is the most popular crag and has the easiest approach. A more recent addition is Lost Boys, 'discovered' in 1994 and situated 25km (15.5 miles) south on Hwy 93A from the junction with Hwy 93. From the parking spot it's a 20-minute hike in to the quartzite crag. For climbers with experience (and preferably a guide), Mt Edith Cavell offers incredible vistas, while Ashlar Ridge and Morro Peak are strictly the terrain of experts.

Rockaboo Adventures CLIMBING
(Map p158; ☑780-820-0092; www.rockaboo. ca; 610 Patricia St, Jasper Town) Jasper's most comprehensive year-round climbing guides offer everything from a four-hour Experience Rock Climbing course (C$125), suitable for kids aged eight and up, to all-day glacier walks on Athabasca Glacier (C$225, ages 12 and up), to two-day climbing photography workshops (C$200), to strenuous ascents of lofty Mt Edith Cavell (from C$600 for two people) and other local peaks.

🏃 Horseback Riding

With horseback riders sharing trails with hikers and bikers, Jasper trumps most other parks when it comes to equestrian adventures. Rival stables on either side of the Athabasca Valley ply routes around Lake Patricia and Lake Annette, while further afield stunning backcountry trips can be organized in the Tonquin Valley, Maligne Pass, Jacques Lake and Bald Hills. Permits and regulations apply.

Jasper Riding Stables HORSEBACK RIDING
(Map p156; ☑780-852-7433; www.jasperstables .com; Stables Rd, Jasper Town; 1/2/3hr rides C$52/95/135; ☉May–mid-Oct) For gentle trail rides through local backcountry, call in at these stables just northwest of Jasper Town on the road to Pyramid Lake. With over 50 horses, they'll match you to a suitable four-legged friend.

🏃 Watching Wildlife

With 69 different mammals, 277 species of birds, and 16 amphibians and reptiles, your chances of spotting wildlife in Jasper National Park are pretty high. A trip down Maligne Rd or Miette Hot Springs Rd may score you a bear, wolf or mountain goat sighting, and elk tend to linger just south of Jasper Town, at the end of Hwy 93. About 0.5km (0.3 miles) north of Jasper Town, on the eastern side of the road, a salt lick is frequented by goats and sheep in summer.

🏃 Ranger Programs

Parks Canada has a proud tradition of staging live theater and free family-geared interpretive programs throughout the summer at Whistlers Campground's outdoor theatre. Due to a comprehensive renovation of the campground, shows have been temporarily suspended, but are scheduled to resume in 2021 when construction work is complete. Contact Parks Canada for current status.

🏃 Golf

Fairmont Jasper Park Lodge Golf Club GOLF
(☑780-852-6090; www.jaspermountaingolf.com; 1 Old Lodge Rd, Jasper Town; green fees from C$210; ☉mid-May–mid-Oct) Overlooking the beautiful green shores of shimmering Lac Beauvert are several golfing greens – 18 to be precise. Designed in 1925 by Stanley Thompson, Jasper's golf course is as stunning as it is challenging. There's also a driving range, and you can rent shoes and clubs. Try not to hit a bear.

🏃 Skiing & Snowboarding

Marmot Basin SKIING
(Map p156; www.skimarmot.com; Marmot Basin Rd; day pass adult/child C$110/89) Jasper's only ski area is located 19km southwest of Jasper Town. A daily shuttle connects the two

---

THE WOODLAND CARIBOU

Jasper's most iconic fauna is also – ironically – one of its most endangered: the woodland caribou, better known to lovers of Father Christmas as the reindeer. Rather like the bison, woodland caribou were once ubiquitous in much of North America, foraging in boreal forests as far south as Idaho. However, hunting and habitat loss have seen their numbers drastically diminished in recent times, leaving them banished to a small pocket of the Rockies largely contained within the confines of Jasper National Park. A member of the deer family, the woodland caribou, in contrast to its more common tundra-roaming cousins, live in smallish groups in subalpine regions, where they subsist on a diet of lichen. Jasper's endangered caribou is split into two groups: a southern herd, numbering less than 50, roams the slopes around Maligne Lake and the Tonquin Valley; a more stable northern group numbering around 140 hides in the park's remote northern mountains. To see them you'll need to get lucky on the Opal Hills, Tonquin Valley or North Boundary hikes.

during the season. Although not legendary, its 95 runs and the longest high-speed quad chair in the Rockies mean Marmot is no pushover – and its relative isolation compared to the trio of ski areas in Banff means shorter lift lines.

The cons: it can get cold (wrap up) and there's no overnight accommodations on site.

🌲 Cross-Country Skiing & Snowshoeing

True to its ethos of multipurpose trails for all, many of Jasper's hiking and biking paths are given over to cross-country skiing and snowshoeing in winter. Trails track-set for classic and skate skiing are centered on three main areas. Close to Jasper Town you can try the 4.5km (2.8-mile) Whistlers Campground Loop or the 10km (6.2-mile) there-and-back Pipeline Trail, sandwiched between Hwy 16 and the Miette River.

Near Maligne Lake is the 10km (6.2-mile) round-trip Beaver and Summit Lakes Trail, following a popular and scenic summer hiking route with little gradient, as well as the easy 2.3km (1.4-mile) Moose Lake Loop.

The third and most comprehensive track-set skiing area can be found on and around Hwy 93A, which is left unplowed in winter for 10.5km (6.5 miles) between the Meeting of the Waters picnic area and Athabasca Falls. Branching off this road is a trail to Moab Lake, or further north you can tackle the steep 12km (7.4-mile) unplowed Edith Cavell Rd, which is skiable as far as Cavell Meadows. For the more adventurous, there's cross-country skiing to the remote Tonquin Valley.

🌲 Other Winter Activities

Half of Jasper shuts down in the winter, while the other half metamorphoses into something just as good (if not better) than its summertime self. Lakes become skating rinks, hiking and biking routes become cross-country skiing trails, waterfalls become ice climbs, wildlife migrates to lower climes, and – last but by no means least – prices become far more reasonable.

There are two hot spots for outdoor skating. The Fairmont Jasper Park Lodge maintains a Zamboni-cleared oval on **Mildred Lake**, on the hotel's north side. Benches are set out here, spontaneous hockey games often erupt and free hot chocolate revives shivering bystanders. For a quieter, more romantic, skate under a full moon, head up to Pyramid Lake (p158), 6km (3.7 miles) northwest of the townsite. You can rent skates at **Jasper Source for Sports** (Map p158; ☑780-852-3654; www.jaspersports.com; 406 Patricia St, Jasper Town; bike rental per day from C$30; ☺9am-9pm).

The area around **Pyramid Bench** is maintained for winter hiking (weather permitting). Along these trails you'll be sheltered by the woods and have a good chance of spotting wildlife. The Mina and Riley Lakes Loop (p139) is well trodden most of the year by enterprising locals, who include it in their early morning jogs.

Slightly less athletic is the iconic three-hour **Maligne Canyon Icewalk** offered by Maligne Adventures (p151). It's a guided walk through a series of frozen waterfalls, viewable from December to April. Extremists tackle these slippery behemoths with rappels and ice axes. **Gravity Gear** (Map p158; ☑780-852-3155; www.gravitygearjasper.com; 625b Patricia St, Jasper Town; ☺10am-9pm) can rent equipment.

BACKCOUNTRY SKIING THE TONQUIN VALLEY

Want a white-knuckle backcountry adventure without heart-stopping risks? Look no further than the Tonquin Valley in winter, when you can ski up frozen Portal Creek to Mac-carib Pass before descending into a rampart-guarded wilderness for a couple of nights at the cozy backcountry Tonquin Valley Backcountry Lodge. From November 1 through mid-February each year, the Tonquin trail is closed to promote caribou conservation, only adding to its remote allure when it reopens for the late winter ski season. Further enhancing its appeal is the trail's relatively low avalanche risk (though it always pays to check ahead) and minimal bear paranoia (they're hibernating). It's 22km (13.7 miles) from the Portal Creek trailhead to the lodge and then another 29km (18.1 miles) out again via the gorgeous Astoria River/Cavell Rd route. You can go it alone, or inquire about joining a guided group. The lodge has a two-night minimum stay in the winter – ideal for less frenetic sidetrips.

◉ SIGHTS

◉ Icefields Parkway

Paralleling the Continental Divide for 230km (143 miles) between Lake Louise and Jasper Town, plain old Hwy 93 is usually branded as the Icefields Pkwy (or the slightly more romantic 'Promenade des Glaciers' in French) as a means of somehow preparing people for the majesty of its surroundings. And what majesty! The Parkway's highlight is undoubtedly the humongous Columbia Icefield and its numerous fanning glaciers, and this dynamic lesson in erosive geography is complemented by weeping waterfalls, aquamarine lakes, dramatic mountains and the sudden dart of a bear, an elk, or was it a caribou?

Completed in 1940, the Parkway is most easily toured by car, meaning it can get busy in July and August. For a clearer vision, consider taking a bus or, even better, tackling it on a bike – the road is wide, never prohibitively steep, and sprinkled with strategically spaced campgrounds, hostels and hotels.

★**Athabasca Glacier**   GLACIER
The tongue of the Athabasca Glacier runs from the Columbia Icefield to within walking distance of the road opposite the Icefield Centre (p147). It can be visited on foot or in an Ice Explorer all-terrain vehicle. It has retreated about 2km since 1844, when it reached the rock moraine on the north side of the road. To reach its toe (bottom edge), walk from the Icefield Centre along the 1.8km **Forefield Trail**, then join the 1km **Toe of the Glacier Trail**.

You can also park at the start of the latter trail. While it is permitted to stand on a small roped section of the ice, do not attempt to cross the warning tape – many do, but the glacier is riddled with crevasses and there have been fatalities.

To walk safely on the Columbia Icefield, you'll need to enlist the help of **Athabasca Glacier Icewalks** (☏780-852-5595; www.icewalks.com; Icefield Centre, Icefields Pkwy; 3hr tour adult/child C$110/60, 6hr tour C$175/90; ⊙late May–Sep), which supplies all the gear you'll need and a guide to show you the ropes. Its basic tour is three hours; there's a six-hour option for those wanting to venture further out on the glacier. Hikers must be at least seven years of age.

The other, far easier (and more popular) way to get on the glacier is to go via the

Columbia Icefield Adventure (www.banffjaspercollection.com/attractions/columbia-icefield; adult/child C$114/57; ⊙9am-6pm Apr-Oct) tour. For many people this is the defining experience of their visit to the Canadian Rockies. The large hybrid bus-truck grinds a track onto the ice, where it stops to allow you to go for a 25-minute wander on the glacier. Dress warmly, wear good shoes and bring a water bottle to try some freshly melted glacial water. Tickets can be bought at the Icefield Centre or online; tours depart every 15 to 30 minutes.

Columbia Icefield Skywalk   VIEWPOINT
(www.banffjaspercollection.com/attractions/columbia-icefield/skywalk; adult/child skywalk only C$37/19, skywalk & glacier tour C$114/57; ⊙10am-5pm mid-Apr–May & Oct, to 6pm Jun–mid-Jul & Sep, to 7pm mid-Jul–Aug) Winner of numerous architectural awards, this glass-floored, glass-sided, open-air lookout and walkway is suspended high above the Sunwapta River opposite Mt Kitchener. While some will find the feeling of standing in midair over the valley pretty thrilling, others find the C$37 price tag excessive. An audioguide fills you in on geology, wildlife and architecture. The Skywalk must be visited via tour bus from the Columbia Icefield Centre. (Drivers along the Parkway are not permitted to stop here.)

Athabasca Falls   WATERFALL
(Map p156) Despite being only 23m high, Athabasca Falls is Jasper's most dramatic and voluminous waterfall, a deafening combination of sound, spray and water. The thunderous Athabasca River has cut deeply into the soft limestone rock, carving potholes, canyons and water channels. Interpretive signs explain the basics of the local geology. Visitors crowd the large parking lot and short access trail. It's just west of the Icefields Pkwy, 30km south of Jasper Town, and at its most ferocious during summer.

Sunwapta Falls   WATERFALL
(Map p156) Meaning 'turbulent water' in the native language of the Stoney First Nations, the 18m Sunwapta Falls formed when the glacial meltwaters of the Sunwapta River began falling from a hanging valley into the deeper, U-shaped Athabasca Valley. Close to the Icefields Pkwy and the Sunwapta Falls Resort and restaurant, the falls are a popular stop for travelers plying the scenic highway. They're also the start of a 25km biking and hiking trail to remote **Fortress Lake** in Hamber Provincial Park.

Jasper National Park Region

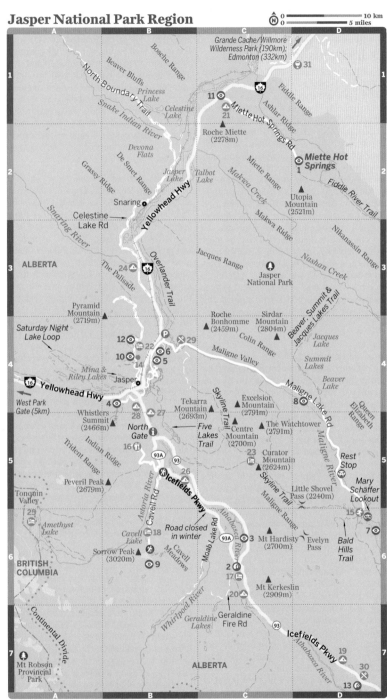

N

0 — 10 km
0 — 5 miles

Grande Cache/Willmore
Wilderness Park (190km);
Edmonton (332km)

31

11

16

Fiddle Range

Ashlar Ridge

21

Miette Hot Springs Rd

Roche Miette
(2278m)

Bosche Range

North Boundary Trail

Beaver Bluffs

Princess
Lake

Celestine
Lake

Snake Indian River

Devona
Flats

De Smet Range

Grassy Ridge

Jasper
Lake

Talbot
Lake

Snaring

Celestine
Lake Rd

Yellowhead Hwy

ALBERTA

The Palisade

24

16

Overlander Trail

Pyramid
Mountain
(2719m)

Saturday Night
Lake Loop

12

22

10

14

6

5

Mina &
Riley Lakes

Jasper

16

Yellowhead Hwy

West Park
Gate (5km)

4

28

27

Whistlers
Summit
(2466m)

North
Gate

16

93A

93

26

Icefields Pkwy

Trident Range

Indian Ridge

Peveril Peak
(2679m)

Tonquin
Valley

25

Amethyst
Lake

BRITISH
COLUMBIA

Sorrow Peak
(3020m)

9

Cavell
Lake

18

Cavell
Meadows

Cavell Rd

Astoria River

Road closed
in winter

Moab Lake Rd

Geraldine
Lakes

Geraldine
Fire Rd

93

Whirlpool River

Continental Divide

Mt Robson
Provincial
Park

ALBERTA

Miette Hot
Springs

1

Miette Range

Makwa Creek

Makwa Ridge

Utopia
Mountain
(2521m)

Fiddle River Trail

Nikanassin Range

Nashan Creek

Jacques Range

Jasper
National Park

Beaver, Summit &
Jacques Lakes Trail

Jacques
Lake

Summit
Lakes

Beaver
Lake

Roche
Bonhomme
(2459m)

Sirdar
Mountain
(2804m)

Colin Range

Maligne Valley

Maligne Lake Rd

8

Queen
Elizabeth
Range

Tekarra
Mountain
(2693m)

Skyline Trail

Excelsior
Mountain
(2791m)

Centre
Mountain
(2700m)

Five
Lakes
Trail

The Watchtower
(2791m)

23

Curator
Mountain
(2624m)

Little Shovel
Pass (2240m)

Maligne Range

Skyline Trail

Maligne River

Rest
Stop

Mary
Schäffer
Lookout

15

7

Bald
Hills
Trail

3

Mt Hardisty
(2700m)

Evelyn
Pass

2

17

Mt Kerkeslin
(2909m)

20

Athabasca River

Icefields Pkwy

19

30

13

Jasper National Park Region

JASPER NATIONAL PARK SIGHTS

Horseshoe Lake   LAKE
(Map p156) This idyllic, blue-green horse-shoe-shaped lake just off the Icefields Pkwy is missed by many visitors, making a stop-over here all the more alluring. A choice spot for a bracing summer swim or a short stroll around the perimeter, the lake is sur-rounded by steep cliffs and is frequented by cliff divers. It's probably safer to watch than join in.

Mt Edith Cavell   MOUNTAIN
(Map p156) Rising like a snowy sentinel over Jasper Town, Mt Edith Cavell (3363m) is one of the park's most distinctive and physically arresting peaks. What it lacks in height it makes up for in stark, ethereal beauty. Ac-cessed via a winding, precipitous road that branches off the Icefields Pkwy 6km south of Jasper, the mountain is famous for its flower meadows and its wing-shaped Angel Glacier.

First climbed in 1915, it was named the following year in honor of a humanitarian British nurse, who was executed by a Ger-man firing squad during WWI after helping to smuggle over 200 wounded Allied sol-diers into neutral Holland.

⊙ Jasper Town & Around

Built in the early 1900s at the confluence of three river valleys, Jasper Town (originally known as Fitzhugh) is surrounded by moun-tains and blessed with one of the most easily accessible trail systems in North America. Characterized by a mishmash of low-rise shops and residential properties – not all of which are attractive – the town these days maintains strict development laws, mean-ing its tenure as an expanding urban hub is well and truly over. While the main sights lie outside the town, it makes a good evening base and, should the weather turn ugly, you can linger in an excellent museum or ponder some interesting railway memorabilia.

Jasper Skytram   CABLE CAR
(Map p156; ☑780-852-3093; www.jaspertram way.com; Whistlers Mountain Rd; adult/child/family C$50/27/125; ☺8am-9pm late Jun-Aug, 9am-8pm mid-May–late Jun, 10am-5pm late Mar–mid-May, Sep & Oct) If the average, boring views from Jasper just aren't blowing your hair back, go for a ride on this sightseeing gondola. The seven-minute journey (departures every nine minutes) zips up through various mountain life zones to the high barren slopes of the

Jasper Town

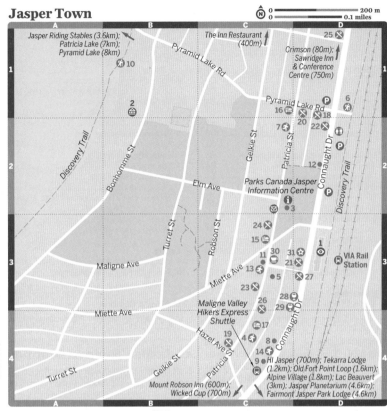

Whistlers. From the gondola's upper station a steep 1.25km hike leads to the mountain's true summit, where views stretch for 75km. Arrive early or late to avoid midday lines. There's a restaurant and gift shop up top.

The Skytram is 7km south of Jasper Town along Whistlers Mountain Rd, off the Icefields Pkwy. If you've got a copy of Gemtrek's *Jasper & Maligne Lake* topo map, bring it along to help make sense of the vast mountain, lake and river panorama that unfolds below.

Jasper Discovery Trail   WALKING

(Map p158) Part walking trail, part outdoor museum, the Jasper Discovery Trail is an 8km partially paved pathway that completely circumnavigates the town, split into three sections highlighting the town's natural, historical and railroad legacies. Interpretive boards en route provide an educational introduction to both town and park. Start from the Discovery Trail info kiosk just north of the train station.

Pyramid Lake   LAKE

(Map p156) Pyramid Lake is popular with canoers and kayakers in summer and ice-skaters in winter. From its eastern shore, a wooden pedestrian bridge leads out to Pyramid Island, a small nature preserve. At night, stargazers congregate on the bridge for unobstructed views of the heavens. It's roughly 7km northwest of Jasper Town.

Patricia Lake   LAKE

(Map p156) Patricia Lake offers abundant water activities, but its most curious feature (hidden deep below the lake's surface) is the wreck of a prototype ice-based aircraft carrier called *Habbakuk,* designed as part of a secret British mission during WWII. It's roughly 6km northwest of Jasper Town.

Lake Annette   LAKE

(Map p156) East across the main highway from Jasper town, Lake Annette is popular for water activities in the summer, with a

Jasper Town

small beach and numerous picnic spots. If you're brave and it's very hot, you might even dare a quick summer dip here – just remember that the water was in a glacier not too long ago! The multiuse trail that circumnavigates the lake is accessible to wheelchairs, cyclists and hikers.

Lake Edith LAKE
(Map p156) On the east side of the highway opposite Jasper town, Lake Edith is a popular summer getaway, ringed by cycling and hiking trails and frequented by kayakers and other boaters. It's equipped with picnic spots and a small beach area.

Lac Beauvert LAKE
Dominated by the Fairmont Jasper Park Lodge and golf course just east of town, crystal-clear Lac Beauvert (literally 'beautiful green' in French) is as gorgeous as the name implies. It's a popular place for boating during summer and ice-skating in winter.

**Jasper-Yellowhead
Museum & Archives** MUSEUM
(Map p158; ☑780-852-3013; www.jaspermuseum.org; 400 Bonhomme St, Jasper Town; adult/child/family C$7/6/15; ☺10am-5pm daily May-Sep, Thu-Sun Oct-Apr) Poke your head into this museum if it's raining, snowing or too hot. Even if the weather is nice, the museum does an excellent job of documenting Jasper's history and recounting the stories of the larger-than-life characters who contributed to making it into the town it is today.

Jasper Train Station LANDMARK
(Map p158; 607 Connaught Dr, Jasper Town) Jasper grew up as a railway town, and the train station (constructed by the Canadian National Railway) is one of its oldest and most attractive buildings. Designed in an unusual 'arts and crafts meets national park' architectural style, it was completed in 1925 to blend into its rustic surroundings. The interior has been upgraded, but remains sympathetic to railroad's golden era, with heavy wooden benches and art-deco travel posters.

◎ Maligne Lake Area

Maligne Lake LAKE
(Map p156) Almost 50km from Jasper at the end of a stunning road that bears its name, 22km-long Maligne Lake is the recipient of a lot of hype. It's the largest lake in the national park and there's no denying its appeal: the baby-blue water and a craning circle of rocky, photogenic peaks are a feast for the eyes.

Although the north end of the lake is heavy with the summer tour-bus brigade, most of the rest of the shoreline is accessible only by foot or boat – and so much quieter. Numerous campgrounds are available lakeside and are ideal for adventurous kayakers and backcountry hikers. Moose and grizzly bears also frequent this area.

The Maligne Lake Boathouse (p152) rents canoes and kayaks for a spin around the lake. Not many people paddle all the way to Spirit

Island – the lake's most classic view – as it would take you all day. Instead most people take it in on the riotously popular boat trip with **Maligne Lake Cruises** (Map p156; www.banffjaspercollection.com/attractions/maligne-lake-cruise; Maligne Lake; adult/child 90min cruise C$79/40, 2hr cruise C$114/57; ⊙ May-Sep). The trips leave the boat dock up to eight times daily and last 1½ to two hours.

Medicine Lake   LAKE
(Map p156) A geological rarity, Medicine Lake is perhaps best described as an intermittent lake with a porous bottom that functions rather like a bathtub without a plug. In summer, when meltwater runoff is high, the lake fills more quickly than it can drain away, and the body of water becomes deep and expansive. In winter, as the runoff slows, the water empties, causing the lake to shrink to the size of a small stream.

What bewildered indigenous peoples and other early visitors was the apparent lack of any water outlet. In fact, the water flows out of the lake via a series of small holes on its floor before passing into a complex underground cave system. The river then re-emerges 16km downstream near Maligne Canyon. In the 1950s a ferry service across the lake was briefly attempted, but efforts to plug the holes with sandbags, mattresses and bundles of magazines all proved futile.

◉ North of Jasper Town

★ **Miette Hot Springs**   HOT SPRINGS
(Map p156; www.pc.gc.ca/hotsprings; Miette Rd; adult/child/family C$7.05/5.15/20.35; ⊙ 9am-11pm mid-Jun–Aug, 10:30am-9pm May–mid-Jun & Sep–mid-Oct) More remote than Banff's historic springs, Miette Hot Springs ('discovered' in 1909) are 61km northeast of Jasper off Hwy 16, near the park's eastern boundary. The soothing waters, kept at a pleasant 37°C (98°F) to 40°C (104°F), are surrounded by peaks and are especially enjoyable when the fall snow is drifting down and steam envelops the crowd. Raining summer evenings also make for stunning, misty conditions.

These are the Canadian Rockies' hottest springs, leaving the mountain at 54°C (129°F) before cooling down. There is a warm pool, a hot pool and a couple of icy ones, just to get the heart going – so it's best to stick a toe in before doing your cannonball. You can rent swimsuits and towels for

C$1.90 each. This area is very popular with bears and you'll often see one on the road or milling around the parking lot.

Pocahontas   HISTORIC SITE
(Map p156) A one-time mining community that produced heaps of poor-quality, smokeless coal for the Allied war effort during WWI, Pocahontas was once the largest settlement in Jasper National Park and home to hundreds of miners. When the market price for coal fell in 1921 the town slipped into a rapid decline, becoming a veritable ghost town nine years later when the 1930 National Parks Act banned mining in the park for good.

All that remains of Pocahontas today are some overgrown ruins, an antiquated superintendent's home and a 1km wheelchair-accessible interpretive trail that meanders around the old mining site. To get here, take the Miette Hot Springs Rd off Hwy 16 and turn at the first right into the parking lot.

☞ TOURS

Jasper Adventure Centre   OUTDOORS
(Map p158; ☑ 780-852-5595; www.jasperadventurecentre.com; 611 Patricia St, Jasper Town; ⊙ 8am-9pm late Jun-Aug, to 6pm May-late Jun & Sep–mid-Oct) Jasper's veteran guiding outfit runs numerous local tours, as well as some further afield to the Icefields and Lake Louise. One of their most popular trips is the three-hour Wildlife Discovery Tour (adult/child C$69/35). In winter they share office space with SunDog Tour Company, from where they organize dogsledding and ice walks in addition to their many year-round tours.

Jasper Walks & Talks   HIKING
(Map p158; ☑ 780-852-4994; www.walksntalks.com; 626 Connaught Dr, Jasper Town; walks per adult C$65-90, per child C$45-50) Longtime local resident and former Parks Canada guide Paula Beauchamp leads small groups on three- to six-hour tours with a focus on such local attractions as Maligne Canyon and Mt Edith Cavell Meadows. Bring a picnic lunch, good walking shoes, your camera and lots of questions for your very knowledgeable guide. Winter snowshoe adventures are also offered.

SunDog Tour Company   TOURS
(Map p158; ☑ 780-852-4056; www.sundogtours.com; 414 Connaught Dr, Jasper Town; ⊙ 8am-5pm)

THE DESOLATE NORTH

Steal a glance at a map of Jasper National Park and you'll see that the whole area to the north of east–west Hwy 16 is almost blank. Although this extensive zone comprises over one-third of the park's total area, it contains no roads, no facilities and warrants virtually no mention at all in any of the standard park literature. So, what's the story?

Covered in a dense mountainscape, Jasper's north is a rugged pastiche of bugs, bogs and roaming caribou, where the infrastructure begins and ends in a handful of primitive campgrounds. For the curious and brave, this is backcountry of the highest order, where you're often three or four days' walk from civilization, and a week or more can pass without seeing another hiker. The only serviceable path through the region is the mythical North Boundary Trail, 192km (120 miles) of brooding backcountry speckled with 20 primitive campgrounds. Long stretches of shadowy forests and mosquito-infested marshes are juxtaposed with reaffirming highlights, such as misty Snake Indian Falls, the glacial intensity of Berg Lake and the meadowed magnificence of Snake Indian Pass. If you hike east–west starting at Celestine Lake, 53km (33 miles) northeast of Jasper Town, you'll save the best part until last: the dramatic north face of Mt Robson rising like an impregnable wall above Berg Lake.

Although lightly trafficked, the North Boundary Trail is well maintained and all river crossings have rudimentary bridges. The hike is unusual in that it runs east–west rather than tracking the Continental Divide. It is generally tackled over eight to 12 days ending near Mt Robson on Hwy 16, 88km (55 miles) west of Jasper Town. Call in at the Jasper Information Centre for trail conditions and maps.

SunDog Tour Company runs a whole host of tours, including trips to the Icefields, train rides, boat rides, wildlife viewing, canoeing, horseback riding and more.

Friends of Jasper WALKING
(Map p158; ☑780-852-4767; www.friendsofjasper
.com; 500 Connaught Dr, Jasper Town) FREE
Friends of Jasper hosts a historical walking tour nightly at 7:30pm throughout the summer, leaving from the Jasper Information Centre (p171). Get tickets in advance at the center; voluntary contributions are gladly accepted. Groups are limited to 30. Other interpretive programs include a junior naturalist program for kids aged six to 10, as well as bird-watching and full-moon walks.

⌂ SLEEPING

Aside from its venerable historic lodge, Jasper has a varied stash of hotels, motels, hostels, cabins, B&Bs and bungalows. Notwithstanding, in July and August you'd be wise to make reservations way in advance. Reservations are also taken for four Jasper campgrounds: Pocahontas, Wabasso, Wapiti and Whistlers (the latter is temporarily closed for renovation). All other campgrounds operate on a first-come, first-served basis.

⌂ Icefields Parkway

Camping

Columbia Icefield Tent Campground CAMPGROUND $
(Icefields Pkwy; tent sites C$15.70; ☺early Jun–mid-Oct) Jasper's sole tent-only campground, a mere 1.5km from the Columbia Icefield, is surprisingly welcoming despite its chilly high-country location and proximity to the tour bus hubbub. Its 33 first-come, first-served sites, including walk-in and disabled-accessible units, are relatively secluded from the parkway, in a forested setting by a rushing creek. Facilities are limited to dry toilets and drinking water.

Wabasso Campground CAMPGROUND $
(Map p156; www.reservation.pc.gc.ca; Hwy 93A; tent/RV sites C$21.50/27.40; ☺May–early Oct) This peaceful, remote campground sits 18km south of Jasper Town on Hwy 93A. Despite having 231 sites (including several with electrical hookups and/or wheelchair access), the grounds are spread out and fairly private. Walk-in tent sites along the river are wooded and lovely. Amenities include hot water and flush toilets, but no showers. Reserve ahead via the Parks Canada website.

JASPER NATIONAL PARK CAMPGROUNDS

CAMPGROUND	LOCATION	DESCRIPTION	NO OF SITES
Columbia Icefield	Icefields Parkway	Tents only and basic facilities, but campground is secluded and views are tremendous	33
Honeymoon Lake	Icefields Parkway	Small and quiet, with a handful of sites on lakeshore	35
Jonas Creek	Icefields Parkway	Close to highway with some seclusion if you choose the right site	25
Mt Kerkeslin	Icefields Parkway	Basic campground with sheltered sites close to Athabasca Falls	42
Wabasso	Icefields Parkway	Well-serviced but relatively remote campground off highway and close to Mt Edith Cavell hikes	231
Wilcox Creek	Icefields Parkway	Close to Columbia Icefield Centre and Wilcox Pass trailhead	46
Wapiti	Jasper Town & Around	Offers 40 serviced sites and showers; 93 sites stay open in winter	364
Whistlers	Jasper Town & Around	A mini-town with every facility imaginable; great for families	781
Pocahontas	North of Jasper Town	Quiet and wooded; close to eastern park entrance	140
Snaring River	North of Jasper Town	Rustic with no RVs; situated off highway 15km (9.5 miles) north of Jasper Town	62

	Drinking Water		Restrooms		Great for Families		Grocery Store Nearby

Honeymoon Lake Campground
CAMPGROUND $

(Map p156; Icefields Pkwy; tent & RV sites C$15.70; ⊙ mid-May–late Sep) With lake access, these rustic first-come, first-served sites are fairly popular. Sites 32, 33 and 35 are right next to the water, and the remaining 32 sites are mostly wooded and relatively large. Dry toilets and drinking water are the only home comforts, but the Sunwapta Falls Resort restaurant (p167) is only 4km to the south.

Mt Kerkeslin Campground
CAMPGROUND $

(Map p156; Icefields Pkwy; tent & RV sites C$15.70; ⊙ mid-May–Sep) Across from its towering namesake, this often overlooked campground offers 42 sheltered sites on a first-come, first-served basis. Facilities are limited to drinking water and dry toilets. Sites 5 through 9 have nice views towards the Athabasca River.

Wilcox Creek Campground
CAMPGROUND $

(Icefields Pkwy; tent & RV sites C$15.70; ⊙ early Jun–late Sep) Located at Jasper National Park's southern tip on the Icefields Pkwy beside the Wilcox Pass trailhead, this woodsy campground offers 46 first-come, first-served sites (some with disabled access) – but no other services beyond drinking water, a cooking shelter, dry toilets and a dump station.

Jonas Creek Campground
CAMPGROUND $

(Icefields Pkwy; tent & RV sites C$15.70; ⊙ mid-May–late Sep) The park's smallest campground has 25 first-come, first-served sites. Unserviced and with no electricity or dump station, it sits near a rushing creek and has an agreeably woodsy feel, despite its location just off the Icefields Pkwy.

Lodging

HI Mt Edith Cavell Wilderness Hostel
HOSTEL $

(Map p156; ☑ 780-852-3215; www.hihostels.ca; Cavell Rd; dm C$38; ⊙ reception 5-8pm mid-Feb–mid-Oct) ☑ Secluded down a dead-end road near the base of Mt Edith Cavell and the Angel Glacier, this rustic place has wood-burning stoves in each of its two 16-bunk cabins and in the propane-lit kitchen-common room, where guests play cards and

ELEVATION	OPEN	RESERVATIONS	DAILY FEE	FACILITIES	PAGE
2012m (6600ft)	Jun-Oct	no	C$15.70		p161
1310m (4300ft)	May-Sep	no	C$15.70		p162
1500m (4920ft)	May-Sep	no	C$15.70		p162
1200m (3936ft)	May-Sep	no	C$15.70		p162
1125m (3690ft)	May-Oct	advisable Jul & Aug	C$21.50-27.40		p161
2012m (6600ft)	Jun-Sep	no	C$15.70		p162
1070m (3510ft)	year-round	advisable Jul & Aug	C$27.40-32.30		p164
1070m (3510ft)	closed until 2021	advisable Jul & Aug	n/a		p164
1200m (3936ft)	May-Sep	advisable Jul & Aug	C$21.50		p166
1050m (3445ft)	May-Oct	no	C$15.70		p166

Restaurant Nearby · Payphone · Summertime Campfire Program · RV Dump Station

share stories of hikes to nearby Cavell Meadows and the remote Tonquin Valley (trailhead directly across the street).

HI Athabasca Falls Wilderness Hostel
HOSTEL $

(Map p156; www.hihostels.ca; Icefields Pkwy; dm C$38, private cabin for 2/4/6 people C$95/135/175; ⊙reception 5-9pm, closed Nov & Tue Dec-Apr) This hostel in the woods 1km down the Icefields Parkway from Athabasca Falls welcomes guests with a big alpine-style kitchen-sitting area, heated dorms in separate wooden cabins, and two private cabins sleeping up to six. There's no running water and the toilets are in outhouses, earning the place a 'rustic' tag – but other features compensate, including solar electricity.

HI Beauty Creek Wilderness Hostel
HOSTEL $

(www.hihostels.ca; Icefields Pkwy; dm C$38; ⊙staffed May–mid-Oct, unstaffed rest of year) As basic as it gets, with two small bunkrooms, a propane-powered communal kitchen and a teensy front-porch common room, Beauty Creek compensates for its minimal indoor space with a dreamy forested setting on the banks of the Sunwapta River. The riverside fire ring brings travelers together every evening, and the stargazing is, well, stellar.

Sunwapta Falls Rocky Mountain Lodge
HOTEL $$$

(Map p156; 780-852-4852; www.sunwapta.com; Icefields Pkwy; r C$259-319; P @) A welcome Icefields rest stop 53km south of Jasper Town, Sunwapta offers a comfortable mix of suites and lodge rooms, each with a fireplace or wood-burning stove, all just a stone's throw from Sunwapta Falls. Clean and comfortable but not fancy, it's got a good restaurant on-site serving breakfast and dinner, and a cafeteria that's popular with the tour-bus crowd.

Glacier View Lodge
HOTEL $$$

(888-770-6914; www.banffjaspercollection.com; Icefield Centre, Icefields Pkwy; d with mountain/glacier view C$489/519; ⊙mid-Apr–mid-Oct; P ☎) The panoramic perspectives over the glacier are unbelievable at this revamped hotel on the top floor of the Icefield Centre. Rooms have been given a total makeover, with loads

JASPER NATIONAL PARK SLEEPING

of Scandinavian-style blonde wood, while the lobby area sports plush chairs and a telescope for admiring spectacular views through the floor-to-ceiling windows.

🛏 Jasper Town & Around

Camping

Jasper's largest campground, **Whistlers** (Map p156; www.reservation.parkscanada.gc.ca; Whistlers Rd; P), has been undergoing a comprehensive renovation. When it reopens (scheduled for 2021, but check status with Parks Canada) it will boast a host of new facilities and hundreds of revamped campsites.

Wapiti Campground   CAMPGROUND $
(Map p156; www.reservation.pc.gc.ca; Hwy 93; tent/RV sites C$27.40/32.30; ⊙ year-round) Jasper's second-biggest campground (364 sites), and the only one currently open year-round, sits just 6km south of Jasper Town, linked by a handy walking-cycling path. Clean, well-maintained toilet and shower facilities are a given here, but Wapiti's main draw is its location on the banks of the Athabasca River. From October through April, 93 sites remain open for winter camping.

Lodging

⭐**HI Jasper**   HOSTEL $
(☑ 587-870-2395; www.hihostels.ca; 708 Sleepy Hollow Rd, Jasper Town; dm/d from C$50/167; P @ ⓢ) 🌱 Jasper's 157-bed HI hostel, opened two blocks from downtown in 2019 to replace the aging Whistlers Mountain facility, is a gem. The sprawling lower level houses a bevy of bright, welcoming common spaces – a guest kitchen and dining area complete with cozy booth seating, pool table, cafe, laundry facilities, free parking with EV charging stations, and more.

Upstairs, pairs of four-bed dorms share their own shower, toilet and sink area, while family rooms, private quads and wheelchair-accessible units are also available. There's excellent wi-fi throughout, along with individual reading lights and charging stations above each bed. A potential downside for light sleepers are the train tracks right outside the back windows – though romantics may appreciate the occasional lonesome locomotive whistle and the families of elk that sometimes bed down in the field across the street.

Jasper Downtown Hostel   HOSTEL $
(Map p158; ☑ 780-852-2000; www.jasperdown townhostel.ca; 400 Patricia St, Jasper Town; dm/d from C$45/140; ⓢ) With Jasper's town center smack on its doorstep, this former residence has been remodeled and expanded to create simple, modern two- to 10-bed dorms, many with en suite bathrooms, along with comfortable private rooms sleeping one to three. Upstairs rooms are brighter, with wooden floors, while common areas include a well-equipped kitchen, a spacious front patio and a simple lounge.

Athabasca Hotel   HOTEL $$
(Map p158; ☑ 780-852-3386; www.athabasca hotel.com; 510 Patricia St, Jasper Town; r without/with bath C$139/239, 1-/2-bedroom ste C$395/425; P @ ⓢ) Around since 1929, the Atha-B (as it's known) is the best budget hotel in town. A taxidermist's dream, with animal heads crowding the lobby, it has small, clean rooms with wooden and brass furnishings and thick, wine-colored carpets. Less expensive rooms share a bathroom. Dated but not worn, it feels like you're staying at Grandma's (if Grandma liked to hunt).

⭐**Tekarra Lodge**   HOTEL $$$
(☑ 780-852-3058; www.tekarralodge.com; Hwy 93A; lodge/cabins from C$249/289; ⊙ May-Oct; P ⓢ 🐾) In business since 1947, these cabins – some of the most atmospheric in the park – sit 1km south of town near the Athabasca River amid tall trees and splendid tranquility. Hardwood floors, wood-paneled walls plus stone fireplaces and kitchenettes inspire coziness. Family-friendly amenities abound, including an on-site playground, evening s'mores and songs by the campfire, bike rentals and a guest laundry.

⭐**Patricia Lake Bungalows**   BUNGALOW $$$
(Map p156; ☑ 780-852-3560; www.patricialake bungalows.com; Patricia Lake Rd; bungalows C$199-510) Reminiscent of an earlier era, this charming assemblage of bungalows sits placidly at the end of a dead-end road on the shores of lovely Patricia Lake, 5km north of Jasper Town. Owned by the same family for nearly half a century, it's the kind of place where you can truly leave the modern world (and the summer crowds) behind.

Cozy up with a good book in one of the red Adirondack chairs looking out at the lake, rent a canoe, kayak or rowboat, or simply settle in for a game of cards and a home-cooked lakeside dinner with your family.

Fairmont Jasper Park Lodge HOTEL **$$$**
(☑780-852-3301; www.fairmont.com/jasper; 1
Old Lodge Rd, Jasper Town; r from C$529; P@⌂)
Sitting on the shore of Lac Beauvert and sur-
rounded by manicured grounds and moun-
tain peaks, this classic old lodge can't quite
match the panache of the Banff and Lake
Louise Fairmonts, although you'll bump into
fewer afternoon-tea-seeking tourists. With a
country-club-meets-1950s-holiday-camp air,
the amenity-filled cabins and chalets are a
throwback to a more opulent era.

The lodge's highlight is its monumental
Emerald Lounge, open to the public and
backed by stupendous lake views. It's filled
with log furniture, chandeliers and fireplac-
es and is the best place in town to write a
postcard over a quiet cocktail. There are of-
ten discounts in the off-season.

Alpine Village CABIN **$$$**
(☑780-852-3285; www.alpinevillagejasper.com;
Athabasca Rd; 2-/4-person cabins from C$230/460;
⊙May-Oct; P⌂) Alpine Village's 58
well-maintained log cabins in a variety of
configurations are a cut above the competition, with an ace location across from the
Athabasca River. Enjoy the tranquility –

BACKCOUNTRY HUTS & LODGES

Jasper offers a handful of huts and lodges modeled on the European alpine tradition. All
situated a good day's hike from the nearest road, these venerable backcountry retreats
offer a unique wilderness experience without the hassle of setting up your tent or listening to things that go bump in the night.

Huts

The Alpine Club of Canada maintains three rustic backcountry huts in Jasper National
Park. For each hut, you must bring your own bedding, food, matches, toilet paper and
dishcloth, and must pack out all of your garbage. Reservations are required (C$30 for
ACC members, C$40 for nonmembers) and can be made through the Alpine Club's
headquarters in Canmore (p269). You are also required to have a Parks Canada wilderness pass.

Wates-Gibson Hut (Tonquin Valley) This beautiful log cabin was built in 1959 and
has 26 bunk beds, a wood-burning stove, sleeping mattresses and a propane-powered
cooking system (utensils available). In summer you can hike here via the 18km (11.2-
mile) Astoria River Trail from the Mt Edith Cavell Wilderness Hostel. Add on another 12km
(7.5 miles) in winter when the Mt Edith Cavell Rd is closed.

Mt Colin Centennial Hut (Colin Range) Used mainly by climbers, this six-bed hut is
accessed by a demanding five- to seven-hour hike off the Overlander Trail. It has a Coleman stove, mattresses and cooking utensils, and is closed from November through May.

Sydney Vallance (Fryatt) Hut Situated 24km (15 miles) up the Fryatt Valley from the
Icefields Pkwy, this is perhaps the most isolated of the huts. It's open year-round, offers
12 beds and facilities include propane cooking and lighting, and a wood-heating stove.

Lodges

In Tonquin Valley, approximately 24km (15 miles) west of the closest road near the
Alberta–British Columbia border, Tonquin Valley Backcountry Lodge (Map p156;
☑780-852-3909; www.tonquinvalley.com; per person incl meals summer/winter C$325/185;
⊙mid-Feb–Mar & Jul–mid-Sep) provides rustic accommodations in historic cabins with
views of Amethyst Lake and the rugged Ramparts. The lodge runs multiday horseback
riding treks in summer, or you can hike in on your own; in winter experienced backcountry skiers can also ski in to the lodge.

Built in 1921 and rebuilt in 1991, the Shovel Pass Lodge (Map p156; ☑780-852-4215;
www.skylinetrail.com; per person incl meals C$255; ⊙late Jun-early Sep), situated halfway
along the emblematic Skyline Trail, is the oldest lodge in the park. With seven guest
cabins plus a main chalet and dining room, the lodge can accommodate up to 18 people. Meals, bed linen and propane lights and heating are provided, though you'll have to
bring your own towel. The price includes three meals daily. It's open June to September;
reserve in advance.

you're just outside the hubbub of town, but close enough to walk. Cabins have plush, country-style decor, with mezzanine bedrooms, renovated bathrooms and stone fireplaces. The nearest neighbors are usually elk.

Pyramid Lake Resort HOTEL **$$$**
(Map p156; ☎587-802-3644; www.mpljasper.com/hotels/pyramid-lake-resort; Pyramid Lake Rd; d from C$273; P 📶 🐾) These chalet-style rooms 6km northwest of Jasper town have fantastic front-row views of Pyramid Lake and great access to it. Rooms have slightly dated decor but many sport balconies and fireplaces. Opportunities for lakeside fun abound, with rental canoes, kayaks and bikes and a small beach to hang out on. There's also a fitness room, hot tub, shop and restaurant.

Park Place Inn BOUTIQUE HOTEL **$$$**
(Map p158; ☎780-852-9770; www.parkplaceinn.com; 623 Patricia St, Jasper Town; r C$249-289; @ 📶) Its ordinary exterior among a parade of downtown shops gives nothing away, but the Park Place starts looking more promising as soon as you ascend the stairs to the open lobby. This building held Parks Canada offices until 2002, and its 14 renovated heritage rooms are elegant, with gleaming wooden floors, claw-foot or Jacuzzi tubs and a general air of refinement and luxury.

Mount Robson Inn MOTEL **$$$**
(☎780-852-3327; www.mountrobsoninn.com; 902 Connaught Dr, Jasper Town; r incl breakfast from C$310; P ❄ @ 📶) This plush option on the western edge of Jasper Town offers everything from sleek queen rooms to family and Jacuzzi suites, along with two outdoor hot tubs and a substantial complimentary breakfast. The overall vibe is rather motel-like, but it wins points for comfort and for its convenient location between the town center and the Icefields Parkway.

WHEN THERE'S NO ROOM AT THE INN

Jasper gets seriously busy in July and August, and finding a room on the spur of the moment can be extremely difficult. Fortunately, aside from the standard clutch of hotels, motels and campgrounds, Jasper Town – which has a permanent population of 4500 – has over 100 B&Bs in private houses. The Jasper Home Accommodations Association (www.stayinjasper.com) maintains an excellent website of inspected B&Bs inside the park, complete with descriptions, contact details and web links. Prices range from C$75 to C$275 in high season and facilities often include kitchenettes, private entrances and cable TV.

Maligne Lake Area

HI Maligne Canyon Wilderness Hostel HOSTEL **$**
(Map p156; www.hihostels.ca; Maligne Lake Rd; dm C$38; ⏲reception 5-9pm, closed Apr & Wed Nov-Mar; P) 🌿 Well positioned for winter cross-country skiing and summer sorties along Maligne Canyon or the Skyline Trail, this very basic hostel is a little close to the road, but thankfully the river next to it drowns out any noise. Fans of rustic living will appreciate the six-bed dorms, outhouse toilets, small cookhouse, frequent bear sightings and friendly long-time hostel manager.

North of Jasper Town

Camping

Pocahontas Campground CAMPGROUND **$**
(Map p156; www.reservation.pc.gc.ca; Miette Hot Springs Rd; tent & RV sites C$21.50; ⏲mid-May–late Sep) If you didn't know, you'd never guess this spacious and densely wooded place near the park's eastern edge has 140 sites. Facilities are minimal, albeit with flush toilets and wheelchair-accessible sites, but it's well maintained. Reserve ahead through the Parks Canada website.

Snaring River Campground CAMPGROUND **$**
(Map p156; Hwy 16; tent & RV sites C$15.70; ⏲mid-May–early Oct; P) This basic campground – the park's most primitive and isolated – has 62 first-come, first-served sites and offers a perfect antidote to the busy campgrounds elsewhere in the park. Riverside sites offer lovely valley views. The minimal amenities include a communal cooking shelter, dry toilets, fire pits and picnic tables. It's 15km north of Jasper Town.

Lodging

Pocahontas Cabins CABIN, RESORT **$$**
(Map p156; ☎587-802-1499; www.mpljasper.com/hotels/pocahontas-cabins; cnr Hwy 16 & Miette Hot Springs Rd; cabins from C$197; 🏊 🐾) Once a

thriving mining community, Pocahontas now consists of this roadside resort, equipped with a restaurant, hot tub, outdoor swimming pool and small grocery store. Clean and comfortable cabins, many with kitchens, are supplemented by basic motel units and more luxurious suites in the classy Cedar Lodge. The Pioneer and Settler's cabins are older, more basic and only open seasonally.

Miette Hot Springs Bungalows CABIN $$
(Map p156; ☑ 780-866-3750; www.miettebungalows.com; Miette Hot Springs Rd; r/chalets/cabins from C$135/165/235; ℗) This low-key 'resort' at the hot springs is a collection of old fashioned but charming log cabins and motel rooms dating from 1938, and chalets from the 1970s. Cabins sleep up to six and have kitchenettes and stone fireplaces (some of the 17 motel rooms also have kitchenettes). The restaurant has reasonably priced standard meals. Bears regularly meander through the grounds.

✖ EATING

While Jasper's culinary scene is far from the bright lights of Calgary and Edmonton, you'll still find plenty to tempt your taste buds. Outside of the small cluster of sterile fast-food franchises and the usual cache of post-hike refueling joints, fine diners can travel the world on cosmopolitan Patricia St, touching down in such exotic locales as Jamaica, Thailand, Italy and Greece.

✖ Icefields Parkway

Sunwapta Falls Rocky Mountain Lodge CANADIAN $$$
(Map p156; ☑ 780-852-4852; www.sunwapta.com /restaurant; Icefields Pkwy; breakfast C$12-18, dinner mains C$25-43; ⊙ 7-11am & 6-9pm May-Nov) With its stone fireplace, plank floors and white tablecloths, this roadside lodge's dining room makes an atmospheric spot for breakfast or dinner (just ignore that it's tucked in between a gift shop and a cafeteria). The locally driven menu features dishes like herb-crusted wild sockeye salmon, slow-roasted chicken with mashed potatoes, or beef and pork pot pie with maple-glazed root vegetables.

The adjacent deli serves breakfast, lunch and dinner cafeteria-style (C$10 to C$15).

✖ Jasper Town & Around

Patricia Street Deli SANDWICHES $
(Map p158; ☑ 780-852-4814; www.facebook.com/ patriciastreetdeli; 610 Patricia St, Jasper Town; sandwiches C$9.50-12; ⊙ 10am-7pm) Come to the Patricia Street Deli hungry – really hungry. Homemade bread is made into generously filled sandwiches by people who are just as generous with their smiles and hiking tips. Choose from a huge list of fillings, including various pestos, chutneys, veggies and meat cuts. Join the queue and satiate your ravenous backcountry appetite.

Wicked Cup CAFE $
(☑ 780-852-1942; www.wickedcup.ca; 912 Connaught Dr; mains C$11-16; ⊙ 7am-2:30pm Mon-Thu, to 5pm Fri-Sun; 🛜) Hidden on the west edge of town, Wicked Cup is one of Jasper's friendliest and coziest places for a bite. Choose between sit-down breakfasts on the dining-room side or all-day sandwiches, flatbreads, soups, smoothies, mixed drinks – and yes, wicked good coffee – in the cafe and front patio area next door. Dependable free wi-fi is just another reason to linger.

The Spice Joint JAMAICAN $
(Map p158; ☑ 780-852-3615; www.facebook.com /TheSpiceJoint; 614 Connaught Dr, Jasper Town; mains C$12-16; ⊙ 10am-9pm) Since opening in 2018, this friendly snack shack decked out in red, yellow and green has brought a welcome dose of Caribbean flavor to Jasper's northern wilds. The menu revolves around Jamaican treats like spicy jerk chicken, barbecued pork, Rasta greens and quinoa salad, all accompanied by fruit smoothies, ginger beer, rum, Red Stripe beer and Blue Mountain coffee.

Bear's Paw Bakery BAKERY $
(Map p158; ☑ 780-852-3233; www.bearspaw bakery.com; 4 Pyramid Lake Rd, Jasper Town; baked goods C$1-8; ⊙ 6am-6pm) Jasper's go-to bakery-cafe is right downtown where you need it most at the end of an energy-sapping activity. The menu features scones, cookies, muffins, focaccia-like breads and super-sweet sticky buns (*too* sweet or just right? – it's your call). The coffee is equally gratifying. Its sister branch opposite the train station, the Other Paw (Map p158; ☑ 780-852-2253; www.bearspawbakery.com; 610 Connaught Dr, Jasper Town; mains C$5-13; ⊙ 7am-6pm), sells similar bakery items plus a wider variety of soups and sandwiches.

AROUND JASPER NATIONAL PARK

Jasper National Park is buffered by additional protected zones to the north and west (Banff National Park borders it to the south). To the west – and in British Columbia – is Mt Robson Provincial Park, home of the Canadian Rockies' highest summit and the headwaters of the mighty Fraser River. To the north and lying wholly within Alberta, Willmore Wilderness Park lures travelers with a penchant for total solitude. To the southwest lies the roadless Hamber Provincial Park, currently inaccessible from Jasper due to a collapsed bridge along the Fortress Lake Trail off the Icefields Pkwy.

Mt Robson Provincial Park

Bordering Jasper National Park in the west and flanked by the Selwyn Range, the drive through Mt Robson Provincial Park follows a historic pathway of fur traders. Rejected by the Canadian Pacific Railway as a route through the Rockies, it was later adopted by Grand Trunk Pacific and Canadian Northern Pacific Railways and is today a major railway route. The views of snowy mountains and glacial lakes are magnificent.

Bisected by Hwy 16 on its way between Jasper and Prince George, **Mt Robson Provincial Park** (☑ 250-964-2243; www.env.gov.bc.ca/bcparks; off Hwy 16) abuts Jasper National Park at the Yellowhead Pass, 24km (15 miles) west of Jasper Town. Covering 2249 sq km (868 sq miles), the park's main hub is an excellent information center near the western border. Here you can pick up trail information, register for hikes with BC Parks staff and take in exhibits on local geography and history – including a short interpretive trail. You'll also find a gas station and cafe situated next door. On clear days the neck-craning views of ice-glazed Mt Robson, glowering like a fiery beacon overhead, are truly amazing.

The tallest mountain in the Canadian Rockies, **Mt Robson**, in British Columbia, towers like a misplaced Everest over the surrounding peaks and valleys, dwarfing other rugged giants in its 3954m (12,969ft) shadow. Approaching from the east, no words can prepare you for the sight of its craggy southern face, which rises like a vertical wall over 2439m (8000ft) above Berg Lake. Visible for less than 14 days a year, the mountain has left onlookers awestruck for centuries; Indigenous people called it 'Mountain of the Spiral Road' and trappers and explorers revered it as unconquerable. It wasn't until 1913 that the mountain was first officially climbed and, even today, only approximately 10% of summit attempts are successful.

Hiking is what draws most visitors to the park. The famous 22km (13.7-mile) **Berg Lake Trail** takes you through the Valley of a Thousand Falls, next to Mt Robson and past

Robinsons Foods SUPERMARKET $
(Map p158; ☑ 780-852-3195; www.robinsonfoods .com; 218 Connaught Dr; ☺ 8am-10pm May-Oct, to 8pm Nov-Apr) Jasper's best supermarket is a great place to shop for trail snacks, picnic supplies or a self-catering dinner – and prices are surprisingly reasonable for a tourist town.

Olive Bistro MEDITERRANEAN $$
(Map p158; ☑ 780-852-5222; www.olivebistro.ca; Pyramid Lake Rd, Jasper Town; mains C$14-35; ☺ 4-10pm May-Oct, 5-9pm Nov-Apr; ☑) This casual restaurant with big booths has a classy menu. Main dishes such as slow-braised organic lamb shank, elk rigatoni or a vegan 'dragon bowl' come sandwiched between appetizers of white truffle scallops and indulgent desserts like a gourmet banana split. In summer, enjoy excellent cocktails during the 4pm to 6pm happy hour; in winter, there's live music twice monthly.

Something Else MEDITERRANEAN $$
(Map p158; ☑ 780-852-3850; www.something elserestaurant.com; 621 Patricia St, Jasper Town; mains C$16-40; ☺ 11am-11pm) A long-standing Jasper favorite founded by a family from northwestern Greece, Something Else wears many hats (steakhouse, Italian, Cajun) but at its core remains authentically Greek. High points include its spacious interior (large enough to accommodate a crowd even on Saturday night), decent beer, copious kids' options and tasty homemade Mediterranean classics like tzatziki, lamb or chicken souvlaki and baklava.

the stunning, glacier-fed lake itself, filled with shorn-off chunks of ice. You must register to undertake the hike, which takes two to three days. Seven backcountry campgrounds are located en route (C$10 per person, per night); reservations for the peak hiking season (mid-May through September) can be made starting on October 1 of the preceding year at www.discovercamping.ca. For more information, see www.env.gov.bc.ca/bcparks/reserve/berg-lake-trail.

For those with less time, the first segment of the Berg Lake Trail (bikes allowed) can be taken as far as the Kinney Lake picnic site and viewpoint at 9km (5.6 miles). Look out for mountain goats, black bears, caribou and porcupine. Alternatively, you can heli-hike; that is, take a helicopter to the Berg Lake area and hike out. For details enquire with Robson Helimagic (www.robsonhelimagic.com).

Boating is popular within the park, although fishing isn't particularly good. Launch your boat in the green waters of Moose or Yellowhead Lakes. Rearguard Falls, just west of the information center, is known for its salmon viewing (mid-August to early September).

On the western border of the park **Mt Robson Mountain River Lodge** (☑ 250-566-9899; www.mtrobson.com; cnr Hwy 16 & Swift Current Creek Rd, Mt Robson; lodges/cabins from C$150/180; ℗ ☻ 🛜) commands stunning views of the eponymous giant peak. There's a main building and a couple of cabins that share a cozy, away-from-it-all atmosphere.

Willmore Wilderness Park

Spreading across the foothills and mountain ranges north of Jasper National Park, **Willmore Wilderness Park** (www.albertaparks.ca/parks/central/willmore) has more wildlife passing through it than people. If you really want to get off the beaten track, consider the 750km (466 miles) of trails crossing this park. Access is by foot only from Rock Lake, Big Berland or Grande Cache. At 95km (59 miles), Mountain Trail is the longest and most continuous route through the park, from Rock Lake to Grande Cache. The scenic 33km (20.5-mile) Indian Trail is popular for hunting and wildlife watching and is in better condition than many of the other trails.

Very little trail maintenance is done here, and while there are designated camping areas, you'll find nothing at them. Water is from lakes and rivers only and must be treated before you consume it. Permits to hike or camp in the park are not required. Be sure to tell someone where you're going and when to expect you back, and be prepared to deal with any emergencies or wildlife you meet on the trail.

Papa George's
AMERICAN **$$**

(Map p158; ☑ 780-852-2260; www.papageorgesjasper.com; 404 Connaught Dr, Jasper Town; breakfast C$9.50-18.50, lunch mains C$12-17, dinner mains C$24-37; ☺ 7am-2pm & 5-10pm; ☑) Almost as old as the park, this stalwart has been in business since 1925, and something about the original rock fireplace, salt-of-the-earth service and comfort food with no surprises still rings true. The menu takes the word 'local' seriously, with elk stroganoff, venison tournedos and wild-boar chops.

★ Raven Bistro
MEDITERRANEAN **$$$**

(Map p158; ☑ 780-852-5151; www.theravenbistro.com; 504 Patricia St, Jasper Town; lunch mains C$16-27, dinner mains C$28-46; ☺ 11:30am-11pm; ☑) This cozy, tastefully designed bistro offers vegetarian dishes, encourages shared plates and earns a loyal clientele with sublime offerings like Kaffir lime–coconut seafood pot or lamb shank glazed with fresh mint, horseradish, honey and Dijon mustard. Not in a lunch-dinner mood? Try the 'late riser' breakfast skillet, or come for happy hour (3pm to 5:30pm daily).

★ Maligne Canyon Wilderness Kitchen
BARBECUE **$$$**

(Map p156; ☑ 844-762-6713; www.banffjaspercollection.com; Maligne Canyon Rd; lunch mains C$16-26, dinner C$55; ☺ 8am-10pm May-Sep, 9am-4pm Sun-Fri, to 10pm Sat Oct-Apr) The outdoor deck at the edge of gorgeous Maligne Canyon is temptation enough to dine at Jasper's newest restaurant. But the real clincher is the cornucopia of local meats, shown off to full advantage in the house special Maligne

Canyon Platter: grilled venison sausage, smoked chicken, glazed baby back pork ribs, and barbecue Alberta beef brisket slow-cooked for 16 hours.

Side dishes are equally scrumptious, from mac and cheese to memorable parsley fries. Prices are more affordable at lunchtime, when simpler fare like Alberta pulled-pork sandwiches.

Evil Dave's Grill FUSION $$$
(Map p158; ☑780-852-3323; www.evildavesgrill.com; 622 Patricia St, Jasper Town; mains C$20-40; ☺5-10pm Mon-Fri, from 4pm Sat & Sun) There's nothing evil about Dave's, other than its attempts to bury Jasper's image as a bastion of family-friendly, post-hiking grub that fills stomachs rather than excites taste buds. The excellent fusion food comes from all over the map, with Caribbean, Middle Eastern and Japanese influences lighting up the fish and beef. Save room for the deadly desserts.

🍷 DRINKING & ENTERTAINMENT

🍷 Jasper Town & Around

★**SnowDome Coffee Bar** COFFEE
(Map p158; ☑780-852-3852; http://snowdome.coffee; 607 Patricia St, Jasper Town; ☺7am-8pm; 🛜) Some of Jasper's best damn coffee is – no joke! – served at this former Coin Clean Laundry, now reincarnated as a cafe-gallery-community hangout. Beyond the stellar espresso, SnowDome bakes killer muffins (still oven-warm at opening time) and promotes good karma with its free mug basket and 'pay it forward' bulletin board where you can prepurchase coffee for a future customer.

Jasper Brewing Co BREWERY
(Map p158; ☑780-852-4111; www.jasperbrewing co.ca; 624 Connaught Dr, Jasper Town; ☺11:30am-1am) 🍺 This brewpub was the first of its kind in a Canadian national park, using glacial water to make its fine ales, including the signature Rockhopper IPA and Jasper the Bear honey beer. It's a perennial favorite hangout for locals and tourists alike, with TVs and a good food menu.

Downstream Lounge BAR
(Map p158; ☑780-852-9449; www.facebook.com/DSjasper; 620 Connaught Dr, Jasper Town; ☺5pm-

2am) This is likely the best-stocked bar in town, with a wide array of whiskeys, vodkas and other alcoholic indulgences – and a bar staff who know how to use them. There's some awesome food to keep your head above water and, often, live music.

Chaba Cinema CINEMA
(Map p158; ☑780-852-4749; 604 Connaught Dr, Jasper Town) A first-run cinema is a rarity in a Canadian national park, so make the most of the popcorn, pop and dating potential at this quaint two-screen affair.

🍷 North of Jasper Town

Folding Mountain Taproom MICROBREWERY
(Map p156; ☑780-817-6287; www.foldingmountain.com; 49321 Hwy 16, Jasper East; ☺11am-10pm) This up-and-coming microbrewery draws a boisterous mix of locals from nearby Hinton and travelers heading to or from the wilderness. Test the waters with a four-beer sampler (choose from Flash Flood IPA, Alpine Cranberry Sour or a dozen other brews on tap), then stick around for excellent burgers, salads and other pub grub. It's just 5km outside Jasper's eastern park gate.

ℹ️ Information

DANGERS & ANNOYANCES

Jasper's biggest dangers – weather, rugged backcountry terrain, wildlife and avalanches – can all be minimized with common sense and planning. Always check trail, weather and wildlife conditions before venturing into the wilderness – even on a day hike – and prepare for fickle weather on trails and roadways any time of year.

MEDICAL SERVICES & EMERGENCY

For emergencies dial ☑911. The 24-hour park warden can be contacted at ☑780-852-6155.
Cottage Medical Clinic (☑780-852-4885; 300 Miette Ave, Jasper Town; ☺8:30am-4pm Mon-Fri) Non-emergency medical assistance on weekdays only.
Seton General Hospital (☑780-852-3344; 518 Robson St; ☺24hr) Round-the-clock emergency care in the heart of town.

MONEY

CIBC (416 Connaught Dr, Jasper Town; ☺bank 9:30am-5pm Mon-Fri, ATM 24hr)

POST

Post Office (Map p158; 502 Patricia St, Jasper Town; ☺9am-5pm Mon-Fri)

TELEPHONE

Cell (mobile) phone reception is patchy to non-existent, especially once you leave Jasper Town. Some park hotels, lodges and nonprimitive campgrounds have public phones. Courtesy phones (local calls only) are located in Jasper Town's visitor center.

TOURIST INFORMATION

Columbia Icefield Discovery Centre (p147) Directly opposite the toe of the Athabasca Glacier, the massive green-roofed Icefield Centre serves as the ticket office and tour departure point for the Columbia Icefield Adventure (p155) and Skywalk (p155). It also houses a hotel, cafeteria, restaurant, gift shop and Parks Canada information desk. It's a bit of a zoo in the summer, with tour coaches cramming the car park.

Parks Canada Has two locations, one at the **Jasper Information Centre** (Map p158; ☑ 780-852-6176; www.pc.gc.ca/jasper; 500 Connaught Dr, Jasper Town; ⊙ 9am-7pm mid-May–early Oct, to 5pm rest of year), a beautiful historic building in Jasper Town dating to 1913, and another 103km (64 miles) south at the **Columbia Icefield Discovery Centre** (☑ 780-852-6288; www.pc.gc.ca/pn-np/ab/jasper; ⊙ 10:15am-5pm mid-May–Sep).

Tourism Jasper (☑ 780-852-6236; www.jasper.travel; 500 Connaught Dr, Jasper Town; ⊙ 9am-7pm mid-May–early Oct, to 5pm rest of year) Adjacent to the Parks Canada downtown office, Jasper's municipal tourist office offers a wealth of information about area activities and accommodations.

❶ Getting There & Away

Most people arrive in Jasper by car, via the three main roads that connect the park to Lake Louise (south), Edmonton (east) and British Columbia (west), the VIA Rail train offers a scenic, adventurous alternative way to reach Jasper Town.

BUS

SunDog (☑ 780-852-4056; www.sundogtours.com; 414 Connaught Dr, Jasper Town; ⊙ 8am-5pm) offers year-round daily bus service to Edmonton airport (C$99, 5½ hours).

Lake Louise, Banff and Calgary are served by SunDog in winter and **Brewster Express** (☑ 877-625-4372; www.banffjaspercollection.com/brewster-express) in summer. From late October through April, SunDog makes the journey, stopping at Lake Louise (C$69, four hours), Banff Town (C$79, five hours) and Calgary airport (C$135, seven hours). From May through mid-October, Brewster Express takes over, running its own daily express bus to Lake Louise (C$97, 3½ hours), Banff (C$120, 4¾ hours), Canmore (C$144, 5¾ hours) and Calgary International Airport (C$167, eight hours).

Bus travel to other destinations was discontinued when Greyhound sharply curtailed its Canadian services in late 2018.

TRAIN

From Jasper Town, **VIA Rail** (☑ 888-842-7245; www.viarail.ca) runs three weekly trains to Vancouver (from C$148, 23½ hours) and Edmonton (from C$97, 6¼ hours), along with two to Toronto (from C$367, 72 hours).

There's also a tri-weekly service to Prince Rupert, BC (from C$156, 33 hours, with obligatory overnight stop in Prince George). Call or check VIA's website for exact details.

❶ Getting Around

Although most people get around the park by private vehicle, with a bit of patience and flexibility, carless travel is possible.

BICYCLE

With numerous bike outlets in Jasper, it's easy to rent a bike to get you around the town and its main sights. Alternatively, you can bring your own.

The park also has one of the most extensive bike-trail networks in Canada. Wide highways with ample shoulders and strict speed limits make road biking easy. The truck-free Icefields Pkwy south to Lake Louise and Banff is a particularly popular ride.

BUS

Brewster buses stop at the Columbia Icefield Centre daily in summer (May to October) on their Jasper–Banff run.

SunDog Tour Company runs shuttles to the Jasper Skytram and many other parts of the park, but to use them you'll generally have to sign up for one of their sightseeing tours. See the website for details.

The Maligne Valley Hikers Express Shuttle (p278) runs daily from Jasper Town to Maligne Lake, stopping en route at Maligne Canyon and the Skyline trailhead (north and south).

CAR & MOTORCYCLE

Speed limits in the park are 90km/h (56mph) on major roads and 30km/h to 60km/h (19mph to 37mph) on secondary roads. Motorists should regularly scan for wildlife either on or crossing the road, and watch for other cars stopping or slowing down to view wildlife.

Jasper Town has a number of gas stations, most along Connaught Dr. Car rental is available at the VIA railway station with National.

TAXI

Caribou Cabs (☑ 780-931-2334; www.facebook.com/cariboucabs) and **Jasper Taxi** (☑ 780-852-3600) offer dependable taxi service; call to arrange pickup.

Glacier National Park

Best Hikes

➡ Highline Trail (p178)

➡ Dawson–Pitamakan Loop (p182)

➡ Iceberg Lake Trail (p183)

➡ Hidden Lake Overlook Trail (p176)

Best Places to Stay

➡ Many Glacier Hotel (p198)

➡ Sperry Chalet (p200)

➡ Lake McDonald Lodge (p196)

➡ Swiftcurrent Motor Inn (p199)

Why Go?

Few places on earth are as magnificent and pristine as Glacier. Protected in 1910 during the first flowering of the American conservationist movement, Glacier ranks with Yellowstone, Yosemite and the Grand Canyon among the United States' most astounding natural wonders.

The glacially carved remnants of an ancient thrust fault have left us a brilliant landscape of towering snowcapped pinnacles laced with plunging waterfalls and glassy turquoise lakes. The mountains are surrounded by dense forests. Grizzly bears still roam in abundance and smart park management has kept the place accessible and authentically wild.

Glacier is renowned for its historic 'parkitecture' lodges, the spectacular Going-to-the-Sun Rd and 740 miles of hiking trails. These all put visitors within easy reach of some 1489 sq miles of the wild and astonishing landscapes found at the crown of the continent.

Road Distance (KM)

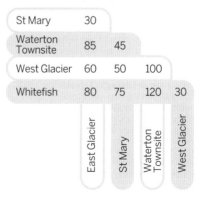

	East Glacier	St Mary	Waterton Townsite	West Glacier
St Mary	30			
Waterton Townsite	85	45		
West Glacier	60	50	100	
Whitefish	80	75	120	30

Note: Distances are approximate

Entrances

Glacier National Park has seven official entrance gates. The two busiest are the West Entrance, just north of West Glacier, and the East Entrance, near St Mary at the opposite end of the iconic Going-to-the-Sun Rd. The other entrances are the Camas Creek Entrance and the Polebridge Ranger Station, both off the Outside North Fork Rd on the park's western side; the Two Medicine Entrance (on Two Medicine Rd, west of Hwy 49); the Many Glacier Entrance (on Many Glacier Rd, west of Hwy 89); and the lesser known Cut Bank Entrance (off Hwy 89, betweeen Two Medicine and St Mary), all on the eastern side.

Boards at entrances indicate which park campgrounds are open or full.

DON'T MISS

Glacier's classic 'parkitecture' lodges – Many Glacier Hotel, Lake McDonald Lodge and Glacier Park Lodge – are living, breathing, functioning artifacts of another – more leisurely – era, when travelers to this wilderness park arrived by train and ventured into the backcountry on horseback. These early 20th-century creations were built with Swiss-chalet features and prototypical Wild West elements. Today they seem to consciously and appealingly conjure up a romantic, almost mythic, vision of rustic comfort – ideal reflections of the beautiful scenery on their doorsteps.

Glacier Park Lodge (p210) sits just outside the park's boundaries, in charming East Glacier, while Lake McDonald Lodge (p193) and Many Glacier Hotel (p198) are both situated within the park on the shores of stunning alpine lakes. The former property is an easy stop while traveling the iconic Going-to-the-Sun Rd and the latter is ensconced in what long-time visitors consider the heart of the park, with nearby trailheads for several of the park's most stunning day and overnight hikes.

When You Arrive

➡ Glacier National Park is open year-round. Entry per car or RV costs $35. People arriving on foot or bicycle pay $20 and those on motorcycle pay $30 per person. In winter, fees are reduced. Both tickets are valid for seven days. Entrance fees are reduced in winter. Fees for Glacier do not include entrance to Waterton Lakes National Park.

➡ Staff at the entrance stations hand out free detailed Glacier & Waterton Lakes National Parks maps, a quarterly newspaper, and the Glacier Explorer, a schedule of events and activities, including ranger-led day trips.

PLANNING TIP

Backcountry camping permits cost US$7 per adult per night, or US$40 with advance reservation online (www.pay.gov/public/form/start/74000984). Otherwise, they can be purchased from the Apgar Backcountry Office, St Mary Visitor Center or the Many Glacier, Two Medicine Valley and Polebridge ranger stations.

Fast Facts

Area 4099 sq km (1583 sq miles)

Highest elevation 3190m (10,466ft)

Lowest elevation 980m (3215ft)

Reservations

Glacier National Park operates 13 campgrounds. Sites at Fish Creek and St Mary Campgrounds can be reserved up to six months in advance, and five group sites at Apgar up to a year in advance. Book through **Recreation.gov** (☑800-365-2267; www.recreation.gov). All other campgrounds are first-come, first-served.

Resources

Glacier National Park (www.nps.gov/glac)

Glacier National Park Lodges (www.glaciernationalparklodges.com)

Glacier National Park

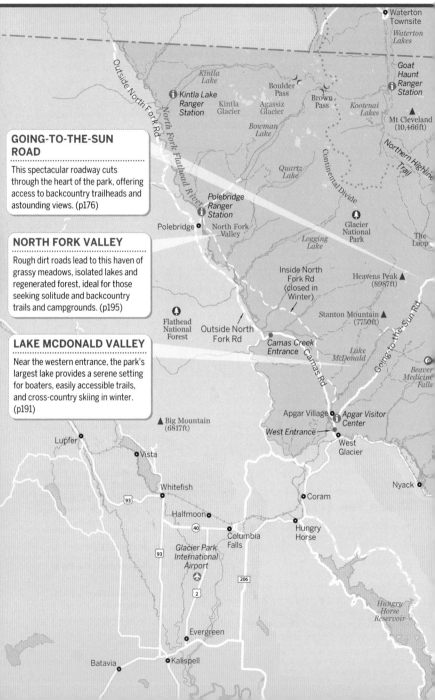

GOING-TO-THE-SUN ROAD

This spectacular roadway cuts through the heart of the park, offering access to backcountry trailheads and astounding views. (p176)

NORTH FORK VALLEY

Rough dirt roads lead to this haven of grassy meadows, isolated lakes and regenerated forest, ideal for those seeking solitude and backcountry trails and campgrounds. (p195)

LAKE MCDONALD VALLEY

Near the western entrance, the park's largest lake provides a serene setting for boaters, easily accessible trails, and cross-country skiing in winter. (p191)

Waterton
Townsite

Waterton
Lakes

Goat
Haunt
Ranger
Station

Kintla
Lake

Boulder
Pass

Brown
Pass

Kootenai
Lakes

Kintla Lake
Ranger
Station

Kintla
Glacier

Agassiz
Glacier

Mt Cleveland
(10,466ft)

Bowman
Lake

Northern Highline
Trail

North Fork Flathead River

Outside North Fork Rd

Quartz
Lake

Continental Divide

Polebridge
Ranger
Station

North Fork
Valley

Glacier
National
Park

Polebridge

Logging
Lake

The
Loop

Inside North
Fork Rd
(closed in
Winter)

Heavens Peak ▲
(8987ft)

Flathead
National
Forest

Outside North
Fork Rd

Stanton Mountain ▲
(7750ft)

Camas Creek
Entrance

Camas Rd

Lake
McDonald

Going-to-the-Sun Rd

Beaver
Medicine
Falls

▲ Big Mountain
(6817ft)

Apgar Village

Apgar Visitor
Center

Lupfer

West Entrance

West
Glacier

Vista

Nyack

Whitefish

93

Coram

Halfmoon

40

Columbia
Falls

Hungry
Horse

93

Glacier Park
International
Airport

206

2

Hungry
Horse
Reservoir

Evergreen

Batavia

Kalispell

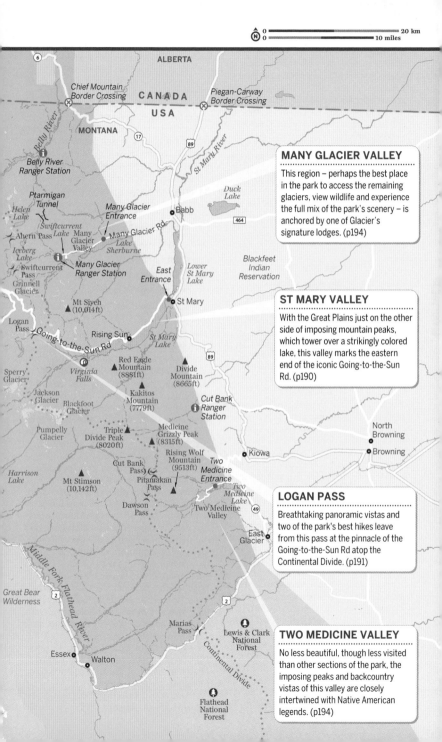

MANY GLACIER VALLEY

This region – perhaps the best place in the park to access the remaining glaciers, view wildlife and experience the full mix of the park's scenery – is anchored by one of Glacier's signature lodges. (p194)

ST MARY VALLEY

With the Great Plains just on the other side of imposing mountain peaks, which tower over a strikingly colored lake, this valley marks the eastern end of the iconic Going-to-the-Sun Rd. (p190)

LOGAN PASS

Breathtaking panoramic vistas and two of the park's best hikes leave from this pass at the pinnacle of the Going-to-the-Sun Rd atop the Continental Divide. (p191)

TWO MEDICINE VALLEY

No less beautiful, though less visited than other sections of the park, the imposing peaks and backcountry vistas of this valley are closely intertwined with Native American legends. (p194)

🚶 DAY HIKES

You don't have to be an aspiring Everest climber to enjoy the well-tramped trails and scenic byways of Glacier National Park. Indeed, two of the park's most popular hikes are wheelchair accessible, while countless more can be easily tackled by parents with children, vacationing couch potatoes or nervous novices.

Going-to-the-Sun Road

🚶 Sun Point to Virginia Falls

Duration Four hours round-trip

Distance 11.5km (7 miles)

Difficulty Easy

Elevation Change 90m (300ft)

Start/Finish Sun Point shuttle stop

Nearest Town St Mary

Transportation Going-to-the-Sun Rd shuttle, car

Summary Shelter from the famous St Mary Lake winds on this sun-dappled trail that takes you to a tempestuous trio of waterfalls, all amidst the burned-out timber of the 2015 Reynolds Creek Fire.

Handily served by the free park shuttle, the myriad trailheads along the eastern side of Going-to-the-Sun Rd offer plenty of short interlinking hikes, a number of which can be pooled together to make up a decent morning or afternoon ramble. Post-fire, wildflowers are beginning to flourish and new vistas, once obscured by foliage, are now available.

This particular variation starts at the Sun Point shuttle stop, where you can track down a quarter-mile trail to a rocky (and often windy) overlook perched above sparkling St Mary Lake. In the 1910s, the Great Northern Railway built some of Glacier's earliest and showiest chalets here in an accommodation chain that stretched from Many Glacier to the Sperry and Granite Park Chalets. Falling into neglect after WWII, the Sun Point chalets were demolished in 1949, though the view remains timeless.

Take the path west through sun-flecked forest along the lake toward Baring Falls, at just past the half-mile mark, for a respite from the sun and/or wind. After admiring the gushing cascades, cross the river and continue on the opposite bank to link

up with the busy St Mary Falls Trail that joins from the right. Undemanding switchbacks lead up through the trees to the valley's most picturesque falls on the St Mary River. Beyond here, the trail branches along Virginia Creek, past a narrow gorge, to mist-shrouded (and quieter) Virginia Falls at the foot of a hanging valley.

Retrace your steps to Sun Point for the full-length hike or, if your legs start to tire, shortcut to the St Mary Falls or Sunrift Gorge shuttle stops and hop on a bus.

🚶 Hidden Lake Overlook Trail

Duration Two hours round-trip

Distance 4.8km (3 miles)

Difficulty Easy–moderate

Elevation Change 150m (494ft)

Start/Finish Logan Pass Visitor Center

Nearest Facilities Logan Pass

Transportation Going-to-the-Sun Rd shuttle, car

Summary A popular hike that's part boardwalk and part path, bisecting lush meadows and melting snowfields before descending to a translucent glacial lake.

For many Glacier visitors, this relatively straightforward hike is the one occasion on which they step out of their cars and take a sniff of the sweet-scented alpine air the area is famous for. Starting at the busy Logan Pass Visitor Center, the hike ascends gradually along a raised boardwalk (with steps) through expansive alpine meadows replete with monkey-flower and pink laurel. Slippery melting snowfields add a challenge for those who decided, misguidedly, to wear flip-flops, but, rain or shine, this trail is a hit with everyone – from toddlers to spry septuagenarians.

After a bit over half a mile, the boardwalk gives way to a gravelly dirt path. If the snow has melted, the diversity of grasses and wildflowers in the meadows around you is breathtaking. Resident trees include Engelmann spruce, subalpine fir and whitebark pine. Hoary marmots, ground squirrels and mountain goats are not shy along this trail. The elusive ptarmigan, whose brown feathers turn white in winter, also lives nearby. Up-close mountain views include Clements Mountain north of the trail and Reynolds Mountain in the southeast.

About 300yd before the overlook, you will cross the Continental Divide – probably

Going-to-the-Sun Road – Day Hikes

GLACIER NATIONAL PARK DAY HIKES

without realizing it – before your first stunning glimpse of the otherwordly, deep-blue **Hidden Lake** (and a realization of what all the fuss is about), bordered by mountain peaks and rocky cliffs. Look out for glistening Sperry Glacier visible to the south.

Hearty souls can continue on to Hidden Lake via a 1½-mile trail from the overlook, steeply descending 765ft.

🚶 Avalanche Lake Trail

Duration 2½ hours round-trip

Distance 6.4km (4 miles)

Difficulty Easy–moderate

Elevation Change 145m (475ft)

Start/Finish Avalanche Creek shuttle stop

Nearest Town Apgar Village

Transportation Going-to-the-Sun Rd shuttle, car

Summary A pleasant, family-friendly

stroll through shady forest to the park's most accessible alpine lake, replete with glacier-strewn boulders and cascading waterfalls.

A handy stop on the shuttle route, the Avalanche Lake Trail provides quick and easy access to one of Glacier National Park's most gorgeous alpine lakes – and you don't have to bust a gut to get there. As a result, the trail is invariably heaving in peak season with everyone from flip-flop-wearing families to stick-wielding seniors making boldly for the tree line. But don't be deceived: while the walk itself might be relatively easy, it's highly recommended you come prepared with bottled water, layered clothing and appropriate footwear.

Starting from Going-to-the-Sun Rd, the path meanders for half a mile along the paved Trail of the Cedars to a signposted three-way junction. Bear right here, diverting into thick rainforest, and follow the path along a scenic section of narrow

HIKING IN GLACIER NATIONAL PARK

NAME	REGION	DESCRIPTION	DIFFICULTY
Sun Point to Virginia Falls	Going-to-the-Sun Rd	Sun-dappled valley trail to a trio of beautiful waterfalls	easy
Hidden Lake Overlook Trail	Going-to-the-Sun Rd	Climb steps and scamper across snow fields to a spectacular lookout	easy-moderate
Avalanche Lake Trail	Going-to-the-Sun Rd	Very popular forested walk to a stunning lake	easy-moderate
Highline Trail	Going-to-the-Sun Rd	Phenomenal alpine scenery all the way to the Granite Park Chalet	moderate
Piegan Pass	Going-to-the-Sun Rd	Dense forest, an above-the-tree-line pass, glacier views, lakes and wildflowers	moderate-difficult
Gunsight Pass Trail	Going-to-the-Sun Rd	See snowfields, glaciers, lakes and more over two riveting days	moderate-difficult
Northern Highline–Waterton Valley	Going-to-the-Sun Rd	Continuation of Highline Trail along the Continental Divide toward the Canadian border	moderate-difficult
Mt Brown Lookout	Going-to-the-Sun Rd	Glacier's steepest day hike to a lofty historic viewpoint	difficult
Swiftcurrent Lake Nature Trail	North of Going-to-the-Sun Rd	Easy stroll along the shores of several lakes in the heart of the park	easy
Iceberg Lake Trail	North of Going-to-the-Sun Rd	Leads to one of the most impressive glacial lakes in the Rockies	easy-moderate
Quartz Lakes Loop	North of Going-to-the-Sun Rd	Rare North Fork loop trail in one of Glacier's most remote corners	moderate
Swiftcurrent Pass Trail	North of Going-to-the-Sun Rd	Pleasant valley ramble followed by sharp climb to the Continental Divide	moderate-difficult
Dawson–Pitamakan Loop	South of Going-to-the-Sun Rd	A lengthy but rewarding hike around the true 'Crown of the Continent'	difficult

🦌 Wildlife Watching   🔭 View   👨‍👩‍👧 Great for Families   🌊 Waterfalls   🚻 Restrooms

GLACIER NATIONAL PARK DAY HIKES

Avalanche Creek. Shaded from the summer sun by mature, old-growth cedar and western hemlock trees, the forest floor is strewn with huge moss-covered boulders, the remnants of a once-powerful glacier.

After hopping over tree roots and fording trickling creeks, you'll emerge, as if by magic, at luminous **Avalanche Lake**, a circle of water fed by cascading waterfalls and overlooked by the steep, rocky escarpments of Bearhat Mountain. The surrounding scenery is sublime and well worth the moderate 2-mile march to get here. Relax on the lakeshore (there's a pit toilet nearby) with a pair of binoculars, keeping a lookout for birds and other wildlife, including fearless Columbian ground squirrels, before heading back down.

🚶 Highline Trail

Duration 7½ hours one way

Distance 18.7km (11.6 miles)

Difficulty Moderate

Elevation Change 255m (830ft)

Start Logan Pass Visitor Center

Finish The Loop

Nearest Facilities Logan Pass

Transportation Going-to-the-Sun Rd shuttle, car

Summary A vista-laden extravaganza that cuts underneath the Garden Wall ridge just below the Continental Divide to the famous Granite Park Chalet.

DURATION	DISTANCE	ELEVATION CHANGE	FEATURES	FACILITIES	PAGE
4hr	11.5km (7 miles)	90m (300ft)			p176
2hr	4.8km (3 miles)	150m (494ft)			p176
2½hr	6.4km (4 miles)	145m (475ft)			p177
7½hr	18.7km (11.6 miles)	255m (830ft)			p178
6hr	20.5km (12.8 miles)	509m (1670ft)			p181
2 days	32km (20 miles)	930m (3000ft)			p180
2-3 days	46km (28.8 miles)	1280m (4200ft)			p186
6hr	17.3km (10.8 miles)	1318m (4325ft)			p181
1hr	4km (2.5 miles)	negligible			p183
4½hr	14.5km (9 miles)	370m (1190ft)			p183
7hr	20.5km (12.8 miles)	765m (2470ft)			p184
6hr	11.6km (7.2 miles)	650m (2100ft)			p184
8hr	30km (18.8 miles)	910m (2935ft)			p182

Icon	Meaning	Icon	Meaning	Icon	Meaning
	Drinking Water		Picnic Sites		Transport to Trailhead
	Ranger Station		Backcountry Campsite		

A Glacier classic, the Highline Trail cuts like an elongated scar across the famous Garden Wall, a sharp, glacier-carved ridge that forms part of the Continental Divide. In summer, the slopes are covered with an abundance of alpine plants and wildflowers. The stupendous views here are some of the best in the park and, with little elevation gain throughout its course, the treats come with minimal sweat.

Cutting immediately into the side of the mountain (a garden hose–like rope is tethered to the rockwall for those with vertigo), the trail presents stunning early views of Going-to-the-Sun Rd and snowcapped Heavens Peak. Look out for the toy-sized red 'jammer' buses motoring up the valley below you and marvel as the sun catches the white foaming waters of 500ft Bird Woman Falls opposite.

After its vertiginous start, the trail is flat for 1.8 miles before gently ascending to a ridge that connects Haystack Butte with Mt Gould at the 3½-mile mark. From here on it's fairly flat as you bisect the mountainside on your way toward the Granite Park Chalet. After approximately 6.8 miles, with the chalet in sight, a spur path (on your right) offers gluttons for punishment the option of climbing up less than 1 mile to the Grinnell Glacier Overlook for a peek over the Continental Divide.

The Granite Park Chalet appears at around 7.6 miles, providing a welcome haven for parched throats and tired feet (stock up at the chalet on chocolate bars and water).

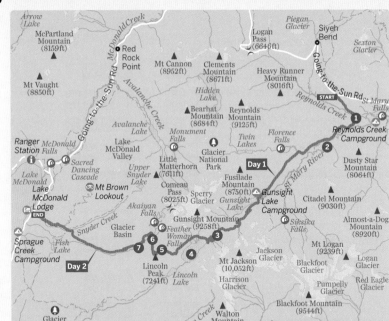

Overnight Hike
Gunsight Pass Trail

START JACKSON GLACIER OVERLOOK
END LAKE MCDONALD LODGE
LENGTH TWO DAYS; 32KM (20 MILES)

This introduction to Glacier's backcountry offers tremendous views and abundant wildlife. Truly bionic hikers knock out the trail in one day, but with copious snowfields, glaciers and lakes to marvel at, two days might be more appropriate. The trail is doable in either direction, but most hikers kick off at the Jackson Glacier Overlook (a designated free shuttle stop) and head west. If you're planning to spend a night at the chalet, you'll need to book in advance.

On the first day follow the trail southeast through fir and spruce forest to Reynolds Creek. The path then follows the creek past **1 Deadwood Falls** to a junction with the Gunsight Pass Trail at the 2km (1.3-mile) mark; take the trail on the right. It crosses a bridge past Reynolds Creek Campground and then heads alongside the **2 St Mary River**. Carry on up the valley below Citadel and Fusilade Mountains, taking in views of glaciers clinging to a high ridge to the south. Soon after the Gunsight Lake Campground, a suspension bridge traverses St Mary River and leads up numerous switchbacks to **3 Gunsight Pass** (2117m/6946ft) on the Continental Divide. Reaching the pass involves walking over cliff ledges, but the trail is broad.

Steeply descending switchbacks lead to the north shore of **4 Lake Ellen Wilson**, a spectacular alpine lake ringed by sheer, glaciated rock walls. The trail continues around the lake's western shore then up the slope to a high shelf overlooking Lincoln Lake. The trail turns gradually to cross **5 Lincoln Pass** (2149m/7050ft), then winds its way down past Sperry Campground. Four scenic sites here overlook Lake McDonald far below and the **6 Sperry Chalet** (p200) is close by.

On day two the trail leads down into fir and spruce forest past **7 Beaver Medicine Falls**. It continues 4km (2.5 miles) down the valley to cross Snyder Creek on a footbridge, then descends through a mossy forest of cedar, hemlock, grand fir, larch and yew to Going-to-the-Sun Rd.

From here you have three options: you can retrace your steps back to Logan Pass, head for Swiftcurrent Pass and the Many Glacier Valley, or descend 4 miles to the Loop, where you can pick up a shuttle bus to all points on Going-to-the-Sun Rd.

🚶 Piegan Pass

Duration Six hours

Distance 20.5km (12.8 miles)

Difficulty Moderate–difficult

Elevation Change 509m (1670ft)

Start Siyeh Bend shuttle stop

Finish Many Glacier

Nearest Facilities Many Glacier

Transportation Going-to-the-Sun Rd shuttle, car

Summary A forest, an alpine meadow, a glacier, a pass and a long descent through Glacier's premier wildlife corridor; Piegan Pass isn't lacking in variety.

A popular hike among Glacier stalwarts, this trail starts on Going-to-the-Sun Rd at a handy shuttle stop on Siyeh Bend east of Logan Pass and deposits you in Glacier's mystic heart, Many Glacier, with transport connections back to St Mary. It also bisects colorful Preston Park, one of the region's prettiest and most jubilant alpine meadows.

The initial climb is through forest from the Siyeh Bend starting point, heading directly for the flower-adorned oasis of **Preston Park**. Turn left and head north at the first trail junction at the 1.2-mile mark, and left again at the 2.7-mile mark, where the Siyeh Pass Trail veers off to the right. The trail crosses a creek and begins to traverse more barren terrain along the base of Mt Siyeh and Cataract Mountain. At the 4½-mile mark you'll reach **Piegan Pass** on a saddle between Piegan Mountain and Mt Pollock. The ruined foundations of a building provide some shelter from the whistling winds. Some people turn around and retrace their steps here, but the savvy descend on the pass's north side to Cataract Creek in the Many Glacier Valley. Morning Eagle Falls is reached at the 7.7-mile mark, and at the 8.8-mile mark you'll enter the Grinnell Lake trail system, popular with boat-hike groups from the Many Glacier Hotel. Stay right at the Grinnell Lake Trail junction and right again at the Lake Josephine link trail and you'll find yourself roaming through classic subal-

pine scenery with glimpses of the turquoise lakes through the trees. The well-signposted trail will ultimately deposit you in the upper parking lot of the Many Glacier Hotel.

🚶 Mt Brown Lookout

Duration Six hours round-trip

Distance 17.3km (10.8 miles)

Difficulty Difficult

Elevation Change 509m (4325ft)

Start/Finish Lake McDonald Lodge

Nearest Town Apgar Village

Transportation Going-to-the-Sun Rd shuttle, car

Summary Glacier's steepest day hike involves no technical skills, but a good level of fitness to reach a sky-high historic lookout on Mt Brown.

This hike is a means to an end; a steep 5.4-mile grunt up through thick forest (things thin out at higher elevations) to a historic 1929 lookout last manned in 1971 (and refurbished in 1999) on the southwest ridge of 8563ft Mt Brown, located about 1076ft below the summit. The views from here are outstanding, and no mountaineering skills are required – just a strong pair of lungs.

The hike starts on Going-to-the-Sun Rd opposite the Lake McDonald Lodge on the heavily used Sperry Chalet trail. Pass the horse corral and head up alongside Snyder Creek, which soon drops away to your right. The Mt Brown Lookout trail is the first of three trails to branch off, swinging left after 1.8 miles and starting a climb that makes your ascent so far seem like a Sunday afternoon stroll. The first five switchbacks are the toughest; after that the 20 or so remaining curves are a little more manageable and occasional glimpses through the trees en route offer hints of the splendor to come. As you approach the lookout, you'll emerge into meadows swaying with beargrass and wildflowers. The **lookout**, with its distinctive pyramid-shaped roof, is perched at 7487ft and is often frequented by mountain goats. The 270-degree view includes the full spread of Lake McDonald and its surrounding mountains. Look out for the Lake McDonald Lodge and the Granite Park Chalet. The summit of **Mt Brown** blocks views northeast. Though it might look close, mountaineering skills are needed to reach it. Take care on the steep and (sometimes) slippery trail as you descend.

South of Going-to-the-Sun Road

🚶 Dawson–Pitamakan Loop

Duration Eight hours round-trip

Distance 30km (18.8 miles)

Difficulty Difficult

Elevation Change 910m (2935ft)

Start/Finish North Shore trailhead, Two Medicine Lake

Nearest Facilities Two Medicine Valley

Transportation East Side shuttle, car

Summary Cross the Continental Divide twice on this strenuous but spectacular hike along exposed mountain ridges that provide prime habitat for grizzly bears.

This lengthy hike can be squeezed into a one-day itinerary, if you're fit and up for it. Alternatively, it can be tackled over two or three days with sleepovers at the No Name Lake and Oldman Lake backcountry campgrounds (permit required). Stretching it out is a double-edged sword: you can go slower, however you'll have to carry overnight gear and food which can weigh you down. Blessed with two spectacular mountain passes

and teeming with myriad plant and animal life, this is often touted by park rangers as being one of Glacier's hiking highlights.

As the hike is a loop, departing from the North Shore trailhead on **Two Medicine Lake**, you must first decide which direction you want to go. Progressing clockwise and tackling Dawson Pass first packs the 3000ft elevation gain into one sharp segment. Head anticlockwise and the same ascent is more drawn out. Walking clockwise, you'll be entering prime grizzly-bear country (rangers have actually used it as a study area), so be on guard and make plenty of noise. Around 5 miles in you'll reach **No Name Lake**, a prime fishing spot. The trail ascends steeply from here, gaining 1200ft in 2 miles during a pulse-racing climb to **Dawson Pass**, an exposed saddle notorious for its high winds – 100mph has been recorded. Follow the narrow, sheer-sided path north along the Continental Divide, taking care with your footing amid stunning high-country scenery. You'll cross the divide again at **Cut Bank** before descending to **Pitamakan Pass** and **Oldman Lake**, a gorgeous blue body of water encased in a cirque and framed by jagged peaks.

From the lake, the hike descends into the **Dry Fork Drainage**, through fields of huckleberries interspersed with clumps of

South of Going-to-the-Sun Road – Day Hike

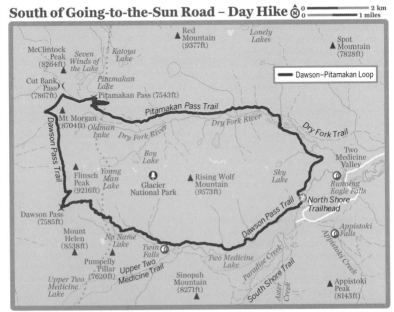

dense forest. Look out for diggings, scat and other evidence of bear activity as you make for Two Medicine Lake and your starting point.

North of Going-to-the-Sun Road

🔥 Swiftcurrent Lake Nature Trail

Duration One hour

Distance 4km (2.5 miles)

Difficulty Easy

Elevation Change Negligible

Start/Finish Many Glacier Hotel

Nearest Facilities Many Glacier

Transportation East Side shuttle, car

Summary From civilization to bear-infested wilderness in less than 60 seconds: natural juxtapositions don't get much more dramatic than this.

Anchoring the trail system that connects Many Glacier's three navigable lakes – Swiftcurrent, Josephine and Grinnell – this easy, flat nature trail offers a potent taste of the valley's rugged essence. Take note: despite heavy usage and its proximity to the hotel, the trail often posts bear warnings.

Heading south from the Many Glacier Hotel along the shoreline of shallow **Swiftcurrent Lake** (30ft at its deepest point), you'll pass an old boathouse and ranger station used as accommodation for summer guides. At a junction for the Grinnell Lake Trail at the southern end of the lake, stay right and take a wooden footbridge across the channel between Swiftcurrent Lake and **Lake Josephine**. Very soon after, you'll pass a small dock used by boat-trip groups organized by the hotel. Continue to the right and finish your lake circumnavigation amid widening mountain views, peeks of the distinctive Salamander Glacier, and possible moose sightings along the willowy shoreline. After skirting close to the Many Glacier campground, the trail turns east and deposits you back in a picnic area adjacent to the handsome hotel.

🔥 Iceberg Lake Trail

Duration 4½ hours round-trip

Distance 14.5km (9 miles)

Difficulty Easy–moderate

Elevation Change 370m (1190ft)

Start/Finish Swiftcurrent Motor Inn

Nearest Facilities Many Glacier

Transportation East Side shuttle, car

Summary A well-trodden, wildlife-studded trail through relatively open terrain to otherworldly Iceberg Lake.

Famed for the bobbing bergs that float like miniature ice cubes in its still waters all summer long, the Iceberg Lake hike has long been a classic Glacier National Park pilgrimage. The popularity of the hike is understandable. Enclosed in a deep glacial cirque and surrounded on three sides by stunning 3000ft vertical walls, the lake is one of the most impressive sights anywhere in the Rockies. The ascent to get there is fairly gentle, and the approach is mostly at or above the tree line, affording awesome views. Wildflower fans will go ga-ga in the meadows near the lake.

The trailhead is just past the Swiftcurrent Motor Inn. Bears are often sighted on this trail, so check at the ranger station before setting out and take all of the usual precautions. Starting steeply, the trail packs most of its elevation gain into the first few kilometers. But once you emerge onto the scrubby slopes above Many Glacier, the gradient is barely perceptible. After 2 miles the path enters a small section of mature forest and arrives at Ptarmigan Creek, crossed by a footbridge, just upstream from **Ptarmigan Falls**. Here you climb gently through pine to the Ptarmigan Tunnel Trail junction, which heads right.

Continuing toward Iceberg Lake, you'll come upon the first of several beautiful meadows under **Ptarmigan Wall**. Descend for a short distance to cross Iceberg Creek via a footbridge, then climb up past **Little Iceberg Lake** before dropping down to the shores of your hallowed destination, the icy-blue cirque lake.

Iceberg Lake is 150ft deep and about three-quarters of a mile across. The glacier is now inactive but, as the lake lies in the shadows on the north side of Mt Wilbur, the area remains cool all through summer. It's not unusual to see a few brave or foolhardy souls take a plunge. After filling your memory card with photos of the lake, retrace your steps to the Swiftcurrent Motor Inn.

North of Going-to-the-Sun Road – Day Hikes

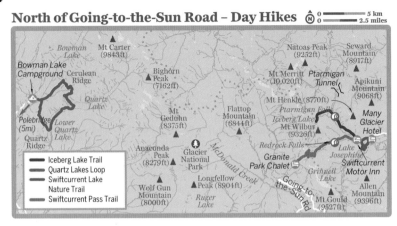

🚶 Quartz Lakes Loop

Duration Seven hours round-trip

Distance 20.5km (12.8 miles)

Difficulty Moderate

Elevation Change 765m (2470ft)

Start/Finish Bowman Lake Campground

Nearest Facilities Polebridge

Transportation Car

Summary Lakes, solitude and scenery are three of the North Fork Valley's primary draws, and all are on display during this multifarious hike. Bring bug spray.

Remote and hard to get to without a car, the wild North Fork Valley is a solitude seeker's utopia. The Quartz Lakes Loop is one of the area's only loop trails, a hiking staple renowned for its wonderful scenery and close-up views of a forest still regenerating after relatively recent (natural) fires.

From the trailhead, cross Bowman Creek before beginning a gradual ascent along the shores of Bowman Lake. After 1 mile or so you'll start a more precipitous climb up Quartz Ridge, which turns into Cerulean Ridge, with an elevation of 5500ft, where you'll be afforded fantastic views of a triumvirate of beautiful lakes – Quartz Lake, tiny Middle Quartz Lake and Lower Quartz Lake – shimmering like tinfoil below. The path drops down to the west side of Quartz Lake, passing in and out of forest which has slowly reasserted itself after the 1988 Red Bench Fire.

Once in the valley, skirt the edges of all three lakes via a clearly marked path ending up, after 3 miles, in a backcountry campground at the south end of Lower Quartz Lake. From here, it's a 1½-mile ascent to the crest of Quartz Ridge – for the second time – before you drop back down to Bowman Creek.

🚶 Swiftcurrent Pass Trail

Duration Six hours one way

Distance 11.6km (7.2 miles)

Difficulty Moderate–difficult

Elevation Change 650m (2100ft)

Start Swiftcurrent Motor Inn

Finish Granite Park Chalet

Nearest Facilities Many Glacier

Transportation East Side shuttle, car

Summary A pleasant meander through the Many Glacier Valley, followed by a steep climb up to the Continental Divide.

This popular trail departs from the west side of the Swiftcurrent Motor Inn parking lot and can be linked up with the Loop or Highline Trails to make an arduous one-day, or slightly less arduous two-day, hike.

Easing in slowly, the first 4 miles of the trail are relatively gentle, bisecting low lodgepole forest sprinkled with aspen, the result of dynamic regrowth following the 1936 Heaven's Peak Fire. Looking around, you'll see the highest visible summit, Mt Wilbur, to the northwest, jagged Grinnell Mountain to the south, and Swiftcurrent Mountain, which this path eventually ascends, to the southwest.

Hiking through the potentially hot open terrain, you will soon find relief amid the foliage, including Engelmann spruce, subalpine fir, fireweed, maple and the shade-giving quaking aspen. Wildflower spotters will enjoy colorful landscapes dotted with forget-me-nots, paintbrush, harebell, yellow columbine and Siberian chive. Watch for stinging nettles along the way and make plenty of noise to ward off Many Glacier's many bears.

Less than 1½ miles into the trail, the path brushes the northern tip of **Red Rock Lake**, and the waterfalls become visible in the distance. Beavers are active along streams in this valley; look out for beaver lodges on the other side of the lake. At the 3.3-mile mark you'll hit **Bullhead Lake** and from here you'll begin a 3-mile climb up to Swiftcurrent Pass, with an elevation of 6770ft, gaining 2000ft in the process. The switchbacks on the ascent are numerous, and the path, which cuts sharply into the mountainside, becomes ever more vertiginous as you climb (if you suffer badly from vertigo, give this route a miss). The Continental Divide at **Swiftcurrent Pass** is marked by an unruly pile of rocks surrounded by dwarf trees. For those still with energy, the optional spur trail up a further set of switchbacks to **Swiftcurrent Lookout** offers one of the park's most tower-topping views. Returning to the pass, head the final 1 mile down to the Granite Park Chalet for a welcome rest (remember to book ahead if you wish to stay overnight) or to link up with other trails.

⚙ CYCLING

Glacier National Park diverges from Banff, Waterton Lakes and Jasper in that none of its trails are open to cyclists. An alternative for two-wheeled travelers is to make use of the park's only allocated bike path (a flat 2.5-mile ramble from West Glacier to Apgar Village), or to ply the limited road network – essentially Going-to-the-Sun Rd – which has further restrictions on when you can and can't use it.

Despite the limitations, committed cyclists can be spied daily throughout summer attempting the 53-mile Going-to-the-Sun Rd, where the spectacular vistas and copious twists and turns are befitting of a challenging Tour de France stage. For safety and congestion reasons, the upper stretches of the road are officially shut to cyclists between 11am and 4pm daily (mid-June to Labor Day), so you'll need to be flexible with your schedule. If you do decide to take the plunge (and it's a memorable ride), start early, pack plenty of water and take extreme care on the long and potentially precarious descents. From a physical point of view, it's easier to start your ride in St Mary and tackle the climb east–west.

On full-moon nights during summer months, Going-to-the-Sun Rd between the Loop and Logan Pass is closed off for cyclists making the memorable run; wear proper gear, including headlamps.

The closest thing to a mountain-biking venture in the park is the Inside North Fork Rd (Glacier Rte 7) to Kintla Lake. Cyclists craving trail rides should consider Waterton Lakes, which has five trails.

You'll encounter plenty of colorfully clad cyclists just outside the park's eastern boundary, plying Hwys 49 and 89, on the edge of the Blackfeet Indian Reservation. Inclines here are gentler, although the stiff winds off the adjacent prairies can be punishing.

Hiker-biker campgrounds (US$5) are available at Apgar, Avalanche Creek, Fish Creek, Many Glacier, Rising Sun, Sprague Creek, St Mary and Two Medicine Campgrounds. You can find cruiser, mountain, road and tandem bikes at **Go Glacier Outfitters** (☑ 406-219-7466; www.goglacieroutfitters.com; 196 Apgar Loop Rd, Apgar Village; ☺ 9am-5pm May-Sep) on the west side of the park in Apgar Village, and a stash of basic machines in the **St Mary KOA Campground** (106 West Shore Rd, St Mary; bikes per hr/day US$2.50/20) on the east side. Better bicycles are available at Glacier Cyclery (p213) in Whitefish, 45 miles southwest.

⚓ OTHER ACTIVITIES

⚓ Boating

McDonald, Bowman, Swiftcurrent, Two Medicine and St Mary Lakes have launching ramps available for boats. Sailors might find St Mary Lake's winds to their liking. Stand up paddling is popular on Lake McDonald – Eddie's Cafe and Go Glacier Outfitters in Apgar rent boards for around US$20 for two hours – and also on Bowman Lake in the North Country.

🎣 White-Water Rafting & Float Trips

The loaded-up school buses ferrying groups from outfitters in and around West Glacier and Hwy 2 give you an idea of rafting's popularity. All tours take place on or outside the park's boundaries, primarily on the North and Middle Forks of the Flathead River. The best water flow is from May to September, with the rapids ranking an unterrifying class I to III. All of the operators can customize highly recommended overnight adventures on the North Fork from near the Canadian border (tents and sleeping gear are provided). Or you can float down McDonald Creek on your own inner tubes.

Glacier Raft Co RAFTING
(☏406-888-5454; www.glacierraftco.com; rafting US$61-130; ☉Jun-Aug) Arguably the most reputable raft company in the area, with offices in the Glacier Outdoor Center on Hwy 2, as well as behind the Alberta Visitor Center in West Glacier Village. Also runs multiday, kayaking and fly-fishing trips.

Wild River Adventures RAFTING
(☏406-387-9453; www.riverwild.com; 11900 Hwy 2, West Glacier; half-day rafting trip adult/child US$60/50) Wild River offers four launch times for half-day trips, as well as a daily full-day trip (adult/child US$99/79). For those who need more autonomy and maybe more of a rush, it also rents inflatable kayaks (you can join up with the rafting tours) and multiday rafting, fishing and horseback-riding trips.

Great Northern Whitewater Raft & Resort RAFTING
(☏406-387-5340; www.greatnorthernresort.com; 12127 Hwy 2, West Glacier; half-day US$60-81, full day US$100-128) Based in a resort of the same name (with a railroad-car cafe on-site), this company offers a wide variety of guided rafting and fly-fishing trips.

🎣 Fishing

The fishing season in streams and rivers is late May to late November, though lakes are open for fishing year-round. While anglers can explore easily accessible waters such as Lake McDonald and St Mary Lake, it is some of the hike-in destinations that are the most tranquil getaways; try Hidden Lake, Oldman Lake or Red Eagle Lake. Most of Glacier's fish were introduced to provide 'sport' for visitors up until the 1960s. Species include

🥾 Overnight Hike
Northern Highline– Waterton Valley

START THE LOOP, GOING-TO-THE-SUN RD
END GOAT HAUNT RANGER STATION
LENGTH TWO TO THREE DAYS; 46KM (28.8 MILES)

This moderately difficult hike follows the splendid Highline Trail beyond the Granite Park Chalet to Waterton, Canada. An extension of the popular 'Garden Wall' section of the Highline Trail, this route, often known as the Northern Highline, forges deeper into the backcountry across open subalpine terrain toward the Goat Haunt region and the US–Canada border. It is also the end point of the 3100-mile Continental Divide Trail (CDT) that runs from Mexico up to Canada, of which Glacier National Park guards the final 110 miles. As you hike, keep an eye out for moose, as well as short-eared owls, American kestrels, mountain bluebirds and pine siskins.

Start this hike from The Loop, a tightly angled switchback on Going-to-the-Sun Rd, 8 miles northwest of Logan Pass, that also serves as a free shuttle stop. An alternative starting point is the trailhead for the Highline Trail at Logan Pass, an option that will add a scenic 3.6 miles to your overall trip.

From The Loop, the climb begins almost immediately through landscape scarred by the 2003 Trapper Fire. Burnt tree trunks characterize a mountainside slowly coming back to life after the inferno. The views are superb. After around half a mile, the Packers Roost Trail joins in from the left. Continue walking uphill gaining 2300ft in elevation within 4 miles to reach the historic ❶ **Granite Park Chalet**, built in 1915 as the last link in a chain of backcountry chalets constructed by the Great Northern Railway (only two remain). The chalet offers hostel accommodation (reserve ahead), a campground, drinks and snacks. There is no running water.

You may want to spend the night at the chalet and incorporate a short side trip up to Swiftcurrent Pass and Lookout. If you're pressing on, get moving quickly, as it's still

11.6 miles to the next campground – Fifty Mountain.

Take the trail to Swiftcurrent Pass and fork almost immediately left to follow the far less crowded Northern Highline Trail as it parallels the Continental Divide through high subalpine terrain, with tremendous vistas of peaks, meadows and safe-from-a-distance wildlife (grizzlies, moose and wolves have all been spotted here). After about 5 miles, an overlook trail to ➋ **Ahern Pass** and a view of Helen Lake forks off to the right; another nearby short spur, just to the north of the one for Helen Lake, leads to the Sue Lake Overlook. If you're not up for either detour, continue straight ahead, climbing up toward the Continental Divide, which you will cross after a short sharp climb 10½ miles from the Granite Park Chalet.

The ➌ **Fifty Mountain Campground** is just over the other side, situated in an alpine bowl below a meadow. It is named for the number of mountains you can see from its stunning viewpoint (count them!) and is arguably the finest backcountry campsite in the park – a grand place to rest your feet after eight or nine hours on the trail.

Wake up amid the moody magnificence of Fifty Mountain and try to tear yourself away from the view and the braver-than-usual deer. Day two (or three, depending on your schedule) involves a 2400ft descent to the Waterton Valley and Goat Haunt on Upper Waterton Lake – a hike of around five to six hours. Most of the descending is in the first 5 miles, as you drop from the Fifty Mountain plateau to the intersection with the Stoney Indian Trail at the 2.7-mile mark – you will pass many avalanche chutes, which open up the scenery for great views. Soon after, you'll come across the Pass Creek ranger hut and footbridge. Back below the timberline is the epiphanic sight of ➍ **Kootenai Lakes** (reached via a short trail on the left), often frequented by day-hikers from Goat Haunt. The lake is renowned for its moose sightings.

Continue along the valley for a further 2.5 miles to the Goat Haunt ranger station, where you can board a boat – or alternatively hike the 7 miles – to Waterton Townsite in Canada.

If doing the hike in the opposite direction, that is, from Waterton in Canada into the US, you'll need to register and have a video conference with Customs and Border Protection via one of the Reporting Offsite Arrival-Mobile (ROAM) kiosks at the Waterton Cruise dock (or download the app on your phone).

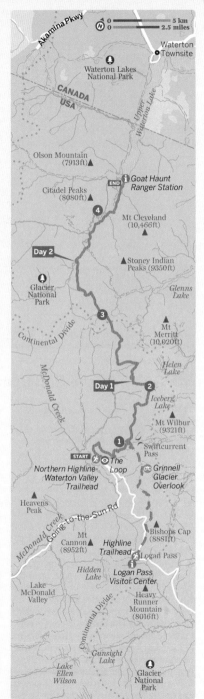

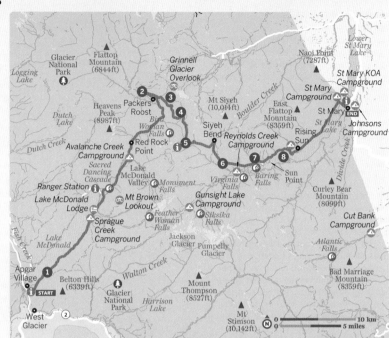

Driving Tour
Going-to-the-Sun Road

START WEST ENTRANCE, NEAR APGAR VILLAGE
END ST MARY VISITOR CENTER
LENGTH THREE HOURS (WITH STOPS); 85KM (53 MILES)

This is, quite literally, one of the most spectacular drives in the US. Going-to-the-Sun Rd starts at the park's western entrance before tracking northeast along **1 Lake McDonald**. Characterized by the famous Lake McDonald Lodge, the valley here is lush and verdant, though a quick glance through the trees will highlight the graphic evidence of the 2003 Robert Fire on the opposite side of the water.

After following McDonald Creek for about 10 miles, the road begins its long, slow ascent to Logan Pass, with a sharp turn to the southeast at **2 The Loop**, a famous hiking trailhead and the start of an increasingly precipitous climb toward the summit. Views here are unfailingly sublime as the road cuts precariously into the **3 Garden Wall**, a 8999ft granite ridge that delineates the west and east regions of the park along the Con-

tinental Divide. Look out for **4 Bird Woman Falls**, stunning even from a distance, and the more in-your-face Weeping Wall, as the gaping chasm to your right grows ever deeper.

Stop at lofty **5 Logan Pass** to browse the visitor center or to stretch those legs amid alpine meadows on the popular Hidden Lake Overlook Trail. Be forewarned: the Logan Pass parking lot gets very busy in July and August.

Descending eastwards, keep an eye out for majestic Going-to-the-Sun Mountain, omnipresent to the north. At the 36-mile mark, you can pull over to spy one of only 25 remaining park glaciers at the **6 Jackson Glacier Overlook**, while a few clicks further on, you can sample narrow **7 Sunrift Gorge** near the shores of St Mary Lake. **8 Wild Goose Island**, a photogenic stub of land, is situated in the center of the lake. The 2015 Reynolds Creek fire, which thinned out much of the east side's tree cover, has also revealed new vistas and perspectives not previously accessible.

The St Mary Visitor Center on the lake's eastern shore is journey's end.

cutthroat trout, northern pike, whitefish, burbot, kokanee salmon, brook trout, rainbow trout, mackinaw and grayling.

A Montana state fishing license is not required within Glacier National Park, though anglers should familiarize themselves with the general park regulations available at any visitor center. Anglers are generally limited to possession of five fish daily, with caps varying by species. Some waters, including Hidden Lake and the North and Middle Forks of the Flathead River, are purely catch-and-release zones. Read the park's Fishing Regulations pamphlet. Portions of the North Fork and Middle Fork of the Flathead River outside the park are subject to Montana state fishing regulations. Part of Lower Two Medicine Lake is on reservation land and subject to Blackfeet Indian Reservation regulations.

Lakestream Fly Fishing (☑406-862-1298; www.lakestream.com; 669 Spokane Ave) in Whitefish, **Montana Fly Fishing Experience** (☑406-249-1482; www.montanaflyfishingexperienc. com), Glacier Guides & Montana Raft Inc (p195) and Glacier Raft Co (p186) are highly recommended for trips and lessons. The very personable Alger Swingley of **Blackfeet Outfitters** (☑406-450-8420; www.black feetoutfitters.com) runs customized trips and can take people out ice fishing in the winter.

Glacier Outdoor Center   FISHING
(☑800-235-6781; www.glacierraftco.com; 12400 Hwy 2, West Glacier; half-/full day US$375/475) You can organize fly-fishing trips, as well as up to week-long customized adventures (US$400 per person per day for three or more), with the Glacier Raft Co; its fishing operation is run out of the Glacier Outdoor Center, the best shop for gear in West Glacier.

Horseback Riding

Glacier may be stingy toward cyclists, but there are far fewer restrictions towards horseback riders – this, after all, is cowboy-land Montana. Equestrian lovers looking for longer multiday trips in similar wilderness scenery should consider the Bob Marshall Wilderness area, not far south of Glacier.

Swan Mountain Outfitters   HORSEBACK RIDING
(☑406-387-4405; www.swanmountainoutfitters. com; from US$40; ☺early May-early Sep) The park's only horseback-riding guides and the largest horseback tour company in Montana, Swan Mountain Outfitters offers a variety of trips lasting from a one-hour circumnavigation of Lake Josephine (US$40) to an all-day

foray to Cracker Lake (US$255). Its three corrals are maintained at Lake McDonald, Many Glacier Corral and Apgar Village. All trips are led by experienced wranglers who'll furnish you with plenty of entertaining tales.

Back in the 'old' days, before Going-to-the-Sun Rd was built, getting around by horse between the various tourist chalets was the primary means of transport, and horses still run a regular supply line up to Sperry Chalet, a route that can be incorporated into an excellent day ride.

Rock Climbing

While Glacier's sharp ridges and steeply stacked cliff faces might look like a rock-climber's paradise, the opposite is often the case. Due to the nature of the Rocky Mountains' loose sedimentary rock – much of it metamorphosed mudstone and limestone – mountaineering, rather than technical climbing, is the sport of choice in the park. Climbers and adrenaline junkies can find solace in the tough but nontechnical ascent of the park's highest peak, 10,466ft Mt Cleveland. Interested parties should enquire at visitor centers and ranger stations, and sign a register before setting out.

Or better yet, climbers looking for technical challenges can head to the Lake Koocunusa area in the Kootenai National Forest west of the park.

Golf

Two golf courses with mountain views – **Glacier Park Lodge Golf Course** (www. glacierparkcollection.com; Glacier Park Lodge, East Glacier; 9 holes US$40, club rental US$16; ☺mid-May–Sep) and **Glacier View Golf Club** (☑406-888-5471; www.glacierviewgolf.com; 9/18 holes US$20/32, club rental US$12/18) – lie just outside the park limits in West and East Glacier.

Skiing & Snowshoeing

Jasper and Banff this is not. From October to May, when Going-to-the-Sun Rd is snowed under, most services in Glacier close, leaving the park to wildlife and intrepid, self-sufficient cross-country skiers and snowshoers, most of whom base themselves in Whitefish or Kalispell.

The one exception are National Park Service–run short guided snowshoe walks on Saturdays and Sundays. They leave from the Apgar Visitor Center (p202) and head down to the oxbow in the river and back.

Snow and cold are no impediments – generally only canceled if the windchill gets below minus 18° F.

The Izaak Walton Inn in Essex, located at a handy Amtrak train stop on the park's southern boundary, maintains its own small network of groomed and partly floodlit cross-country skiing and snowshoeing trails – 20½ miles worth – from November to April. Instructors based here can organize private ski lessons (US$50) or take you on customized backcountry skiing or snowshoeing trips (US$125 per person for two to eight people) into the almost-deserted winter park. The inn rents out snowshoes/skis for US$15/30 per day.

Self-sufficient cross-country skiers can choose from a number of popular marked but ungroomed trails in the park itself, the bulk of them emanating from Apgar Village and Lake McDonald. A well-used favorite is to ski along an unplowed section of Going-to-the-Sun Rd from the (closed) Lake McDonald Lodge to Avalanche Creek. The road is always plowed as far as the lodge, allowing easy access by car. Another regularly tackled trail is the 11½-mile McGee Meadow Loop heading up the unplowed Camas Rd and back down the Inside Fork Rd to Apgar Village. Far more difficult is the steep 5.2-mile ascent to the Apgar Lookout.

Other lesser-used park penetration points are St Mary for the Red Eagle Lake Trail, Polebridge for the Bowman Lake Trail, and Two Medicine for the unplowed Two Medicine Rd as far as Running Eagle Falls.

Although all hotels and restaurants stay closed, and the park registers only a handful of visitors, Glacier's mountains and valleys remain gloriously open all winter to those intrepid enough to breach them. For ultimate safety, organize a guided backcountry ski tour with **Glacier Adventure Guides** (☑ 877-735-9514; www.glacieradventureguides.com; 729 Nucleus Ave, Columbia Falls; per person from US$180), which operates out of Columbia Falls, MT. Day rates hover at around US$180 per person.

⊙ SIGHTS

⊙ Going-to-the-Sun Road

If it were possible to mathematically measure 'magnificence,' Going-to-the-Sun Rd would surely hit the top end of the scale. Chiseled out of raw mountainside and punctuated by some of the most vertiginous drop-offs in the US, this vista-laden artery of asphalt that bisects the park west to east is an engineering marvel without equal. In the circumstances, it is hardly surprising that it's considered by many motorists to be the best drive in the country.

St Mary Lake   LAKE
Located on the park's dryer eastern side, where the mountains melt imperceptibly into the Great Plains, St Mary Lake lies in a deep, glacier-carved valley famous for its astounding views and ferocious winds. Overlooked by the tall, chiseled peaks of the Rockies and with the northern slopes dramatically thinned from the lake shore to Going-to-the-Sun Rd by the 2015 Reynolds Creek fire, the valley views are still spectacu-

---

GLACIER'S GLACIERS

Today's visitors could be some of the last to actually see a glacier in the park. Current figures suggest that, if current warming trends continue, the park could be glacier-free by 2030. Thanks to a Glacier Research Monitoring program carried out by the US Geological Survey, the Montana park's icy monoliths have been more studied than any of their counterparts. The estimates are based on research undertaken on the Sperry, Agassiz, Jackson and Grinnell Glaciers, all of which have lost approximately 35% of their volume since the mid-1960s. Many are surprised to learn that the park's current number of glaciers – 26 (35 were identified and named in 1966) – is significantly less than other American national parks, including the North Cascades (with over 300) and Mt Rainier (with 25 on one mountain).

However, whatever scenario ultimately transpires, the park – contrary to popular opinion – will not have to change its name. The 'glacier' label refers as much to the dramatic ice-sculpted scenery as it does to its fast-melting rivers of ice, and these remarkable geographical features ought to be dropping jaws for a good few millennia to come.

lar and punctuated by numerous trailheads and viewpoints.

St Mary's gorgeous turquoise sheen, easily the most striking color of any of Glacier's major bodies of water, is due to the suspension of tiny particles of glacial rock in the lake's water that absorbs and reflects light.

Wild Goose Island   ISLAND
(St Mary Lake) This tiny stub of an island with a handful of lopsided trees perches precariously in the middle of St Mary Lake, providing a perfect photo op for incurable camera-clickers.

Rising Sun   LANDMARK
You'll welcome this handy pit stop on Going-to-the-Sun Rd, with useful tourist facilities including a motel, restaurant, showers, small grocery and boat launch. At the peculiarly named Two Dog Flats nearby, thick trees give way to grassy meadows, making it much easier to spot bears, coyotes and elk.

Sun Point   VIEWPOINT
This rocky, often windy promontory overlooks St Mary Lake and was the site of some of the park's earliest and most luxurious chalets (now demolished). Trails link to Baring Falls and St Mary Falls.

Sunrift Gorge   CANYON
Just off Going-to-the-Sun Rd and adjacent to a shuttle stop lies this narrow canyon carved over millennia by the gushing glacial meltwaters of Baring Creek. Look out for picturesque Baring Bridge, a classic example of rustic Going-to-the-Sun Rd architecture, and follow a short trail down to misty Baring Falls. Most of the tree cover in this area was thinned out by the 2015 Reynolds Creek fire.

Jackson Glacier Overlook   VIEWPOINT
This popular pull-over, located a short walk from the Gunsight Pass trailhead, offers telescopic views of the park's fifth-largest glacier, which sits close to its eponymous 10,052ft peak – one of the park's highest.

★Logan Pass   LANDMARK
Perched above the tree line, atop the wind-lashed Continental Divide, and blocked by snow for most of the year, 6646ft Logan Pass – named for William R Logan, Glacier's first superintendent – is the park's highest navigable point by road. Two trails, Hidden Lake Overlook (p176), which continues on to Hidden Lake itself, and Highline (p179),

lead out from here. Views are stupendous; the parking situation, however, is not – you might spend a lot of time searching for a spot during peak hours.

Garden Wall   LANDMARK
The sharp, steep-sided ridge that parallels Going-to-the-Sun Rd as it ascends to Logan Pass from the west was carved by powerful glaciers millions of years ago. Its western slopes, bisected by the emblematic Highline Trail, are covered by a quintessential Glacier Park feature: steep velvety meadows embellished by an abundance of summer wildflowers.

Weeping Wall   WATERFALL
Located 2000ft below the iconic Garden Wall, the glistening Weeping Wall creates a seasonal waterfall that was formed when Going-to-the-Sun Rd construction workers drilled their way across a network of mountain springs. The water has subsequently been diverted over the lip of a 9m (30ft) artificial cliff, and frequently gives unwary cars and motorbikes a good soaking.

Bird Woman Falls   WATERFALL
Standing at the artificially created Weeping Wall, look across the valley to this distant natural watery spectacle; the spectacular Bird Woman Falls drops 500ft from one of Glacier's many hanging valleys. There are several pullouts along the western side of Going-to-the Sun Rd to view the falls.

The Loop   LANDMARK
This sharp hairpin bend acts as a popular trailhead for hikers descending from the Granite Park Chalet and the Highline Trail. Consequently, it's normally chock-a-block with cars. The slopes nearby were badly scarred by the 2003 Trapper Fire, but nature and small shrubs are beginning to reappear.

Lake McDonald Valley   FOREST
Greener and wetter than the St Mary Valley, the Lake McDonald Valley harbors the park's largest lake and some of its densest and oldest temperate rainforest. Crisscrossed by a number of popular trails, including the wheelchair-accessible, 0.8-mile Trail of the Cedars, the area is popular with drive-in campers, who frequent the Sprague Creek and Avalanche Creek campgrounds, as well as winter cross-country skiers who use McDonald Creek and Going-to-the-Sun Rd as seasonal skiing trails.

Glacier National Park Region

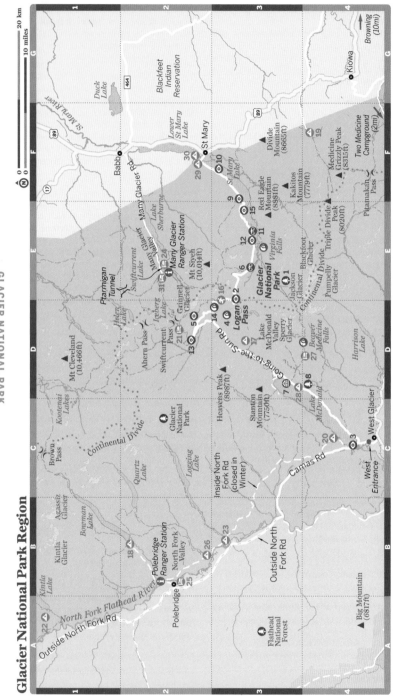

20 km
10 miles

Browning (10mi)

Kiowa

Blackfeet Indian Reservation

Duck Lake

464

St Mary River

Lower St Mary Lake

89

St Mary

89

17

Babb

Many Glacier Rd

Lake Sherburne

30

29

10

St Mary Lake

Divide Mountain (8665ft)

19

Medicine Grizzly Peak (8315ft)

Two Medicine Campground (2mi)

Kakitos Mountain (7779ft)

Pitamakan Pass

9

15

Red Eagle Mountain (8881ft)

Swiftcurrent Lake

Many Glacier Ranger Station

31

24

12

11

Virginia Falls

Blackfoot Glacier

Triple Divide Peak (8020ft)

Ptarmigan Tunnel

Mt Siyeh (10,014ft)

6

2

Glacier National Park

Continental Divide

Pumpelly Glacier

Helen Lake

Grinnell Glacier

16

Jackson Glacier

Iceberg Lake

21

14

4

Logan Pass

Ahern Pass

Swiftcurrent Pass

5

Going-to-the-Sun Rd

Lake McDonald

Sperry Glacier

Beaver Medicine Falls

Harrison Lake

Mt Cleveland (10,466ft)

13

27

Kootenai Lakes

Glacier National Park

Heavens Peak (8987ft)

Stanton Mountain (7750ft)

28

7

8

Lake McDonald

Brown Pass

Continental Divide

Quartz Lake

Lagging Lake

Inside North Fork Rd (closed in Winter)

20

3

West Glacier

West Entrance

Agassiz Glacier

Bowman Lake

Camas Rd

Outside North Fork Rd

Big Mountain (6817ft)

Kintla Glacier

North Fork Valley

Polebridge Ranger Station

North Fork Flathead River

18

23

26

North Fork Flathead River

25

Polebridge

Outside North Fork Rd

22

Kintla Lake

Flathead National Forest

Glacier National Park Region

The 2018 Howe Ridge fire, ignited by lightning, burned for more than a month in the area northwest of the lake and destroyed more than a dozen historic landholdings; the Upper McDonald Creek trail was still closed as of June 2019.

Lake McDonald Lodge   HISTORIC BUILDING
(www.glaciernationalparklodges.com; Lake McDonald) On the northeastern shore of the lake, this rustic lodge, first built in 1895 as the Glacier Hotel, is the park's oldest hotel. Replaced by a newer Swiss-style structure in 1913, before any roads had penetrated the region, the current lodge's imposing entrance was built facing the lake, meaning modern-day road travelers must enter via the back door. It's worth a visit simply to admire the lobby-lounge area with a classic Old West aesthetic, featuring taxidermied wildlife and a massive fireplace.

Apgar Village   VILLAGE
Supporting little more than a couple of lodges, a gift shop or two, a recommended outdoor gear outfitter and a restaurant with an adjoining window for ice cream and shakes to go, this collection of tourist facilities sits quietly on the southern shores of Lake McDonald. Dimon Apgar, for whom

the settlement is named, built the first road from Belton to the lake in 1895, allowing a handful of early homesteaders to establish themselves on Salish and Kootenai tribal territory.

A fire destroyed much of the early settlement in 1930, but it spared the original schoolhouse, dating from 1915, which is now a gift shop. Nearby, the tiny Discovery Cabin (1929) acts as an activity center for children. Junior ranger programs start here at 9am and 1pm in July and August.

South of Going-to-the-Sun Road

With no hotels, no restaurants and only one dead-end road, the Two Medicine Valley is a favorite haunt for ambitious hikers intent on reaching one of a trio of high-altitude passes that guard the gusty Continental Divide. More intrepid hikers forge further west, beyond Cut Bank Pass, where faintly marked trails descend into the barely visited Nyack Creek Wilderness. It's a rough mélange of fordable rivers and primitive campsites that surround the isolated hulk of Mt Stimson, the park's second-highest peak at 10,142ft.

DON'T MISS

RIDING THE RAILS

Glacier National Park owes its existence to the Great Northern Railway constructed by Canadian-born entrepreneur James J Hill in the 1890s and later used to carry the park's first pioneering visitors into some of America's most uncompromising backcountry. Still running daily between West Glacier and East Glacier Park train stations, the line remains one of the best ways to view the park's impressive southern perimeter, demarcated by the Middle Fork of the Flathead River and guarded by the rampart-like mountains of the Lewis Range. On the south side of the line lies the even wilder Great Bear Wilderness Area, a roadless landscape, uninhabited bar for its bears, beavers et al.

The journey of one hour and 40 minutes between the two stations costs US$16 for reclining business-class seats and access to an onboard cafe and observation car on the legendary *Empire Builder*; board the train in West Glacier, about half a mile from the park's western entrance, and let the geographical drama unfold. The Flathead River is your constant companion as the train labors its way up to Marias Pass, the mythical mountain crossing that once eluded Lewis and Clark. On the way, you'll pass Essex Station, the only flag stop (request stop) on the *Empire Builder* route between Seattle and Chicago. Clearly visible from the train is the Izaak Walton Inn, built by the Great Northern in 1939 and now a favored stopover for train buffs who stay in old cabooses restored as luxury accommodation.

Soon after Essex, the train reaches the 5220ft Marias Pass, the country's lowest pass over the Continental Divide. An obelisk stands next to an imposing statue of the green-before-his-time US president, Theodore Roosevelt, the darling of the early US conservationist movement. The vegetation quickly thins out as you approach East Glacier Park train depot, a historic station that marks the sudden, almost incongruous, meeting of mountains and prairie. Disembark here and walk 400yd across manicured lawns to the classic 'parkitecture' East Glacier Lodge; it's an apt end to a magnificent journey.

Two Medicine Valley

Before the building of Going-to-the-Sun Rd in the 1930s, the Two Medicine Valley was one of the park's most accessible hubs, situated a mere 12 miles by horseback from the Great Northern Railway and the newly inaugurated Glacier Park Lodge. Famous for its healthy bear population and deeply imbued with Native American legends, the region is less visited these days, though it has lost none of its haunting beauty. Hikers can grab a picnic at the historic Two Medicine Campstore, once the dining hall for the now defunct Two Medicine Chalets and the venue for one of President FD Roosevelt's famous 'fireside chats.' Towering authoritatively over sublime Two Medicine Lake is the distinctive hulk of Rising Wolf Mountain, named for Canadian-turned-Piegan Native American, Hugh Monroe, who was the first white person to explore the region in the mid-19th century.

Located around 3 miles to the northwest, 8020ft Triple Divide Peak marks the hydrologic apex of the North American continent. Empty a bucket of water on its summit and it will run into three separate oceans: the Pacific, the Atlantic and the Arctic.

☉ North of Going-to-the-Sun Road

You can penetrate the park's rugged north from both east and west sides. The northeast is accessible through the popular Many Glacier nexus and is crowned by a historic lodge. The northwest is more remote and requires a good car, self-sufficiency and an adventurous spirit.

Many Glacier Valley

Dubbed the 'heart and soul' of Glacier by park purists, Many Glacier Valley is a magical mélange of lush meadows and shimmering lakes, whose pièce de résistance is the strategically positioned Many Glacier Hotel, constructed by the Great Northern Railway in 1915. Known traditionally for its 'rivers of ice' – though there aren't quite so many of them these days – the valley nurtures some of the park's most accessible glaciers, including the rapidly shrinking Grinnell Glacier, spotted by conservationist and naturalist George Bird Grinnell in 1885, and the Salamander Glacier that sits tucked beneath the saw-toothed Ptarmigan Ridge, so named for its distinctive amphibian-like shape. Other 'unmissables' include Iceberg Lake, where turquoise waters are fed from a surrounding snowfield, and the Ptarmigan Tunnel, a 56m (183ft) corridor through the rock, blasted out of the mountain in the 1930s to cut some distance off the hike to Belly River Valley (an environmental anomaly that would win few backers today).

Many Glacier is probably the best place in the park to spot wildlife. Avalanche chutes around the lakes attract bears, and mountain goats are easy to pick out on the steep scree slopes above Swiftcurrent Lake.

North Fork Valley

Glacier's most isolated nook is a riot of grassy meadows and regenerated forest that protects the park's only pack of wolves and hides some of its best backcountry trails and campgrounds. North and east of Polebridge, bone-rattling roads lead to a couple of secluded lakes. Bowman Lake is Lake McDonald without the tourists, an ideal spot to enjoy a picnic, launch a canoe or scan the horizon for wildlife. Meanwhile, 14 miles further north, Kintla Lake is a secret haven for solitude-seeking fishermen. Stalwart hikers venture out from here along the backcountry Boulder Pass Trail.

ⓖ TOURS

Red Bus Tours   BUS
(☑855-733-4522; www.glaciernationalparklodges. com/red-bus-tours; adult US$46-100, child US$23-50; ☺mid-May–end Oct) ⚐ Glacier's stylish red 'Jammer' buses (so-called because drivers had to 'jam' hard on the gears) are iconic park symbols. Guided tours take visitors along a dozen routes, from the Western Alpine Tour, a 3½-hour trip between Lake McDonald Lodge and Logan Pass, to the Big Sky Circle Tour, an 8½-hour journey that circles the park via Hwy 2. Book online.

The open-roof buses were introduced on Going-to-the-Sun Rd between 1936 and 1939. They have thus been serving the park loyally for 80 years, save a two-year sabbatical in 1999 when the fleet was reconfigured by the Ford Motor Company. After an extensive makeover, they are safer, sturdier and 93% more environmentally friendly (now running on propane gas); some are being periodically pulled off the road to be converted to electrical.

The drivers provide excellent information about what you are seeing during the drive, though the four-person seats can be cramped and you may not have the best views from the middle.

Glacier Park Boat Co   BOATING
(☑406-257-2426; www.glacierparkboats.com; adult/child US$18.25/9.25) Six historic boats – some dating back to the 1920s – ply five of Glacier's attractive mountain lakes, and some of them combine the float with a short guided hike led by interpretive, often witty, ranger guides. For those looking for a bit of a workout, it also rents rowboats (US$18 per hour), kayaks (US$18 per hour) and paddleboards (US$10 per hour) at Lake McDonald, Mary, Many Glacier and Two Medicine.

One of the best excursions leaves from the Many Glacier Hotel twice daily (July to September), chugging across Swiftcurrent Lake. Groups disembark on the southern shore and stroll to Lake Josephine, where another boat whisks you to another landing; from here your guide leads you a further 1½ miles overland to Grinnell Lake for wondrous glacial views.

Sun Tours   BUS
(☑406-732-9220; www.glaciersuntours.com; adult/child from US$60/35; ☺end May-late Sep) Blackfeet tribal members lead these interpretive tours of Going-to-the-Sun Rd. Air-conditioned buses leave from various points in East Glacier, St Mary and Browning; half- and full-day tours available.

Kruger Helicop-Tours   SCENIC FLIGHTS
(☑406-387-4565; www.krugerhelicopters.com; 11892 Hwy 2; per person 30min/1hr US$150/295) To get a view from above the eagles' nests, consider a helicopter tour run by this outfit, which has an office on Hwy 2, 1 mile west of West Glacier.

**Glacier Guides &
Montana Raft Inc**   FISHING
(☑406-387-5555; www.glacierguides.com; 11970 Hwy 2; fishing half-/full day US$400/515) This company runs fishing trips to the Middle and North Forks of the Flathead River, and beginners can sign up for half- or full-day lessons (US$400/515; part-classroom, part-practical). It's also recommended for rafting trips (half-day US$53 to US$87, full day US$100) and guided hikes in the park.

🛏 SLEEPING

In the early 1910s, James Hill's Great Northern Railway built a series of grand hotels to lure rich tourists to Glacier National Park. Two of these so-called 'parkitecture' structures, Many Glacier Hotel and Lake McDonald Lodge, still stand within the park boundaries, conjuring up nostalgic memories of times gone by.

There are 13 NPS campgrounds. For comprehensive information about camping in the park, see www.nps.gov.

🛏 Going-to-the-Sun Road

Camping

Rising Sun Campground   CAMPGROUND $
(Rising Sun Campground Rd; tent & RV sites US$20; ⊙mid-Jun–mid-Sep) Sites at this campground above the north side of St Mary Lake vary, with lush and diverse vegetation providing some shade. A host of facilities, including the Rising Sun Motor Inn, an excellent store, shower facilities, a restaurant and a boat launch, are nearby. A handful of sites, including 35, 37 and 39 especially, offer outstanding views of Red Eagle Mountain.

Sprague Creek Campground   CAMPGROUND $
(Going-to-the-Sun Rd, Lake McDonald; tent sites US$20; ⊙May–mid-Sep) Off Going-to-the-Sun Rd on the shore of Lake McDonald, the park's smallest campground draws mostly tents – no vehicles over 21ft are allowed – and feels more intimate than many of the park's other options, at least at night when the passing traffic goes to bed.

Arrive early to claim a site overlooking the lake. Hiker/biker sites US$5.

Avalanche Creek
Campground   CAMPGROUND $
(tent & RV sites US$20; ⊙mid-Jun–mid-Sep) This lush campground abutting the park's old-growth cedar forest gets more rainfall than most. Some sites are overshadowed by old stands of hemlock, cedar and Douglas fir, but you're close to Lake McDonald and right in the path of a couple of very popular trailheads. Expect no quiet or privacy during the daytime.

Apgar Campground   CAMPGROUND $
(☑406-888-7800; www.recreation.gov; tent & RV sites US$20; ⊙year-round) This large wooded campground, the park's largest, is a good choice for its proximity to the conveniences of Apgar Village and West Glacier, as well as for being only a short stroll to Lake McDonald. It feels, however, far from a wilderness experience.

St Mary Campground   CAMPGROUND $
(☑406-732-7708; www.recreation.gov; St Mary Campground Rd; tent & RV sites US$23; ⊙year-round) Cottonwood and aspen dot this mostly flat and exposed campground with reservable sites (up to six months in advance) just west of St Mary entrance station. It can be breezy and sunny, but does have unobstructed views of the lower valley. Showers for registered campers. It's only half a mile walk to the St Mary Visitor Center.

Lodging

Lake McDonald Lodge   HISTORIC HOTEL $$
(☑855-733-4522; www.glaciernationalparklodges. com; r US$85-190, cabins US$140-205, ste US$329; ⊙mid-May–Sep; 🐾) 🐾 Fronting luminous Lake McDonald and built in classic US 'parkitecture' style, the lodge welcomes its guests through a more mundane backdoor setting – they originally disembarked from a boat on the lakeside. Once inside the main building, a huge fireplace, Native American-themed paintings and taxidermied animal heads ensure you know you're out West. Small, comfortably rustic rooms are complemented by cottages and a 1950s motel.

Built on the site of an earlier lodge commissioned by park pioneer George Snyder in the 1890s, the present building was constructed in 1913 and rooms remain sans air-con and television – it's worth requesting one of the more than two dozen rooms and cabins renovated for the 2016 season. Deluxe ones even boast some boutique stylings, including tiled bathrooms, extremely comfy king-sized beds and a touch of art. Two restaurants are on-site and evening ranger programs are held nightly in the summer. The lakefront location is fairly ideal and close to trailheads on Going-to-the-Sun Rd.

Village Inn at Apgar   MOTEL $$
(☑855-733-4522; www.glaciernationalparklodges. com; Apgar Village; r US$179, ste US$240-302; ⊙Jun–mid-Sep) When you lean out on your sunrise-facing balcony at this motel, occupying a serene setting at the southern end of Lake McDonald in Apgar Village, you are quite literally within spitting distance of the park's largest and most tranquil lake. The

rooms, rustic and gadget-free, underwent a top-to-bottom renovation in 2015, including new carpeting and bedding.

Rising Sun Motor Inn MOTEL **$$**
(📞855-733-4522; www.glaciernationalparklodges.com; r & cabin US$175; ☺Jun–mid-Sep; 🐾) One of two classic 1940s-era motor inns in the park, the Rising Sun's recent makeover has brought it tastefully up-to-date without sacrificing its historic character. The 71 motel and cabin rooms are set in the back of the compound across the road from the upper north shore of St Mary Lake. The summer camp-like cabin exteriors are deceptive; inside it's plush bedding and historic park posters and photos.

The motel is part of a small complex that includes an excellent general store, campground and boat launch (the 2015 Reynolds Creek Fire burned all the way to the property's backside). The lobby (the only place with wi-fi) and check-in is in the same building as the gift shop and the excellent, also updated restaurant.

Apgar Village Lodge MOTEL **$$**
(📞406-892-2525; www.glacierparkcollection.com; r US$95-150, cabins US$150-380; ☺mid-May–Sep) This lodge (one of two in Apgar Village) offers a variety of well-maintained motel-style rooms and cabins. The family cabins are spacious and come with kitchenettes, while the smaller rooms are rustic, if decidedly cozy, with large back windows looking out on McDonald Creek, and Adirondack chairs out front for catching some afternoon rays.

🛏 South of Going-to-the-Sun Road

Cut Bank Campground CAMPGROUND **$**
(tent sites US$10; ☺May-Sep) Strangely enough, considering its appealing out-of-the-way feel, park rangers at Glacier's visitor centers sometimes forget about this small, peaceful site. It's accessed via a 5-mile-long gravel road off Hwy 89, halfway between St Mary and the junction for Two Medicine. Several recommended hikes, including the much-favored Medicine Grizzly Lake, leave from here.

Two Medicine Campground CAMPGROUND **$**
(Two Medicine Valley; tent & RV sites US$20; ☺end May-Oct) This campground below Rising Wolf Mountain, 3 miles southwest of Two Medicine entrance station, is your only accommodation in the park's relatively ignored southwest corner. It's a picturesque area with nicely wooded sites and easy lake and creek access. A camp store with prepared foods is close by. Primitive camping allowed through end of October.

🛏 North of Going-to-the-Sun Road

Camping

All campgrounds are first-come, first-served, except Fish Creek.

⭐**Bowman Lake**
Campground CAMPGROUND **$**
(North Fork; tent & RV sites US$15; ☺mid-May–early Sep) Rarely full, this campground 6 miles up Inside North Fork Rd from Polebridge offers very spacious sites in forested grounds, and beautiful Bowman Lake is only steps away. It has a visitors information tent with reference books and local hiking information. The road from Polebridge can be especially rough after heavy rain. Also offers primitive camping through to end of October.

Many Glacier
Campground CAMPGROUND **$**
(Many Glacier Campground Rd; tent & RV sites US$23; ☺end May-Sep) With access to phenomenal trails, this heavily wooded campground is one of the park's most popular. It lies within strolling distance of the Swiftcurrent Motor Inn complex, which includes a restaurant, hot showers, a laundry and camp store. Primitive camping available through the end of October.

Half of the sites are reservable (www.recreation.gov), including numbers 94 and 92, which are the best spots along the river.

Fish Creek
Campground CAMPGROUND **$**
(tent & RV sites US$23; ☺Jun-early Sep) Cocooned inside a dense cedar-hemlock forest along Lake McDonald and only 2.5 miles from Apgar Village, this large campground with showers (located in loop A and a long walk from other locations) offers registered campers sites that are tucked among the trees. Some have quick access to the lake and views, but loop C is rocky with few level spots.

GLACIER NATIONAL PARK CAMPGROUNDS

CAMPGROUND	LOCATION	DESCRIPTION	NO OF SITES
Apgar	Going-to-the-Sun Rd	The park's largest campground is near trails, a lake and Apgar Village	192
Avalanche Creek	Going-to-the-Sun Rd	In old-growth forest and close to hikes; also has an outdoor amphitheater for evening programs	87
Rising Sun	Going-to-the-Sun Rd	Part-open, part-covered sites close to camp store, restaurant and boat launch	84
Sprague Creek	Going-to-the-Sun Rd	No RVs allowed; tranquil lake views are hindered by proximity to Going-to-the-Sun Rd	25
St Mary	Going-to-the-Sun Rd	Large and fairly open, with cracking views; visitor center nearby	148
Bowman Lake	North of Going-to-the-Sun Rd	Remote and basic, but great for tent campers; pit toilets available; bring mosquito repellent	48
Fish Creek	North of Going-to-the-Sun Rd	Large, wooded campground that offers plenty of privacy	180
Kintla Lake	North of Going-to-the-Sun Rd	The park's most remote campground; listen to the howls of wolves at night	13
Logging Creek	North of Going-to-the-Sun Rd	Small and primitive with no services, although there are pit toilets	13
Many Glacier	North of Going-to-the-Sun Rd	One of the park's most popular campgrounds, set in a beautiful valley with facilities nearby	110
Quartz Creek	North of Going-to-the-Sun Rd	Smallest campground in the park, primitive; RVs not recommended	7
Cut Bank	South of Going-to-the-Sun Rd	Small, quiet and secluded campground; access to several trailheads; no RVs	19
Two Medicine	South of Going-to-the-Sun Rd	Secluded campground with space for larger RVs, and an evening ranger program	100

 Drinking Water   *Restrooms*   *Great for Families*   ♿ *Wheelchair Accessible*

Kintla Lake Campground CAMPGROUND $
(Inside North Fork Rd; tent sites US$15; ⊙early Jun-early Sep) If you've come to Glacier to dip your nose into *Ulysses* and *War and Peace*, you'll find little to disturb you at this primitive campground, at the top of Inside North Fork Rd around 15 miles north of Polebridge. Primitive camping allowed through end of October.

Logging Creek Campground CAMPGROUND $
(Inside North Fork Rd; tent sites US$10; ⊙ Jul-end Sep) It takes some determination to reach this primitive campground, on Inside North Fork Rd, 17 miles north of Fish Creek Campground, but it is worth it if you're looking for tranquility amid the trees. The atmosphere is very still here, but for the sound of a flowing creek.

Quartz Creek Campground CAMPGROUND $
(Inside North Fork Rd; tent sites US$10; ⊙ Jul-Oct) The campground here, on Inside North Fork Rd, is tranquil. The sites, surrounded by thick vegetation, feel private.

Lodging

★**Many Glacier Hotel** HISTORIC HOTEL $$
(📞 303-265-7010; www.glaciernationalparklodges. com; 1 Many Glacier Rd; r US$207-322, ste US$476; ⊙mid-Jun–mid-Sep; 🐾) Enjoying the most wondrous setting in the park, this massive, Swiss chalet–inspired lodge (some of the male staff wear lederhosen) commands the northeastern shore of Swiftcurrent Lake. It was built by the Great Northern Railway in 1915, and the comfortable, if rustic, rooms have been updated (restoration work contin-

ELEVATION	OPEN	RESERVATIONS	DAILY FEE	FACILITIES	PAGE
960m (3153ft)	May-Oct & Nov-Mar	no	US$15-20		p196
1067m (3500ft)	Jun-Sep	no	US$20		p196
1463m (4800ft)	Jun-Sep	no	US$20		p196
1067m (3500ft)	May-Sep	no	US$20		p196
1372m (4500ft)	year-round	available	US$23		p196
1372m (4500ft)	year-round	no	US$15		p197
1067m (3500ft)	Jun-Sep	available	US$23		p197
1372m (4500ft)	year-round	no	US$15		p198
1372m (4500ft)	Jul-Sep	no	US$10		p198
1372m (4500ft)	May-Sep	no	US$23		p197
884m (2900ft)	Jul-Oct	no	US$10		p198
1562m (5125ft)	May-Sep	no	US$10		p197
1585m (5200ft)	Apr-Oct	no	US$20		p197

Grocery Store Nearby	Restaurant Nearby	Summertime Campfire Program	RV Dump Station

ues) over the last 15 years. The deluxe rooms feature boutique-style elements, including contemporary tiled bathrooms.

The raised stone hearth with a unique chimney system from the 1940s marks the center of the large lobby and lounge area where guests gather to take in the shimmering snow and glacier-capped peaks (anyone can try out the lobby piano circa 1877). Some of the park's most iconic hikes leave from nearby. Several restaurants are part of the complex, and hikers can stock up on food and other supplies at the cafe and shop downstairs.

Those who want their video downloads in the wilderness will be happy to know that hi-speed wi-fi will be available in the rooms in 2020.

Swiftcurrent Motor Inn MOTEL $$
(☑ 855-733-4522; www.glaciernationalparklodges .com; cabin with/without bath US$140/115, r US$175; ☺ mid-Jun–mid-Sep; ☎) After an extensive renovation, the Swiftcurrent, ideally located next to numerous Many Glacier trailheads, has retained the facade of classic roadside relic, while its mixture of cabins and motel-style rooms offer a version of upscale contemporary rusticity. Cabins come with colorful bedding, black-and-white historical photos and deep sinks in the bathrooms; some have pull-out couches sleeping four. True to park tradition, no TV and air-con.

Directly outside the front door is a handy store, a restaurant and a laundry facility, all of which are also heavily frequented by guests at the campground across the street.

BACKCOUNTRY ACCOMMODATIONS

Sperry Chalet (☎888-345-2649; www.sperrychalet.com; Lake McDonald Valley; s/d incl full board US$135/332; ☉Jul–early Sep) Constructed by the Great Northern Railway in 1914, much of this 17-room historic Swiss-style chalet burned down in a 2017 fire. Its historic features will be maintained in the planned rebuild (expected to reopen by the 2020 season). It's a good three-hour hike from the nearest road, and guests must either walk or horseback ride here via an ascending 6½-mile trail that begins at Lake McDonald Lodge.

With no lights, heat or water, staying at Sperry rates alongside a night in the African bush. Part of an old accommodations network that once spanned the park before the construction of Going-to-the-Sun Rd, Sperry offers phenomenal views. Be sure to bring a flashlight for midnight trips to the outdoor toilets. Rooms are private; walls, however, are paper thin. Rates include three excellent meals (box lunches are available) and mules can be hired to carry gear.

Granite Park Chalet (☎888-345-2649; www.graniteparkchalet.com; 1st person US$108, extra person US$80; ☉Jul–mid-Sep) A popular stopping point for hikers on the Swiftcurrent Pass and Highline trails, this very basic chalet (pit toilets) dates back to the park's early 20th-century heyday. A rustic kitchen is available for use (with propane-powered stoves), though you must bring and prepare your own food. Snacks and freeze-dried meals are available for purchase. Twelve guest rooms sleep from two to six people each.

Bedding costs US$25 extra per person. Book in advance as it gets busy, and remember to bring as much of your own water as possible (bottled water and sodas are available to buy). Reservations should be made online.

✖ EATING

✖ Going-to-the-Sun Road

Jammer Joe's Grill & Pizzeria PIZZA $
(Lake McDonald Lodge; sandwiches & pizza US$12; ☉11am-9pm late May-early Sep; ♠) Only steps away, but light-years from Lake McDonald Lodge's decor and vibe, Jammer Joe's (named for Joe Kendall, who drove the park's iconic Red Buses for 16 years) looks like a pizzeria from a Midwestern suburban strip mall circa 1970. However, it's a pleasant apparition for tired hikers enamored by the simple no-frills menu, which, in addition to whole-grain pizzas, includes burgers, pasta and salads.

Two Dog Flats Grill AMERICAN $$
(Rising Sun Motor Inn; mains US$11-26; ☉6:30am-10am & 11am-10pm mid-Jun–mid-Sep; ♠) With a clientele made up primarily of famished hikers and tour-bus passengers happy just to stretch their legs, Two Dog doesn't have to try too hard to satisfy. However, with an emphasis on organic and locally sourced ingredients, it offers typical Montana fare with a twist, like the organic tofu scrambler, sautéed local trout and huckleberry pulled-pork sandwich.

Also has a good selection of local microbrews and wines from the American west.

Eddie's Cafe AMERICAN $$
(236 Apgar Loop Rd, Apgar Village; mains US$13-12; ☉7am-9pm late May–mid-Sep; ♠) Summer jobbers man the diner-style tables inside Apgar Village's only eating joint, serving up meatloaf, fish and chips and buffalo burgers from a kitchen where quantity rules over quality. We prefer it for breakfast, especially the hearty burrito. There's usually a line at the side window, which dishes out quality ice cream, lemonade, tea and coffee.

Russells Fireside Dining Room INTERNATIONAL $$$
(Lake McDonald Lodge; mains US$12-30; ☉6:30am-9:30pm late May–mid-Sep; ✐) ✿ Lake views and stuffed animal heads characterize the interior of this handsome restaurant. You can enjoy hash browns for breakfast, huckleberry-elk burger for lunch, and steelhead trout and the southwest rotini skillet (corn, organic pinto beans, spinach, tomato, peppers and cheddar cheese) for dinner.

✖ South of Going-to-the-Sun Road

Two Medicine Campstore SANDWICHES, GROCERY $
(Two Medicine Valley; sandwiches US$8; ☉7am-9pm mid-Apr–Sep) While the Two Medicine Valley has no standard restaurants, you can forgo al-

fresco campground cooking and chow down on excellent chili, soups and sandwiches, at this historic building-cum-grocery-store and gift shop that once served as a dining hall for the erstwhile Two Medicine Chalets. Your can also grab coffee, ice cream and ingredients to make up a decent picnic.

President FD Roosevelt, accompanied by John D Rockefeller Jr, chose to give one of his famous 'fireside chats' here in the 1930s.

✖ North of Going-to-the-Sun Road

'Nell's   AMERICAN $
(Swiftcurrent Motor Inn; mains US$10-14; ⊙6:30am-10pm mid-Jun–mid-Sep) Recently made over from top to bottom, 'Nell's menu is geared to famished hikers and campers looking for a quick meal on the go or to take with them on the trail. The menu, including egg sandwiches and oatmeal for breakfast and burgers, mac & cheese, pizza, salads, wraps and sandwiches, is displayed on the screen above the counter where you order.

Ptarmigan Dining Room   INTERNATIONAL $$$
(Many Glacier Hotel; mains US$15-43; ⊙6:30am-9:30pm mid-Jun–mid-Sep) With magnificent lakeside views, this spacious and handsomely designed restaurant with vaulted ceilings is the most refined of the park's lodges. Enjoy 7, 10 or 14oz prime rib, grilled wild Alaskan salmon, surf and turf burger, craft cocktails and microbrews, and watch bears munch on berries in the bushes outside. The staff, mostly international and seasonal, have service kinks to work out early in the summer.

🍷 DRINKING & ENTERTAINMENT

Both the Many Glacier Hotel and Lake McDonald Lodge have cozy bars, good for a post-hike alcoholic beverage. In West Glacier, **Freda's** (West Glacier Bar; Going-to-the-Sun Rd; ⊙noon-11pm) and the Belton Chalet (p207) are the liveliest for drinks; East Glacier has a couple of restaurants with bars, including in the Glacier Park Lodge.

The park visitor centers give out a free newspaper listing evening programs, including ranger talks and Native American Speaks. Summer events kick off nightly between 7:30pm and 8:30pm, rotating between locations.

🛍 SHOPPING

Montana House   ARTS & CRAFTS
(☎406-888-5393; www.montanahouse.info; 198 Apgar Loop Rd; ⊙9am-7:30pm Jun-Sep, 10am-5pm May-Oct) A Glacier Park institution since 1960, Montana House offers a wide selection of quality jewelry, Montana-inspired artwork and photography, and books about Glacier for adults and kids. On the second floor, the new space hosts community meetings, film screenings, live music and talks about subjects like wildfires and the grizzly bear population. Check the website for the event schedule.

Importantly, Montana House is the only place open in Apgar and West Glacier in the winter. You can stop in here for a hot chocolate, coffee, granola bar and a selection of snacks. After a day out cross-country skiing in below freezing temps with nary another human in sight, entering the warm shop can feel unreal.

ℹ Information

DANGERS & ANNOYANCES
Glacier is prime grizzly-bear country and, although you're more likely to be involved in a car accident than be maimed by a bear, attacks have happened. Bear spray costs US$49 and is available in all outdoor stores in and around the park; a few stores rent spray by the day. Your best bet is Go Glacier Outfitters (p185); bear spray rental is US$9.25 for 24 hours and US$28 for three to seven days, with a shop near the baggage claim in FCA Airport and another in Apgar Village. It also has a bin to return rental bear spray in East Glacier.

Another option, suggested by airline employees at FCA, is to ask departing travelers before they have to throw their spray away (you can't fly with it or travel across the border to Canada).

Solo backcountry hikes aren't advised. The larger your hiking group, the less likely you are to encounter a bear.

Water poses the greatest danger in the park, from hikers testing out no-longer-frozen-solid icy lakes to scampering over slippery rocks and through rushing water.

Going-to-the-Sun Rd is crowded and vertiginous with a steep drop-off. As it is a historic monument there are no modern guard rails. Drive with care.

INTERNET ACCESS
Mobile wi-fi signals generally don't extend far past park entrances. The visitor center in Apgar provides free service, and the park lodges make their wi-fi available to guests only. There are also internet points in St Mary and West Glacier.

LAUNDRY & SHOWERS

St Mary (p196) and Fish Creek (p197) have showers for registered campers. The camp stores at Rising Sun (p197) and Swiftcurrent (p199) motor inns have showers open to the public. The latter also has laundry facilities. Also, Glacier Campground (p207) in West Glacier and the KOA campground (p209) in St Mary have showers available for US$5 for non-guests.

MEDICAL SERVICES

North Valley Hospital (☑ 406-863-3500; www.nvhosp.org; 1600 Hospital Way, Whitefish; ⊙ 24hr) A 24-hour facility in Whitefish.

West Glacier Clinic (p259) The most convenient place to head to for medical attention for minor injuries.

MONEY

Canadian currency is not widely accepted in Glacier. The nearest banks are in Columbia Falls and Browning. West Glacier, East Glacier and St Mary have 24-hour ATMs, as do Many Glacier Hotel, Swiftcurrent Motor Inn, Rising Sun Motor Inn and Lake McDonald Lodge. There's also an ATM at the camp store at Eddie's Cafe in Apgar Village.

TELEPHONE

All park lodges and nonprimitive campgrounds have public phones.

Cell (mobile) phone service in the park is unreliable; however, most networks have sporadic reception near the entrances, and Verizon even further into the park.

TOURIST INFORMATION

The park has three informative visitor centers and three fully staffed ranger stations scattered within its midst. All are overseen by knowledgeable and helpful rangers during peak season. Visitor centers usually offer other amenities such as restrooms, drinking water, bookstores, maps and interpretive displays.

Apgar Backcountry Permit Center (☑ 406-888-7800; www.nps.gov/glac; Apgar Village; ⊙ 7am-5pm Jun-late Sep, 8am-4pm May & Oct) Get information on backcountry camping everywhere in Glacier and purchase permits if you haven't already booked online. Check out the binder with detailed information and photos of every route and site.

Apgar Visitor Center (☑ 406-888-7939; west end of Going-to-the-Sun Rd; ⊙ 8am-6pm daily mid-May–mid-Oct, hours vary Sat & Sun mid-Oct–mid-May) This LEED–certified center with a large parking lot and free wi-fi signal is 1½ miles north of West Glacier at the west end of Going-to-the-Sun Rd. Catch the **free park shuttle** (www.nps.gov/glac; ⊙ 7am-7pm Jul & Aug) here for all points along Going-to-the-Sun Rd to Logan Pass, where you transfer to continue to

St Mary Visitor Center. Rangers hold periodic demonstrations about how to use bear spray. In the winter, Saturday morning **snowshoe** trips leave from here.

Logan Pass Visitor Center (☑ 406-888-7800; Going-to-the-Sun Rd; ⊙ 9am-7pm late Jun-late Aug, 9:30am-4pm Sep) In the most magnificent setting of all the park's visitor centers, the building has park information, interactive exhibits and a good gift shop. The Hidden Lake Overlook Trail (p176) and Highline (p179) trails begin here.

Many Glacier Ranger Station (☑ 406-732-7740; ⊙ 7am-4:30pm late May-late Sep) Call here for local hiking information and details of recent bear activity.

Polebridge Ranger Station (☑ 406-888-7842; ⊙ 9am-4:30pm late May-late Sep) A small historic station with North Fork information; also issues backcountry permits. One of the rangers is the owner of the nearby North Fork Hostel.

St Mary Visitor Center (east end of Going-to-the-Sun Rd; ⊙ 8am-6pm late May-early Sep, to 5pm Sep-early Oct) Houses interesting exhibits on wildlife, geology and Native American culture and history, as well as an auditorium featuring slide shows and ranger talks. For over 35 years, the **Native America Speaks** program has connected visitors with the stories, history and culture of the Blackfeet, Salish, and Kootenai tribes. Check the seasonal schedule for days and times. Also has a good gift shop.

An astronomical observatory was opened at the visitor center in late August 2019; expect public programs to begin soon to take advantage of the dark, starry nights here.

Two Medicine Ranger Station (☑ 406-226-4484; ⊙ 7am-4:30pm Jun-late Sep) A good source for Two Medicine area hikes.

❶ Getting There & Away

Glacier Park International Airport (p275) in Kalispell has year-round service to Salt Lake, Minneapolis, Denver, Seattle and Las Vegas, and seasonal service to Atlanta, Oakland, LA, Chicago and Portland. Alaska, Allegiant, American Airlines, Delta and United have flights to FCA.

The Great Falls International Airport (p275) is 140 miles south of East Glacier.

Amtrak's *Empire Builder* (www.amtrak.com) stops daily at **West Glacier** (⊙ year-round) and **East Glacier Park** (⊙ Apr-Oct), with a whistle stop in Browning. Xanterra provides a shuttle (adult US$6 to US$10, child US$3 to US$5, 10 to 20 minutes) from West Glacier to their lodges on the west end, and Glacier Park Collection by Pursuit offers shuttles (from US$15, one hour) connecting East Glacier Park to St Mary and Whitefish.

🛈 Getting Around

Glacier National Park runs a free hop-on, hop-off shuttle bus from **Apgar Transit Center** to St Mary over Going-to-the-Sun Rd during summer months; it stops at all major trailheads. Xanterra concession operates the classic guided Red Bus Tours (p195).

If driving a personal vehicle, be prepared for narrow, winding roads, traffic jams, and limited parking at most stops along Going-to-the-Sun Rd.

BICYCLE

Getting around by bike is feasible on Going-to-the-Sun Rd at certain times of the day – although the ride is tough. With all trails out of bounds, cyclists are confined to plying the park's scant road network. A 2½-mile paved bike path runs between Apgar Village and West Glacier.

BUS

Free park shuttle buses ferry visitors between spots on Going-to-the-Sun Rd, which means all of the park's major trailheads (bar those in the remote North Fork area) are well served by public transportation from July 1 to Labor Day. Service in 23-seater buses between the Apgar Visitor Center (via Apgar Village) leave every 30 minutes from 9am to 5:45pm. For non-stop service to Logan Pass, several smaller buses leave in the morning between 7am and 7:30am (the last bus leaves Logan Pass at 7pm). To continue on down to the St Mary Visitor Center, you have to transfer to another bus. The buses have air-conditioning, are wheelchair accessible and run on biodiesel. Most of the shuttles have bike racks. Clear route maps are provided at every shuttle stop or can be viewed on the park website at www.nps.gov/glac.

On the park's eastern side, **Glacier Park Collection by Pursuit** (☑844-868-7474; www.glacierparkcollection.com) runs the East Side Shuttle (US$15 to US$30 depending on distance) between Glacier Park Lodge, Two Medicine and St Mary Lodge (reservations can be made up to 24 hours in advance) and **Xanterra** (Glacier National Park Lodges; ☑855-733-4522; www.glaciernationalparklodges.com) runs its own first-come, first-served shuttle (adult US$6 to US$10, child US$3 to US$5) connecting Many Glacier Hotel and the Swiftcurrent Motor Inn with the St Mary Visitor Center. All shuttles run from early June to mid-/ late September.

CAR & MOTORCYCLE

The only paved road to completely bisect the park is the 85-kilometer (53-mile) Going-to-the-Sun Rd. The partly unpaved Inside North Fork Rd links Apgar with Polebridge. To connect with any other roads, vehicles must briefly leave the park and re-enter via another entrance.

A decades-plus-long upgrade of Going-to-the-Sun Rd means construction and minor delays aren't uncommon. Also, because of forest fires or other natural events, unexpected road closures do happen.

Hwy 2 is fairly well maintained in the winter, which means you can drive between West and East Glacier, but it still means winter driving; chains or studded tires are recommended.

The car rental counters at Glacier International Park Airport are just before baggage claim. The pick-up and drop-off process generally runs remarkably smoothly. The Dollar Rent A Car (p211) office is a few minutes drive from the airport, but staff are waiting to pick you up and get you moving quickly. Hertz (www.hertz.com) and Budget (www.budget.com) can also deliver cars to the West Glacier and East Glacier train stations (you can leave them here as well). Other outlets can be found in the nearby town of Whitefish.

TRAIN

Largely responsible for opening up the region in the 1890s, the train has been a popular method of transport to Glacier since the park's inception in 1910. Amtrak's *Empire Builder* continues to ply the Great Northern Railway's historic east–west route from Chicago to Seattle once daily (in either direction), stopping in both East Glacier (6:45pm westbound, 9:54am eastbound; stops mid-spring to mid-fall) and West Glacier (8:23pm westbound, 8:16am eastbound). The same train also connects with Whitefish and (by request only) Essex.

From the East Glacier Park station, you can get the **East Side Shuttle** (www.glacierparkcollection.com) to Two Medicine (US$15, 30 minutes) or St Mary (US$30, one hour), where you can transfer to the free park shuttle. And from West Glacier, a Xanterra shuttle can take you to Lake McDonald Lodge (adult/child US$10/5) or Village Inn at Apgar (adult/child US$6/3). From either location you can hop aboard the free park shuttle to your choice of campgrounds, most of which have hiker sites.

Note: the westbound train arrives after the free park shuttle stops, meaning you'll need to overnight in either East Glacier or West Glacier; if arriving at the latter, it is possible to walk to Apgar Campground (half a mile).

GLACIER NATIONAL PARK GETTING AROUND

EB ADVENTURE PHOTOGRAPHY / SHUTTERSTOCK ©

1. Kayaking on Lake McDonald (p39)
Canoeing and kayaking are the best ways to get out on the water.

2. Lake McDonald Lodge (p196)
Situated on the northeastern shore of the lake in Glacier National Park, this is the park's oldest hotel.

3. Iceberg Lake Trail (p183)
A popular trail, with good reason – the lake features bobbing icebergs surrounded by 3000ft vertical walls.

4. Going-to-the-Sun Road (p188)
One of the most spectacular drives imaginable, it shows off vistas, waterfalls and glaciers.

Around Glacier National Park

Best Places to Stay

➡ Izaak Walton Inn (p210)

➡ St Mary Tiny Homes (p209)

➡ North Fork Hostel & Square Peg Ranch (p208)

➡ Belton Chalet (p207)

➡ Brownie's (p210)

➡ Garden Wall Inn (p214)

Best Places to Eat

➡ Whitefish Lake Restaurant (p215)

➡ Belton Chalet Grill & Taproom (p207)

➡ Serrano's Mexican Restaurant (p211)

➡ Abruzzo Italian Kitchen (p214)

Why Go?

After you spend a day exploring Glacier's natural wonders, you'll find the communities surrounding the park provide a welcome taste of civilization in the Montana wilderness. The tiny towns of West Glacier, East Glacier and St Mary may look like little more than blips on the map, but they provide a wealth of tourist services, including campgrounds, motels and restaurants.

The more substantial town of Whitefish, on the park's western fringes, cranks things up a notch, with a lively downtown, a wider range of accommodations and eateries, a summer farmers market and a host of outdoor activities, from downhill skiing to cycling to swimming in the local parks. East of Glacier, Browning is home to the Blackfeet Nation and the fascinating Museum of the Plains Indian.

When to Go

Glacier National Park

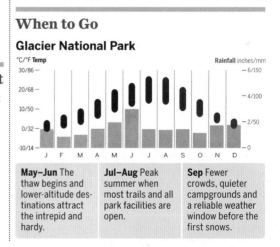

May–Jun The thaw begins and lower-altitude destinations attract the intrepid and hardy.

Jul–Aug Peak summer when most trails and all park facilities are open.

Sep Fewer crowds, quieter campgrounds and a reliable weather window before the first snows.

West Glacier

Lying a bit over half a mile from the park's busiest entrance gate and equipped with an Amtrak train station, West Glacier is the park's most pleasant gateway town, with an attractive cluster of serviceable facilities and the base for white-water rafting and kayak trips. Known as Belton until 1949, the settlement was the site of the park's oldest hotel, the Belton Chalet, built in 1910 and still hosting guests. The village anchors the western terminus of Going-to-the-Sun Rd. Whitefish, a charming and sophisticated year-round outdoor adventurer destination in its own right, and a possible base for forays into the park, lies only 26 miles west.

🛏️ Sleeping

Glacier Campground   CAMPGROUND $

(☑ 406-387-5689; www.glaciercampground.com; 12070 Hwy 2; tent/RV sites US$28/45, cabins US$45-65; 🛜) This well-run and friendly campground, located 1 mile west of West Glacier and off Hwy 2, sits on 40 acres of densely wooded grounds. Sites (all have electrical outlets) come in a variety of sizes and configurations, so it's best to check out several before committing. It also offers basic wooden cabins (you'll need to bring your own bedding).

Hearty grub, such as gumbo and catfish po'boys, is served from 7am to 3:30pm Tuesday to Sunday in the **Sunflower Cafe** restaurant (mains US$10), an outdoor pavilion open to nonguests as well.

Nonguests can shower here for US$5.

★ Belton Chalet   HISTORIC HOTEL $$

(☑ 406-892-2525; www.beltonchalet.com; 12575 Hwy 2; r US$145-210, cottages US$350) 🏳️ Built and opened the same year as the national park (1910), this Swiss chalet overlooking the railroad tracks in West Glacier was Glacier's first tourist hotel. Other incarnations followed, including time as a pizza parlor, and it lay rotting until a late-1990s refurb, which dusted off 25 traditional yet elegant rooms, arts-and-crafts-style furnishings, a spa and a celebrated taproom.

Glacier Highland Resort Motel   MOTEL $$

(☑ 406-888-5427; www.glacierhighland.com; 12555 Hwy 2; r US$145; 🛜) The majority of the rooms at this popular place are in a low-slung motel-style building just up the hill from the West Glacier train station. It

has a faux log cabin exterior, whereas the blandly furnished, carpeted rooms offer little suggestion you're out West; it does have flat-screen TVs.

Glacier Guides Lodge   B&B $$

(☑ 406-387-5555; www.glacierguides.com; Highline Blvd; r US$229; ❄️🛜) 🏳️ One of West Glacier's nicest properties, Glacier Guides Lodge is set in a quiet pocket just off Hwy 2, opposite the West Glacier train station. It's an attractive wooden B&B-style lodge (built to LEED standards) with a stylish, rustic authenticity that doesn't forsake creature comforts such as wi-fi, air-con and TV. Rooms are discounted to US$169 during spring and autumn.

West Glacier Motel & Cabins   MOTEL $$

(☑ 844-868-7474; www.glacierparkcollection.com; cnr Going-to-the-Sun Rd & River Bend Dr; d US$95-115, cabins US$135-240) A bed and a Bible are the only two guarantees at the closest motel to the park entrance, located on the north side of the railroad tracks in West Glacier Village. Motel-style rooms are situated in the retro building in the village, while cabins are perched on a bluff overlooking Flathead River. No TVs, fridges, coffee machines or wi-fi.

🍴 Eating & Drinking

Great Northern Railway Cafe   CAFE $

(12125 Hwy 2; sandwiches US$8; ⏰ 8am-8pm Jun-Sep) Housed in a bright red Great Northern Railway train caboose, with a kitchen the size of a food truck's, this little cafe serves up excellent breakfast sandwiches, crepes and simple paninis and salads. It's attached to the Great Northern Rafting company office and has a large outdoor patio.

West Glacier Restaurant   AMERICAN $

(200 Going-to-the-Sun Rd; mains US$8-17; ⏰ 7am-10pm mid-May–Oct; 👶) Recently renovated and redesigned, both in terms of its menu and decor, the blandly named West Glacier Restaurant is now one of the more enjoyable places to eat on this side of the park. Choose from burgers (elk, bison, lentil or good 'ol Western beef) or an excellent homemade chili. Looking to load up on calories? Go for a sundae, float, frappe or milkshake.

★ Belton Chalet Grill & Taproom   AMERICAN $$$

(☑ 406-888-5000; www.beltonchalet.com; 12575 Hwy 2, West Yellowstone; mains US$24-35; ⏰ 5-9pm, tap room from 3pm) 🏳️ West Glacier's finest dining option, housed in one of its most historic buildings, has evolved with

POLEBRIDGE

Glacier's most isolated outpost is populated with more wildlife than people (although if you plan your journey around Polebridge's raucous July 4th celebration, the opposite may be true). Sandwiched between the towering Livingstone and Whitefish mountain ranges, the 'town' is a low-key place really consisting of two hubs: the Northern Lights Saloon (offering ales, tall tales and a standard pub-grub menu) and the historic Polebridge Mercantile (a combination store, post office, gas station and local gathering spot).

Camping is free along the North Fork of the Flathead River or you can stop by Glacier's quirkiest lodgings – the **North Fork Hostel & Square Peg Ranch** (Map p192; ☑ 406-888-5241; www.nfhostel.com; 80 Beaver Dr, Polebridge; tent sites/dm/tipis & trailers US$27/30/75, cabins US$75-105; ☺ end May-Sep 15; ☎ ☀) 🖉; expect no electricity, few facilities and even fewer worries.

Polebridge is located on the Outside North Fork Rd, 26 miles northwest of the park's western entrance. The Polebridge Ranger Station lies 1 mile to the east, next to the park entrance. Driving a car is the only reliable way of getting to Polebridge, although you'll need good snow tires in the winter. The North Fork Hostel sometimes runs a shuttle service from West Glacier.

the times, the faux Swiss milkmaid waitress uniforms aside. The head chef, a Whitefish native now in his second season at the helm, has created a sophisticated menu featuring locally sourced ingredients and mains such as bison meatloaf with broccolini and bacon lardons (strips of fatty bacon).

The adjoining taproom is a more casual, economical affair that offers some inventive sandwiches, microbrews and craft cocktails.

🏪 Shopping

Glacier Outdoor Center SPORTS & OUTDOORS
(☑ 406-888-5454; www.glacierraftco.com; 11957 Hwy 2; ☺ 7:30am-9pm) Just outside the park, about half a mile from the train station on US 2, this is the best one-stop shop for outdoor gear. It rents and sells everything you could need for rafting, fishing, mountain biking, camping and backpacking. It shares premises with and is owned and operated by Glacier Rafting Co.

ℹ Information

Most basic facilities can be found here, including a gas station, a grocery store, a post office and an ATM. There's also a coin-operated laundry in the back of the parking lot where the Alberta Information Centre is located.

Alberta Information Centre (☑ 406-888-5743; off Hwy 2; ☺ 8am-7pm; ☎) A large and comprehensive visitor center for wilderness junkies keen on heading north to Waterton Lakes, Banff and Jasper National Parks, as well as other destinations in Alberta and British Columbia. Staff here can also answer Glacier trail queries. Has a strong, free wi-fi signal.

Glacier National Park Headquarters (☑ 406-888-7800; www.nps.gov/glac; West Glacier; ☺ 8am-4:30pm Mon-Fri) Inhabits a small complex just south of the park's West Entrance. No longer the focus for visitor information, but might be worth checking out in winter months.

West Glacier Clinic (☑ 406-888-9924; 100 Rea Rd, West Glacier Fire Hall; ☺ 9am-5pm) The most convenient place to head to for medical attention for minor injuries such as sprains and infections when on the western side of the park. Staffed by nurse practitioners and physician assistants and affiliated with the North Valley Hospital in Whitefish.

ℹ Getting There & Around

A 4km (2.5-mile) paved cycle path links West Glacier with Apgar Village and transit center inside the park, from where you can catch free Going-to-the-Sun Rd shuttles. Amtrak's *Empire Builder* stops at the West Glacier train station once a day traveling in either direction.

Hertz has cars available for rent parked at the train station.

St Mary

Sitting on the Blackfeet Indian Reservation just outside the park's east entrance, St Mary makes a handy base for exploring Glacier's dryer eastern side. Though less a cozy village than its western counterpart, West Glacier, the views of the mountains are better here, and it's a shorter walk (0.6 miles) to the first free shuttle stop on Going-to-the-Sun Rd (outside the St Mary visitor and transit center). A cluster of handy services (all but the gas station are closed in winter) not found inside the park crowd around the junction of Hwy 89 and Going-to-the-Sun Rd, including campgrounds, a motel, a supermarket, a gas station, a relatively swanky modern lodge and a charming collection of pastel-colored 'mini-homes.' Two shuttle services provide easy access to the Swiftcurrent Motor Inn, East Glacier, Two Medicine and Many Glacier.

🛏️ Sleeping & Eating

Johnson's of St Mary CAMPGROUND $
(☎406-732-4207; www.johnsonsofstmary.com; 21 Eagle Rd, off Hwy 89; tent/RV sites US$32/45, cabins US$70-187; ☺May-Sep; 🛜) Set on a knoll overlooking St Mary, RV sites here get gorgeous views of St Mary Lake with the crenellated peaks of the Continental Divide glimmering in the background. Tent sites, well-suited to large groups, are shaded peacefully by alder trees. This long-running family operation also includes cabins, a cottage and Johnson's of St Mary World Famous Restaurant.

St Mary KOA Campground CAMPGROUND $
(Map p192; ☎406-732-4122; www.koa.com/camp grounds/st-mary; 106 West Shore Rd; tent/RV sites US$60/100; ☺mid-May–Sep; 🛜) Set in an open meadow 1 mile down a paved road, beside St Mary's eponymous river, this unshaded campground can accommodate tents and RVs and also offers a variety of cottages and cabins. A plethora of other services includes bike rental (per hour/day US$2.50/20), canoe rental (US$10 per hour), a grocery store, coffee counter, laundry, hot tub, playground and the A-OK Grille. Wi-fi is unreliable.

St Mary Lodge & Resort HOTEL $$
(☎406-892-2525; www.glacierparkcollection.com; cnr Hwy 89 & Going-to-the-Sun Rd; r US$139-345; ☺mid-May–Sep; ❄🛜) Despite mountains looming in the background and the park entrance a half-mile away, this hotel's location at the junction of Hwy 89 and the eastern terminus of Going-to-the-Sun Rd is surprisingly mundane. It's part of a large, paved lot with a gas station, gift shop and grocery store. However, in terms of modern comforts, it outdoes the rustic park lodges.

⭐St Mary Tiny Homes CABIN $$$
(☎844-868-7474; www.glacierparkcollection. com; 3 Going-to-the-Sun Rd; cabins US$290; 🛜) 🌿 These pastel colored cabins with separate individual fairly luxurious bathhouses wouldn't be out of place on the cover of an upscale design magazine. But the views of Glacier's east-side mountains and proximity to Going-to-the-Sun Rd can't be captured in print. Four can sleep easily on the living-room pull-out couch and the bedroom separated by sliding barn doors.

Everything is designed with efficiency and access to the outdoors in mind, including large windows to frame the scenery. It's such a cozy and comfortable refuge that you might return home looking to downsize.

Cabin 8 has possibly the most ideal location – you can hear the gurgling of the Divide Creek just in back and views of the mountains are unobstructed.

Johnson's of St Mary
World Famous Restaurant AMERICAN $
(☎406-732-5565; 21 Red Eagle Rd; mains US$9-17; ☺11am-9pm Mon-Thu, from 8am Fri-Sun mid-May– late Sep) It feels like you've stepped onto the set of a John Wayne western. Well, the plastic chairs are a giveaway. But this log-cabin restaurant perched above St Mary is charmingly heavy on the classic decor. Burgers and sandwiches are better and bigger than average and the Sunday fried chicken meal is a gut buster. Do not order a dessert pie unless you're sharing.

Rising Sun Pizza PIZZA $$
(☎406-732-9995; Hwy 89, St Mary; pizza from US$16; ☺4-11pm; 🛜) Small-town locals generally greet any new joint with curiosity and excitement, but this pizzeria's positive reviews have outlived the initial honeymoon period. The menu, only salads and whole pies produced with homemade sauce and dough, is as basic as the completely unadorned dining room.

Park Café AMERICAN $$
(www.parkcafeandgrocery.com; 3147 Hwy 89, St Mary; mains US$9-18; ☺7am-9pm Jun-Sep) Owned and operated by the same family since 1952, it's now the grandchild of the Park's founder who's in charge. The charming dilapidated diner decor remains. A variety of berry pies, including of course huckleberry, are still the speciality, along with hearty breakfasts (US$8 for a short stack of huckleberry pancakes) and burgers. Reasonably priced mains such as a hot roast-beef sandwich and fish and chips are also good.

Snowgoose Grille STEAK $$$
(cnr Going-to-the-Sun Rd & Hwy 89, St Mary; mains lunch US$14, dinner US$15-32; ☺6:30am-9:30pm mid-May–Sep) If you're craving an

AROUND GLACIER NATIONAL PARK ST MARY

IZAAK WALTON INN

Perched on a hill within snowball-throwing distance of Glacier National Park's southern boundary, **Izaak Walton Inn** (☑ 406-888-5700; www.izaakwaltoninn.com; 290 Izaak Walton Inn Rd, Essex; r US$109-179, cabins & cabooses US$199-249; ☺year-round; ☎) is a historic mock-Tudor inn that was originally built in 1939 to accommodate local railway personnel. It remains a daily flag stop (request stop) on Amtrak's *Empire Builder* route – a romantic way to arrive. Caboose cottages with kitchenettes are available, along with a historic GN441 locomotive refurbished as a luxury four-person suite (US$329).

One caveat: sleep might be hard to come by, especially on the track-side, since trains pass by every half-hour to hour through the middle of the night.

Located close to the Park Creek area, the lodge became something of an incongruity after WWII, when a plan to build a new southern park entrance in the vicinity never materialized. Dubbed the 'Inn between' in the years since, the Izaak has enjoyed a modern renaissance with cozy rooms, a sauna and easy access to miles of some of the only groomed cross-country skiing trails in the area.

opportunity to break away from the hikers' breakfast/picnic lunch monotony, try this wheelchair-accessible restaurant in the St Mary Lodge & Resort, where the steaks are succulent and the footwear is equally heels as hiking boots. The bison meatloaf and rainbow trout are standouts on the dinner menu, and it's worth postponing the day's hike for a breakfast of huckleberry pancakes and bison chorizo.

East Glacier

A summer-only stop on Amtrak's Empire Builder route, East Glacier grew up around the train station (which splits the small, slightly scruffy settlement in half) and the adjacent Glacier Park Lodge. While its eating and sleeping options offer more variety than West Glacier, its location away from Going-to-the-Sun Rd makes quick forays into the park less convenient. However, the closest entrance, only 10 miles to the north, is the spectacular Two Medicine Valley.

Other facilities include a post office, ATMs and a couple of gas stations.

🛏 Sleeping & Eating

★**Brownie's**   HOSTEL **$**
(☑ 406-226-4426; www.brownieshostel.com; 1020 Hwy 49; dm/d/q US$25/49/79; ☺May–Sep; ☎) Above Brownie's Deli & Bakery, this casual HI hostel is packed with travelers staying in the coed six-and eight-person dorms or small, rustic private doubles. It has a common room, kitchen and balcony with a hodgepodge of secondhand furniture. Linen is provided free of charge. The son of the

original longtime owners has taken over and added a few traveler-friendly features, like more soundproofing and updated flooring and baths and showers.

Downstairs is the excellent **bakery and deli** (www.brownieshostel.com; 1020 Hwy 49; sandwiches US$5-8; ☺7am-10pm mid-May–Sep; ☎) of the same name.

Glacier Park Lodge   HISTORIC HOTEL **$$**
(☑ 406-892-2525; www.glacierparkcollection.com; East Glacier; r US$169-256; ☺Jun-Sep; ☎⛵) ◢ Set in attractive, perfectly manicured flower-filled grounds overlooking Montana's oldest golf course, this historic 1914 lodge was built in the classic national-park tradition, with a splendid open-plan lobby supported by lofty 900-year-old Douglas fir timbers (imported from Washington State). Eye-catching Native American artwork adorns the communal areas, and a full-sized tipi is wedged incongruously onto a 2nd-floor balcony.

In keeping with national-park tradition, the rooms here are 'rustic' with no TVs or air-con; bathrooms and showers, especially, are small. The configuration of the rooms, including where furniture and the beds go, can be a little quirky, especially at the beginning of the season when kinks are being worked out by the mostly seasonal staff. Rocking chairs are dispersed inside, and out on the shaded porch where the views of the Glacier peaks are worth the price of admission alone; the pool out back has little shade.

Two restaurants and a bar are also open to nonguests.

Rock n Roll Bakery BAKERY $
(Dawson Ave, East Glacier; muffins & scones US$3; ⏲7:30am-2pm; 🐾) Doubling as a small outdoor gear shop, this bakery will satisfy sweet and semi-healthy cravings with its cookies, hearty muffins, cakes and pies (the latter are made by the well-regarded former pie maker at the Park Cafe in St Mary). It offers Montana Coffee Traders espresso drinks as well.

★**Serrano's Mexican Restaurant** MEXICAN $$
(📞406-226-9392; www.serranosmexican.com; 29 Dawson Ave, East Glacier; mains US$14-21; ⏲5-10pm May-Sep; 🐾) East Glacier Park's most buzzed-about restaurant serves a mean chile relleno. Renowned for its excellent iced margaritas, Serrano's also has economical burritos, enchiladas and quesadillas in the vintage Dawson house log cabin, originally built in 1909. Expect a wait.

Out back there are three spartan backpacker cabins for rent (dorm/room US$20/50) in the adjoining yard.

Great Northern Dining Room INTERNATIONAL $$
(Glacier Park Lodge; mains US$17-24; ⏲6:30am-9:30pm Jun-Sep) This big restaurant in the Glacier Park Lodge serves upscale classics, such as prime rib, and more Montana-influenced dishes like braised bison ribs, as well as pasta and fish and chips. A good way to start off the meal is with the roasted brussel sprouts or a classic caesar salad. Much of the menu is available in the more casual Empire Lounge and bar a few steps away.

ℹ **Getting There & Around**

The three-times-daily East Side Shuttle links East Glacier with Two Medicine (US$10), Cut Throat Creek (US$20), St Mary (US$30), Many Glacier (US$40) and Waterton (US$50). The Amtrak (www.amtrak.com) *Empire Builder* stops at the train station once daily traveling in either direction. **Dollar Rent A Car** (📞406-892-0009; www.dollar.com; 5506 Hwy 2 West, Columbia Falls) has an office in East Glacier.

Blackfeet Indian Reservation

The short-grass prairie east of Glacier is home to the Blackfeet Nation, which includes the Northern Piegan (Blackfeet), Southern Piegan and Blood tribes that came south from the Alberta area in the 1700s. Originally an agrarian people, the Blackfeet took quickly to horses and guns, eventually developing a reputation as the fiercest warriors in the West. Today approximately 10,000 tribal members reside on or around the reservation (www.blackfeetcountry.com), where unemployment is high and the struggling economy is primarily driven by ranching, farming and the sale of oil, natural gas, lumber and other mineral rights. Tribal members are rightfully proud of the Chief Mountain Hotshots, an elite fire-fighting crew of Blackfeet sent to the front lines of wilderness blazes throughout the West.

Browning, an ordinary if rundown town 18 miles east of Glacier National Park, is where most of the reservation's amenities lie. Attractions are scarce, so it's worth mentioning the skate park sponsored by Jeff Ament, one of the founders of Pearl Jam. The winter months can be fairly brutal, when strong, cold winds blow unimpeded across the plains and the town's two casinos begin looking like welcome refuges.

Every second weekend of July there's a pow-wow, a celebration of tribal arts, culture and food, held on the grounds to the north of the newly built Holiday Inn Express. Heart Butte, 28 miles to the south, holds its annual pow-wow on the second weekend of August.

Browning is worth a detour if for no other reason than the excellent **Museum of the Plains Indian** (📞406-338-2230; www.doi.gov/iacb/museum-plains-indian; Hwy 89/West Central Ave; adult/child US$6/2; ⏲9am-4:45pm Tue-Sat Jun-Sep, 10am-4:30pm Mon-Fri Oct-May), which honors the culture of the Crow, Cree, Sioux, Cheyenne and, above all, the Blackfeet. Housed in a bland building that looks like a 1970s-era suburban elementary school, the museum provides extensive descriptions for exhibits of costumes, art and craftwork. Ernie Heavy Runner sits at the desk in front and can act as a guide if you choose. You can also chat with local artisans working in an attached gallery.

As far as overnighting in Browning, it's a no-brainer. Bed down in one of the tipis set rather majestically onto the plains at the **Lodgepole Gallery & Tipi Village** (📞406-338-2787; www.blackfeetculturecamp.com; Hwy 89; s/d/tr US$75/91/107), a large property 2 miles west of Browning. The owners, Darrell, a Blackfeet member, and his friendly and knowledgeable wife, Angelika, are both talented artists and show their works in the attached gallery. They can help arrange horseback-riding trips in the area.

AROUND GLACIER NATIONAL PARK BLACKFEET INDIAN RESERVATION

NATIVE AMERICANS: LIVELIHOODS ON THE LAND

Where the grassy plains of the prairies meet the saw-toothed mountains of Glacier National Park, three legendary Native American tribes once intermingled – and the results weren't always peaceful.

One of the most populous tribes in the Montana region was the Blackfeet (Niitsítapi), a westward-dwelling subset of the Algonquian-speaking Plains Native Americans, a linguistic group that included the Crow, Cheyenne and Sioux. Warlike and highly mobile, the Blackfeet acquired horses in the 1730s from the Shoshoni people, and they used their new bounty to hunt buffalo and assert territorial rights over the mountains east of the Continental Divide, where numerous sacred sites (including Two Medicine and Chief Mountain) were integral to the tribe's creation story.

Glacier's western slopes (this includes the present-day site of Apgar Village), meanwhile, were the domain of the more peaceful Plateau Native Americans, most notably the Flathead and Kootenai tribes. The former were Salish people, related through language to a much larger family of tribes that spread west as far as the Pacific coast. The latter were a cultural anomaly whose anthropological roots remain sketchy, and whose language is a linguistic isotope unrelated to any other Native American tongue.

The Salish and Kootenai were skilled fishermen and canoeists who subsisted on a diet of salmon plucked from the region's teeming rivers, but who sometimes crossed the Rockies to hunt buffalo. It was on these eastern forays that they came into contact and – inevitably – conflict with the more numerous Blackfeet. Though the Flatheads, over time, adopted some Plains Native American characteristics (horses and tipis for instance), the superior firepower of the Blackfeet meant that they slowly pushed the Plateau tribes back west.

In 1805–06, all three tribes had their first contact with white settlers when the Lewis and Clark expedition passed through the region on an abortive attempt to find a northern route over the Rockies. Relations were initially cordial, particularly among the Salish and Kootenai, with whom the explorers traded horses, but events took a turn for the worse on the expedition's return leg when a small party led by Lewis got into a skirmish with a group of Blackfeet and two very young braves were killed. Tellingly, they were the only fatalities of the group's two-year adventure.

All three tribes suffered during the westward expansion of white settlers in the early 19th century and the near extinction of the buffalo that ensued. Relying increasingly on government money, Native Americans had little choice but to agree to one-sided treaties in 1855. The Salish and Kootenai were signatories to the ambiguous Hellgate Treaty, which merged them into the Confederated Salish and Kootenai tribes of the Flathead Nation (no Native American identifies as 'Flathead') on the Flathead Indian Reservation in northwest Montana. The Blackfeet, meanwhile, signed the Lame Bull Treaty the same year, creating a sprawling reservation a little larger than Delaware. The reservation originally included all of the Glacier National Park region east of the Continental Divide; however, in 1896, due to continuing economic difficulties, the Blackfeet sold a further 2000 sq miles of this land for US$1.5 million to the US government, which was intent on prospecting for copper and gold. When no minerals were found, the government, recognizing the area's potential as a tourist destination, formed Glacier National Park in 1910.

Today, approximately 10,000 Blackfeet live on a 3812-sq-mile reservation immediately to the east of the park. The reservation includes important park access points such as St Mary and East Glacier (another 5000 or so live elsewhere, including many who have relocated to Seattle); Browning is the largest town and commercial hub. Unlike many Native American reservations, this is the Blackfeet's traditional territory. Despite their dispossession, the land in and around the east side of Glacier holds significant ceremonial and cultural significance. A battle that began in the early 1980s to prevent oil and natural gas drilling in the area continues to this day. You can learn more about the issue at www.badger-twomedicine.org.

To the southwest, approximately 6800 Flathead and Kootenai Native Americans inhabit a 1938-sq-mile reservation between Kalispell and Missoula.

Browning is a seasonal stop on Amtrak's Empire Builder route, operating from April to October with daily trains to Seattle and Chicago.

Whitefish

To be both 'rustic' and 'hip' within the same square kilometer is a hard act to pull off, but tiny Whitefish (population 8000) makes a good stab at it. Once sold as the main gateway to Glacier National Park, this charismatic New West town has earned enough kudos to merit a long-distance trip in its own right. Aside from grandiose Glacier (which is within an easy day's cycling distance), Whitefish is home to an attractive stash of restaurants, a historic train station and an underrated ski resort.

◎ Sights

City Beach Park   BEACH
Glued to the southern shore of Whitefish Lake, this busy sandy stretch is where the whole town comes to date and debate in the summer months. The swimming area is roped off and kayak and paddleboard rentals are available. Parking (more spaces are being added) is free.

Les Mason State Park   PARK
(www.stateparks.mt.gov/les-mason; 2650 E Lakeshore Dr; ⊙8am-8pm) Ideal Whitefish Lake swimming spot with an anchored wood 'raft', great for big jumps as well as mid-swim rests, and a cobblestone beach.

🕈 Activities

Whitefish Mountain Resort   SKIING
(✐406-862-2900; www.skiwhitefish.com; Big Mountain Rd; ski/bike lift US$81/41) Big Mountain skiing at Whitefish Mountain Resort (formerly Big Mountain), is a laid-back old-school affair, great for families, as well as expert skiers and snowboarders willing to hike up in order to rip up off-piste double-black-diamond glades. The mountain is known for its foggy days, but views from the summit are unsurpassed (when clear). On fresh powder days, locals ditch work and other responsibilities to make fresh tracks.

Whitefish Trail   HIKING
(✐406-862-3880; www.whitefishlegacy.org) Locals are deservedly proud of this 40-miles-and-growing trail system surrounding Whitefish Lake. It was developed by a pub-lic-private partnership on previously used public access lands and offers opportunities for hiking, biking and horseback riding, with groomed nordic skiing in the winter. Soon, the Whitefish Trail will be connected to the Spencer Trail and the Big Mountain trails (Whitefish Mountain Resort) for a total of 80-plus miles.

Glacier Cyclery   CYCLING
(✐406-862-6446; www.glaciercyclery.com; 326 E 2nd St; per day/week from US$40/190; ⊙9am-6pm) A superfriendly and knowledgeable bike store (with rentals available) located in the center of Whitefish that extols the virtues and benefits of cycling in and around Whitefish and Glacier.

Dog Sled Adventures   DOG SLEDDING
(✐406-881-2275;www.dogsledadventuresmontana .com; per person US$75) Jeff Ulsamer, the self-described backwoods guy mushing Alaskan huskies since the late 1970s, cares for his hundred-plus dogs with affection and care. By all accounts, the dogs love to pull and those left out of trips are anxious to join in. During winter, Jeff runs three daily trips (10am, 1pm and 3:30pm) on old logging roads into Stillwater State Forest.

Wave Aquatic & Fitness Center   SWIMMING
(✐406-862-2444; www.whitefishwave.com; 1250 Baker Ave; day pass adult/child US$15/8; ⊙5am-9pm Mon-Fri, 7am-8pm Sat & Sun Jun-Aug, 5am-10pm Mon-Fri, 7am-8pm Sep-May) One-stop shop for all your fitness needs and surprisingly large for a town of Whitefish's size. Adults can swim laps in the pool, while kids enjoy the mini-water park under the same light-filled atrium space. In the back is a counter serving healthy smoothies and fruit juices.

🛏 Sleeping

Recommended local motels include **Cha-let Motel Whitefish** (✐406-862-5581; www. whitefishlodging.com; 6430 Hwy 93 S; r US$199; ✻☎☒) and the **Downtowner Inn** (✐406-862-2535; www.downtownermotel.cc; 224 Spokane Ave; r from US$100; ✻@☎☒). Hotels stretch along Hwy 93 to the south, with a few options in downtown Whitefish. There's a small, cramped hostel on Lupfer Ave, and a bicyclist's paradise out near Beaver Lake.

Whitefish Lake State Park Campground   CAMPGROUND **$**
(✐406-862-3991; State Park Rd; tent & RV sites US$18; ⊙year round) On the southwest edge of Whitefish Lake are 26 shady forested

grounds, including one that is wheelchair friendly. Reservations can be made up to nine months in advance for the summer months; walk-ins, first-come, first-served other times.

⭐ Garden Wall Inn
B&B $$

(☑406-862-3440; www.gardenwallinn.com; 504 Spokane Ave; r US$255-295, ste from US$395; 🛜) Now in its 32nd year, this elegant and meticulously run five-room B&B is ideally located in a shady spot just a few blocks south of the town center. The owners, Rhonda and Chris, are charming storytellers and fonts of knowledge regarding Whitefish and Glacier. They've retained the home's original woodwork, maple floors and light fixtures from 1923. Enjoy art-deco rooms, log fires blazing in the living room on cold days, and gourmet breakfasts prepared by a chef (preceded by a wake-up coffee tray delivered to your room).

Firebrand
BOUTIQUE HOTEL $$

(☑406-863-1900; www.firebrandhotel.com; 650 E 3rd St; r from US$140; ❄@🛜) Easily downtown Whitefish's nicest hotel, this handsome brick structure shelters large and supremely comfortable rooms, a spa and fitness center, a rooftop hot tub, a bar-restaurant and a genuine touch of class.

Good Medicine Lodge
B&B $$

(☑406-862-5488; www.goodmedicinelodge.com; 537 Wisconsin Ave; r US$245, ste US$300; ❄@🛜) There's no doubt you're out West at this intimate chalet-style inn just north of downtown Whitefish and rightly known for its gourmet breakfast. From the antler-head chandelier to the horse saddle slung over a railing, Good Medicine is the antithesis of bland chain hotels. The friendly owners, Woody and Betsy Cox, anticipate every need; the rooms and suites are designed in a homey luxury style.

Kandahar Lodge
LODGE $$$

(☑406-862-6098; www.kandaharlodge.com; 3824 Big Mountain Rd; r US$250; ❄@🛜) Nothing feels more luxurious to a skier than finishing the day's last run at the back door of their lodge, then popping into the outdoor hot tub before sipping a drink in front of the fire. This ski-in-ski-out resort up at the base of Whitefish Mountain Resort covers all those bases and has efficiently designed and warmly decorated rooms to match.

🍴 Eating

Tuesdays are the busiest nights of the summer in downtown Whitefish because of this **farmers market** (www.whitefishfarmersmarket. com; Central Ave at Depot Park; ⊙5-7:30pm Tue late May-late Sep) of around 100 local vendors held in the plaza just south of the train depot. The founder and organizer is Rhonda Fitzgerald of the Garden Wall Inn.

Stumptown Marketplace
FOOD HALL $

(www.stumptownmarket.com; 12 Spokane Ave; mains US$7-15; ⊙8am-6pm Mon-Thu, to 9pm Fri & Sat) Grab a table and choose from three quality artisan food kiosks: **Zucca Bistro**, with Mediterranean style soup, sandwiches and salads; **Tea Kettle Cafe** with highly recommended Asian noodle bowls; and **Glacier Ginger Brew**, with healthy smoothies, juices and vegetarian bowls.

Abruzzo Italian Kitchen
ITALIAN $$

(☑406-730-8767; 115 Central Ave; mains US$14-32; ⊙4-10pm Sun-Thu, to 11pm Fri & Sat) Upscale and classy fine dining in Whitefish doesn't mean warmth and hospitality are sacrificed, and this trattoria opened in 2017 delivers on all counts. Wood-fired pizza, homemade pasta and mains like pork shank confit and a veal dish with pancetta, prosciutto, fontina and duck-fat potatoes are served up at big, comfy booths with tables good for groups.

Buffalo Café
CAFE $$

(☑406-862-2833; www.buffalocafewhitefish.com; 514 E 3rd St; breakfast US$5-13, mains US$10-18; ⊙7am-2.30pm & 5-9pm Tue-Sat, 7am-2.30pm Mon, 8am-2pm Sun) Hopping with neighborly locals, the Buffalo is what you get when a standard chain diner hires someone who actually knows how to cook. For breakfast try the original Buffalo Pie: a mountain of poached eggs and various add-ins (cheese, veggies, bacon) piled atop a wedge of hash browns. You won't leave hungry.

Wasabi Sushi Bar & the Ginger Grill
JAPANESE $$

(☑406-863-9283; www.wasabimt.com; 419 E 2nd St; mains US$12-21; ⊙5-11pm Tue-Sat) Yes, you're in Montana and, yes, this is exceptionally good sushi. Confirming Whitefish's cosmopolitan credentials, this place delivers the fish in both traditional and fusion styles. For those who don't crave it raw, you can choose from an array of cooked pan-Asian main dishes. Reservations are recommended.

Whitefish Lake Restaurant STEAK $$$
(☑ 406-862-5285; www.whitefishlakerestaurant.
com; 1200 Hwy 93 N, Whitefish Lake Golf Club;
mains US$23-48; ☺ 5:30pm-late) A golf-course
clubhouse isn't the typical location for a
special-occasion steakhouse. But Whitefish
locals know this is the place to make reserva-
tions for holidays, engagements and the like.
The prime rib, lamb chops and rib-eye are
the best in town and the historic log-cabin
dining room adds to the Western feel.

🍷 Drinking & Nightlife

Bonsai Brewing Project MICROBREWERY
(☑ 406-730-1717; 549 Wisconsin Ave; ☺ noon-8pm
Tue-Sun; 🐾) This husband-and-wife-owned
place just north of the center of town has a
homey and welcoming vibe and is especial-
ly popular with locals and their dogs when
both can enjoy the nice outdoor garden
area. Check the chalkboard for descriptions
of an interesting selection of mostly local
craft brews (try a flight for variety); the food
menu (mains US$11 to US$16) is equally ec-
lectic with bowls, salads and tacos.

Montana Coffee Traders COFFEE
(☑ 406-862-7667; www.coffeetraders.com; 110
Central Ave; ☺ 7am-6pm Mon-Sat, 8am-4pm Sun;
🐾) Whitefish's homegrown microroaster
runs this always-busy cafe and gift shop in
the old Skyles building in the center of town.
The organic, fair-trade beans are roasted in
an old farmhouse on Hwy 93 that you can
tour (10am Friday by reservation).

Great Northern Bar & Grille BAR
(☑ 406-862-2816; www.greatnorthernbar.com; 27
Central Ave; mains US$8-10; ☺ 11am-2am) The
hipsters have taken over the biker bar! Not
to be confused with the brewery of the same
name down the street, this classic saloon
sees a generally friendly crowd most nights,
even when there isn't live music on the patio.
It's a fun place to hang out, but get your food
elsewhere. Ping-pong and billiards inside.

Casey's BAR
(☑ 406-862-8150; www.caseyswhitefish.com; 101
Central Ave; ☺ 11am-2am) Each of Casey's three
floors has a different identity. The first is a
restaurant with an upscale menu; the sec-
ond is a large performance space with live
music and a bar; and the third, the pièce de
résistance, is a rooftop lounge and bar with

fantastic views and a good selection of craft
beers, as well as an eclectic menu.

Great Northern Brewing Co BREWERY
(☑ 406-863-1000; www.greatnorthernbrewing.
com; 2 Central Ave; ☺ tours 1pm & 3pm Mon-Thu)
Stop at this high-ceilinged brewpub and
tasting room for a pint or sampler anytime,
or join a tour to up your beer-nerd game.

ⓘ Information

Whitefish Visitors Center (☑ 877-862-3548;
www.explorewhitefish.com; 307 Spokane Ave;
☺ 9am-5pm Mon-Fri) The professional and
helpful office is worth a visit; the excellent web-
site has loads of information on news, events,
activities, and places to stay and eat.

ⓘ Getting There & Away

AIR
Glacier Park International Airport (p275),
located 11 miles south of Whitefish, has daily
service to Denver, Minneapolis, Salt Lake and
Seattle. Additional summer-only destinations
include Chicago, Dallas and Los Angeles.

BUS
SNOW Bus (☑ 406-201-5669; www.bigmtn
commercial.org; Whitefish Library; ☺ Jun-early
Sep) offers daily summertime shuttle services
between Whitefish (the most convenient stop
is the Whitefish Library) and the Apgar Visitor
Center in Glacier National Park.

TRAIN
The most scenic way to get here is via **Amtrak**
(☑ 406-862-2268; www.amtrak.com/empire
-builder-train; 500 Depot St; ☺ 6am-1:30pm,
4:30pm-midnight) on the *Empire Builder* line,
which also connects to Glacier National Park via
West Glacier (US$7.50, 30 minutes) and East
Glacier (US$16, two hours).

ⓘ Getting Around

The **Whitefish Shuttle** (☑ 406-212-0080; www.
whitefishshuttle.com) has new service with ex-
tremely convenient pick-ups (7:30am, 8:30am,
9:30am, 2pm, 3pm and 4pm) at all Whitefish
area hotels and bike shops, with stops at Apgar
Village, Apgar Transportation Center, Lake
McDonald Lodge and the Avalanche trailhead
off Going-to-the-Sun Rd (the latter stop only for
cyclists). Return trips leave more or less three
hours after each location's drop-off time. Also
has trips to Polebridge in the North Fork section
of the park.

Waterton Lakes National Park

Best Local Spots

➡ Thirsty Bear Saloon (p231)

➡ Wieners of Waterton (p231)

➡ Welch's Chocolates, Ice Cream & Desserts (p231)

➡ Waterton Lakes Opera House (p231)

Best Views

➡ Prince of Wales Hotel (p230)

➡ Cameron Lake (p227)

➡ Carthew-Alderson Trail (p219)

➡ Lineham Ridge (p224)

Why Go?

Here flat prairies collide dramatically with the Rockies, with a sparkling lake and a hilltop castle that may make you wonder if you've fallen into a fairy tale. However, Waterton Lakes National Park is rarely known to outside visitors, remaining a pocket of sublime tranquillity. Visitor numbers took a hit after the 2017 Kenow Wildfire which burned over 19,000 hectares of the park, destroying infrastructure and damaging 80% of the trail network.

Established in 1895 and now part of a Unesco World Heritage site, Unesco Biosphere Reserve and International Peace Park (with the USA's Glacier National Park), this 525-sq-km reserve lies in Alberta's southwestern corner. The park is a sanctuary for numerous iconic animals – grizzlies, elk, deer and cougar – along with 800-odd wildflower species.

Road Distance (KM)

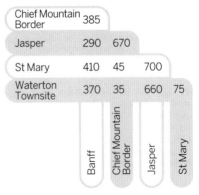

	Banff	Chief Mountain Border	Jasper	St Mary
Chief Mountain Border	385			
Jasper	290	670		
St Mary	410	45	700	
Waterton Townsite	370	35	660	75

Note: Distances are approximate

🥾 DAY HIKES

Waterton is a hiker's haven. There are around 200km (125 miles) of trails in Waterton, and a number of them are multipurpose routes, accommodating hikers, horseback riders, cross-country skiers and cyclists. Short, easy hikes lie in the vicinity of the townsite, while further afield, day hikes such as the much-lauded Crypt Lake Trail can rival anything in Glacier or Banff National Parks for variety of scenery. The area was badly damaged by the 2017 Kenow Wildfire; most trails are open but check www.parkscanada. gc.ca/waterton-open for the most up-to-date information.

🥾 Rowe Lakes

Duration Three hours round-trip (Lower Lake), five hours (Upper Lake), four hours (Rowe Meadow)

Distance 8km/5 miles round-trip (Lower Lake), 12.6km/7.9 miles (Upper Lake), 10.4km/6.5 miles (Rowe Meadow)

Difficulty Easy–moderate

Elevation Change 250m (820ft)

Start/Finish Akamina Pkwy

Nearest Town Waterton Townsite

Transportation Tamarack hiker shuttle, car

Summary A tempting foray to the cusp of Waterton's easily accessible backcountry that may have you coming back for more.

This fine hike starts innocuously enough on the Akamina Pkwy approximately halfway between Waterton Townsite and Cameron Lake. The first section to Lower Rowe Lake is moderately easy. Beyond this, you can hike further up to Rowe Meadow and Upper Rowe Lake. For backcountry hikers, this is the start and end point of the multiday Tamarack Trail.

From the Akamina Pkwy, follow a sinuous but well-defined trail through a mix of larch and evergreen trees alongside Rowe Creek. The path can be muddy after rain, but with only 250m (820ft) of elevation gain spread over the first 4km (2.5 miles) to Lower Rowe Lake, the ascent is only gradual.

After 3.8km (2.4 miles) a trail branches off to the left. Follow this side trail 200m (220yd) to reach **Lower Rowe Lake**, a small, beautifully clear body of water laid out in a natural amphitheater. A 150m (492ft) waterfall links it with Upper Rowe Lake, which sits in a hanging valley above.

Back at the main trail you have a choice. Turn right and retrace your steps to the parkway or turn left toward **Rowe Meadow**,

WATERTON LAKES NATIONAL PARK DAY HIKES

Waterton Lakes – Day Hikes

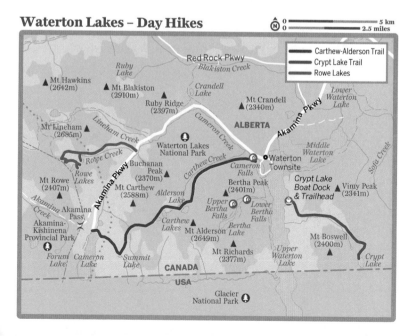

Waterton Lakes National Park

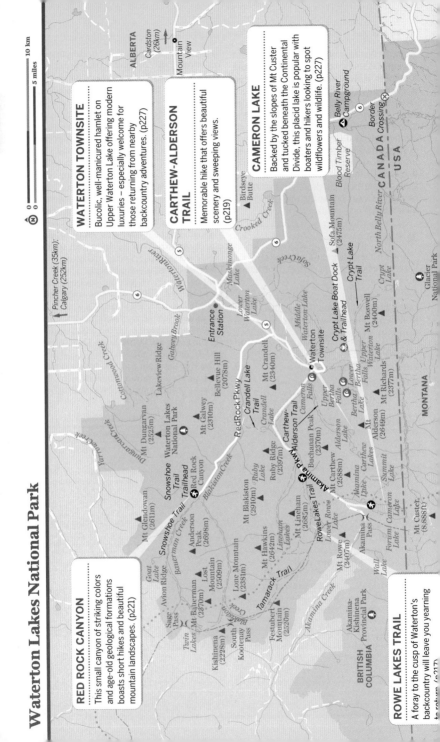

RED ROCK CANYON
This small canyon of striking colors and age-old geological formations boasts short hikes and beautiful mountain landscapes. (p221)

WATERTON TOWNSITE
Bucolic, well-manicured hamlet on Upper Waterton Lake offering modern luxuries – especially welcome for those returning from nearby backcountry adventures. (p227)

CARTHEW-ALDERSON TRAIL
Memorable hike that offers beautiful scenery and sweeping views. (p219)

CAMERON LAKE
Backed by the slopes of Mt Custer and tucked beneath the Continental Divide, this placid lake is popular with boaters and hikers looking to spot wildflowers and wildlife. (p227)

ROWE LAKES TRAIL
A foray to the cusp of Waterton's backcountry will leave you yearning to return. (p217)

a wonderful array of wildflowers situated on the edge of the timberline. After crossing a creek at the far end of the meadow, you'll encounter another junction. The Tamarack Trail goes right here up to Lineham Ridge. A left turn offers a last steep climb to **Upper Rowe Lake**, actually two alpine lakes backed by the vertiginous cliffs of the Continental Divide. Look out for marmots and bighorn sheep along the way.

Retrace your steps to the parkway. Strong, speedy hikers might want to climb a further 3.4km (2.1 miles) from the trail junction below Upper Rowe Lake to **Lineham Ridge**, one of the highest paths in the park, with views stretching for 50km (31 miles).

🥾 Carthew-Alderson Trail

Duration Six hours one way

Distance 20km (12.5 miles)

Difficulty Moderate

Elevation Change 610m (1968ft)

Start/Finish Cameron Lake/Cameron Falls

Nearest Town Waterton Townsite

Transportation Tamarack hiker shuttle

Summary A panoramic parade through myriad forests, lush meadows and rough scree, showcasing the best of Waterton Lakes National Park.

Long considered one of North America's best mountain day hikes, it comes as no surprise to find that many seasoned hikers make this scenic sojourn the subject of many repeat visits. As a result, the trail is well trafficked, though this takes nothing away from its multifarious beauty and incredible sweeping views.

Damaged by the 2017 Kenow Wildfire, only the top half of the trail (from Cameron Lake to a few kilometres short of Alderson Lake) was reopened by midsummer 2019. It's likely that the entire trail will be accessible some time in 2020. Once open, the section from Alderson Lake to Cameron Falls which was burned in the fire will be more exposed and hotter than previous years.

Most hikers embark from **Cameron Lake** in the west (at the end of Akamina Pkwy) and tramp east back to Waterton Townsite (thus incorporating a gentler elevation gain). This scenario is made possible courtesy of the Tamarack hiker shuttle that runs from Waterton to Cameron Lake daily at 8:15am (9:15am in September) in summer.

The trail heads southeast from the Cameron Lake boat ramp (and tiny store) and enters a pine-encased slope alongside the lake's eastern shore, before ascending through a series of switchbacks to the smaller **Summit Lake**. This pool, surrounded by meadow and pine, incorporates the bulk of the hike's elevation gain.

Turn left (northeast) here for the Carthew Lakes Trail, a more gradual ascent through scrub, grass and then just open mountainside, with stupendous views over Montana, British Columbia and Alberta, while the distinctive form of Mt Cleveland frames the backdrop. The ascent culminates in several switchbacks followed by a sharp scramble up loose scree to the ridgeline, where you'll get an expansive panorama including northern Glacier National Park summits to the south and Carthew Lakes to the north.

After the climbing is done, the trail descends from the ridge and weaves between the two starkly located **Carthew Lakes**, where snow can linger all summer and marmots can be seen scampering about. A steep cliff is negotiated at the exit of the Carthew basin before **Alderson Lake** becomes visible below. The trail reenters the trees shortly before the lake; a detour of 500m (0.3 miles) leads to the water itself.

From here, the narrow path follows the Carthew Valley, descending gradually through the forest to Waterton Townsite. A fitting end to the day is the impressive Cameron Falls.

🥾 Crypt Lake Trail

Duration Six hours round-trip

Distance 17.2km (10.6 miles)

Difficulty Difficult

Elevation Change 710m (2329ft)

Start/Finish Crypt Lake Boat Dock & Trailhead

Nearest Town Waterton Townsite

Transportation Water taxi

Summary A veritable obstacle course that incorporates a ride in a water taxi, a climb up a ladder and a crawl through a narrow rocky tunnel to gorgeous Crypt Lake.

Crypt Lake or Carthew–Alderson? The choice is a toss-up. Indeed, both hikes have gained kudos from leading outdoor writers for their interesting nooks and delightful scenery. No doubt the rating of Crypt Lake by National Geographic as one of the world's

HIKING IN WATERTON LAKES NATIONAL PARK

NAME	REGION	DESCRIPTION	DIFFICULTY
Carthew–Alderson Trail	Cameron Lake	Memorable hike that offers beautiful scenery and sweeping views	moderate
Rowe Lakes	Waterton Townsite	Quick access to forested trails and shimmering alpine lakes	easy-moderate
Tamarack Trail	Waterton Townsite	Waterton's big backcountry adventure through glacial moraines and kaleidoscopic wildflower displays	moderate-difficult
Crypt Lake Trail	Waterton Townsite	Involves tunnel crawling and a cable-assisted walk along sheer cliffs	difficult

🦌 *Wildlife Watching*   🔭 *View*   🎣 *Fishing*   🚻 *Restrooms*

top 20 hikes in the 'Thrilling Trails' category in 2014 has only added to its popularity.

Once an overnight jaunt, Crypt Lake Trail is now tackled in a single day thanks to a water-taxi service that transports hikers to the trailhead from the townsite marina twice daily, at 9am and 10am. The return taxi is in the afternoon, allowing hikers time for a relaxed lunch break at Crypt Lake.

From the trailhead, the ascent begins quickly, forging through thick green vegetation and copious clumps of wildflowers. Make plenty of noise here, as this trail has been known to attract the odd bear. Once in more open terrain, you'll take in up-close views of waterfalls, mountains and an unnamed lake below.

The hike now turns into something of an obstacle course. First, you must climb up a narrow ladder to a small tunnel that will take you – via a combination of crawling or crouching – to a glacial cirque (the tunnel, though natural, was enlarged in the 1960s). On the other side you'll encounter a sheer rock face that must be negotiated with the assistance of a cable. It's not as terrifying as it sounds, but take extra care when it's raining. The cirque encloses gorgeous Crypt Lake, nestled in an amphitheater-like setting close to the international boundary (which crosses the lake's southern shore). Plenty of other hikers will, no doubt, be enjoying lunch in the exquisite natural surroundings. Choose your spot and soak up the beauty.

Ensure that you allow enough time for your return trip down, as the boats to the townsite are the only easy way back!

🚗 DRIVING

With only three paved roads, none of which measure more than 24km (15 miles) in length, opportunities for lengthy road trips in Waterton are limited. Even more so since the 2017 Kenow Wildfire burned through the Akamina and Red Rock Pkwys and the surrounding areas, meaning both are closed until extensive repairs can be made.

🚗 Akamina Parkway

Duration 20 minutes one way

Distance 16km (10 miles)

Speed Limit 50km/h (30mph)

Start Waterton Townsite

Finish Cameron Lake

Nearest Town Waterton Townsite

Summary Winter cross-country skiing trail and summer wildlife corridor, the Akamina makes for a dreamy afternoon motoring trip.

Severely impacted by the 2017 Kenow Wildfire, the Akamina isn't expected to be fully open to private vehicles until the summer of 2021 (it's possible shuttle buses will be used in the interim). Like the Red Rock Pkwy, hikers and cyclists can use the roadway and access all trailheads.

The road begins 500m (0.3 miles) from the townsite center. After you've climbed the first 500m (0.3 miles), you'll get a sideways glance at the town and lake below. Rocky cliff faces on the right and tree-packed

DURATION	DISTANCE	ELEVATION CHANGE	FEATURES	FACILITIES	PAGE
6hr	20km (12.5 miles)	610m (1968ft)			p219
3hr	8km (5 miles)	250m (820ft)			p217
2 days	31.6km (19.6 miles)	1460m (4700ft)			p224
6hr	17.2km (10.6 miles)	710m (2329ft)			p219

Drinking Water　　Transport to Trailhead　　Ranger Station　　Backcountry Campsite

slopes on the left predominate during the first few kilometers, and soon you'll glimpse **Cameron Creek**.

The curious structure at the 7.6km (4.7-mile) mark is the **Lineham Discovery Well National Historic Site**, the first oil well in western Canada. It was struck in 1902, along with premature optimism that led to dubbing the area 'Oil City.' After two years the flow was poor, and the last time the well

dripped was 1936. The parkway ends at the stellar **Cameron Lake**.

🚗 Red Rock Parkway

Duration 20 minutes one way

Distance 15km (9 miles)

Speed Limit 50km/h (30mph)

Start Waterton Townsite

Akamina Parkway

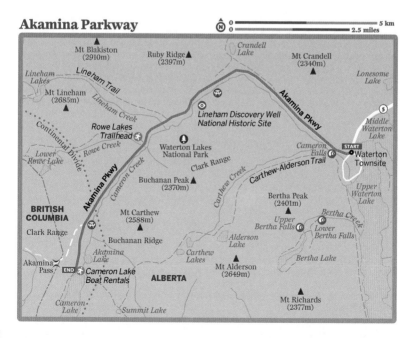

Red Rock Parkway

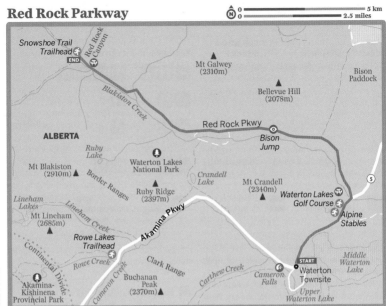

Finish Red Rock Canyon

Nearest Town Waterton Townsite

Summary A short but sweet sojourn to Red Rock Canyon, driving past over 500 million years of geological history.

At the time of research, Red Rock was closed to vehicles, but open to hikers and cyclists. It's expected to open to all traffic early 2020 but check www.parkscanada.gc.ca/waterton -open for the latest information.

Red Rock Pkwy originates at a junction with Hwy 5, about 8km (5 miles) southwest of the park entrance. This road, running alongside Blakiston Creek for much of its route, is full of wildflower-speckled prairie spilling onto incredible mountains. South of the parkway, the awe-inspiring Mt Blakiston is Waterton's tallest peak at 2910m (9547ft). A few picnic spots are dotted along the way, and at the 4.9km (3-mile) mark, **Bison Jump** – a small native history exhibit – is worth a stop.

Most visitors persevere to the end of the road, 15km (9 miles) in, where **Red Rock Canyon** sits colorfully aglow. A 700m (0.4-mile) self-guided loop trail circuits the edge of the canyon. Consisting of ancient Grinnell argillite, the canyon is a fantastic introduction to one of the geologically wondrous aspects of Waterton.

🚴 CYCLING

In contrast to Glacier, Waterton has five trails open for cycling. On top of the two we've described, you'll also find the Akamina Pass Trail, which is 1.3km (0.8 miles) one way; the Wishbone Trail, which is 21km (13 miles) round-trip; and the 6.9km (4.3-mile) Kootenai Brown Trail, which parallels the entrance road from the park gate to the townsite.

Cyclists on park trails should adhere to a few basic rules. Ride single file to prevent trail damage or erosion; alert hikers ahead of you when passing; and when encountering a horse, get off your bike and stand aside until it passes. Always stay on the trail and be careful not to surprise wildlife.

Mountain bikes can be rented in Waterton at Pat's (Map p226; ☎ 403-859-2266; www. patswaterton.com; 224 Mt View Rd; rental per hr/ day from C$15/50). Helmets are included.

🚴 Red Rock Parkway Loop

Duration Three hours round-trip

Distance 20.6km (12.8 miles)

Difficulty Moderate

Start/Finish Waterton Townsite

Nearest Town Waterton Townsite

Summary Mix road biking with single-track on a multifarious romp around Waterton's classic parkways.

Incorporating the hikeable Crandell Lake Trail with the paved Akamina and Red Rock Pkwys, this popular loop can be tackled from one of three starting points: Waterton Townsite, the closed Crandell Mountain Campground (off the Red Rock Pkwy), or a trailhead 6.4km (4 miles) along the Akamina Pkwy.

All three approaches make for a varied and pleasant half-day ride that mixes 6.4km of rocky off-road with 10km (miles) of smooth asphalt. The only technicalities come with the ascent to the lake (less steep if you travel anticlockwise), which involves a 100m elevation gain from the respective parkways. The clear Crandell Lake, with Mt Crandell visible to its southeast, is a serene setting with sandy areas and rocks perfect for a picnic perch. Cyclists should beware of hikers on the Crandell Lake Trail and wildlife (including bears) on both parkways.

🚴 Snowshoe Trail

Duration 1½ hours round-trip

Distance 16.4km (10.2 miles)

Difficulty Moderate

Start/Finish Red Rock Canyon parking lot

Nearest Town Waterton Townsite

Summary Tackle part of the Tamarack Trail on this short but steep sojourn into Waterton's northwestern corner.

This fine Waterton cycle follows Bauerman Creek on an abandoned fire road from the Red Rock Canyon parking lot. The turnaround point is at Snowshoe Warden Cabin, 8.2km (5.1 miles) further on.

Don't be deceived by the initial wideness of the track; the gradient gets noticeably steeper beyond the Goat Lake turnoff, and there are also a couple of rocky streams that will need to be forded in late spring and early summer.

Wedged into the park's northwestern corner, mountain views are excellent throughout this ride, and vibrant wildflowers add color during summer. Although bikes aren't allowed on any of the connecting trails (including Castle Divide and Twin Lakes), the ride makes for a popular bike-hike excursion, with cyclists locking their bikes close to the trail junctions, before continuing along spur paths to destinations such as Goat Lake and Avion Ridge.

⚓ OTHER ACTIVITIES

Waterton offers all the activities available in Glacier, with a couple of hidden extras thrown in for good measure. Golf is possible inside the park perimeter or you can take to the trails on horseback. Even scuba diving is possible – committed divers brave the frigid waters of Upper Waterton Lake at Emerald Bay, where Gertrude, a 1900 paddle wheeler, sits 20m (66ft) below the surface.

Because its sedimentary rock is soft and crumbly, Waterton is not hugely popular

---

INTERNATIONAL PEACE PARK HIKE

A unique opportunity to visit two parks – and two different countries – in one day, the International Peace Park Hike leads participants on a free guided 13.7km (8.5-mile) walk alongside twinkling Upper Waterton Lake, from Waterton Townsite in Canada to Goat Haunt in Glacier National Park in the US. Led by a duo of rangers from both nations, hikers follow an undulating path (with some moderately difficult uphill sections) south through sun-dappled forest and scenic shoreline, to the unguarded border (passengers weren't allowed to disembark during the 2019 summer season because of water and staffing shortages here). When landings are allowed in subsequent seasons, you'll need to have previously registered and had a video conference with Customs and Border Protection via one of the Reporting Offsite Arrival-Mobile (ROAM) kiosks at the Waterton Shoreline Cruise (p227) dock (or download the app on your phone). Then you are free to soak up the impressive mountainscape and examine exhibits in a small 'peace pavilion' at the boat dock. When making your reservation, you will have assured passage on the 5:25pm boat back to Waterton (adult/child C$34/18).

The International Peace Park Hike departs from the Bertha Trailhead in Waterton at 10am every Tuesday and Friday from early July to late August. Places are available for up to 30 people, but reserve beforehand at the Parks Canada Visitor Centre (p232) as the hike is perennially popular.

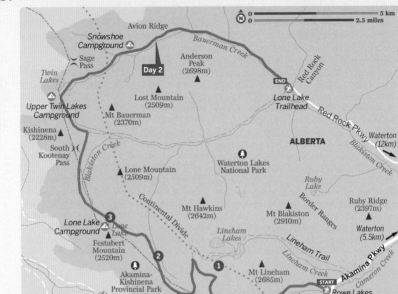

Overnight Hike
Tamarack Trail

START ROWE LAKES TRAILHEAD
END LONE LAKE TRAILHEAD
LENGTH TWO DAYS; 31.6KM (19.6 MILES)

Waterton's only real backcountry adventure is this moderately difficult hiking trail with an overall elevation change of 1460m (4700ft) – usually tackled over two days. Glacial moraines and wildflowered meadows, lakes and larch, and perhaps even an animal or two, are viewed along the way. Tricky descents over scree, extreme winds at high altitude and long stretches without treatable water sources are potential difficulties that must be considered before heading out.

Choose between two starting points: the Rowe Lakes Trail off Akamina Pkwy for a clockwise loop, or the Lone Lake Trail from Red Rock Canyon for a counterclockwise alternative. Early autumn is the best time to make this journey, when the namesake Tamarack tree or alpine larch (a deciduous conifer) sheds its needles in a riot of rustic yellows. The reservation-only Tamarack

hiker shuttle can deliver you to your chosen trailhead.

From the Rowe Lakes trailhead, the hike junctions with the main Tamarack Trail at the 5.1km mark, before ascending ❶ **Lineham Ridge**. Offering breathtaking panoramic views, this ridge is a huge highlight. The trail soon leaves the ridge and traverses open slopes, then descends to the west bank of ❷ **Blakiston Creek**. From here, it's mostly a steep ascent to a saddle with Festubert Mountain in the background before descending to ❸ **Lone Lake Campground**, on the north side of Lone Lake. You can overnight here or carry on another 7.3km to Upper Twin Lakes Campground, beautifully situated just under Kishinena Peak. Lone Lake to Twin Lakes involves an easy descent past the South Kootenay Pass and Blakiston Creek trail junctions, the fording of a creek, a moderate climb to a saddle west of Mt Bauerman and then a hike down scree. A third campground – Snowshoe – is only another 4.6km from here, and the striking colors of Red Rock Canyon are an easy 8.2 km from there along Bauerman Creek.

for rock climbing, but the upper and lower bands of Bear's Hump offer 10 approaches ranging from grades 5.4 to 5.8; aficionados rave about the park's ice-climbing potential.

Waterton Lakes Golf Course   GOLF
(Map p228; ☑ 403-859-2114; www.golfwaterton. com; green fees 9/18 holes C$25/50) Sterling scenery will take your eye off the ball at this 18-hole course. It's 4km north of town, just off Hwy 5.

Alpine Stables   HORSEBACK RIDING
(Map p228; ☑ 403-859-2462; www.alpinestables. com; guided rides per 1hr/4hr from C$40/115) Displaced from their longtime home by the Kenow wildfire, this third-generation family business is now operating out of the lower parking lot of the Waterton Lakes Golf Course. If you're keen to experience the park on horseback, it has over 50 horses suitable for riders of all levels; tours range from one (C$70) to eight hours (C$240) and overnight pack trips.

Construction to rebuild the stables, which were completely destroyed by the fire, continues apace.

Awesome Adventures   DIVING
(☑ 403-328-5041; www.awesomeadventures.ca; 314 11th St S, Lethbridge; scuba equipment rental per day/weekend C$55/100) With no in-park scuba-dive specialists, your closest equipment rental is with this company located in Lethbridge. Most divers head to Cameron Bay or Upper Waterton Lake.

🎣 Fishing & Boating

Fishing is popular in Waterton Lakes National Park, with the waters hosting 24 species of fish, including northern pike, whitefish and various types of trout.

A Parks Canada permit is required to fish in Waterton. Permits cost C$9.80 for the day or C$34.30 for the season and can be purchased at the visitor center, park headquarters or at campground entry booths. Not all lakes are open to fishing and there are some seasonal regulations; check at the visitor center. There has been a general move toward more catch-and-release fishing among anglers in recent years.

A popular hike-in destination for anglers is Bertha Lake (and Carthew Lakes, which remain closed because of fire damage).

Motorboats and water skis are permissible only on Upper and Middle Waterton Lakes. Wear a wetsuit as the water is cold.

Waterton Shoreline Cruises (p227) manage the docking facilities at the townsite's marina.

Blakiston & Co Adventure Rentals   BOATING
(Map p226; ☑ 800-456-0772; www.blakistonand company.com; Crandell Mountain Lodge, 102 Mt View Rd; stand-up paddleboard rental per 1/4hr C$30/85; ☺ Jun-Aug) Offers stand-up paddleboard (SUP), canoe and kayak (including ones with glass bottoms) rentals for Emerald Bay, the mostly calm patch of water across the street from the Crandell Mountain Lodge (from where this shop operates). E-bikes are also now available (one/two hours C$35/50).

Cameron Lake Boat Rentals   BOATING
(Map p228; ☑ 403-627-6443; www.cameronlake boatrentals.com; rental per hour C$35-45; ☺ 8am-6:30pm Jul & Aug, 9am-5pm Jun & Sep) Rents out boats for kayaking, canoeing or rowing on the exquisitely situated Cameron Lake, as well as boards for stand up paddleboarding (SUP). There's a simple snack bar and souvenir shop as well.

🎿 Winter Activities

In winter, Akamina Pkwy is the most popular access point for cross-country skiing, while the Cameron Lake area is a favorite for snowshoeing. Waterton (along with Kootenay, Jasper and Banff) is considered to be one of the world's premier waterfall ice-climbing destinations. Since the sport comes loaded with a number of inherent risks, aspiring climbers are encouraged to check avalanche bulletins. *Waterfall Ice: Climbs in the Canadian Rockies* by Joe Josephson is the definitive text on the topic.

ℹ️ WILDERNESS PERMITS & REGULATIONS

Permits are not required for day hikes, but overnight trips do require them. Up to 24 hours before the start of your journey, make arrangements at the visitor center. The nightly fee is C$9.80 per adult. Kids 16 years and under get free permits. Campsites (only Bertha Bay, Bertha Lake and Boundary Bay are open) are reservable, and advance reservations can be made up to 90 days ahead; an extra fee of C$11.70 is charged.

Waterton Townsite

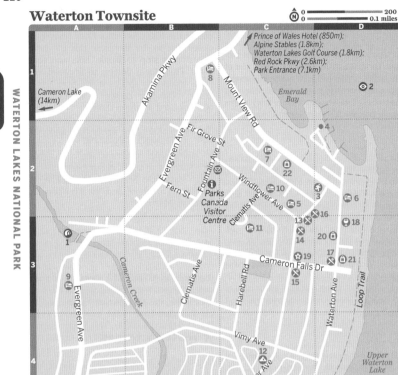

WATERTON LAKES NATIONAL PARK

Waterton Townsite

◉ SIGHTS

The 2017 Kenow Wildfire burned 19,000 hectares of the park, including 50% of the park's vegetated area, which led to significant closures. However, by the end of the summer of 2019, most of the trail system was reopened, even if the two major parkways were still closed to vehicle traffic. Check www.parkscanada.gc.ca/waterton-open for closures.

◉ Waterton Townsite

The diminutive town of Waterton is a manicured and peaceful little place. Of course, it wouldn't warrant a visit if not for the gorgeous alpine scenery and outdoor adventures on its doorstep. Low-key and walkable – really nothing more than a few streets – its wintertime population shrinks to the size of an extended family (only around 35 residents). A number of short walking trails make the most of lakeside vistas. A 3.2km (2-mile) loop trail along Upper Waterton Lake and around the townsite provides a good introduction to the area. There's also the shorter 2km (1.2-mile) Emerald Bay Loop.

Cameron Falls   WATERFALL
(Map p226; Cameron Falls Dr) At the west end of Cameron Falls Dr (a short hop from the center of town) is this dramatically poised torrent of foaming water, notable among geologists for harboring the oldest exposed Precambrian rocks in the Canadian Rockies. Estimates suggest they are 1.5 billion years old, give or take the odd millennium. The lookout here is paved for wheelchair access and the falls are lit up at night.

Upper Waterton Lake   LAKE
(Map p226) Visible from all over town, this is the deepest lake in the Canadian Rockies, sinking to a murky 120m. One of the best vantage points is from the Prince of Wales Hotel, where a classic view is framed by an ethereal collection of Gothic mountains, including Mt Cleveland, Glacier National Park's highest peak. A more placid spot is **Emerald Bay**, famous for its turquoise waters and ever-popular with scuba divers.

◉ Cameron Lake

Cameron Lake   LAKE
(Map p228) Backed by the sheer-sided slopes of Mt Custer, placid Cameron Lake is tucked tantalizingly beneath the Continental Divide

at the three-way meeting point of Montana, Alberta and British Columbia. Poised at the end of the 16km Akamina Pkwy (currently closed due to fire damage), this is where day-trippers stop to picnic, hike and rent boats. From foam flowers to fireweed, copious wildflower species thrive here, while grizzly bears are known to frequent the lake's isolated southern shores.

There are some interesting interpretive displays outlining the area's flora and fauna under a shelter adjacent to the parking lot, along with restrooms and a hut that sells snacks and sodas. A number of hiking trails start from here, including the short Cameron Lakeshore and the ever-popular Carthew–Alderson.

⟲ TOURS

Waterton Shoreline Cruises   CRUISE
(Map p226; ☑ 403-859-2362; www.watertoncruise.com; adult/youth/child C$53/26/18; ☺ May-Oct) Sail across the shimmering waters of Upper Waterton Lake to the far shore of Goat Haunt, Montana (USA). This family-owned business offers a scenic, 2¼-hour trip on the vintage MV *International* (1927), with lively commentary. Bring your passport: it docks in the USA for about 30 minutes (passengers weren't allowed to disembark during the 2019 summer season because of water and staffing shortages). July and August have four cruises daily (10am, 1pm, 4pm and 7pm).

The company also provides a water shuttle (adult/child C$27/14) to the trailhead for the Crypt Lake hike, with three departures in the morning (8:30am, 9am and 10am) and two returns in the afternoon (4pm and 5pm). If you take the boat one way, hiking to or from Goat Haunt, you'll need to download and use the ROAM app or check in at the marina kiosk.

Tickets can only be purchased in person at the company's office at the town marina.

⨯ SLEEPING

Only two campgrounds, the Waterton Townsite Campground (p228) and Belly River Campground (p228) 29km away near the US border, remain open after the 2017 Kenow Wildfire. Much of the backcountry also burned so campsites are limited. The

Waterton Lakes National Park Region

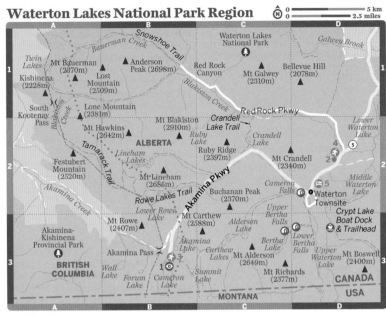

Waterton Lakes National Park Region

iconic Prince of Wales Hotel (p230) sits majestically just above Upper Waterton Lake and several quality hotels and small resorts are in town. Basic motels in fairly dispiriting Pincher Creek, 56km to the north, will do in a pinch.

Camping

In high season Waterton Townsite Campground can fill by late morning. If staying at Crandell Mountain or Belly River Campgrounds, you can use the showers at Waterton Townsite Campground free of charge.

Belly River Campground   CAMPGROUND $
(☑ 403-859-5133; www.pc.gc.ca; Hwy 6/Chief Mountain International Hwy; tent sites C$4.90; ☺ May–Sep) Located 26km outside the park on the way to the US border, this primitive campground sits in placid parkland terrain with aspen trees and far-off views of the mountains. Availability is first-come, first-served.

Waterton Townsite
Campground   CAMPGROUND $
(Map p226; ☑ 877-737-3783; www.reservation.parkscanada.gc.ca; Vimy Ave; tent/RV sites C$22.50/38.20; ☺ May–Oct; ℗) Dominating the southern end of Waterton village, this campground is mainly an enormous, gopher hole–covered field aimed at RV campers. It has all the charm of camping in a grassy parking lot at a music festival – but the location is incredibly convenient. There are some tree-shaded sites near the edges, but by midsummer you'll be lucky to get anything. Book ahead.

Lodging

There's a moratorium on development in the park, including in and around the townsite where all of the lodging is located, so it's unlikely there will be any expansion in alternatives anytime soon. Three lodges stay open year-round.

Bayshore Inn Resort & Spa
HOTEL $$

(Map p226; ☎403-859-2211; www.bayshoreinn. com; 111 Waterton Ave; r C$169-259; ☺Apr-Oct; P@☎) A large, spread-out place, the Bayshore has lakefront rooms that have very comfy beds and balconies – ask for a recently remodeled one with lake views; mountain-view rooms take in the parking lot with the peaks beyond. Walls are thinner than ideal, so noise can be an issue if a wedding or other party is happening. There's a spa, an upscale restaurant and a Starbucks on site.

Aspen Village Inn
HOTEL $$

(Map p226; ☎403-859-2255; www.aspenvillage inn.com; 111 Windflower Ave; r from C$230; ☺May–mid-Oct; ☎) These dated, motel-style rooms aren't really good value, but when space is limited and you don't want to camp... It's good for families, with an on-site kids playground and resident deer finding shade in the grounds. Barbecues and picnic tables offer a touch of ambiance on warm summer nights and many rooms have kitchenettes.

★ Northland Lodge
B&B $$

(Map p226; ☎403-859-2353; www.northland lodgecanada.com; 408 Evergreen Ave; r C$196-249; ☺mid-May–mid-Oct; ☎) On the edge of town within earshot of gushing Cameron Falls is this cozy house that Louis Hill (the genius behind the Prince of Wales Hotel) built for himself. A B&B with a wide range of quaint rooms (some with shared bath) and a creaking staircase, it's steeped in character. The welcoming host's freshly baked breakfast is fabulous.

The Danish Blue Boy and Dutch Treehouse double rooms are especially nice.

Crandell Mountain Lodge
HOTEL $$

(Map p226; ☎403-859-2288; www.crandell mountainlodge.com; 102 Mt View Rd; r from C$200; P☎) With homemade cookies in the lobby, this 1940s lodge is doing a good impersonation of a Tudor cottage plucked from a quiet English village. The Crandell has old-fashioned rooms with quilts like Grandma used to make, fireplaces and a front deck facing Emerald Bay across the street. Service is very welcoming.

Bear Mountain Motel
MOTEL $$

(Map p226; ☎403-859-2366; www.bearmountain motel.com; 208 Mt View Rd; r C$140-175; ☺mid-May–Sep; P✳✻) Upfront about its offerings, Bear Mountain is a standard, retro-style motel with immaculate rooms and friendly service. There are barbecues and picnic tables; some rooms are pet friendly and some have kitchenettes. This is about as 'budget' as you get in Waterton.

Wi-fi is free, compliments of the Waterton town network.

THE LONELIEST BORDER CROSSING IN THE US

Welcome to what must be the most low-key and pleasant border crossing in the US – and with not a car in sight! Goat Haunt is a rare foot-traffic-only land border between the US and Canada, located at the southern end of Upper Waterton Lake, 9.6km below the 49th parallel international boundary. The nearest US road to this lonely outpost is the Going-to-the-Sun Rd, 46km to the south via a steep but visually stunning trail. Consequently most people arrive here from Canada on the *MV International*, a historic boat that sails south from Waterton Townsite four times daily (summer only). The boat has a 30-minute scheduled stopover that allows visitors to check out the 'haunt's' very basic facilities: a boat dock, restrooms, a hikers' shelter, drinking water, the peace pavilion interpretive exhibit (chronicling the history of the park and exploring the meaning of the word 'peace' worldwide) and a tiny ranger station that doubles up as one of North America's smallest border posts (passengers weren't allowed to disembark during the 2019 summer season because of water and staffing shortages here).

And it's likely that the ranger station won't be staffed in the future. Rather, anyone disembarking will have to have gained permission in advance via the ROAM (Reporting Offsite Arrival Mobile) app, either at one of kiosks at the Waterton Shoreline Cruise (p227) dock in Waterton townsite, or via the app on your phone.

Short- and long-term hiking options abound. You can walk 11.2km back to Waterton along the lakeshore, undertake a wild backcountry adventure up Waterton Valley beneath the shadow of 3190m Mt Cleveland (the highest peak in the peace park), or indulge in one of half-a-dozen shorter hikes before catching a later boat back to Waterton.

★**Prince of**
Wales Hotel   HISTORIC HOTEL $$$

(Map p228; ☑ 403-859-2231; www.princeofwales
waterton.com; Prince of Wales Rd; r from C$249;
⊙ May-Sep; P 🛜) With a Hogwarts-like set-
ting on a wind-buffeted bluff overlooking
Upper Waterton Lake, the grand Prince of
Wales Hotel blends Swiss-style architecture with
the atmosphere of a Scottish castle. The old-
world charms extend to serving staff in kilts
and high tea in the main lounge – very civ-
ilized. The large lake-facing windows frame
the wilderness that awaits.

The carpeted rooms, spread over five
floors, aren't particularly inspiring, though
– the charm is in the setting and common
areas which retain much of the original
hand-carved woodwork. All of the bath-
rooms, most quite small with sinks outside
per the architect's design, have been reno-
vated in the last two years. This regal hotel
was the brainchild of Louis Hill; built in 1927
by the US-owned Great Northern Railway, it
was the only Canadian link in its chain of
historic accommodations.

Waterton Lakes
Lodge Resort   RESORT $$$

(Map p226; ☑ 403-859-2150; www.watertonlakes
lodge.com; 101 Clematis Ave; lodge C$249, ste
C$300; P 🛜 ⓢ) A family-oriented sprawler
with the kind of ample facilities that will
make you feel a million miles from the
trailhead, this place has a gym, indoor pool,
hot tub and snazzy on-site lounge and grill.
Large lodge rooms that sleep up to four
people come in standard or deluxe – the latter have fireplaces and Jacuzzis. Suites have
kitchenettes.

Waterton Glacier Suites   HOTEL $$$

(Map p226; ☑ 403-859-2004; www.waterton
suites.com; 107 Windflower Ave; ste from C$259;
P @ 🛜 ⓢ) This year-round lodge counts
26 spacious, suite-like rooms, all fully
equipped with whirlpool bath, satellite TV,
gas fireplace, fridge, microwave and air-
con. It doesn't have a lot of character, but
if you prefer a little front-country luxury,
this could be your bag. Outside high season,
rates drop significantly.

FROM EXPLORATION TO CONSERVATION

Englishman Peter Fidler, of the Hudson Bay Company, is thought to be the first Europe-
an to have explored this southern portion of the Canadian Rockies, setting out in 1792.
Explorer Thomas Blakiston first came upon Waterton Lakes in 1858, naming them after
famous British naturalist Charles Waterton.

The seed to designate the area a reserve was sown by Fredrick William Godsal, a
rancher and conservationist in southern Alberta who had the prescience to see that, if
the beautiful lakes region was not hastily set aside as protected land, private interests
would soon take hold. In 1893 he wrote a letter to William Pearce, the superintendent of
mines who, in turn, urged government officials in Ottawa to consider the issue and, in
1895, what is now known as Waterton Lakes was given protective status by the Canadian
federal government as a forest park.

In the days before the 1930 National Parks Act, Cameron Valley had a brief stint as
an 'Oil City,' beginning in 1902, when copious barrels of the liquid gold poured out from
western Canada's first oil well. The oil discovery also led to the foundation of a townsite,
whose first structures included a cookhouse, stable and blacksmith's shop. In 1910, 150
town lots were offered for leasehold at C$15 per annum and the settlement opened up
its first hotel. When the oil dried up prematurely a few years later, local businesses quick-
ly turned their attention to tourism.

Fortunately, the changes occurred just as Louis W Hill, son of Great Northern Railway
magnate and 'Empire Builder' James J Hill, was formulating a plan to link Waterton to his
great chain of railway-inspired hotels as a means of circumventing Prohibition in the US.
A Swiss-style hotel, occupying a prime perch overlooking windy Upper Waterton Lake,
opened in 1927 and was named for the then Prince of Wales (later Edward VIII).

Linked with Glacier in the world's first International Peace Park in 1932, Waterton had
the distinction of becoming the first Canadian national park to be designated a Unesco
Biosphere Reserve in 1979. In 1995 it was declared, along with Glacier, a Unesco World
Heritage site.

✕ EATING

Wieners of Waterton
HOT DOGS $

(Map p226; www.wienersofwaterton.com; 301 Wind-flower Ave; hot dogs C$6-8; ☉ 11am-11pm; 🖋) Not all wieners are made equal and those served here approach gourmet level, including locally smoked and breakfast-dog varieties. Get 'em with a side of sweet-potato fries. Rightfully popular, it commonly sees lines out the door during summer.

★ Welch's Chocolates, Ice Cream & Desserts
DESSERTS $

(Map p226; cnr Windflower Ave & Cameron Falls Dr; desserts C$3-12; ☉ 9am-10pm May-Oct) In a ranch-style house at the end of Windflower Ave, this family-run Waterton institution is filled with a Willy Wonka's worth of home-made chocolates, fudge and candy. It's also been dishing out ice cream, pies and pastries for 50 plus years, all scoffed down on the wraparound deck.

Pearl's
CAFE $

(Map p226; www.pearlscafe.ca; 305 Windflower Ave; mains C$9-15; ☉ 7am-11pm mid-May–Sep; 🖘) Enjoy Waterton's best breakfast spot on the sunny front patio for good strong coffee and several hearty, innovative variations on French toast and pancakes. Sandwiches, salads and specialty pizzas are available the rest of the day.

★ 49° North Pizza
PIZZA $$

(Map p226; ☎ 403-859-3000; www.49degrees northpizza.com; 303 Windflower Ave; pizzas C$12-30; ☉ noon-9pm Mon-Fri, from 5pm Sat & Sun May-Sep) Seriously satisfying pizza with all of the expected renditions, plus some creative gourmet options such as bison and Saska-toon berries, as well as a choice of salads and a make-your-own 'power bowl' (brown rice with a bunch of vegetarian add-ons). Service is top-notch and there's a good beer selection; if the handful of tables and patio are full, you can get takeout.

Zum's Eatery
CANADIAN $$

(Map p226; ☎ 403-859-2388; 116b Waterton Ave; mains C$15-22; ☉ 8am-9:30pm May–mid-Oct) Good, home-style cooking of the burger, pizza and fried-chicken variety makes Zum a staple in Waterton. For breakfast there's corned beef and hash; tortillas with eggs, sausage and chili; or waffles. The lack of sophistication is made up for by the character of the decor: several hundred North American license plates embellish almost every centimeter of wall.

🍷 DRINKING & ENTERTAINMENT

Evenings can be surprisingly lively in Waterton, with hikers celebrating their return to civilization with a pint or three; this is less noticeable these days, however, because the 2017 Kenow Wildfire has impacted the number of visitors and hikers to the park. Everything is within staggering distance.

Thirsty Bear Saloon
PUB

(Map p226; ☎ 403-859-2211; 111 Waterton Ave; ☉ 4pm-2am Mon-Sat mid-May–Sep) This large barn-like pub attached to the Lakeside Convention Center is where what passes for wild Waterton nights happen, aided by live music, good craft beer and a convivial vibe.

Waterton Lakes Opera House
CINEMA

(Map p226; ☎ 403-859-2467; 309 Windflower Ave; tickets adult/child C$10/7; ☉ May-Sep) Waterton has its own small movie theater, showing two films nightly, as well as live classical music and the occasional play. Cash only. Check the Facebook page to see what's on.

🛍 SHOPPING

Akamina Gifts & Book Nook
GIFTS & SOUVENIRS, BOOKS

(Map p226; ☎ 403-859-2361; 108 Waterton Ave; ☉ 9am-7pm mid-May–Sep) One of many souvenir shops that can satisfy any desires for maple syrup, kitschy gifts and replacement T-shirts, along with park-related literature.

Tamarack Outdoor Outfitters
SPORTS & OUTDOORS

(Map p226; ☎ 403-859-2378; www.hikewaterton. com; 214 Mt View Rd; ☉ 8am-8pm May-Sep) Waterton's most comprehensive equipment store stocks everything from backpacks to bear spray. It offers guides for one-day and multi-day treks and shuttle buses to many trailheads in the park – including Chief Mountain (C$30), which you can book online. Tamarack and the free shuttles to all hikes on the Akarama Pkwy are on hold until the area opens up again. It also exchanges US currency.

Blackfoot Cultural Centre
BOOKS

(Map p226; ☎ 403-859-5133; 117 Waterton Ave; ☉ 9am-9pm mid-May–late Sep) A gift shop, bookstore and information desk for the Blackfeet Nation, this center is run by the nonprofit Waterton Natural History Association. You'll find local maps and affordable artwork, too.

ℹ️ WHEN YOU ARRIVE

The park is open 24 hours a day, 365 days a year, although many amenities and a couple of park roads close in winter. Entry costs are family/adult/child C$15.70/7.80/free per day (C$11.75/5.80/free during the shoulder seasons). An annual Waterton pass costs C$39.20 (adult). Park admission is free on Canada Day (July 1) and Parks Day (third Saturday in July). Passes, to be displayed on your vehicle's windshield, are valid until 4pm on the date of expiration.

If you enter the park when the booth is shut, get a pass early the next morning at the Parks Canada Visitor Centre.

ℹ️ Information

INTERNET

The town itself provides free, if generally weak, wi-fi. Many of the restaurants and cafes also have their own.

MEDICAL SERVICES & EMERGENCY

Cardston Health Centre (☑ 403-653-4411; www.albertahealthservices.ca; 144 2nd St W, Cardston) Located 54km east of Waterton, this is the closest hospital.

Pincher Creek Health Centre (☑ 403-627-1234; www.albertahealthservices.ca; 1222 Bev McLachlin Dr) Located 57km north of the park.

MONEY

Most businesses in Waterton Townsite will accept US dollars. The caveat, however, is that they won't calculate the conversion rate, which means you lose out; debit and credit cards are good options. Pat's, Prince of Wales Hotel, Caribou Clothes, Bayshore Inn and Tamarack Outdoor Outfitters have ATMs; the latter is also one of the only places in town to exchange money.

POST

Post Office (Map p226; 102a Windflower Ave; ⊙ 8:30am-12:30pm & 1-4:30pm Mon-Fri)

TOURIST INFORMATION

Parks Canada Visitor Centre (Map p226; ☑ 403-859-2378; www.pc.gc.ca/waterton; Fountain Ave; ⊙ 8am-6pm May-Sep) The central stop for information on everything from trail conditions to hotels. It's in a temporary stucture until a new large, contemporary-designed building opens in the spring of 2021.

My Waterton (www.mywaterton.ca) Waterton Lakes' Chamber of Commerce website with up-to-date visitor information.

ℹ️ Getting There & Away

Waterton lies in Alberta's southwestern corner, 130km from Lethbridge and 156km from Calgary. The one road entrance into the park is in its northeastern corner, along Hwy 5. Most visitors coming from Glacier and the USA reach the junction with Hwy 5 via Hwy 6 (Chief Mountain International Hwy) from the southeast, after crossing at the **Chief Mountain border crossing** (Chief Mountain Hwy; ⊙ 7am-10pm Jun-Labour Day, 9am-6pm mid-May–late May & Labour Day-Sep 30). A passport, enhanced driver's license or NEXUS card is required for US and Canadian citizens; all others must present passports and fill out an I-94 or I-94W form (available for C$6 at the border). From Calgary, to the north, Hwy 2 shoots south toward Hwy 5 into the park. From the east, Hwy 5, through Cardston, heads west and then south into the park.

There is no public transportation from Canadian cities outside the park. **Pincher Creek Taxi** (☑ 403-632-9738) does provide service from the town of Pincher Creek to Waterton town for C$75. The shuttle service that previously connected the Prince of Wales Hotel and Glacier Park Lodge in Montana is no longer offered.

ℹ️ Getting Around

BICYCLE

In marked contrast to Glacier, biking in Waterton is both popular and encouraged. Indeed, you can rent out everything from mountain bikes to large two-person rickshaws from Pat's (p222) in the townsite. The multipurpose Kootenai Brown Trail links the park gate with the townsite and there are four further designated trails open to bicycles.

CAR & MOTORCYCLE

The speed limit in the townsite is 30km/h (19mph) unless otherwise posted; campgrounds post 20km/h (12mph) limits.

The town's only gas station is at Pat's on Mount View Rd and is open May to October. To fuel up in winter, head to Mountain View. Parking is simple around town; there are no meters or any unusual restrictions, and the town has a few free parking lots (no parking between 11pm and 6am).

PUBLIC TRANSPORTATION

Waterton Shoreline Cruises (p227) operates a water shuttle service to the east shore of Upper Waterton Lake for the Crypt Lake trailhead. The boat leaves Waterton marina at 8:30am, 9am and 10am and picks up returns at 4pm and 5pm during July and August. The round-trip fare is C$27/14 per adult/child.

Tamarack Outdoor Outfitters (p231) runs hiker shuttles that depart daily from the store in season. The Cameron Express (C$13.50) to Cameron Lake leaves daily at 8:15am or 9:15am.

Understand Banff, Jasper & Glacier

The Parks Today

Banff, Jasper and Glacier are experiencing a tourist boom. On the plus side, the parks inspire millions of visitors annually, teaching respect for wildlife and the beauty of untamed wilderness. At the same time, certain areas such as Lake Louise are getting overrun, causing traffic snarls and tempting the tourism industry to capitalize on higher demand by raising prices. Meanwhile, Jasper's recent pine beetle infestation and forest fires in Glacier and Waterton point to the ongoing detrimental effects of human-influenced climate change.

Best on Film

Brokeback Mountain (2005) Cowboy tale partly filmed in Kananaskis Country.

The Shining (1980) The opening scene tracks a car winding along the Going-to-the-Sun Rd in Glacier National Park.

River of No Return (1954) Marilyn Monroe's peroxide glamor is pitted against Banff and Jasper's natural beauty.

The Revenant (2015) A trapper's harrowing wilderness journey after a grizzly attack, partially filmed in Canmore and the Kananaskis.

Best in Print

The Melting World (Christopher White; 2013) What the warming climate is doing to Glacier's glaciers.

People Before the Park (Sally Thompson, Kootenai Cultural Committee & Pikunni Traditional Association; 2015) Tribal histories of Glacier before it was a park.

Old Indian Trails of the Canadian Rockies (Mary Schäffer; 1911) Early 20th-century account of Schäffer's wilderness adventures.

Mark of the Grizzly (Scott McMillion; 2011) Tales of real-life human-grizzly encounters, collected over a span of four decades.

Managing Crowds at Banff

As Canada's oldest and busiest national park, Banff is no stranger to crowds – but tourism here has soared to new heights. In 2017, Banff became the first Canadian park to receive over 4 million annual visitors, a level it has now maintained for three years running.

On the ground, this translates into bigger crowds – and in the case of Lake Louise and Moraine Lake – actual traffic jams. Anyone hoping to snag a parking spot at either lake needs to set out early. When the lots start filling in early to midmorning, an army of traffic workers begin sending drivers straight back down the hill to overflow lots where they can catch shuttle buses back uphill to Lake Louise – and if their stamina holds out, take a *second* connecting shuttle to Moraine Lake.

The shuttle bus system has been working...to a point. Still, on the busiest days, wait times for the shuttle itself can last an hour or more. In 2018, Banff's public transit company Roam launched a bus service from Banff to Lake Louise to relieve some of the pressure, and Parks Canada continues to look at ways to address the overcrowding. In the meantime, visitors can take matters into their own hands by scheduling visits for off-peak hours, or by walking, cycling or using public buses.

Rising from the Ashes

Both Glacier and Waterton Lakes have suffered significant wildfires in recent years, and the road to recovery in both parks is still ongoing. Waterton was especially hard hit. The massive Kenow fire rampaged through the park in September 2017, burning over 190 sq km, destroying the visitor center, ravaging the Akamina and Red Rock Pkwys and impacting 80% of Waterton's trails.

In Glacier, large conflagrations struck two years in a row, with the 2017 Sprague fire and the 2018 Howe Ridge fire burning nearly 69 sq km and 57 sq km, respectively.

The most news-grabbing impact of the Sprague Fire was its destruction of the century-old Sperry Chalet, a backcountry lodge that had been welcoming hikers since its construction by the Great Northern Railway in 1914.

By summer 2019, much of Waterton Lakes was functioning normally again, but recovery was incomplete, with many of Waterton's trails at least partially closed – including the iconic Carthew-Alderson Trail – and other trailheads along the Akamina and Red Rock Pkwys still only accessible by foot or bicycle. By the time you read this, the situation will have doubtless improved; check with Parks Canada for details. Meanwhile, down in Glacier, the Sperry Chalet is being rebuilt for a scheduled 2020 reopening.

Who Owns the Parks?

Banff, Jasper, Glacier and Waterton Lakes have long contracted with private entities to run certain park services, including hotels, restaurants and bus transport – but lately these deals have been provoking greater scrutiny.

In May 2019, American-owned Viad Corp announced that it would assume a majority stake in Mountain Park Lodges (MPL), owner of 31% of the hotel rooms in Jasper. Viad already operates several of the most high-profile and lucrative national-park properties on both sides of the border, including the Brewster sightseeing bus company, Banff Gondola, the Columbia Icefield Adventure, boat cruises on Lake Minnewanka and Maligne Lake, the Prince of Wales Hotel in Waterton Lakes and several other hotels in Banff and Glacier.

The recent MPL hotel deal has set off alarm bells for some locals, who still remember the 2012 controversy over Viad's successful proposal to build the Columbia Icefield Skywalk – an elevated platform over the Athabasca River valley that has since become one of Jasper's top tourist attractions. At the time, over 130,000 Canadians signed a petition against construction of the Skywalk on the grounds that Viad's commercial aspirations were at odds with the parks' core mission to promote conservation and universal access to public lands.

Parks Canada and the Ministry of the Environment ultimately approved the Skywalk, allowing Viad to privatize what had formerly been a public viewpoint and require visitors to pay a fee to visit this section of the Icefields Pkwy.

Against that backdrop, some observers are distrustful of the Viad–MPL deal, fearing that Viad is now veering dangerously close to monopoly control of the Banff–Jasper corridor.

Whatever the ultimate impact, Viad's growing market share within the parks is an ongoing fact of life, and one all travelers will encounter as they travel through the Rockies.

BANFF AREA: **6641 SQ KM (2564 SQ MILES)**

JASPER AREA: **11,228 SQ KM (4335 SQ MILES)**

GLACIER AREA: **4100 SQ KM (1583 SQ MILES)**

WATERTON LAKES AREA: **505 SQ KM (195 SQ MILES)**

ecoregions of Banff
(% of national park)

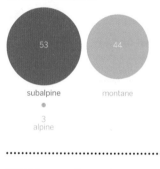

53 subalpine

44 montane

3 alpine

if 100 people come to Banff

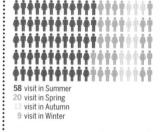

58 visit in Summer
20 visit in Spring
13 visit in Autumn
9 visit in Winter

population per 100 sq km

BANFF   JASPER   CANADA

≈ 40 people

History

First Nations people lived for millennia in scattered nomadic indigenous groups in the areas that later became Jasper, Banff, Glacier and Waterton Lakes. In the late 18th century European expeditions edged inexorably west. Exploration quickly led to exploitation, and some of the pristine land was mined for minerals, while other parts were earmarked by cross-continental railroad companies. All four parks were inaugurated between 1885 and 1910 through an unconventional alliance between foresighted conservationists and railway entrepreneurs eager to market the region as America's very own Swiss Alps.

Banff National Park

The history of Banff National Park begins in 1875 with the selection of Kicking Horse Pass, just west of the present-day park, over the more northerly Yellowhead Pass (in present-day Jasper), as the route for the nascent Canadian Pacific Railway (CPR). It was during the building of this railway in 1882 that three railroad laborers, William and Tom McCardell and Frank McCabe, stumbled upon the Cave and Basin hot springs at the base of Sulphur Mountain.

While the Stoney indigenous people had known about the springs and their supposed healing powers for centuries, it took the entrepreneurship of the trio to bring the waters to national attention. But, caught up in an acrimonious battle over ownership rights, the workers' tentative proposal to develop the springs as a lucrative tourist destination was rudely quashed by a Canadian government that had already, surreptitiously, made similar plans of its own.

In 1885, as the last spike was driven into the transcontinental railway at Craigellachie in British Columbia, a 26-sq-km (10-sq-mile) federal reserve was established around Banff Springs by the Conservative government of John A MacDonald. Sensing a tourist bonanza, not just from the recuperative springs, but from the astounding mountainscapes that surrounded them, the fledgling CPR was quick to jump on the bandwagon. 'If we can't export the scenery, we'll import the tourists,' announced CPR president William Van Horne portentously in 1886. His idea was to build a luxurious chain of grand hotels across the railway network that would lure

For a comprehensive history of the Rocky Mountain parks go to the website of Parks Canada (www.pc.gc.ca) or the US National Park Service (www.nps.gov).

TIMELINE	10,000 BC	1750	1793
	First Nations indigenous groups begin to settle and hunt throughout the Rockies. Groupings include the Kootenay and Stoney from the high plateaus and the bison-hunting Piegan from the plains.	European explorers and traders arrive in the area via the fur trade. The introduction of modern weapons, European diseases and horses filters down to First Nations indigenous groups, causing disruption.	British explorer Alexander Mackenzie becomes the first European to cross the Rocky Mountains via the Peace and Fraser River systems on his journey to the Pacific coast in British Columbia.

in wealthy tourists and repay the railway's outstanding loans. The plan clearly worked. Opened in 1888 as the grandest and most expansive hotel in the chain, the chateau-style Banff Springs Hotel was a runaway success and quickly established itself as an icon of Canadian architecture.

By 1888 over 5000 tourists had been ferried into the embryonic park to be rejuvenated in the magic spring water, and Banff Town listed 300 permanent residents, as well as churches, hotels, saloons and shops. The national park, which had been Canada's first – and the world's third – when it was created in 1885, was expanded in 1892 to include the area surrounding Lake Louise and, before long, Banff had spawned another of Van Horne's fairy-tale hotels, the beguiling Chateau Lake Louise.

In 1885 Banff became the world's third national park (and the first in Canada), after Yellowstone in the US, inaugurated in 1872, and Royal National Park in Australia, founded in 1879.

Welcoming the Masses

A coach road was opened to Banff in 1911, and the following year public traffic was allowed into the park. Suddenly the wilderness was accessible to all kinds of visitors, rather than just wealthy Victorians, and the opportunities for outdoor recreation multiplied. Campsites were set up on Tunnel Mountain and at Two Jack Lake, and affordable lodging began to appear in the Bow Valley. Pursuits diversified: skiing, the arts and short-lived sports like ice boating all drew participants and spectators. A road was built to Norquay ski slopes, and Lake Louise soon began to welcome skiers as well. The year 1917 saw the initiation of the Banff Winter Carnival, lasting a week and featuring everything from dances to dogsled races.

Throughout WWI, immigrants from enemy countries were detained in camps below Castle Mountain and near Cave and Basin hot springs. Forced to labor, they established much of the infrastructure throughout the park, including making horse trails car-friendly. In the 1930s similar work was taken up by relief workers during the Depression, when the Icefields Pkwy was first initiated. Relief workers also built gardens in Banff Town and an airfield for private planes.

The National Parks Act, passed in 1930, established the boundaries of the park much as they are today, along with many of the conservation laws that are still in place. While the number of tourists to the park diminished during WWII, Banff became a popular honeymoon destination in the 1940s and 1950s, attracting returning war veterans and their brides. By 1962, when the Trans-Canada Hwy officially opened, the park had begun to market itself as an international holiday destination.

Banff unsuccessfully bid for the Winter Olympics three times: in 1964, 1968 and 1972. The controversial 1972 bid was ultimately withdrawn when environmental groups lobbied the government.

Balancing Act

Banff gained further global recognition as a summer and winter resort with the 1988 Winter Olympics in nearby Calgary. Although events were actually held at Nakiska ski resort in Kananaskis Country and the Nordic Centre in neighboring Canmore, the Olympics drew tourists and

1800s	1805–06	1811	1813
Dislocated First Nations indigenous groups begin to settle in their hunting grounds along the Athabasca Valley using the area's various passes and valleys as migratory routes.	The Lewis and Clark Expedition passes close to the Glacier area, but misses Marias Pass. On their return journey Lewis gets into a skirmish with the Blackfeet indigenous group and two young braves are killed.	Heading west from a post near present-day Jasper Town, David Thompson becomes the first European to cross the Athabasca Pass on his way to the Columbia River and the Pacific.	The Northwest Company opens up a permanent trading post on Brulé Lake near present-day Pocahontas; by 1817 it is known as 'Jasper's House' after the presiding clerk Jasper Hawse.

publicity to the park. Banff Town's economy boomed, further strengthening the tourism infrastructure. In 1990, after more than a century of being governed federally, Banff Town was granted the right to become a self-governing community. That year, the CPR train service, which had played such an important role in the town's late 19th-century take-off, was discontinued. Tourism in Banff has grown rapidly in recent years – witness the 28% increase in visitors between 2014 and 2018 – leading to concerns about ecological imbalance. As a result, the public zeitgeist has changed and the park today energetically promotes environmental as well as economic concerns.

Jasper National Park

First Nations peoples traditionally used the land that is now Jasper National Park as seasonal hunting and gathering grounds. It wasn't until the 1800s, when fur traders began to push west across the continent, dislocating various indigenous groups, that some First Nations groups began utilizing the Athabasca Valley as a more permanent base.

Soon after, a dispute with Piegan people over access to Howse Pass near present-day Banff led British-Canadian explorer David Thompson to look for a new route across the Rockies to link up with lucrative trading centers on the west coast. Veering north during the winter of 1810, he trudged with his party through deep snow to the top of Athabasca Pass, crossing the Continental Divide in January 1811.

Before departing for Athabasca Pass, Thompson left fellow explorer William Henry in the Athabasca Valley, where he established Henry House, the region's first staging post, situated close to Old Fort Point, near present-day Jasper Town. In 1813 the Northwest Company established a more permanent post, 40km (25 miles) to the east, at Jasper House on Brulé Lake, which remained in operation until 1884.

In an effort to build good trade relations, the traders were encouraged to take indigenous wives. In doing so, a distinct Métis (French for 'mixed blood') culture was formed, and the unique language of Michif arose. Descendants of the Métis continued to farm in the Athabasca Valley well into the 20th century, greatly influencing the area's development. In 1910 they were given compensation payments and forced to leave their land, which by then had become a federal reserve.

Adventurers & Mountaineers

In the early 1860s, around 200 pioneers set out from Ontario with their sights on the gold rush in British Columbia. The Overlanders, as they would come to be known, passed through Jasper and struggled over Yellowhead Pass, the park's present-day boundary with Mt Robson Provincial Park. The planned two-month journey turned into six months of

1882	1885	1885	1888
Three railway workers, Tom and William McCardell and Frank McCabe, find the Cave and Basin hot springs near present-day Banff and unwittingly usher in the age of tourism.	The Trans-Canada Railway is completed, and a federal reserve is established around Cave and Basin hot springs in response to a dispute about who has the right to develop them commercially.	Naturalist George Bird Grinnell visits the Glacier area and comes across the Grinnell Glacier in the Many Glacier Valley. He coins the term 'Crown of the Continent' and lobbies for protective status.	Banff Springs Hotel opens as an original 'log cabin' hotel constructed by the Canadian Pacific Railway. The hotel is rebuilt in its more grandiose stone palace style in 1914.

MARY SCHÄFFER

Breaking the mould in an era when most women didn't even have the right to vote, Mary Schäffer was a rather unlikely park pioneer who, according to some, was Jasper's and the Rocky Mountains' first real tourist. A spirited Philadelphia widow, Schäffer first ventured to Jasper in the early 20th century to – in her own words – 'turn the unthumbed pages of an unread book.' Her quest was an elusive mountain lake known to the Stoney people as Chaba Imne. Guided by a map sketched from memory 14 years earlier by a Stoney man, Sampson Beaver, she became the first non-indigenous person to set eyes on Maligne Lake in July 1908. Her subsequent book about her brave and sometimes turbulent adventures, *Old Indian Trails of the Canadian Rockies*, was republished on its 100th anniversary in 2011 and still resounds with poignant, poetic aphorisms.

near starvation. Poorly equipped and inexperienced, a number of men died en route, some swept away by turbulent rivers, others succumbing to hypothermia. The only woman to accompany the group managed to survive, giving birth upon reaching Kamloops.

With the fur trade in decline and a new national park in Banff prospering to the south, mountaineers and adventurers began heading into Jasper's rugged wilderness in search of unnamed peaks and fabled glacial lakes. In 1906 Irish-born mountaineer and surveyor AO Wheeler founded the Alpine Club of Canada and began organizing periodic assaults on Mt Robson. Three years later he was instrumental in helping two colorful local characters, Reverend Kinney and Donald 'Curly' Phillips, in their brave but ultimately abortive attempt on the summit. The mountain was eventually climbed by Austrian Conrad Kain in 1913.

The Emergence of a Park

Jasper's founding, rather like Banff's, is closely entwined with the development of the railway. Passed over in the 1880s by the CPR in favor of Kicking Horse Pass in Banff, Jasper got its revenge in 1903 when Wilfred Laurier's government gave the go-ahead for the Grand Trunk Pacific Company to build a line from the west coast through Yellowhead Pass. All too aware of how the railway had significantly boosted the fortunes of Banff, the Ministry of the Interior opportunistically created Jasper Forest Park in 1907, the Canadian Rockies' fifth – and Canada's sixth – national park.

Built between 1910 and 1913, the railway reached the tiny settlement of Fitzhugh at mile marker 113 in 1911, bringing an immediate influx of adventurers, mountaineers and railway workers. Almost overnight the burgeoning town jumped from a population of 125 to around 800 and

The term 'parkitecture' was used to describe the type of rustic architecture used in national parks in the early 20th century. Employing local materials in order to blend in with the forests whence they sprang, the buildings took root in numerous national parks including Glacier and Waterton Lakes.

1892	1895	1896	1907
The Banff reserve, which originally measured only 26 sq km (10 sq miles), is enlarged to include Lake Louise as alpinists brought over from Europe begin scaling the area's peaks.	Upon the urging of rancher and conservationist Frederick William Godsal, Waterton Lakes is given protective status by the Canadian federal government.	The Blackfeet reluctantly accept the US government's offer to purchase all of the land east of the Continental Divide in what is now Glacier National Park for US$1.5 million.	Jasper Forest Park is established as Canada's sixth national park, although it doesn't acquire its present-day boundaries until the passing of the National Parks Act in 1930.

DAVID THOMPSON

The history of Jasper National Park will always be synonymous with indefatigable British-Canadian explorer David Thompson, born in London in 1770, but resident in Canada from 1784, where he was nicknamed 'Stargazer' by First Nations people and 'the greatest mapmaker who ever lived' by those who had the good fortune to follow in his footsteps.

Thompson developed his prodigious navigational skills working as a fur trader, first for the Hudson Bay Company and later for its bitter rivals the Northwest Company, which gave him the task of establishing fur-trading posts along the hotly contested US–Canada border. In 1806, in response to the American-sponsored Lewis and Clark Expedition, Thompson was sent west to establish new Northwest Company posts closer to the Pacific, a journey that soon turned into a race over which group would reach the mouth of the Columbia River first. The explorer's biggest challenge was crossing the Rocky Mountains through precipitous terrain still largely controlled by Native American indigenous groups. Thompson found his preferred southern route over Howse Pass near Banff blocked by the hostile Piegan indigenous group, forcing him to tack north toward the uncharted lands of what is now Jasper National Park. Enlisting the help of a local indigenous man, Thomas the Iroquois, Thompson forged a route across Athabasca Pass in January 1811, becoming the first white person to cross the Rockies via a northerly route. For the next 50 years, until the advent of the railway era, Athabasca Pass became the preferred route of fur traders making for the Pacific.

was promptly renamed Jasper after Jasper Hawse, a fur-trading manager who had been based at the Jasper House trading post in the 1820s.

Before the passage of the National Parks Act in 1930, the park faced far fewer limitations on its industrial and commercial development. Consequently, in the 1910s, local outfitters and guides, eyeing a potential business bonanza, sprang up all over the Athabasca Valley intent on bringing the wilderness to the masses. Plans for an enlarged town were laid out, a school was built, and clearing began for roads and climbing trails. The first grocery store opened in 1914, meaning that residents no longer had to wait for a month's supply by train from Edmonton. The following year, 10 crudely constructed tents were set up for visitors on the shores of Lac Beauvert, an encampment that would soon metamorphose into the Jasper Park Lodge.

In 1910 a coal mine was established at Pocahontas, near the eastern boundary of the park. A small mining town grew up in the vicinity, but was short-lived. The coal that was mined from the area burned at a high heat and was virtually smokeless, making it useful for warships during WWI. But, with the war over by 1918, and competition heating up with larger operations in the industrial east, the mine was shut down and the town dismantled by 1921.

1908	1910	1911	1912
Mary Schäffer visits Maligne Lake with her Stoney indigenous guide and opens up what is to become one of Jasper's most alluring sights and tourist attractions.	US President Taft signs a bill creating Glacier as the nation's 10th national park. William Logan is named as the park's first superintendent.	Grand Trunk Pacific's railway reaches the shantytown of Fitzhugh, which is renamed Jasper two years later. Almost simultaneously the Canadian Northern Railway builds a second line through the park.	The Great Northern Railway begins building grand hotels and chalets within Glacier National Park (and, later, Waterton Lakes) to promote its railway line and open up the region to tourism.

Sharing the Limelight

The road from Jasper to Edmonton was opened in 1928 and by the onset of WWII, legions of Depression-era workers had completed the legendary Icefields Pkwy linking Jasper to Lake Louise. In 1930 the National Parks Act was passed, fully protecting Jasper as the largest park in the nation, and tourists began visiting in droves; famous guests included King George VI, Marilyn Monroe and Bing Crosby. By 1948 the Athabasca Glacier had become a major sight, and the Banff-based Brewster brothers manufactured a ski-equipped Model A Ford truck to cart tourists out over the ice.

Since the 1950s, Jasper's tourism infrastructure has been gradually strengthened. Major highways into the park have been paved and roads to sights like Maligne Lake and Miette Hot Springs have been cleared or upgraded. In 1961 the Marmot Basin ski area got its first rope tow while, three years later, the Jasper Tramway took its first trip to the top of Whistlers Mountain.

Since 2001 Jasper Town has been governed jointly by the Specialized Municipality of Jasper and Parks Canada. These days there are strict development laws in place (eg no second homes are allowed) and, in 2010, the two bodies drafted the town's first Community Sustainability Plan.

Winter sports were first ignited in the Rockies at the Banff Winter Carnival in 1917. Skiing began at Mt Norquay in the 1920s and at Sunshine Village in the 1930s. Norquay installed Canada's first chairlift in 1948 and, in 1961, Jasper added its own ski resort, Marmot Basin.

Glacier National Park

The ancestors of Montana's present-day Native Americans have inhabited the Glacier region for over 10,000 years. At the time of the first European contact, two main indigenous groups occupied the Rocky Mountains region. The valleys in the west were the hunting grounds of the Salish and Kootenay people, while the prairies in the east were controlled by the Blackfeet, a fiercely independent warrior indigenous group whose territory straddled the border with Canada. Linked spiritually to the land, the Blackfeet knew Glacier as the 'Backbone of the World,' and within the area of the park, many sites – including the oddly shaped Chief Mountain – were considered sacred to the people.

In the mid-18th century, when trappers and explorers began to arrive out west, the Blackfeet controlled most of the northern plains and adjacent mountain passes. Although they resisted the European invaders at first, a catastrophic smallpox epidemic in 1837 dealt them a deadly blow, wiping out 6000 of their 30,000 population. Eventually both the Blackfeet, and Salish and Kootenay, were forced into one-sided treaties that sequestered them to reservation lands.

The romantic wanderer James Willard Schultz spent many years living among the Blackfeet people, whom he considered his relatives and closest friends. As a result, he became one of the first European

History & Culture Museums

....

Whyte Museum of the Canadian Rockies (Banff)

....

Museum of the Plains Indian (Browning)

....

Jasper-Yellowhead Museum & Archives (Jasper)

....

Waterton Heritage Centre (Waterton Townsite)

1914–18	1920s	1932	1940
Prisoners of war – most notably from Germany, Austria and the Ukraine – are detained in camps within Banff National Park; their labor is used to improve the park's infrastructure.	Automobile organizations lobby for a road through Jasper, and in 1922 the first car breaches the Yellowhead Pass. The road to Edmonton opens in 1928 and the Yellowhead Hwy in 1970.	The Going-to-the-Sun Rd is completed east–west across Glacier National Park. Two new motels are constructed at Rising Sun and Swiftcurrent Lake to cater for the new influx of auto traffic.	The Icefields Pkwy opens, linking Lake Louise with Jasper Town to the north; this remarkable feat of engineering is named for the copious icy behemoths visible from the roadside.

American men to lay eyes on much of Glacier's interior. In the 1880s he introduced the area to Dr George Bird Grinnell, a leading conservationist who lobbied Congress vociferously for a decade until, in 1910, President Taft signed the bill that created Glacier National Park.

Historic Lodges & Hotels

Chateau Lake Louise, 1913

Lake McDonald Lodge, 1913

Banff Springs Hotel, 1914

Many Glacier Hotel, 1915

Assiniboine Lodge, 1928

Skoki Lodge, 1931

From Gilded-Age Railroads to Modern-Age Cars

Visitors began coming regularly to the park around 1912, when James J Hill of the Great Northern Railway instigated an intense building program to promote his newly inaugurated line. Railway employees built grand hotels and a network of tent camps and mountain chalets, each a day's horseback ride from the next. Visitors would come for several weeks at a time, touring by horse or foot, and staying in these elegant but rustic accommodations.

But the halcyon days of trains and horse travel weren't to last. In response to the growing popularity of motorized transportation, federal funds were appropriated in 1921 to connect the east and west sides of Glacier National Park by a new road. Over a decade in the making, the legendary Going-to-the-Sun Rd was finally opened in 1932, crossing the Continental Divide at 2026m (6646ft) Logan Pass and opening up the park to millions.

That same year, thanks to efforts from Rotary International members in Alberta and Montana, Glacier joined with Waterton Lakes in the world's first International Peace Park, a lasting symbol of peace and friendship between the USA and Canada.

WWII forced the closure of almost all hotel services in the park, and many of Glacier's rustic chalets fell into disrepair and had to be demolished. Fortunately, nine of the original 13 'parkitecture' structures survived and – complemented by two wood-paneled motor inns that were added in the 1940s – they form the basis of the park's accommodations today.

Founded in 1906 by Irish-born surveyor and mountaineer AO Wheeler, the Alpine Club of Canada still stands at the sharp end of mountaineering in the Canadian Rockies. Check out its excellent website, www.alpineclubof canada.ca.

Over the years, the Going-to-the-Sun Rd has been the primary travel artery in the national park and, for many, its scenic highlight. Still sporting its original stone guardrail and embellished with myriad tunnels, bridges and arches, the road has been designated a national historic landmark. In the 1930s a fleet of bright red 'Jammer' buses was introduced onto the road to enable tourists to gain easy access to the park's jaw-dropping scenery; the same buses (being retrofitted to run on electric hybrid motors) still operate today.

1984	1990	2014	2017
Banff, along with Jasper, Yoho and Kootenay, is declared a Unesco World Heritage site, adding an extra layer of protection, but invoking more environmental commitments.	Banff Town becomes self-governing, though it is still subject to national park planning and development laws. The Canadian Pacific Railway passenger service is discontinued after 105 years.	Native American indigenous groups in Alberta and Montana sign a treaty to reestablish the bison's migratory patterns across the US–Canada border.	Devastating wildfires hit Glacier and Waterton Lakes, destroying Glacier's historic Sperry Chalet and impacting 80% of Waterton's hiking trails.

Geology

Majestic, indomitable and bursting with life, the Canadian Rockies are environmentally unique. Formed over 170 million years ago when a massive collision in the earth's crust caused a giant lateral displacement known as the Lewis Overthrust, the mountains today are the product of several million years of glaciation. Anointed rather regally with the title 'Crown of the Continent,' the parks are home to a plethora of glaciers, dwindling in number and size, relics of a colder and mightier age.

The Land

The Canadian Rockies are a rock-lover's paradise, a striking mix of towering mountain chains and multicolored terrain that is considered to be one of the most important fossil localities in the world. Everywhere you look you'll see graphic evidence of 1.5 billion years of the earth's history laid out like hieroglyphics in well-preserved sedimentary strata. Even more dramatic are the region's crenellated peaks and U-shaped valleys, a lasting testimony to the formidable power of ancient glaciers and ice fields.

The First Supercontinent

In the beginning there was nothing much at all. And then, approximately 1.5 billion years ago, sediments began to be laid down in an inland sea within a hypothesized supercontinent known as Rodinia (a combination of landmasses that later broke apart into the continents we recognize today). Consisting of sands, silts and cobbles, these ancient sedimentary layers are now so deeply buried that they appear on the earth's surface in only a few places, two of which are Waterton Lakes and Glacier National Parks.

On the west side of the parks, the oldest layer is known as the Pritchard Formation and preserves evidence of a deep sea visible in thin layers of fine green rock along MacDonald Creek. Other strata such as the Altyn, Appekunny and Snowslip Formations are also evident in places such as St Mary Lake and Logan Pass. Perhaps the most eye-catching and easy-to-recognize layer of rock is the brick-red coloration of the Grinnell Formation, which is spectacularly exposed in Red Rock Canyon in Waterton Lakes National Park.

The Big Breakup

About 750 million years ago, the supercontinent Rodinia began to break up along a giant rift, creating a new shoreline where North America split off from the future continents of Australia and Antarctica. Various sediments accumulated in an ancient sea during this epoch and, over time, these deposits hardened to form limestone, mudstone and sandstone.

A significant transition occurred around 570 million years ago, with the onset of the Cambrian period, a transitional era that sparked an incredible proliferation of complex new fauna in what became known as the 'Cambrian explosion.' Embedded in the region's rock, many well-preserved fossils of multicellular organisms remain from this period, and have taught scientists much about evolution and the development of species diversity worldwide. Some of the planet's best Cambrian fossils were uncovered at the Burgess Shale site in Yoho National Park in 1909.

The Rocky Mountain Trench is a large valley up to 25km (15.6 miles) wide that runs from Montana up to the Yukon/BC border, separating the Rocky Mountains from the Columbia/Cassiar Mountains to the west. Although partially glaciated, it was caused primarily by faulting.

Situated on the western side of the Continental Divide, Yoho National Park receives over 884mm (35in) of rain annually; meanwhile, drier Banff National Park on the eastern side gets 472mm (19in).

The Cambrian era was followed by a long period of relative stability as desert landmasses eroded and sedimentary layers accumulated along the continental coastline. For a period of over 350 million years the dozens of different rock layers that comprise the bulk of the peaks in today's Canadian Rockies were laid down in contrasting bands, documenting an encyclopedia of geological history, a record that shows how seas advanced and retreated numerous times across the region.

A common feature of a hanging valley is a waterfall caused when a river drops from the higher side valley down to the U-shaped valley below. Visible from Glacier National Park's Going-to-the-Sun Rd, 152m (500ft) Bird Woman Falls near Mt Oberlin is a classic example.

Collision Course

This period of stability came to a close around 200 million years ago when the continental plate began a steady march westward, pushing against the part of the earth's crust that lies under the Pacific Ocean. Like a slow-motion collision, the leading edge of the continental plate buckled against the impact. At first, the buckled edge may have simply created folds in the earth's crust, but over time these folds became steeper and started to fracture under the stress.

Extending progressively eastward, the fractures reached the region of the Canadian Rockies about 100 million years ago where dynamic tectonic movement pushed up a huge wedge of rock and displaced it over 80km (50 miles) to the east, forming the basis of the mountains we see today.

The main period of compression reached its apex 60 to 80 million years ago, then subsided slowly, leaving behind layers of deep old Paleozoic rock wedged up on top of younger Mesozoic rock. This compressing process is known as thrust faulting and it geologically sets the northern Rockies apart from their smoother southern cousins, which were formed by broader tectonic uplifting.

Glaciers

For the past 60 million years, the primary force in the Canadian and northern US Rockies has been erosion, not deposition. The most dramatic erosive process has been that of glaciation, precipitated by the great glaciers and ice fields of the Ice Age that have sculpted rugged peaks and gouged out deep valleys from Pocahontas to Marias Pass. Two million years ago, huge sheets of ice covered much of the region. These giant sheets produced incredible amounts of weight and pressure, and as tongues of ice crept across the landscape they tore apart rocks and transformed narrow V-shaped ravines into broad open valleys. Trillions of tons of debris were left behind when the ice finally retreated 10,000 years ago, much of it forming distinctive ridges called moraines, such as the one that the chateau at Lake Louise is perched on.

Nearly every feature seen in the region today is a legacy of the Ice Age. Peaks that were simultaneously carved on multiple sides left behind

ROCKY MOUNTAINS GLACIERS UP CLOSE

Four of the parks' glaciers are easily accessible to day hikers:

Victoria Glacier (Banff) The crystal crown of Banff is visible from the Chateau Lake Louise at the far end of the eponymous lake, or in close-up on the Plain of Six Glaciers trail.

Sperry Glacier (Glacier) Perched astride Gunsight Mountain, this dwindling glacier is accessible by a steep but rewarding hike across high-alpine terrain.

Grinnell Glacier (Glacier) Named for the famous US naturalist, this river of ice is Glacier National Park's most photographed and precarious. An 8.8km (5.5-mile) trail leads out from the Many Glacier Hotel.

Athabasca Glacier (Jasper) The Rockies' most famous glacier dips its toe close to the Icefields Pkwy from where you can arrange excursions to walk or drive (yes, drive!) on it with an Ice Explorer tour.

THE GLACIAL LANDSCAPE OF THE ROCKIES

The Rocky Mountains national parks provide a perfect outdoor classroom for wannabe students trying to digest the geomorphological (surface) features created by glacial erosion. Here are some of the best examples, although there are plenty more:

FEATURE	DEFINITION	BEST EXAMPLE
Arête	A thin sharp ridge that forms between two parallel glaciers	Garden Wall (Glacier)
Glacial cirque	A bowl-shaped amphitheater formed at the head of a valley glacier	Iceberg Cirque (Glacier)
Glacial horn	A pyramidal peak formed when three glacial cirques form together	Mt Assiniboine (Mt Assiniboine Provincial Park)
Glacial lake	A lake left behind when glaciers retreat	Lake Louise (Banff)
Hanging valley	Small side valleys left 'hanging' above a deeper U-shaped glacier-carved valley	Maligne Valley (Jasper)
Moraine	An accumulation of glacial rock and soil	Moraine Lake (Banff)
Roche moutonnée	Tear-shaped hills formed when a glacier erodes down to the bedrock	Old Fort Point (Jasper)
U-shaped valley	A steep-sided, flat-bottomed valley formed by a glacier moving downhill	St Mary Valley (Glacier)

sharp spires called horns, as can be seen at Mt Assiniboine. Mountains that had glaciers cutting along two sides ended up as sharp ridges known as arêtes. Side streams flowing into valleys that were deepened by glaciers were often left hanging in midair, creating hanging valleys, with the streams pouring out as waterfalls down over sheer cliffs.

Glaciers Today

Even though the Ice Age ended 10,000 years ago when the great ice fields gradually retreated, the story of ice and glaciers in the Canadian Rockies is far from over. Mini ice ages have regularly altered the climate in the years since, the most recent of which peaked in the 1840s when the frozen tip of the Athabasca Glacier reached as far as the present-day Icefield Centre – it has retreated 1.6km (1 mile) since 1844. Even today, along the spine of the Continental Divide, smaller ice fields continue to craft and shape the landscape and the relatively larger ice fields in Banff and Jasper are probably safe for a good couple of centuries, whatever the warming effects from climate change.

However, intensifying concerns and research suggest that the glaciers in Glacier National Park (which now number only 25) will be all but extinct by the year 2030 (Waterton Lakes National Park is already a glacier-free zone). The degree of the loss is quite affecting to contemplate. These grand and seemingly indomitable monuments formed over millennia are now vanishing before our eyes. In 1850 northwest Montana was home to nearly 150 glaciers, and when Sperry Glacier was first photographed in 1887 surely the photographer never imagined it would some day vanish. Harrison is now the largest and Weasel Collar, just east of Mount Carter, is predicted to be the last surviving – south-facing glaciers with more sun exposure are the most vulnerable. Research scientists studying the park's glaciers are part of a global network sharing data with the World Glacier Monitoring Service (WGMS; www.wgms.ch), which is tracking global trends. Of course, the melting glaciers aren't simply an aesthetic concern. The downstream impact on water systems, surrounding ecosystems and the survival of various species of wildlife are all threatened.

Highest Peaks

Jasper:
Mt Columbia
3747m (12,293ft)

Banff:
Mt Assiniboine
3618m (11,870ft)

Yoho: Mt Goodsir
3567m (11,703ft)

Kootenay:
Deltaform
Mountain 3424m
(11,234ft)

Glacier:
Mt Cleveland
3190m (10,466ft)

Waterton Lakes:
Mt Blakiston
2910m (9547ft)

Wildlife

Rising like snow-coated sentinels above the plains and prairies of Alberta and Montana, the Rockies protect a narrow, wildlife-rich corridor that stretches down the continent from northern Canada to Mexico. With the adjacent lowlands taken over by roads, farms and cities, the mountains have provided a final refuge for wolves, mountain lions, bears, elk, deer and many other large mammals. While populations of these animals are only a fraction of their former numbers, they are still impressive enough to lure wildlife enthusiasts.

Animals

Above Bears, Jasper
National Park

The Canadian Rockies support nearly 70 species of mammal, and the prospect of seeing 'charismatic megafauna' is one of the region's biggest draws. In the fall and winter, many large mammals move down into valleys; high concentrations can be seen along the Icefields Pkwy.

Bears

The black bear roams montane and subalpine forests throughout the Canadian Rockies in search of its favorite foods: grasses, roots, berries and the occasional meal of carrion. They can frequently be seen along roadsides feeding on dandelions. While most black bears are black in color, they can also be light reddish brown (cinnamon). Black bears are somewhat smaller than grizzlies and have more tapered muzzles, larger ears and smaller claws. These claws help them climb trees to avoid their main predator, grizzly bears, which are known to drag black bears out of their dens to kill them. Although they are generally more tolerant of humans and less aggressive than grizzlies, black bears should always be treated as dangerous.

Grizzly bears once roamed widely in North America, but most were killed by European settlers who feared this mighty carnivore. Thanks to conservation efforts, their numbers have increased since they were listed as endangered in 1975. Today, an ongoing and complicated legal battle wends its way through the courts as to whether to 'delist' them or classify them as threatened. Even with rebounding populations, they aren't particularly easy to see or count, in part because males roam 3885 sq km (1500 sq miles) in their lifetimes. Male grizzlies reach up to 2.4m (8ft) in length (from nose to tail) and 1.05m (3.5ft) high at the shoulder (when on all fours) and can weigh more than 315kg (700lb) at maturity. Although some grizzlies are almost black, their coats are typically pale brown to cinnamon, with 'grizzled,' white-tipped guard hairs (the long, coarse hairs that protect the shorter, fine underfur). They can be distinguished from black bears by their concave (dish-shaped) facial profile, smaller and more rounded ears, prominent shoulder hump and long, nonretractable claws.

Both bears are omnivorous opportunists and notorious berry eaters, with an amazing sense of smell that's acute enough to detect food miles away. Their choice of meal varies seasonally, ranging from roots and winter-killed carrion in early spring to berries and salmon in the fall. Before hibernation, bears become voracious. Black bears will eat for 20 hours straight and gain an incredible 1.8kg (4lb) each day before retiring to their dens; grizzly bears are known to eat 200,000 buffalo berries a day.

Sometime in October, bears wander upslope to where snows will be deep and provide a thick insulating layer over their winter dens. There the bears scrape out a simple shelter among shrubs, against a bank or under a log and sink into deep sleep (not true hibernation, as their body temperatures remain high and they are easily roused). Winters are particularly hard, since bears live entirely off their fat and lose up to 40% of their body weight. A female who has been able to gain enough weight will give birth to several cubs during the depths of winter, rearing the cubs on milk while she sleeps.

Coyotes & Wolves

The cagey coyote is actually a small opportunistic wolf that devours anything from carrion to berries and insects. Its slender, reddish-gray form is frequently seen in open meadows, along roads and around towns and campgrounds. Coyotes form small packs to hunt larger prey such as elk calves or adults mired in deep snow. Frequently mistaken for a wolf, the coyote is much smaller – 11.3kg to 15.8kg (25lb to 35lb), versus 20.3kg to 65.3kg (45 to 145lb) for a wolf – and runs with its tail carried down (a wolf carries its tail straight out).

The gray wolf, once the Rocky Mountains' main predator, was nearly exterminated in the 1930s, then again in the 1950s. It took until the mid-1980s for them to reestablish themselves in Banff, and today they

There have been 10 human fatalities from bear attacks in Glacier National Park's 106-year history. By remarkable coincidence two of them occurred on the same night – 13 August 1967 – 10 miles apart in separate attacks by different bears. Both victims were 19-year-old females.

Latest figures (2017) for grizzly bear numbers in Alberta Province, Canada (including Jasper, Banff and Waterton National Parks) are cited as fewer than 1000, while up to 16,000 are in British Columbia.

are common only from Jasper National Park north; in Glacier National Park, wolves can be found in North Fork Valley. Colors range from white to black, with gray-brown being the most common hue. They roam in close-knit packs of five to eight animals ruled by a dominant (alpha) pair. The alpha pair are the only members of a pack to breed, though the entire pack cares for the pups. Four to six pups are born in April or May, and they remain around the den until August. Packs of wolves are a formidable presence, and they aren't afraid of using their group strength to harass grizzly bears or kill coyotes, but more often they keep themselves busy chasing down deer, elk or moose.

The Canadian Rockies are home to the only fully protected caribou herds in North America. Two tiny herds roam British Columbia's Glacier and Mount Revelstoke parks, whereas Jasper has four herds, a northern one and three southern ones totaling around 125 head.

Bighorn Sheep & Mountain Goats

Living on high slopes near rocky ridges and cliffs, bighorn sheep are generally shy creatures of remote areas. Unlike in other parts of their range, however, bighorn sheep in the Canadian Rockies come down to roadsides in search of salts, invariably causing traffic jams of excited visitors. Males, with their flamboyant curled horns, spend summer in bachelor flocks waiting for the fall rut, when they face off and duel by ramming into each other at 96km/h (60mph). Their horns and foreheads are specially modified for this brutal but necessary task. When not hanging around roadsides looking for salt and handouts (strictly forbidden), bighorn sheep use their extraordinary vision and smell to detect humans up to 300m (1000ft) away, making them extremely difficult to approach.

Occupying even steeper cliffs and hillsides, pure white mountain goats are a favorite with visitors, but are seldom observed close up. Their cliffside habitat provides excellent protection from predators, and both adults and kids are amazingly nimble on impossibly sheer faces. Occasionally they descend to salt licks near roads. In Jasper they occur in high densities on Mt Kerkeslin; around Banff try scanning the slopes of Cascade Mountain; and in Glacier National Park you might see goats at Logan Pass.

Deer

Two species of deer are common in valleys and around human dwellings throughout the region. More common by far are the mule deer of dry, open areas. Smaller, and with a large, prominent white tail, are the white-tailed deer of heavily forested valley bottoms. Both species graze extensively on grasses in summer and on twigs in winter. Delicate, white-spotted fawns are born in June and are soon observed following their mothers. Adult males develop magnificent racks of antlers in time for their mating season in early December.

Three members of the cat family are found in the parks: the mountain lion (cougar), the Canadian lynx and the bobcat. All are elusive and rarely seen by humans, moving mainly at night. The Canadian lynx has been listed as threatened since 2000. Lynx hunt hares, while mountain lions prefer deer.

Elk & Moose

Weighing up to 450kg (1000lb) and bearing gigantic racks of antlers, male elk are the largest mammals that most visitors will encounter in these parks. Come September, valleys resound with the hoarse bugling of battle-ready elk, a sound that is both exciting and terrifying, as hormone-crazed elk are one of the area's most dangerous animals. Battles between males, harem gathering and mating are best observed from a safe distance or from your car. While numbers increase dramatically in winter, quite a few elk now spend their entire year around towns like Banff and Jasper, where they can be seen grazing in yards and on golf courses.

At 495kg (1100lb), the ungainly moose is the largest North American deer. Visitors eagerly seek this odd-looking animal with lanky legs and periscope ears, but they are uncommon and not easily found. Moose spend their summers foraging on aquatic vegetation in marshy meadows and shallow lakes, where they readily swim and dive up to 6m (20ft).

Moose, Glacier National Park

Visitors can look for moose in Jasper's Miette Valley and Maligne Lake corridor, around Banff's Upper Waterfowl Lake and in Glacier's McDonald Valley. The male's broadly tined antlers and flappy throat dewlap are unique, but like their close relative the elk, moose can be extremely dangerous when provoked. Moose numbers have dwindled due to vehicle traffic (roadkills), a liver parasite and the suppression of the wildfires that rejuvenate their favorite foods.

Pikas, Marmots & Beavers

Hikers into the realm of rock and open meadow will quickly become familiar with two abundant mammals. When you encounter a pika, you are likely to hear its loud bleating call long before you spot the tiny, guinea-pig-like creature staring back at you with dark beady eyes. Pikas live among jumbles of rocks and boulders, where they are safe from predators, but they still have to dart out into nearby meadows to harvest grasses that they dry in the sun to make hay for their winter food supply.

Another rock dweller is even more of a tempting morsel for predators. Hoary marmots are plump and tasty, but they have a system for protecting themselves. First, they stay near their burrows and dart in quickly when alarmed. Second, all the marmots on a hillside cooperate in watching out for predators and giving shrill cries whenever danger approaches. Marmots may shriek fiercely when humans come near, warning everyone in the neighborhood. Whistlers, a mountain outside Jasper, is named after these common rodents.

The aquatic beaver has a long history of relations with humans. Prized by early trappers for its fur and reviled for its relentless efforts to block creeks, the Canadian Rockies' largest rodent is now widely recognized as a 'keystone species' – an animal whose activities have a tremendous influence on the lives of many other species. Beavers' shallow-water dams

Nonthreatened
Mountain goat, bighorn sheep, elk, moose, deer, hoary marmot, white-tailed deer, beaver, pika, black bear, mountain lion

Endangered
Grizzly bear, Canadian lynx, wolverine, gray wolf, woodland caribou, Banff Springs snail

create vibrant wetlands, mini-ecosystems that promote biodiversity, and dozens of animals, including ducks, frogs, fish, moose and mink, depend on beavers for their livelihood. Although their numbers have declined as much as 90% in recent decades, beavers are still fairly common around marshes and ponds in valley bottoms. Here, each beaver cuts down as many as 200 aspens and willows per year, feeding on the sweet inner bark and using the trunks and branches to construct dams.

Estimated Species Numbers in Banff

....

Grizzly bears: 65

....

Black bears: 40

....

Mountain lions: un-known, but widely distributed

....

Wolves: 25-40

Birds

More than 300 bird species have been found in the Canadian Rockies. Casual observers will notice some of the more conspicuous species without even trying.

At campsites and picnic tables throughout the parks, you'll quickly be approached by gray jays hoping for a handout. They stash most of their food away in small caches for winter. The stash master, however, is the larger Clark's nutcracker. Each nutcracker buries up to 98,000 seeds in thousands of small caches across miles of landscape, then returns to dig them up over the course of several years – an unbelievable test of memory.

Two large raptors are frequently encountered. Working their way along rivers and lakes are white and brown fish hawks, better known as ospreys. Fairly common during May to September thaw, ospreys specialize in plunging feet first into the water and grabbing fish up to 90cm (3ft) deep, before flying off to eat on a high perch. Osprey nests are enormous mounds of sticks piled on top of dead trees or artificial towers.

In recent years the Canadian Rockies have gained fame for the spectacular golden eagle migration. Each year 6000 to 8000 golden eagles migrate both north and south along a narrow corridor on the east side of the main mountain divide (the official count site is near Mt Lorette, in Kananaskis Country). Spring migration peaks at the end of March, and fall migration peaks in October. While migrating, golden eagles do little feeding, though some pairs stay for the summer and nest on high, remote cliffs.

FISH TALES

Despite the classic image of a philosophical fisher sitting with rod and line beside a back-country lake, high mountain lakes do not naturally support native fish. Instead, countless non-native species were introduced to the national parks over a period of 50 years in a bid by wildlife and park agencies to 'improve' the visitor experience and attract more fishing tourists. Today Banff counts at least 119 lakes stocked with non-native fish (when only 26 contained fish historically). As a consequence, native fish populations and aquatic ecosystems in lower lakes have suffered, while non-native fish have thrived. Though the fish stocking policies have been phased out (in 1971 in Glacier and 1988 in Banff and Jasper), millions of non-native fish remain.

Surviving native fish include the threatened bull trout, whose dwindling populations are protected by law. Once the Canadian Rockies' most widespread native fish, bull trout are now seen at only a few sites. Your best bet is Peter Lougheed Provincial Park, south of Canmore, where they migrate up creeks out of Lower Kananaskis Lake from late August to mid-October. They are distinguished from other trout by their lack of black lines or spots. Return them to the water if you accidentally catch one.

Among the nine non-native fish that have become most common, brook trout can be recognized by their olive-green color, reddish belly and yellow squiggly lines along their back; they are found in most low-elevation streams and lakes. Also thriving in the Canadian Rockies is the mountain whitefish, a bottom-feeder that preys on small invertebrates in the major watercourses and lakes.

BEST PLACES TO SEE WILDLIFE

WHAT	WHERE	WHEN
Bighorn Sheep	Lake Minnewanka (Banff), Highline Trail (Glacier)	Nov–Apr
Black Bear	Bow Valley Pkwy (Banff), Maligne Lake Rd (Jasper)	May–Oct
Caribou	Tonquin Valley (Jasper)	Nov–May
Elk	Vermilion Lakes (Banff), Maligne Lake Rd (Jasper)	Mar–May
Grizzly Bear	Many Glacier (Glacier), Carthew-Alderson Trail (Waterton)	May–Oct
Marmot	Skyline Trail (Jasper), Highline Trail (Glacier)	May–Sep
Moose	Moose Lake (Jasper), Kootenai Lake (Glacier)	May–Aug
Mountain Goat	Logan Pass (Glacier), Icefields Pkwy (Jasper)	Year-round
Wolf	North Fork Valley (Glacier), Lake Minnewanka (Banff)	Nov–Apr

WILDLIFE PLANTS

Of the region's eight species of owl, only the great horned owl is familiar to most visitors. Fearless around humans, highly vocal and sometimes active in the daytime, these large birds are a perennial sight around towns and campgrounds at lower elevations.

Plants

The Canadian Rockies are home to over 1000 species of plants, comprising a fairly diverse mix for such a relatively cold, northern climate. One of the main reasons for this mix is that the Continental Divide not only creates a strong elevational gradient, but also splits the region into westside and eastside habitats, with a wet, ocean-influenced climate on the west side and a dry, interior climate on the east side. Adding to the region's botanical diversity are alpine plants from the Arctic, grassland plants of the eastern prairies, and forest plants from the Pacific Northwest.

Trees

Except for areas of rock, ice or water, landscapes of the Canadian Rockies are mostly covered with coniferous forest. Only a handful of species are present, and these are easy to identify – recognizing these species makes it easier to understand the layout of life zones and to predict where you might find specific animals.

Montane and subalpine forests are dominated by two spruces – white and Engelmann. Both have sharp-tipped needles that prick your hand if you grasp a branch. White spruce occurs mainly on valley bottoms, and Engelmann spruce takes over on higher slopes, but the two frequently overlap and hybridize. Cones on white spruces have smooth, rounded tips on their scales, but Engelmann spruces have narrow, jagged tips on theirs. Many animals feed on spruce seeds or rely on spruce forests for their livelihood in some way.

Sharing the higher slopes with the Engelmann spruce is the subalpine fir, the namesake tree of the Canadian Rockies' subalpine zone. Recognized by their flattened, blunt-tipped needles, subalpine firs have narrow, conical profiles. This shape allows the trees to shed heavy winter snows so their branches don't break off under the weight.

At the uppermost edges of the subalpine forest, mainly growing by themselves on high, windswept slopes, are whitebark pines. Intense wind and cold at these elevations can cause these trees to grow in low, stunted mats. Their squat, egg-shaped cones produce highly nutritious seeds favored by Clark's nutcrackers and grizzly bears, but an introduced disease is threatening this important tree and the animals that depend on it.

Estimated Species Numbers in Jasper

Bighorn sheep: 1200

Grizzly bears: 109

Black bears: 90

Moose: 180

Woodland caribou: 150

Estimated Species Numbers in Glacier

Bighorn sheep: 800

Grizzly bears: 1000

Black bears: 600

Wolves: 60

Wildflowers, Icefields Pkwy, Jasper National Park

One of the oddest trees of the Canadian Rockies is the a rare tree found most easily in Larch Valley, just west of Moraine Lake. Although it's a conifer, this remarkable tree has needles that turn golden in September and then drop off for the winter in October. This makes places like Larch Valley a photographer's paradise during the peak display. Other good places to spot larches include Saddleback (south of Lake Louise) and Healy Pass near Banff's Sunshine Village.

After fires or other disturbances, lodgepole pines quickly spring up and form dense 'doghair' thickets. In some areas, lodgepoles cover many square kilometers so thickly that the forests are nearly impossible to walk through. These conditions eventually promote hot fires that create seedbeds for more lodgepoles; in fact, lodgepole cones are sealed in resin that only melts and releases seeds after a fire.

The Rockies feature three different life zones: the montane (warm, dry tree-filled valley bottoms), the subalpine (wetter forests of smaller stunted trees) and alpine (high windy slopes of flower meadows and barren rock).

A beautiful tree of dry, open areas, the quaking aspen has radiant, silver-white bark and rounded leaves that quiver in mountain breezes. Aspen foliage turns a striking orange-gold for just a few weeks in fall.

Shrubs

Half a dozen species of blueberry occur in the Canadian Rockies, with common names like huckleberry, grouseberry, bilberry and cranberry. Often these plants grow in patches large enough that berries for a batch of pancakes or muffins can be harvested within minutes.

Closely related and similar in appearance to blueberry plants is the kinnikinnik, also known as bearberry. This ground-hugging shrub has thick glossy leaves and reddish woody stems. Its leaves were once mixed with tobacco to make a smoking mixture, and the berries have been a staple food for many First Nations peoples.

It's something of a surprise to encounter wild roses growing deep in the woods, but in keeping with Alberta's official nickname (Wild Rose

Country) at least five types grow here. All look like slender, somewhat scraggly versions of what you'd see in a domestic garden.

Wildflowers

The flowering season in the Canadian Rockies begins as soon as the snows start to melt. Though delicate in structure, the early rising glacier lily pushes up so eagerly that the stems often unfurl right through the snow crust. Abundant in montane and subalpine forests or meadows, each lily produces several yellow flowers, with six upward-curled petals. Wherever lilies occur in great numbers, grizzlies paw eagerly through the soil in search of the edible bulbs.

Within days of snowmelt, pretty purple pasqueflowers (aka prairie crocuses) cover montane slopes. Growing close to the ground on short, fuzzy stems, these brilliant flowers stand out because of their yellow centers. Later in the summer, 'shaggy mane' seed heads replace the flowers. All parts of this plant are poisonous and may raise blisters if handled.

One of the most photographed flowers of Glacier National Park is the striking bear grass. From tufts of grasslike leaves, the plant sends up 1.5m-high (5ft) stalks of white, star-shaped flowers that may fill entire subalpine meadows. Grizzlies favor the tender spring leaves, hence the plant's common name.

Hike almost anywhere in these mountains and you're bound to encounter the easy-to-recognize bluebell, with its large, bell-like flowers held up on a long, skinny stem. After flowering, seeds are produced in capsules that close in wet weather, then open in dry winds to scatter the seeds far and wide.

Many visitors know the familiar Indian paintbrush for its tightly packed flowers (technically speaking, these are actually bracts, or modified leaves) in colors ranging from bright red to pink, orange or crimson. The plant is a semiparasite that taps into neighbors' roots for nourishment, allowing it to grow luxuriantly in desolate places like roadsides or dry meadows. Paintbrush patches are also one of the best sites for finding hummingbirds.

The big, showy cow parsnip can grow to an impressive height of 1.8m (6ft). Its huge, celery-like stalks and umbrella-shaped flower clusters are a familiar sight along streams and in moist aspen groves throughout the region. The stems are eaten by many animals and favored by grizzlies (avoid tasting yourself because of their similar appearance to other deadly species).

More localized in its distribution, but sometimes confused with cow parsnip, because it has the same large leaves, is the devil's club. This stout, 2.7m-high (9ft) plant practically bristles with armor. Completely covered in poisonous spikes (even the leaves are ribbed with rows of spines) that break off in the skin when contacted and cause infections, this plant further announces itself with its strong odor and large clusters of brilliant red berries. Despite these features, devil's club has a rich and important history of medicinal use among First Nations people of the area.

The mountain pine beetle is an insect that attacks and kills mature trees (turning their needles a distinctive red color). Rather like wildfires, this process is a natural part of the Rocky Mountain ecosystem, so park management bodies have tried to let it continue with minimal interference.

Synonymous with the expansive evergreen forests of Alberta and British Columbia, the Douglas fir tree is named after Scottish botanist David Douglas (1799–1834), who first visited Jasper in 1827, when he wrongly declared Mt Brown and Mt Hooker to be the highest peaks in North America.

WILDLIFE PLANTS

Conservation

Despite their remoteness and relatively late colonization, the Rocky Mountains parks were conceived in the infancy of the evolution of wilderness protection. And as the public perception of wilderness changed, so too have the parks. Banff was Canada's first – and the world's third – national park when it was inaugurated in 1885, while Jasper, Waterton and Glacier (all given protective status by 1910) were three more early beneficiaries of the nascent North American conservation movement.

The Early Conservationists

The American environmental movement was born during the progressive era at a time when early eco-thinkers were separating into two philosophical camps: the conservationists led by US president Theodore Roosevelt and his chief environmental advisor Gifford Pinchot, and the more radical preservationists epitomized by John Muir, founder of the Sierra Club. The former proposed federal intervention in order to manage and conserve natural resources; the latter considered nature to be sacred and tourism sustainable only under strict limits.

While Muir remains an icon to modern environmentalists, it was the conservationists who had the biggest impact on the public zeitgeist during the early flowering of the North American national park network in the 1890s. In the Rocky Mountains, their chief exponent was George Bird Grinnell, an anthropologist and naturalist from New York City who was more at home mingling with the Blackfeet Native Americans and leading sorties into the mountains of northwest Montana than he was tramping the streets of Manhattan. It was Grinnell who christened the Glacier/ Waterton region 'the Crown of the Continent' and, using his influential position as editor of *Field and Stream* magazine, he badgered the US Congress relentlessly for protective status. His entreaties were rewarded in 1910 when Glacier became the nation's 10th national park. In 1911 the Canadian government formed the Dominion Parks Branch (an early incarnation of Parks Canada) as the world's first national park coordinating body, and in 1930 the National Parks Act laid down the first firm set of ground rules for conservation and preservation. The huge debt owed to Grinnell and his contemporaries by our current generation is immeasurable.

But, with conflicting commercial interests and an inordinate influence wielded by the all-powerful cross-continental railway companies, early park rules were sketchy and haphazard. While the parks today still promote recreation and education as a crucial part of the overall wilderness experience, the concept of ecological integrity has taken center stage with a shift toward a more populist strand of environmentalism in the 1980s.

When Lewis and Clark traversed America in the early 1800s, there were approximately 100,000 grizzly bears roaming the lower 48 states of the US. Now there are around 1800 occupying an area that is less than 2% of their traditional range.

Environmental Issues

Tourism Boom

Fatefully, the work of Grinnell et al was just the beginning of a protracted process. Tourism and the ongoing impact of millions of visitors trampling through important wildlife corridors is one of the parks' most ticklish issues in modern times and nowhere is this problem more apparent than in Banff. Hosting an incorporated town with a permanent population of nearly 8000 people, along with main roads, a ski resort and over four million annual visitors, Banff's environmental credentials have long been a subject for hot debate. Comparisons with Glacier (governed by the US parks system) further south are particularly telling.

In 1996 a two-year investigation by the Banff–Bow Valley study group provided a crucial turning point in Banff's modern evolution. Putting forward 500 urgent recommendations – a list that included everything from population capping to quotas on hiking trails – the study prompted the implementation of a 15-year development plan designed to redress the park's ecological imbalance and save its priceless wilderness from almost-certain long-term damage. Almost two decades later, progress has certainly been made, though growing concerns and awareness about climate change give the issue even more urgency.

Long lauded as one of the continent's most pristine parks, Banff's smaller American cousin is a veritable wilderness, with no population center, no fast-food franchises and no water-sapping golf courses. Glacier bans bikes from all park trails, runs an environmentally friendly free shuttle service to minimize car pollution, and has barred its historic lodges from installing modern 'luxuries' such as TVs and room phones. Supplementing these efforts, the US Geological Survey conducts ongoing studies at the Northern Rocky Mountain Science Center on Glacier's ecosystems, management policies and environmental concerns such as eroding glaciers. Not surprisingly, the park is frequently acclaimed for its rich biodiversity, and its grizzly bear population is said to be one of the healthiest in the whole of North America.

Jasper sits somewhere between the two extremes. While it is closer to Banff in infrastructure and park policies (it hosts a townsite, golf course, pubs and restaurants), its superior size and smaller annual visitor count (roughly 60% of Banff's) means environmental pressures are less corrosive. Its most symbolic conservation issue is the preservation of the woodland caribou, a species no longer present in Banff, but still

Of all the Rocky Mountains parks, Waterton-Glacier is the best protected, with four different conservation designations: as a National Park (1895 Waterton, 1910 Glacier), International Peace Park (1932), Unesco Biosphere Reserve (1979) and Unesco World Heritage site (1995).

SUSTAINABILITY TIPS

The behavior of individual visitors in the parks can play a vital role in ensuring their long-term health and sustainability. Here are a few green recommendations:

➡ Glacier National Park runs a free shuttle bus designed to ease congestion on the increasingly traffic-choked Going-to-the-Sun Rd. The Canadian parks have a number of paying shuttles, and Banff runs public buses between Banff Town and Lake Louise.

➡ Stay on friendly terms with bears by using bear-proof containers and recycling bins, making noise on the trails, and giving bears a wide and respectful berth.

➡ Look into local volunteer organizations. Many people work tirelessly to protect fragile park wildernesses from degradation and neglect, and it's easy to join them.

➡ By staying in a Glacier National Park–run hotel you are lodging with a profoundly 'green' organization, whose policies include large-scale garbage recycling, use of low-energy light fixtures and donation of old furniture to charity.

➡ Jasper and Glacier National Parks can still be reached by using the train. The VIA/Amtrak services are economical, scenic, 'green' and comfortable.

➡ Glacier's propane-fueled red Jammer buses already emit 93% less pollutants than their gas-powered equivalents, and will soon reduce emissions further by converting to electric hybrid motors.

➡ Stay on the trail – wandering 'off-piste' or bushwhacking your own path damages flora and causes erosion.

surviving precariously further north. Jasper Town was made a Specialized Municipality in 2001 and began drafting a similarly comprehensive Community Sustainability Plan in the late 2000s.

Despite the very developed nature of little Waterton Townsite, tourism in Waterton Lakes, the smallest of the parks, will be limited as long as the moratorium on new accommodations and buildings remains in effect.

The Human Hand

Climate change and its attendant cascade of environmental impacts, which even in a best-case scenario points to a staggering number of potential losses, is one of the most important ways human behavior is threatening these wilderness areas. However, it's far from the only one. Often, the direst threat to an individual species' sustainability, whether flora or fauna, is disguised, at least to the untrained eye, as natural and endemic. But whether it's a fungus that arrived in the early 20th century or a fish stocked in lakes by park authorities in the 1960s, invasive species can potentially alter ecosystems, lead to hybridization and decimate habitats for true endemics.

Just one example in Waterton-Glacier is the whitebark pine population, ravaged by a combination of forces, including a foreign fungus, decreased mortality of native pine beetles that feed on the trees' bark (this because warmer winters ironically mean that more pine beetles survive the cold months), and the many decades previous when best forestry practice called for fire suppression (whitebark pines need the sunlight created by canopy-destroying wildfires). The risk is not simply that attractive trees are being killed, but that healthy whitebark pines are integral to the health of their particular ecosystem.

But it is the rapid pace of warming that complicates all other conservation issues. Fires are becoming more frequent and more intense. High alpine meadows are being colonized by seedlings that formerly couldn't have survived dense snowpacks. Pika, cute rodent-like mammals, are running out of alpine tundra and room to construct their burrows to escape the life-threatening summer temperatures. Wolverines lose habitat to roam. Earlier snowmelt leads to less runoff in summer, which means streams warm and fish that depend on cold water adapt or die. Avalanche patterns are disrupted and so on and on. Research scientists worry that their surveys and studies cumulatively point to the impending loss of biodiversity. While this is a concern the world over, these national parks serve as laboratories to witness and document the change, as well as ideal environments to experiment with localized interventions.

Solutions

There's no silver bullet obviously, and each park faces its own particular challenges. And no matter the prospect for small successes, what happens outside the park boundaries matters just as much. However, each national park system continues to address how to limit the carbon footprint of its visitors, improve energy efficiency and increase alternative-energy use. As habitats change and shift and animals roam looking for more suitable climes, conservation authorities have looked to maintain and create suitable corridors outside the park boundaries. Large landowners have been enlisted and efforts to limit mining and oil and natural gas exploration have intensified. Volunteers are planting thousands of whitebark pine seedlings grown disease-free in greenhouses in order to restore the population of this important linchpin tree species. Fishing and boating regulations are strictly enforced to stop the spread of invasive aquatic species. And tourism-dependent businesses do their best to educate the public. After all, their survival also depends on that of the wilderness around them.

Unhindered by human-created forces, wildfires are perfectly natural events that open up new habitats, promote the growth of fresh seedlings and replenish soil nutrients with decomposed organic matter. Understanding this, park authorities today carefully monitor annual blazes and let them run their natural course, unless they have been human-ignited or are directly threatening property and livelihoods.

Survival Guide

Health & Safety

If you have an emergency while staying in the national parks dial ☑911. Major centers like Banff, Jasper and Waterton have medical facilities.

BEFORE YOU GO

If you require medications bring them in their original, labeled containers. A signed and dated letter from your physician describing your medical conditions and medications, including generic names, is a good idea. If carrying syringes or needles, be sure to have a physician's letter documenting their necessity.

Some of the walks in this book are physically demanding and most require a reasonable level of fitness. Even if you're tackling the easy or easy–moderate walks, it pays to be relatively fit, rather than launch straight into them after months of fairly sedentary living. If you're aiming for the demanding walks, fitness is essential.

If you have any medical problems, or are concerned about your health in any way, it's a good idea to have a full checkup before you start walking.

Medical Checklist

➡ acetaminophen (paracetamol) or aspirin

➡ adhesive bandages (Band-Aids)

➡ adhesive medical tape

➡ antibacterial ointment for cuts and abrasions

➡ antibiotics

➡ antidiarrheal drugs (eg loperamide)

➡ antihistamines (for hay fever and allergic reactions)

➡ anti-inflammatory drugs (eg ibuprofen)

➡ bandages, gauze swabs, gauze rolls

➡ DEET–containing insect repellent for the skin

➡ elasticized support bandage

➡ iodine tablets or water filter (for water purification)

➡ moleskin for blisters

➡ nonadhesive dressing

➡ oral rehydration salts

➡ paper stitches

➡ permethrin-containing insect spray for clothing, tents and bed nets

➡ pocket knife

➡ scissors, safety pins, tweezers

➡ sterile alcohol wipes

➡ steroid cream or cortisone (for allergic rashes)

➡ sunblock

➡ sutures

➡ syringes and needles

➡ thermometer

Recommended Vaccinations

There are no required vaccinations for travel to the United States or Canada; however, an up-to-date tetanus shot is highly recommended for anyone planning to engage in outdoor activities.

Health Insurance

If you're traveling out of your home country, be sure to purchase medical insurance before you leave. It is also important to read the policy's fine print and ascertain exactly what you are covered for. Medical services in Canada and the US are not reciprocal.

Further Reading

➡ *Medicine for Mountaineering & Other Wilderness Activities* (James Wilkerson) An outstanding reference book for the layperson; describes many of the medical problems typically encountered while trekking.

➡ *Hypothermia, Frostbite and Other Cold Injuries* (James Wilkerson) Good background reading on the subject of cold and high-altitude problems.

➡ *Backcountry Bear Basics: The Definitive Guide*

to Avoiding Unpleasant Encounters (Dave Smith) Good on the basics of bear behavior and biology.

➡ *Mountaineering: The Freedom of the Hills* (The Mountaineers) Comprehensive guide to mountaineering, with a substantial section covering safety, first aid and alpine rescue.

IN THE PARKS

Visiting city dwellers will need to keep their wits about them in order to minimize the chances of suffering an avoidable accident or tragedy. Dress appropriately, tell people where you are going, don't bite off more than you can chew and, above all, *respect* the wilderness and the inherent dangers that it conceals.

Crime is far more common in big cities than in sparsely populated national parks. Nevertheless, use common sense: lock valuables in the trunk of your vehicle, especially if you're parking it at a trailhead overnight, and never leave anything worth stealing in your tent.

Medical Assistance

Banff National Park

For medical emergencies, head to the modern **Mineral Springs Hospital** (☑403-762-2222; www.covenanthealth.ca/hospitals-care-centres/banff-mineral-springs-hospital; 305 Lynx St, Banff Town; ⊙24hr).

Jasper National Park

The two local hospitals are **Seton General Hospital** (☑780-852-3344; 518 Robson St; ⊙24hr) and **Cottage Medical Clinic** (☑780-852-4885; 300 Miette Ave, Jasper Town; ⊙8:30am-4pm Mon-Fri).

Glacier National Park

Basic first aid is available at visitor centers and ranger stations in the park. The closest hospitals to the west side are **Kalispell Regional Medical Center** (☑406-752-5111; www.krh.org/krmc; 310 Sunnyview Lane, Kalispell) and **North Valley Hospital** (☑406-863-3500; www.nvhosp.org; 1600 Hospital Way, Whitefish; ⊙24hr) in Whitefish. The **West Glacier Clinic** (☑406-888-9924; 100 Rea Rd, West Glacier Fire Hall; ⊙9am-5pm) can provide treatment for minor injuries.

If you're in the northeast, you may find that **Cardston Health Centre** (☑403-653-4411; www.albertahealthservices.ca; 144 2nd St W, Cardston), in Alberta, Canada, is the closest bet, though customs could consume time en route.

Waterton Lakes National Park

Full medical help is available at **Cardston Health Centre** (☑403-653-4411; www.albertahealthservices.ca; 144 2nd St W, Cardston) and **Pincher Creek Health Centre** (☑403-627-1234; www.albertahealthservices.ca; 1222 Bev McLachlin Dr).

Infectious Diseases

Giardiasis

While water running through the mountains may look crystal-clear, much of it carries *Giardia lamblia*, a microscopic parasite that causes intestinal disorders. To avoid getting sick, boil all water for at least 10 minutes, treat it with water tablets or filter at 0.5 microns or smaller. Note that iodine in cold water doesn't destroy giardiasis.

Symptoms of giardiasis include stomach cramps, nausea, a bloated stomach, watery, foul-smelling diarrhea and frequent gas. Giardiasis can appear several weeks after you have been exposed to the parasite. The symptoms may disappear for a few days and then return;

this can go on for several weeks.

Seek medical advice if you think you have giardiasis, but where this is not possible, tinidazole or metronidazole are the recommended drugs. Treatment is a 2g single dose of tinidazole, or 250mg of metronidazole three times daily for five to 10 days.

Environmental Hazards

Altitude

Altitude sickness can strike anyone heading up into the mountains. Thinner air means less oxygen is reaching your muscles and brain, requiring the heart and lungs to work harder. Many trailheads begin at high elevations, meaning that you don't have to go very far before feeling the effects.

Symptoms of acute mountain sickness (AMS) include headache, lethargy, dizziness, difficulty sleeping and loss of appetite. AMS may become more severe without warning and can be fatal. Severe symptoms include breathlessness, a dry, irritating cough (which may progress to the production of pink, frothy sputum), severe headache, lack of coordination and balance, confusion, irrational behavior, vomiting, drowsiness and unconsciousness. There is no

WATER PURIFICATION

To ensure you are getting safe, clean drinking water in the backcountry you have three basic options:

Boiling

Water is considered safe to drink if it has been boiled at 100°C for at least 10 minutes. This is best done when you set up your camp and stove in the evening.

Chemical Purification

There are two types of chemical additives that will purify water: chlorine or iodine. You can choose from various products on the market. Read the instructions carefully first, be aware of expiration dates and check you are not allergic to either chemical.

Filtration

Mobile devices can pump water through microscopic filters and take out potentially harmful organisms. If carrying a filter, take care it doesn't get damaged in transit, read the instructions carefully and always filter the cleanest water you can find.

hard-and-fast rule as to what is too high – AMS has been fatal at 3000m (9843ft) – although 3500m to 4500m (11483ft to 14764ft) is the usual range.

Treat mild symptoms by resting at the same altitude until recovery, usually a day or two. Paracetamol or aspirin can be taken for headaches. If symptoms persist or become worse, however, *immediate descent* is necessary; even 500m (1640ft) can help. Drug treatments should never be used to avoid descent or to enable further ascent.

The drugs acetazolamide and dexamethasone are recommended by some doctors for the prevention of AMS; however, their use is controversial. They can reduce the symptoms, but they may also mask warning signs; severe and fatal AMS has occurred in people taking these drugs. In general we do not recommend them for travelers.

To prevent acute mountain sickness:

➡ Ascend slowly – have frequent rest days, spending two to three nights at each

rise of 1000m (3281ft). If you reach a high altitude by trekking, acclimatization takes place gradually and you are less likely to be affected than if you fly directly to high altitude.

➡ It is always wise to sleep at a lower altitude than the greatest height reached during the day, if possible. Also, if traveling above 3000m (9843ft), care should be taken not to increase the sleeping altitude by more than 300m (984ft) per day.

➡ Drink extra fluids. The mountain air is dry and cold and moisture is lost as you breathe; evaporation of sweat may occur unnoticed and result in dehydration.

➡ Eat light, high-carbohydrate meals for more energy.

➡ Avoid alcohol and sedatives.

Bites & Stings
MOSQUITOES

Mosquitoes can be rampant in all parks, particularly on summer evenings. In Banff and Jasper, you'll notice them around lakes and on wooded hikes; they are

particularly prevalent in the Tonquin Valley and along parts of the remote North Boundary Trail. In Glacier and Waterton Lakes, mosquitoes tend to be more annoying on the west side of the park than in the windier east. Use repellent, wear light-colored clothing and cover yourself in the evening.

TICKS

Ticks are most active from spring to autumn, especially where there are plenty of sheep or deer. They usually lurk in overhanging vegetation, so avoid pushing through tall bushes.

If you find a tick attached to your skin, press down around its head with tweezers, grab the head and gently pull upward. Avoid pulling the rear of the body as this may squeeze the tick's gut contents through its mouth into your skin, increasing the risk of infection and disease. Smearing chemicals on the tick will not make it let go and is not recommended.

Lyme disease is a tick-borne illness that manifests itself in skin lesions and, later on, intermittent or persistent arthritis. To avoid contracting it, use all normal mosquito preventative measures, including wearing long-sleeved shirts and trousers, checking clothing for ticks after outdoor activity, and using an effective brand of DEET or insect repellent.

Rocky Mountain spotted fever is another tick-borne disease that is potentially lethal, but usually curable if diagnosed early. Symptoms include fever and muscle pain followed by the development of a rash. Treatment is with antibiotics, but to prevent it take the usual anti-tick measures, especially when walking in areas of tall grass or brush.

Cold
HYPOTHERMIA

This occurs when the body loses heat faster than it can produce it and the core temperature of the body falls.

It is frighteningly easy to progress from very cold to dangerously cold due to a combination of wind, wet clothing, fatigue and hunger, even if the air temperature is above freezing. If the weather deteriorates, put on extra layers of warm clothing; a windproof and/or waterproof jacket, wool or fleece hat and gloves are all essential. Have something energy-giving to eat and ensure that everyone in your group is fit, feeling well and alert.

Symptoms of hypothermia are exhaustion, numb skin (particularly toes and fingers), shivering, slurred speech, irrational or violent behavior, lethargy, stumbling, dizzy spells, muscle cramps and violent bursts of energy. Irrationality may take the form of sufferers claiming they are warm and trying to take off their clothes.

To treat mild hypothermia, first get the person out of the wind and/or rain, remove their clothing if it's wet and replace it with dry, warm clothing. Give them hot liquids – not alcohol – and some high-energy, easily digestible food. Do not rub victims: instead, allow them to slowly warm themselves.

FROSTBITE

This refers to the freezing of extremities, including fingers, toes and nose. Signs and symptoms of frostbite include a whitish or waxy cast to the skin, or even crystals on the surface, plus itching, numbness and pain.

Warm the affected areas by immersion in warm (not hot) water, or with blankets or clothes, only until the skin becomes flushed. Frostbitten parts should not be rubbed. Pain and swelling are inevitable. Blisters should not be broken. Get medical attention right away.

Heat

HEATSTROKE

This is a serious, occasionally fatal, condition that occurs if the body's heat-regulating mechanism breaks down and the body temperature rises to dangerous levels. Long, continuous periods of exposure to high temperatures and insufficient fluids can leave you vulnerable to heatstroke.

The symptoms are feeling unwell, not sweating very much (or at all) and a high body temperature of around 39°C to 41°C (102°F to 106°F). Where sweating has ceased, the skin becomes flushed and red. Severe, throbbing headaches and lack of coordination will also occur, and the sufferer may be confused or aggressive. Eventually the victim will become delirious or convulse. Hospitalization is essential but, in the interim, get victims out of the sun, remove their clothing, cover them with a wet sheet or towel, and then fan continually. Give fluids if they are conscious.

DEHYDRATION & HEAT EXHAUSTION

Dehydration is a potentially dangerous and generally preventable condition caused by excessive fluid loss. Sweating combined with inadequate fluid intake is one of the common causes in trekkers, but other causes are diarrhea, vomiting and high fever.

The first symptoms are weakness, thirst and passing small amounts of very concentrated urine. This may lead to drowsiness, dizziness or fainting on standing up, and finally, coma.

It's easy to forget how much fluid you are losing via perspiration while you are trekking, particularly if a strong breeze is drying your skin quickly. You should always maintain a good fluid intake – a minimum of 3L a day is recommended.

Dehydration and salt deficiency can cause heat exhaustion. Salt deficiency is characterized by fatigue, lethargy, headaches, giddiness and muscle cramps. Salt tablets are overkill; just adding extra salt to your food is probably sufficient.

Snow Blindness

This is a temporary, painful condition resulting from sunburn of the surface of the eye (cornea). It usually occurs when someone walks on snow or in bright sunshine without sunglasses. Treatment is to relieve the pain – cold cloths on closed eyelids may help. Antibiotic and anesthetic eye drops are

---

WALK SAFETY – BASIC RULES

➡ Allow plenty of time to accomplish a walk before dark, particularly when daylight hours are shorter.

➡ Study the route carefully before setting out, noting the possible escape routes and the point of no return (where it's quicker to continue than to turn back). Monitor your progress during the day against the time estimated for the walk, and keep an eye on the weather.

➡ It's wise not to walk alone. Always leave details of your intended route, number of people in your group and expected return time with someone responsible before you set off, and let that person know when you return.

➡ Before setting off, make sure you have a relevant map, compass and whistle, and that you know the weather forecast for the area for the next 24 hours. In the Rockies always carry extra warm, dry layers of clothing and plenty of emergency high-energy food.

BEAR ISSUES

Although people have an inordinate fear of being hurt by bears, the Canadian Rockies are a far more dangerous place for the bears themselves. In Banff National Park alone, 90% of known grizzly-bear deaths have occurred within 400m (0.25 miles) of roads and buildings, with most bears either being killed by cars or by wardens when bears and people got mixed up. Cross-continental trains traveling through the parks have also killed many of these magnificent beasts.

Bears are intelligent opportunists that quickly learn that humans come with food and tasty garbage. Unfortunately, once this association is learned, a bear nearly always has to be shot. Remember: 'A fed bear is a dead bear,' so never feed a bear, never improperly store food or garbage, and always clean up after yourself.

Bears are also surprisingly fast creatures that can sprint the length of a football field in six seconds. Although such encounters are rare, bears will readily attack if their cubs are around, if they're defending food or if they feel surprised and threatened. Your best defenses against surprising a bear are to remain alert, avoid hiking at night (when bears feed) and be careful when traveling upwind near streams or where visibility is obscured.

To avoid an encounter altogether, hike in groups (bears almost never attack hiking groups of more than four people) and make noise on the trail, preferably by talking or singing. Jangling bear bells aren't really loud enough to be effective.

If you do encounter a bear, there are several defensive strategies to employ, but no guarantees. If the bear doesn't see you, move a safe distance downwind and make noise to alert it to your presence. If the bear sees you, slowly back out of its path, avoid eye contact, speak softly and wave your hands above your head slowly. Never turn your back to the bear, never kneel down and never run.

Sows with cubs are particularly dangerous, and you should make every effort to avoid coming between a sow and her cubs. A sow may clack her jaws, lower her head and shake it as a warning before she charges.

If a bear does charge, do not panic and do not scream (which may frighten the bear and make it more aggressive), because the bear may only be charging as a bluff. Drop to the ground, crouch face down in a ball, and play dead, covering the back of your neck with your hands and your chest and stomach with your knees. Do not resist the bear's inquisitive pawing – it may get bored and go away.

If the bear continues to attack you, it may be a (rare) predatory bear, in which case you should fight back aggressively. Park authorities recommend hikers carry bear spray, which can be used as a last resort. It has proved to be effective if aimed into the face of a charging bear from a range of about 10m (33ft). For more bear advice, check www.nps.gov/subjects/bears/safety.htm.

not necessary. The condition usually resolves itself within a few days and there are no long-term consequences.

Sun

Protection against the sun should always be taken seriously. Particularly in the rarefied air and deceptive coolness of the mountains, sunburn occurs rapidly. Slap on the sunscreen and a barrier cream for your nose and lips, wear a broad-brimmed hat and protect your eyes with good-quality sunglasses with UV lenses, particularly when walking near water, sand or snow. If,

despite these precautions, you get yourself burnt, apply calamine lotion, aloe vera or other commercial sunburn-relief preparations to the affected area.

SAFE HIKING

Avalanches

Avalanches are a threat during and following storms, in high winds and during temperature changes, particularly when it warms in spring. Educate yourself about the dangers of avalanches before

setting out into the back-country. Signs of avalanche activity include felled trees and slides.

For up-to-date information on avalanche hazards in all the Canadian Rockies national parks, visit avalanche. pc.gc.ca. Alternatively, for Banff, Kootenay and Yoho call ☑403-762-1470, for Jasper ☑780-852-6155 and for Waterton Lakes ☑888-927-3367. For other areas, contact **Avalanche Canada** (☑250-837-2141; www.ava lanche.ca) or local park information centers.

For Glacier National Park avalanche info, check the

Flathead Avalanche Center website (www.flathead avalanche.org) or call ☎406-257-8402. Local radio stations broadcast reports on area avalanche conditions studied by the Northwest Montana Avalanche Warning System.

If you are caught in an avalanche, your chance of survival depends on your ability to keep yourself above the flowing snow and your companions' ability to rescue you. The probability of survival decreases rapidly after half an hour, so the party must be self-equipped, with each member carrying an avalanche beacon, a sectional probe and a collapsible shovel.

Crossing Streams

Sudden downpours are common in the mountains and can speedily turn a gentle stream into a raging torrent. If you're in any doubt about the safety of a crossing, look for a safer passage upstream or wait. If the rain is short-lived, it should subside quickly.

If you decide it's essential to cross (late in the day, for example), look for a wide, relatively shallow stretch of the stream rather than a bend. Take off your trousers and socks, but keep your boots on to prevent injury. Put dry, warm clothes and a towel in a plastic bag near the top

of your pack. Use a walking pole, grasped in both hands, on the upstream side as a third leg, or go arm in arm with a companion, clasping at the wrist, and cross-side-on to the flow, taking short steps.

Lightning

If a storm brews, avoid exposed areas. Lightning has a penchant for crests, lone trees, small depressions, gullies, caves and cabin entrances, as well as wet ground. If you are caught out in the open, try to curl up as tightly as possible with your feet together and keep a layer of insulation between you and the ground. Place metal objects such as metal-frame backpacks and walking poles away from you.

Rescue & Evacuation

If someone in your group is injured or falls ill and can't move, leave somebody with them while others go for help. Those leaving the scene should take clear written details of the location and condition of the victim, and of helicopter landing conditions. If there are only two of you, leave the injured person with as much warm clothing, food and water as it's sensible to spare, plus the whistle and torch. Mark

the position with something conspicuous – an orange bivvy bag, or perhaps a large stone cross on the ground.

SAFE CYCLING

One of the most common problems cyclists will encounter is unobservant motorists busy gawping at the scenery and wildlife. The arterial Going-to-the-Sun Rd in Glacier, built in the early days of the motor car, is notoriously precipitous and narrow, with no shoulders for cyclists. Jammed with dawdlers and oversized SUVs, the highway is a cycling obstacle course and, as a result, cyclists are prevented from using it between 11am and 4pm (June to September), largely for their own safety.

Wildlife is another problem, particularly for off-roaders who run the risk of surprising large animals such as moose or bears when progressing rapidly along twisting forested trails. To avoid potentially dangerous encounters with foraging megafauna, cyclists are encouraged to take heed of posted trail warnings and make plenty of noise on concealed corners and rises (remember, a bear can easily outsprint a cyclist).

Helmets are mandatory in all North American national parks. Off-roaders may also want to invest in elbow and knee pads.

Clothing & Equipment

Visitors to the Rockies should prepare themselves for fickle weather and wildlife encounters, whatever the season. Double down on this if you're planning on backcountry camping. Take the time to get properly kitted out and you're guaranteed to have a safer and more comfortable trip. Most importantly, make certain you've got good boots, rain gear and plenty of layers, plus a canister of pepper spray to use as a last resort against aggressive wild animals, especially bears.

Clothing

Layering

A secret of comfortable walking is to wear several layers of light clothing, which you can easily take off or put on as you warm up or cool down. Most walkers use three main layers: a base layer next to the skin; an insulating layer; and an outer-shell layer for protection from wind, rain and snow.

For the upper body, the base layer is typically a shirt of synthetic material that wicks moisture away from the body and reduces chilling. The insulating layer retains heat next to your body, and is usually a (windproof) fleece jacket or sweater. The outer shell consists of a waterproof jacket that also protects against cold wind.

For the lower body, the layers generally consist of either shorts or loose-fitting trousers, thermal underwear and waterproof overtrousers.

When purchasing outdoor clothing, one of the most practical fabrics is merino wool. Though a little pricier than other materials, natural wool absorbs sweat, retains heat even when wet, and is soft and comfortable to wear. Even better, it doesn't store odors like other sports garments, so you can wear it for several days in a row without inflicting antisocial smells on your tent mates.

Waterproof Shells

Jackets should be made of a breathable, waterproof fabric, with a hood that is roomy enough to cover headwear, but that still allows peripheral vision. Other handy accessories include underarm zippers for easy ventilation and a large map pocket with a heavy-gauge zipper protected by a storm flap.

Waterproof pants are best with slits for pocket access and long leg zips so that you can pull them on and off over your boots.

Footwear, Socks & Gaiters

Running shoes are OK for walks that are graded easy or moderate. However, you'll probably appreciate, if not need, the support and protection provided by hiking boots for more demanding walks. Nonslip soles (such as Vibram) provide the best grip.

Buy boots in warm conditions or go for a walk before trying them on, so that your feet can expand slightly, as they would on a hike. It's also a good idea to carry a pair of sandals to wear at night for getting in and out of tents easily or at rest stops. Sandals are also useful when fording waterways.

Gaiters help to keep your feet dry in wet weather and on boggy ground; they can also deflect small stones or sand and maintain leg warmth. The best are made of strong fabric, with a robust zip protected by a flap, and secure easily around the foot.

Walking socks should be free of ridged seams in the toes and heels.

Equipment

Backpacks

For day walks, a day pack (30L to 40L) will usually suffice, but for multiday walks you will need a backpack of between 45L and 90L capacity. Even if the manufacturer claims your pack is waterproof, use heavy-duty liners.

Navigation Equipment

MAPS & COMPASS

You should always carry a good map of the area in which you are walking, and know how to read it. Before setting off on your walk, ensure that you are aware of the contour interval, the map symbols, the magnetic declination (difference between true and grid north), plus the main ridge and river systems in the area and the general direction in which you are heading. On the trail, try to identify major landforms such as mountain ranges and valleys, and locate them on your map to familiarize yourself with the geography.

Buy a compass and learn how to use it. The attraction of magnetic north varies in different parts of the world, so compasses need to be balanced accordingly. Compass manufacturers have divided the world into five zones. Make sure your compass is balanced for your destination zone. There are also 'universal' compasses on the market that can be used anywhere in the world.

GPS

Originally developed by the US Department of Defense, the Global Positioning System (GPS) is a network of more than 20 earth-orbiting satellites that continually beam encoded signals back to earth. Small, computer-driven devices (GPS receivers) can decode these signals to give users an extremely accurate reading of their location – to within 30m, anywhere on the planet, at any time of day, in almost any weather. The cheapest handheld GPS receivers now cost less than US$40 (although these may not have a built-in averaging system that minimises signal errors). Other important factors to consider when buying a GPS receiver are its weight and battery life.

Remember that a GPS receiver is of little use unless used with an accurate topographical map. The receiver simply gives your position, which you must then locate on the local map. GPS receivers will only work properly in the open. The signals from a crucial satellite may be blocked (or bounce off rock or water) directly below high

ROUTE FINDING

While accurate, our maps are not as detailed as commercially available topographic maps. Whichever map you use on the trail, some basic route-finding techniques will also come in handy:

➡ Be aware of whether the trail should be climbing or descending.

➡ Check the north-point arrow on the map and determine the general direction of the trail.

➡ Time your progress over a known distance and calculate the speed at which you travel in the given terrain. From then on, you can determine with reasonable accuracy how far you have traveled.

➡ Watch the path – look for boot prints and other signs of previous passage.

cliffs, near large bodies of water or in dense tree cover and give inaccurate readings. GPS receivers are more vulnerable to breakdowns (including dead batteries) than the humble magnetic compass – a low-tech device that has served navigators faithfully for centuries – so don't rely on them entirely.

Bear Spray

Most of the hikes/activities in the parks are also in bear country. As a last resort, bear spray (pepper spray) has been used effectively to deter aggressive bears, and park authorities often recommend that you equip yourself with a canister when venturing into backcountry. Be sure to familiarize yourself with the manufacturer's instructions before use, and only use as a last resort (ie on a charging bear approximately 9m to 15m/30ft to 50ft away from you). Most shops in or around the parks stock bear spray. Prices typically range from C$35 to C$50 in Canada, or US$35 to US$45 in the US; some places also rent it by the day. It is best kept close at hand on a belt around your waist.

Tent

A three-season tent will fulfill most walkers' requirements. The floor and the outer shell,

or fly, should have taped or sealed seams and covered zips to stop leaks. The weight can be as low as 1kg for a stripped-down, low-profile tent, and up to 3kg for a roomy, luxury, four-season model.

Dome- and tunnel-shaped tents handle windy conditions better than flat-sided tents.

Sleeping Bag & Mat

While down fillings are generally warmer than synthetic ones for the same weight and bulk, synthetic fillings have two main advantages: they retain warmth when wet and are free from the animal cruelty concerns associated with down. Mummy-shaped bags are best for weight and warmth. The temperature rating (-5°C, for instance) is the coldest temperature at which a person should feel comfortable in the bag (although the ratings are notoriously unreliable).

An inner sheet helps keep your sleeping bag clean, as well as adding an insulating layer; silk is lightest, but liners also come in cotton or synthetic fabric.

Self-inflating sleeping mats work like a thin air cushion between you and the ground; they also insulate from the cold. Foam mats are a low-cost, but less comfortable and less compact, alternative.

EQUIPMENT CHECKLIST

This list is a general guide to the things you might take on a walk. Your list will vary depending on the kind of walking you want to do, whether you're camping or planning to stay in hostels or B&Bs, and on the terrain, weather conditions and time of year.

Clothing

- ☐ boots and spare laces
- ☐ gaiters
- ☐ warm hat, scarf and gloves
- ☐ waterproof pants
- ☐ rain jacket
- ☐ athletic or trail shoes and sandals
- ☐ shorts and trousers
- ☐ socks and underwear
- ☐ sunhat
- ☐ sweater or fleece jacket
- ☐ thermal underwear
- ☐ T-shirt and long-sleeved shirt with collar

Equipment

- ☐ backpack with waterproof liner
- ☐ bear spray
- ☐ first-aid kit
- ☐ flashlight (torch) or headlamp, spare batteries and bulb (globe)
- ☐ food and snacks (high energy) and one day's emergency supplies
- ☐ insect repellent
- ☐ map, compass and guidebook
- ☐ map case or clip-seal plastic bags
- ☐ plastic bags (for carrying rubbish)
- ☐ pocket knife
- ☐ sunglasses
- ☐ sunscreen and lip balm
- ☐ survival bag or blanket
- ☐ toilet paper and trowel
- ☐ water container
- ☐ whistle

Overnight Walks

- ☐ cooking, eating and drinking utensils
- ☐ dishwashing items
- ☐ matches and lighter
- ☐ sewing/repair kit
- ☐ sleeping bag and bag liner/inner sheet
- ☐ sleeping mat and inflatable pillow
- ☐ spare cord
- ☐ stove and fuel
- ☐ tent, pegs, poles and guy ropes
- ☐ toiletries
- ☐ towel
- ☐ water-purification tablets, iodine or filter

Optional Items

- ☐ backpack cover (waterproof, slip-on)
- ☐ binoculars
- ☐ camera, film and batteries
- ☐ candle
- ☐ cell (mobile) phone
- ☐ emergency distress beacon
- ☐ GPS receiver
- ☐ groundsheet
- ☐ mosquito net
- ☐ swimsuit
- ☐ walking poles

Stoves & Fuel

The easiest type of fuel to use is butane or propane gas in disposable containers; true, it doesn't win many environmental points, but it's much easier to come by than liquid fuels. The most widely used brands are Coleman, MSR and Camping Gaz, available from outdoor gear shops and, in some remote areas, from small supermarkets.

Liquid fuel includes Coleman fuel, methylated spirits and paraffin. Again, outdoor gear shops, possibly hard-ware stores or even small supermarkets are the best places to look for it.

Airlines prohibit the carriage of any flammable materials and may well reject empty liquid-fuel bottles or even the stoves themselves.

Buying & Renting Locally

Specializing in the great outdoors, the national park towns offer some stellar options for buying and renting gear. More specialized gear such as bikes, snowshoes, hiking poles and climbing harnesses can usually be rented in the parks or the surrounding settlements.

Kayaks, canoes and stand up paddleboards (SUP), including inflatable options of all three, are available for rental in many locations.

In addition to the outfitters selling the latest name-brand gear, some shops, such as **Switching Gear** (Map p116; ✆403-678-1992; www.switchinggear.ca; 718 10th St; ⊙11am-6pm) in Canmore, also sell high-quality used equipment.

Directory A–Z

Accessible Travel

Visiting Banff, Jasper and Glacier still presents quite a few challenges for people with auditory, visual or physical disabilities and for people with restricted mobility, but all of the parks have made strides towards greater accessibility.

Your best bet is to contact the parks' visitor centers directly with questions on specific activities, and to consult online resources such as www.nps.gov/glac/planyourvisit/accessibility.htm (Glacier), www.banfflakelouise.com/accessibility (Banff), and www.pc.gc.ca/en/pn-np/ab/jasper/visit/installations-facilities/accessible (Jasper). Another helpful website is the Disabled Traveler's Companion (www.tdtcompanion.com).

➡ Most hotels have wheelchair-accessible rooms.

➡ Several national-park campgrounds, including Fish Creek and Apgar in Glacier; Two Jack Lakeside, Tunnel Mountain, Johnston Canyon and Lake Louise in Banff; and Whistlers, Wabasso, Wapiti, Pocahontas, Wilcox and Icefield in Jasper, have facilities for disabled users, including wheelchair-friendly campsites and washrooms.

➡ Download Lonely Planet's free Accessible Travel guides from http://lptravel.to/AccessibleTravel.

Banff

Most of the main sights in Banff, including Lake Louise, Banff's museums, Upper Hot Springs Pool and Peyto Lake along the Icefields Pkwy are wheelchair accessible, as is the main visitor center.

➡ Paved trails ideal for wheelchair users include the Bow Riverside Trail, the Fenland Trail, the Banff Legacy Trail, the lower section of Johnston Canyon, the paved section of the Lake Minnewanka Shoreline Trail, the Lake Louise Shoreline Trail and the mixed-use Sundance Trail in Banff.

➡ In Kananaskis Country, William Watson Lodge has been designed specifically to give people with disabilities access to the great outdoors. Alberta residents get priority at the lodge's 22 fully accessible cabins and 11 accessible campsites, but anyone can use their 20km (12.4-mile) network of accessible trails.

Glacier & Waterton Lakes

➡ In Glacier, two short, scenic trails are paved for wheelchair use: Trail of the Cedars, off Going-to-the-Sun Rd, and the Running Eagle Falls Trail in Two Medicine. The cycling path between Apgar Village and the visitor center is also accessible.

➡ Hearing-impaired visitors can get information at ☎406-888-7806.

➡ Park visitor centers have audio guides for visually impaired visitors.

➡ At least one or two ground-floor, wheelchair-friendly rooms are available at all in-park lodges.

➡ All shuttles in Glacier are ADA accessible, as is the 'Jammer' bus.

➡ The Waterton Townsite campground has accessible bathroom facilities.

➡ Waterton's Linnet Lake Trail, Waterton Townsite Trail and Cameron Lake Day area are wheelchair accessible.

Jasper

Jasper's museum, Miette Hot Springs, Maligne Lake, Medicine Lake, Jasper Tramway and the visitor center are all wheelchair accessible, as is Athabasca Falls and the Icefield Centre along the Icefields Pkwy.

➡ Several trails are good for wheelchair users, including the initial paved section of the Mary Schäffer Loop, Maligne Lake, the Clifford E Lee Trail at Lake Annette and Pyramid Isle in Pyramid Lake.

➡ Few accommodations in Jasper have dedicated rooms for wheelchair users, although most have elevators, and there are usually ground-floor rooms that can accommodate disabled visitors.

➡ Jasper's restaurants are on the ground floor and have accessible toilets.

Accommodations

Banff, Jasper and Glacier offer a wide-ranging mix of accommodations. All should be booked well in advance from mid-June to September.

B&Bs & Guesthouses

Staying with locals can be a great way to immerse yourself in the park and get some insiders' tips on the best things to see and do during your stay. Many residents offer B&B rooms in their own homes to travelers, but standards vary widely. Some places are fairly basic, while others will give many top-end hotels a run for their money. B&Bs are less common in Glacier than the Canadian parks.

➡ Breakfast is nearly always included in room rates, but if you have special requirements, let the owners know in advance.

➡ Not all B&B rooms have private bathrooms, so check before booking if that's important to you.

➡ Remember to check the B&B's policies on pets, kids and credit cards. Some will accept all three, while others won't accept any.

Camping

FRONTCOUNTRY CAMPING

Camping is a wonderful (and popular) way of experiencing the national parks. All of the Canadian and US parks offer a good range of frontcountry campgrounds that are accessible from the main roads.

Facilities vary widely: large campgrounds might have flush toilets, drinking water, public phones, fire pits and RV hookups, while others might only have pit toilets and a standpipe for drinking water. In general, the better equipped campgrounds (especially those close to tourist centers) fill up faster than simpler ones further afield.

➡ In the Canadian parks, the only campgrounds that accept reservations are Tunnel Mountain, Two Jack, Johnston Canyon, Lake Louise and Rampart Creek (in Banff); Pocahontas, Wapiti and Wabasso (in Jasper); and the townsite campground in Waterton.

➡ Whistlers, the largest campground in Jasper, is undergoing major renovations but will again accept reservations when it reopens (most likely in 2021).

➡ Two Jack Lakeside and Tunnel Mountain II (Banff) also offer oTENTiks, small A-frame tents with hot water and electricity (C$120).

➡ Reservations can be made starting in January each year via the **Parks Canada Reservation Service** (📞877-737-3783; www.reservation.pc.gc.ca); there's a reservation fee of C$11 for reservations made online, or C$13.50 for those made via the call center.

➡ In Glacier National Park, reservations can be made up to five months in advance for Fish Creek, St Mary and half the sites at Many Glacier campground via www.recreation.gov.

➡ All other sites operate on a first-come, first-served basis and typically fill by midmorning, particularly in July and August. Arrive before checkout time at 11am for the best chance of securing a site. Campground availability bulletins are available at visitor centers and on park radio.

➡ Most campgrounds are suitable for tents, camper vans and RVs, although not all have pull-throughs or paved sites.

➡ At more remote campgrounds, facilities are generally limited to pit toilets and drinking water, although some have recycling bins and bear-proof storage lockers.

➡ Some campgrounds operate on a self-registration basis. Find an available site first, then fill in your details (name, site number, length of stay, registration number) on the payment envelope and drop it in the box near the entrance. Credit cards are accepted.

➡ The maximum stay at any campground is 14 days.

➡ Fires are usually allowed in designated fire pits. In Canada you'll need to buy a fire permit (per day C$8.80); the permit includes a bundle of wood.

BACKCOUNTRY CAMPING

Backcountry campgrounds are mainly geared for hikers exploring the trails, so facilities are extremely rudimentary. Most only offer cleared tent pads and a pit privy; some also have food-storage bins or cables where you should suspend toiletries, garbage and food items to avoid attracting bears to the campground.

➡ Overnight backcountry stays require a special permit, known in Canadian parks as a wilderness pass (C$9.80 per person per night) and in US parks as a backcountry permit (US$40 per trip per group if reserved in advance, plus a US$7 per person per night camping fee). Popular spots fill up quickly in peak months so advance reservations are highly recommended. Select 'Backcountry Camping' on the Parks Canada reservation site (www.reservation.pc.gc.ca) or visit Glacier's Backcountry Advance Reservations page (www.nps.gov/glac/

planyourvisit/backcountry-reservations.htm) to begin planning your trip.

➡ Visitor numbers on backcountry trails are limited, so you'll usually need to specify your campgrounds when you purchase your wilderness pass. The maximum stay at any one campground is generally three nights.

➡ In some very remote areas of the parks, wild camping is allowed – choose a site at least 50m from the trail, 70m from water sources and 5km (3 miles) or more from the trailhead.

➡ See the useful Leave No Trace website (www.leavenotrace.ca) for tips on how to travel responsibly in the backcountry.

Condos & Vacation Apartments

Local bylaws prohibit the rental of vacation homes or apartments in Banff, Lake Louise and Jasper, but many hotels offer suites or chalets that are specifically intended for families, often including a full kitchen, bathroom and two or three bedrooms.

Vacation apartments and condos are available outside the park borders (eg in Canmore, Kootenay or Whitefish), but only certain properties are licensed to be used for the purpose. Make sure you use a legitimate operator, avoid arranging anything directly with the owner or paying anything up front, and always check the terms and conditions carefully before booking. Whitefish properties available on popular booking sites are especially sought after by skiers in winter months (a resort tax might be applied to rentals).

Hostels

Another cheap way of visiting the parks is to stay in a hostel. They're not just for backpackers and hikers these days: most are happy to rent

out whole dorms and private rooms, making them ideal for families or couples on a budget. The region's largest network of hostels is in the Canadian parks; operated by Hostelling International (HI; www.hihostels.ca), it includes flagship hostels in Banff Town, Lake Louise and Jasper Town (the latter newly opened in 2019). Dorm rooms cost between C$35 and C$60 depending on the season.

➡ Accommodations are usually in dorms with four to 12 beds, with a communal kitchen and lounge. Some also have cafes, games rooms and TV rooms.

➡ Dorms are sometimes gender segregated, sometimes mixed; where both dorm types exist in the same hostel, you can specify your preference at the time of booking. Bathrooms and showers are shared. Some hostels have en suite bathrooms for each dorm, while others have communal bathrooms down the corridor.

➡ HI members qualify for discounts on nightly rates. Annual membership costs C$35 and is free for young people 17 and under.

➡ HI also runs 10 wilderness hostels in Banff, Jasper and Yoho National Parks – typically wood cabins with a kitchen, dining area and communal lounge, often supplemented by an outdoor fire ring or cozy wood-burning stove. Facilities are usually extremely basic (no

showers or running water, propane lighting, limited solar electricity or none at all), though wilderness hostel guests do have the right to take a free shower at the nearest in-town HI facility.

➡ The **Alpine Club of Canada** (☑403-678-3200; www.alpineclubofcanada.ca; Indian Flats Rd) operates its own flagship hostel in Canmore, along with a network of rustic backcountry huts, mostly used by climbers and hikers. Reservations are essential.

➡ The Canadian Rockies also have some excellent non-HI-affiliated hostels, in places such as Canmore and Jasper.

➡ The closest hostels to Glacier National Park are in East Glacier, Polebridge and Whitefish.

Hotels

There's no shortage of hotels in Banff, Jasper and Glacier, but they're generally not cheap. Room rates, especially in Banff, are notoriously expensive, and always shoot upward in the peak season between May and September. Things are a bit more affordable in Jasper, as well as in the neighboring provincial parks.

➡ Nearly all hotel rooms come with en suite bathroom, telephone and cable TV, and most places offer free wi-fi for guests. Breakfast is often charged as an extra.

➡ Room rates are nearly always quoted per room, but without sales tax.

SLEEPING PRICE RANGES

The following price ranges are based on a double room with private bathroom in high season; cheaper rates may be available in shoulder and low seasons. Prices are based on Canadian dollars (C$) in Canada and US dollars (US$) in the United States.

$ less than $100

$$ $100–$250

$$$ more than $250

Climate

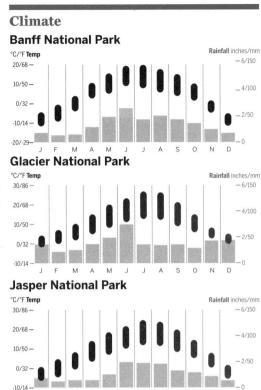

Banff National Park

Glacier National Park

Jasper National Park

Customs Regulations

➡ There are strict restrictions on the import of plants, seeds and animal products to prevent the spread of pests and diseases. This also applies to firewood.

➡ If traveling overland, you can bring bear spray across the border as long as the specific intended usage is clearly indicated. Air travelers are prohibited from bringing bear spray aboard planes in checked or carry-on luggage.

Food

Restaurants, diners and cafes are plentiful around the park townsites, but choice is a lot more limited once you get out into the rest of the national parks. If you're eating out, remember that service is usually not added to your bill – a tip of 15% to 20% is the expected norm.

The following price indicators reflect the cost of a main dish. Prices are based on Canadian dollars (C$) in Canada and US dollars (US$) in the United States.

$ Less than $15

$$ $15–$25

$$$ more than $25

Insurance

Travel insurance is always a worthwhile investment if you're visiting another country. Worldwide travel insurance is available at www. lonelyplanet.com/travel -insurance. You can buy, extend and claim online any time – even if you're already on the road.

➡ Choose your policy carefully, especially for coverage against flight delays, 'acts of God' or force majeure events, and baggage loss, and check the excess to be paid in the event of a claim.

➡ If you're undertaking outdoor activities such as hiking, cycling, climbing or water sports, and especially if you're skiing or snowboarding, make sure your travel insurance policy covers you against medical treatment and emergency repatriation, as hospital bills are cripplingly expensive.

➡ Most standard US health plans aren't valid for treatment in Canada, so you'll need to ensure you're covered under a separate travel insurance policy.

➡ Auto insurance purchased in Canada and the US is usually applicable to either country, but confirm this with your provider before you leave home.

➡ Many auto insurance policies extend to rental cars, and some credit-card providers provide coverage if you pay for the rental with your card.

Internet Access

Access is widespread around both of the Canadian parks, and around Waterton townsite, but it's patchy around Glacier.

➡ Most hotels including the historic 'parkitecture' lodging in Glacier offer free wireless access to customers with their own laptops, and wi-fi hot spots are common in cafes and restaurants.

➡ The wi-fi icon denotes wireless access is available.

➡ The internet icon denotes that there is a computer available for public use.

➡ Most public libraries offer free internet access.

Electricity

Canada and the US both use plugs with either two or three pins. Adaptors to convert power plugs are easily available from electrical outlets and travel shops.

Type A
120V/60Hz

Type B
120V/60Hz

Legal Matters

➡ It's illegal to remove any flora or fauna from the national parks, including rocks, minerals and fossils, as well as bird eggs, plants and wildflowers.

➡ Tree bark and pine cones harbor destructive parasites such as pine beetle, so don't collect them.

➡ Hunting and firearms are not permitted in the national parks.

➡ As of October 2018, recreational use of cannabis is legal in Canada; however, Canada's national parks still have regulations governing the use of cannabis on their property. For example, individuals may use cannabis at their own registered campsite, but not during quiet hours (11pm to 7am). Use is also prohibited any time of day or night in campground common areas such as restrooms, cooking shelters and playgrounds. Individual municipalities may enforce additional cannabis restrictions. For example, the towns of Banff and Jasper prohibit the use of cannabis on public property, while Waterton and Lake Louise have no such controls in place. For a list of current regulations, see www.pc.gc.ca/en/voyage-travel/regles-rules/cannabis.

LGBTIQ+ Travelers

Attitudes towards LGBTIQ+ travelers are generally very open and friendly in the national parks. Banff and Jasper in particular welcome LGBTIQ+ travelers with rainbow flags and prominent traffic crosswalks painted in rainbow colors, and Jasper holds a four-day Pride festival (www.jasperpride.ca) in April each year. Canada legalized same-sex marriage in 2005, and Montana did the same in 2014.

Maps

For the Canadian parks, the best topographical maps are produced by Gem Trek Publishing (www.gemtrek.com). Maps range in scale from 1:35,000 to 1:100,000 and cover Banff and Mt Assiniboine, Jasper and Maligne Lake, Waterton Lakes, Lake Louise and Yoho, Bow Lake and Saskatchewan River Crossing, the Columbia Icefield, Canmore and Kananaskis Country.

All major trails and points of interest are clearly marked on the maps, which are waterproof and tear-proof (although in practice they'll only take so much punishment). They're available everywhere, including from retail stores, bookstores, grocery stores and many gas stations.

National Geographic's *Trails Illustrated* series offers topographical, waterproof, tear-proof maps of Glacier and Waterton Lakes (the smaller maps within this series that only cover a region such as Two Medicine Valley are recommended because they include water hazards), while the United States Geological Survey (USGS) publishes a 1:100,000 topographical map for Glacier National Park.

Map Art Publishing (www.mapart.com) produces a range of road maps covering the Canadian Rockies.

Note that Lonely Planet's maps aren't intended for serious backcountry hikes; we highly recommend you purchase one of the options above.

Money

Canada

Banks and ATMs are fairly widespread in the main townsites, and you'll find branches of at least one major bank (CIBC, ATB, Scotiabank or Bank of Montreal) in Jasper, Banff, Canmore and other park gateway towns.

INTERNATIONAL VISITORS

Entering the US & Canada by Air

➡ Visitors from 54 countries, including the US, most European Union nations, the UK, Australia and New Zealand do not require a visa to enter Canada. However, with the exception of US citizens, all visa-exempt foreign nationals arriving by air need to apply for an eTA (electronic travel authorization). For details, visit www.canada.ca/en/immigration-refugees-citizenship/services/visit-canada/eta/apply. You are usually permitted to remain in Canada for six months, after which you will have to apply for an extension to your stay.

➡ Visitors arriving in the US from the UK, Australia, New Zealand, Chile, Japan, Singapore, South Korea, Taiwan and most European Union nations qualify for entry under the Visa Waiver Program. This will qualify you to remain in the US for a stay of up to 90 days. Citizens of the 38 countries in the US Visa Waiver Program need to register with the government online (www.cbp.gov/travel/international-visitors/esta); apply at least 72 hours in advance (notification is usually immediate and registration is valid for two years).

➡ Citizens of other countries will need to apply for a visitor's visa from either the Immigration and Citizenship Service Canada (www.canada.ca/en/immigration-refugees-citizenship/services/visit-canada) or the US Citizenship and Immigration Services (www.uscis.gov), or apply directly to the embassy or consulate in their own country.

➡ There's a comprehensive list of Canadian consular offices at www.cic.gc.ca/english/information/offices/apply-where.asp and of US embassies at http://travel.state.gov/content/travel/en/us-visas/visa-information-resources/list-of-posts.html.

Entering the US & Canada via the Land Border

Most US-based visitors heading for Canada cross via the land border, either by train, bus or, more likely, by car. With thousands of people crossing the border on a daily basis it's one of the busiest land borders in the world and, unsurprisingly, queues at some points of entry can be horrendously long. You can get the heads-up on the likely delays at specific checkpoints by searching for 'current border wait times' at the Canada Border Services Agency website (www.cbsa-asfc.gc.ca).

At the checkpoint, you'll need to present your passport, plus driver's license, insurance and registration if you're arriving by car. Note that if you're bringing a rental car across the border, you might have to have this cleared with the rental company beforehand, and you may be asked to present your rental agreement to border officials for inspection. If you're on public transportation, you will generally have to disembark and carry your own luggage across the border.

Be prepared to answer standard questions from border guards about the purpose of your visit, length of stay and any items you're intending to bring across the border.

ATMs can also be found at many gas stations and supermarkets, at Samson Mall in Lake Louise Village and at Saskatchewan Crossing on the Icefields Pkwy. For exchange services in Waterton, head to **Tamarack Outdoor Outfitters** (Map p226; ☑403-859-2378; www.hikewaterton.com; 214 Mt View Rd; ⊙8am-8pm May-Sep). The closest banks are in Cardston and Pincher Creek.

➡ Cards affiliated with the Cirrus or Maestro networks can be used to withdraw cash from ATMs bearing these logos, but fees can be high.

➡ Visa and MasterCard are accepted practically everywhere; American Express is slightly less widely accepted.

➡ Prices for almost everything in Canada are quoted without GST.

USA

In Glacier, the nearest banks are in Columbia Falls and Browning. West Glacier, East Glacier and St Mary have 24-hour ATMs, as do Many Glacier Hotel, Swiftcurrent Motor Inn, Rising Sun Motor Inn, Lake McDonald Lodge and the camp store at Eddie's Cafe in Apgar Village.

➡ Credit cards are widely accepted.

➡ There's no sales tax in Montana.

➡ For Glacier visitors crossing over to Waterton, bear in mind that most Canadian businesses accept US currency, but don't bother to calculate the exchange rate, which means you lose out.

➡ Canadian currency is not widely accepted in Glacier.

Opening Hours

Opening hours noted in reviews are for high season. Low-season hours may be reduced, or businesses may close altogether.

Shops 9am to 5:30pm, although grocery and convenience stores, tourist services, gift shops, cafes and chain stores often open later

Banks 9am to 5:30pm Monday to Friday

Restaurants From around 7am to 10:30am for breakfast, 11am to 3pm for lunch and 5pm to 10pm for dinner

Bars From 4pm onwards to around midnight or later

Post

Mail services are much the same as in the national parks as in the rest of the US and Canada, although it can take longer for letters to arrive in winter, when heavy snow sometimes causes delays. Banff, Jasper, Waterton and Glacier all have large, efficient post offices, while you'll find smaller branches in most gateway towns.

Public Holidays

Both Canada and the US observe a number of national holidays, when most shops, visitor attractions and services shut or operate on limited hours, and banks, schools and post offices are all closed.

Canada
New Year's Day January 1

Good Friday March/April

Easter Monday First Monday after Good Friday

Victoria Day Monday preceding May 25

Canada Day July 1

Labour Day First Monday in September

Thanksgiving Day Second Monday in October

Remembrance Day November 11

Christmas Day December 25

Boxing Day December 26

USA
New Year's Day January 1

Martin Luther King Day Third Monday in January

President's Day Third Monday in February

Memorial Day Last Monday in May

Independence Day July 4

Labor Day First Monday in September

Columbus Day Second Monday in October

Veterans' Day November 11

Thanksgiving Day Fourth Thursday in November

Christmas Day December 25

Telephone
Cell Phones
➡ Canadian and US cell-phone networks are generally compatible. If you're bringing a phone from abroad, check that it works with the cell phone systems in the US and Canada.

➡ Most networks provide sporadic coverage in and around the entrances to Glacier National Park, and good coverage in Banff and Jasper Towns.

➡ Service is nonexistent in remote areas including backcountry trails and the Icefields Pkwy.

➡ Verizon offers the best service in the US; Telus, Bell and Rogers have the best service in Canada.

➡ Make sure your plan covers the country you're in; if not, a temporary pay-as-you-go SIM card is the best way to avoid expensive roaming charges.

Pay Phones
You'll still find a few pay phones in remote areas without cell service.

Phone Codes
Area codes are denoted by the first three digits of phone numbers (eg 403 or 780 in Alberta, 406 in Montana). If you're outside the area code, you'll need to dial it along with the relevant phone number.

Other commonly used codes include 1 which is the International prefix, used for calling the US and Canada from abroad; and 800, 888, 877, 866 etc which are common toll-free prefixes

Time
Alberta, Montana and parts of eastern British Columbia are in the Mountain Time zone, one hour ahead of Pacific Time (used by the US West Coast and western parts of British Columbia), one hour behind Central Time, two hours behind Eastern Time (the US East Coast) and seven hours behind GMT (Greenwich Mean Time).

Alberta, British Columbia and Montana all observe daylight-saving time between the second Sunday in March and the first Sunday in November. The clocks are put forward one hour during this period so nightfall is later.

Toilets
➡ Free public toilets are common in the major townsites, at tourist

PRACTICALITIES

Newspapers The most widely read dailies in Alberta are the *Calgary Herald* (www.cal garyherald.com) and *Edmonton Journal* (www.edmontonjournal.com), plus the *Calgary Sun* (www.calgarysun.com) and *Edmonton Sun* (www.edmontonsun.com) tabloids. Regional news sources include the historic *Crag & Canyon* (www.thecragandcanyon.com) and the *Rocky Mountain Outlook* (www.rmoutlook.com). In Montana pick up the *Whitefish Pilot* (www.whitefishpilot.com) and *Daily Inter Lake* (www.dailyinterlake.com).

Radio The nationwide Canadian Broadcasting Company (CBC) is the main radio service in Canada, although reception is patchy across the parks; try 96.3FM for CBC Radio One in Banff and 98.1FM in Jasper. The volunteer-run Banff Park Radio is on 101.1FM. In Montana KJJR (880AM) has news and talk, while KNMC (90.1FM) is a college station with some National Public Radio programming.

Taxes A goods and services tax (GST) of 5% is added to most goods in Alberta and British Columbia. Montana has no sales tax.

Weights & Measures Distances in Canada are quoted in kilometers, with elevations in meters. In the US it's miles and feet. Both countries quote weights in imperial pounds.

---

attractions and visitor centers.

➜ You'll find pit toilets (outhouses) at most trailheads and backcountry campsites.

Tourist Information

For general information on the national parks, visit the websites of Parks Canada (www.pc.gc.ca) and the US National Park Service (www. nps.gov). Local tourism websites in places like Banff-Lake Louise (www.banfflakelouise. com) and Waterton Lakes (www.mywaterton.ca) are also helpful.

For more specific information, park visitor-center staff tend to be hugely knowledgeable, and can provide handouts on practically every imaginable activity in the park. All the provincial parks have their own visitor centers.

Volunteering

Many organizations volunteer their efforts to ensure the continuing welfare of the parks. Among the best known are **Friends of Jasper** (www.friendsofjasper.com), **Friends of Kootenay** (www. friendsofkootenay.ca) and the **Parks Canada volunteer program** (www.pc.gc.ca/en/ agence-agency/benevolat -volunteering). These organizations undertake everything from administrative work and fundraising to trail maintenance, and are often looking for volunteers to help with current programs.

Banff Volunteer Program (www.pc.gc.ca/pn-np/ab/banff/ activ/benevole-volunteer) Parks Canada offers park-wide volunteer opportunities, ranging from campground hosting to trail repairs to removal of litter and invasive weeds. Need is greatest between April and October. See the website for application forms and further details.

Alberta Institute for Wildlife Conservation (☑403-946-2361; www.aiwc. ca; Madden) Wildlife charity that helps protect native species through animal rehabilitation, habitat protection and volunteer training.

American Hiking Society (☑800-972-8608; www. americanhiking.org) A national advocacy organization that arranges volunteering 'vacations' to maintain hiking trails.

Glacier National Park Associates (www.gnvpa.org) Volunteer group that tackles projects such as trail maintenance, building preservation and habitat regeneration.

Glacier Institute (☑406-755-1211; www.glacierinstitute. org; Apgar Village) The Glacier Institute, founded in 1983, offers one-/two-/three-day/week-long workshops, youth camps and courses year-round from US$65 to US$1125 on subjects from wildflowers to fly fishing.

Transportation

GETTING THERE & AWAY

Air

Airports & Airlines

BANFF & JASPER NATIONAL PARKS

➡ Calgary (www.yyc.com) and Edmonton (www.flyeia.com) are the closest international airports to Banff and Jasper respectively.

➡ It's feasible to fly into Vancouver (www.yvr.ca), but you'll have a long drive – it's 859km (534 miles) to Banff and 807km (501 miles) to Jasper.

➡ Air Canada (www.aircanada.com) and WestJet (www.westjet.com) cover the majority of Canadian routes, and connect through Montreal and Toronto to many European destinations.

➡ US-based airlines, including United (www.united.com), American (www.aa.com), Alaska Airlines (www.alaskaair.com) and Delta (www.delta.com) connect through major American cities.

➡ British Airways (www.ba.com) mainly serves London Heathrow.

GLACIER NATIONAL PARK

Glacier's only nearby airport is Glacier Park International Airport (www.iflyglacier.com), halfway between Whitefish and Kalispell. It's served by Delta (www.delta.com), American (www.aa.com), Alaska Airlines (www.alaskaair.com) and United (www.united.com). Year-round destinations include Salt Lake City, Minneapolis, Denver and Seattle, plus seasonal flights to Chicago and Atlanta.

Glacier Park International Airport (FCA; ☏406-257-5994; www.iflyglacier.com; 4170 Hwy 2 East, Kalispell; ☞) Glacier's most convenient airport is between Kalispell and Whitefish, MT, and approximately 26 miles from the park's West Entrance. It has year-round service to Salt Lake, Minneapolis, Denver, Seattle and Las Vegas, and seasonal service to Atlanta, Oakland, LA, Chicago and Portland.

Great Falls International Airport (GTF; www.flygtf.com) Located 140 miles from East Glacier.

Missoula International Airport (MSO; ☏406-728-4381; www.flymissoula.com; 5225 Hwy 10 W) Missoula International Airport, 5 miles west of Missoula, serves Salt Lake City, Denver, Phoenix, LA, San Francisco, Portland, Seattle and Minneapolis, among others. Seasonal service to Atlanta and Chicago.

WATERTON LAKES NATIONAL PARK

The closest airport to Waterton Lakes, 129km (80 miles) to the northeast, is Lethbridge Airport (www.lethbridgeairport.ca). It's served by Air Canada (www.aircanada.com) and WestJet (www.westjet.com), but the limited flight schedule usually means it's more convenient (and cheaper) to fly into Calgary, 266km (165 miles) north of Waterton.

Bus

Banff & Jasper National Parks

AIRPORT SHUTTLES

There are a number of shuttles from Calgary International Airport to Banff, with the **Banff Airporter** (www.banffairporter.com) and **Brewster Express** (www.banffjaspercollection.com/brewster-express) providing the most frequent service.

Sundog Tours (www.sundogtours.com) offers similar service from Edmonton's airport to Jasper Town.

PUBLIC BUSES

At the time of research, **Greyhound** (www.greyhound.ca) had discontinued its long-haul routes in western Canada, leaving Banff and Jasper with no dependable bus service to Vancouver or other Canadian cities.

Glacier & Waterton Lakes National Parks

AIRPORT SHUTTLES

Public transport from Glacier Park International Airport (www.iflyglacier.com) is limited; the airport website maintains a list of companies offering shuttle and taxi service.

From Calgary, **Airport Shuttle Express** (☑403-509-4799; www.airportshuttle express.com; from C$85) runs scheduled bus and van transfers to Waterton Lakes and Glacier in summer, plus year-round chartered sedans and vans along the same route.

Car & Motorcycle

Major Routes

BANFF & JASPER NATIONAL PARKS

There are various road routes into the parks.

➡ Trans-Canada Hwy (Hwy 1) runs from Calgary to Canmore, Banff and Lake Louise, before continuing west into Yoho National Park.

➡ Hwy 93 – known as the Icefields Pkwy in its 230km northern section between Jasper and Lake Louise – merges with the Trans-Canada Hwy for 30km between Lake Louise and Castle Junction, then branches south to Kootenay National Park and Radium Hot Springs.

➡ Hwy 11 heads west from Red Deer and enters Banff National Park on the Icefields Pkwy, just south of the border with Jasper.

➡ To reach Jasper from Edmonton, take Hwy 16 west.

GLACIER & WATERTON LAKES NATIONAL PARKS

The west side of Glacier is most easily reached from Whitefish, Kalispell and Flathead Lake; the east side is closer to Great Falls and Helena. West Glacier and East Glacier are connected by US 2, below the southern boundary of the park.

If you're traveling north into Waterton Lakes, you'll have to cross the border on the eastern side of Glacier (the crossing north of Polebridge in the northwest has been closed for decades), passing through customs en route. You'll need two forms of ID (driver's license and passport are standard).

Port of Piegan/Carway
(☑in Canada 403-653-3009, in US 406-732-5572; ☺7am-11pm) On Trans-Canada Hwy 2 (US Hwy 89); open year-round.

Car Rentals

The vast majority of people visiting the parks rent a car. It's the most convenient way to travel, allowing you to explore at your own pace and visit even the most remote sights, though you have to factor in fuel costs, traffic and breakdown.

All the major car-rental agencies have branches at the main airports and townsites. Airport branches generally stay open from around 6am to midnight; town branches keep regular business hours.

➡ Booking online will get the best rates, but check carefully for hidden extras such as high excess, mileage

caps, limits on interstate travel and GST. Most deals these days include unlimited mileage.

➡ One-way rentals will incur a 'drop fee,' the price of which varies depending on the vehicle and how far you're taking it.

➡ Airport rentals charge a different tax rate, so it's worth checking equivalent rates with town branches (such as in Banff and Canmore); it can work out cheaper for long rentals, even with the one-way drop fee.

➡ Think about whether you need Collision Damage Waiver (CDW); you may be covered by your own auto or travel insurance, or by your credit-card company if you use the card to pay for the rental.

➡ If considering doing any off-roading or merely getting off the major arteries, a 4WD or at least a vehicle with high clearance is recommended.

Recreational Vehicles & Campervan Rentals

Cruising the parks in a recreational vehicle (RV) or camper van has many advantages – you won't incur hotel bills, you can cook your own meals and you can experience a taste of the outdoors without having to rough it too much.

There are drawbacks, though: RVs in particular are big, unwieldy, heavy on fuel, and slow, and can be difficult to maneuver if you're

---

CLIMATE CHANGE & TRAVEL

Every form of transport that relies on carbon-based fuel generates CO_2, the main cause of human-induced climate change. Modern travel is dependent on airplanes, which might use less fuel per kilometer per person than most cars but travel much greater distances. The altitude at which aircraft emit gases (including CO_2) and particles also contributes to their climate change impact. Many websites offer 'carbon calculators' that allow people to estimate the carbon emissions generated by their journey and, for those who wish to do so, to offset the impact of the greenhouse gases emitted with contributions to portfolios of climate-friendly initiatives throughout the world. Lonely Planet offsets the carbon footprint of all staff and author travel.

not used to driving a large vehicle. Camper vans offer a more nimble alternative.

➡ Make sure you get a full rundown on the vehicle before you leave the rental agency.

➡ Check that the campground you're staying at has spaces suitable for RVs.

➡ Rates spike in peak season. Deals are often available at other times.

➡ Rental agencies often get booked out in summer, so reserve well ahead.

➡ Mileage is nearly always extra to the quoted rental rates.

Popular rental agencies include Cruise America (www.cruiseamerica.com) and CanaDream (www. canadream.com).

CanaDream (☑888-480-9726, international calls 925-255-8383; www.canadream. com) Rents truck campers, campervans and motor homes from locations in Calgary, Edmonton and various other places. Prices start at around C$200 per day for a small, economy RV. Discounts may be available online.

Cruise Canada (☑403-291-4963; www.cruisecanada.com) Rents three sizes of RV from locations in Calgary and Vancouver. Rates start at around C$240 to C$330 per night depending on the size of the vehicle. Three-night minimum rental.

Train
Banff National Park
The only passenger rail service to Banff and Lake Louise is the luxury-priced Rocky Mountaineer tourist train.

Rocky Mountaineer Rail Tours (☑877-460-3200; www. rockymountaineer.com; 2-day tours from C$1665; ☺May-Oct) Scenic train trips through the Rockies, Banff and Jasper. Most of the travel is done during daylight hours, and prices include park passes, hotel accommodations and day trips.

Jasper National Park
VIA trains (www.viarail.com) serve Jasper from Vancouver, Edmonton and Toronto. Amtrak serves Glacier with its transcontinental *Empire Builder* service.

Mainline intercity trains operated by **VIA Rail** (☑888-842-7245; www.viarail.com) stop in Jasper twice or thrice weekly on their way between Vancouver, Edmonton and Toronto. You can connect to this route from other US and Canadian cities. Sample advance-purchase fares from Jasper:

TO	ONE WAY (C$)	TIME (HR)
Edmonton	97	6¼
Saskatoon	128	17½
Vancouver	148	23½
Winnipeg	197	32½
Toronto	367	72

Glacier & Waterton Lakes National Parks
Amtrak (www.amtrak.com) operates the cross-country *Empire Builder* line from Seattle to Chicago, serving stations in East Glacier, West Glacier and Whitefish.

Eastbound trains run in the early morning; westbound trains travel through in the early evening. There are ticket offices at East Glacier and Whitefish, but you'll have to prebook or buy on board from West Glacier.

Fares start around US$7.50 from Whitefish to West Glacier (30 minutes), US$16 from Whitefish to East Glacier (two hours), and US$16 from East Glacier to West Glacier (1½ hours). Long-haul base fares from West Glacier include Seattle (US$102, 15 hours) and Chicago (US$177, 31 hours).

GETTING AROUND

Most visitors travel by car or camper van (brought from home or rented). Getting around the parks without your own vehicle can be challenging, but is not impossible.

Car & Motorcycle All of the parks are accessible on clearly signposted, well-maintained roads. Rental vehicles are available at townsites including Banff, Jasper and Whitefish.

Bus Glacier has an excellent free park shuttle linking most of the trailheads (summer only). In Canada, buses connect Banff with Lake Louise and Jasper. Public transportation elsewhere is limited to taxis and commercial shuttle buses.

Bicycle Cycling in Glacier is limited to main highways like Going-to-the-Sun Rd. In the Canadian parks, off-road cycling is also possible.

Bicycle
Cycling is a popular and eco-friendly way of getting around the parks, especially in and around the main townsites. Further afield, the distances between sights are long and better suited to serious long-distance cycle touring.

➡ Bikes are readily available for rent in Banff, Jasper, Glacier and Waterton. Prices start around C$10 (US$8) per hour or C$35 (US$27) per day.

➡ Bikes are banned on all trails (but not roads) in Glacier.

➡ In the Canadian parks, some trails are open to cyclists without restrictions, while others such as Banff's Sundance Canyon and Redearth trails are only partially open to cyclists; in the latter case, bike racks are generally provided at the junction where the trail switches from mixed use to hikers only.

➡ Banff and Jasper have several excellent paved long-distance cycling routes, including the Legacy Trail between Banff and Canmore, the Bow Valley

Pkwy between Banff and Lake Louise and the Icefields Pkwy between Jasper and Lake Louise.

Bus

Getting around by bus in the parks is possible, but takes some planning.

Banff to Jasper

One daily public bus, operated by Brewster Express (www.banffjaspercollection.com/brewster-express) in summer and Sundog Tours (www.sundogtours.com) in winter, connects Banff and Jasper towns via the Icefields Pkwy.

Banff National Park

Banff has an excellent and ever-expanding public bus system known as **Roam** (☑403-762-0606; www.roamtransit.com; Canmore to Banff adult/child C$6/3). All routes travel via Banff Ave, and serve destinations including the Banff Gondola and Hot Springs, Tunnel Mountain campgrounds, Lake Minnewanka, Cave and Basin Historic Site and the Banff Centre, as well as further-flung destinations such as Canmore, Johnston Canyon and Lake Louise.

Free summer and winter shuttle buses carry skiers and hikers from Banff to the Sunshine and Norquay ski areas; similar services run between Lake Louise village and the Lake Louise gondola.

White Mountain Adventures (☑403-760-4403; www.whitemountainadventures.com; 137 Eagle Cres; excursions from C$79; ☺8am-5pm Mon-Fri) runs a regular shuttle from the Mt Shark trailhead for hikers returning from Mt Assiniboine. To get to other trailheads, you'll have to drive or organize your own transport with a local taxi company.

Jasper National Park

Public transit in Jasper is fairly limited. Free or low-cost shuttles run from Jasper Town to the Jasper Tramway and Maligne Canyon, while the **Maligne Valley Hikers Express Shuttle** (Map p158; ☑780-852-3331; www.maligneadventures.com; one way adult/child C$35/17.50; ☺late Jun-late Sep) travels from Jasper townsite to Maligne Lake.

Glacier National Park

Glacier is the easiest park to get around by bus.

Free park shuttle buses ferry visitors between spots on the Going-to-the-Sun Rd, which means all of the park's major trailheads (bar those in the remote North Fork area) are well served by public transportation from July 1 to Labor Day. Service in 23-seater buses between the Apgar Visitor Center (via Apgar Village) for all westside stops leaves every 30 minutes from 9am to 5:45pm. For non-stop service to Logan Pass, several smaller buses leave in the morning between 7am and 7:30am (the last bus returns from Logan Pass at 7pm). To continue on down to the St Mary Visitor Center you have to transfer to another bus. The buses have air-conditioning, are wheelchair accessible and run on biodiesel. Most of the shuttles have bike racks. Clear route maps are provided at every shuttle stop or can be viewed on the park website at www.nps.gov/glac.

On the park's eastern side, Pursuit runs the East Side Shuttle (US$15 to US$30 depending on distance, reservable up to 24 hours in advance) between Glacier Park Lodge, Two Medicine and St Mary Lodge, while Xanterra runs its own first-come, first-served shuttle (adult US$6 to US$10, child US$3 to US$5) connecting Many Glacier Hotel and the Swiftcurrent Motor Inn with the St Mary Visitor Center. All

shuttles run from early June to mid-/late September.

In addition, Glacier's signature red 'Jammer' buses (www.glaciernationalparklodges.com/red-bus-tours) ferry passengers throughout the park on regularly scheduled tours. These serve the east side of the park from early June to late September, and the west side from mid-May through mid-October.

Car & Motorcycle

Automobile Associations

The **Alberta Motor Association** (☑403-240-5300; https://ama.ab.ca; 4700 17th Ave SW) is the province's main motoring organization and is affiliated with the Canadian Automobile Association (CAA). It can help with queries on driving in Alberta, as well as arrange breakdown cover and insurance for members; members also sometimes qualify for special rates on hotels and other services.

The **American Automobile Association** (www.aaa.com) is the US equivalent, and offers a similar range of services. There are other branches in Missoula, Great Falls and Bozeman.

Driver's License

➔ Foreign driver's licenses can be used in Alberta for up to three months. International driver's licenses can be used for up to 12 months.

➔ It's required that you carry your license and vehicle registration at all times.

Fuel & Spare Parts

➔ Gas is readily available in the main townsites, but make sure you fill your tank before setting out on a driving tour, especially if traveling the 230km-long Icefields Pkwy.

➔ There are gas stations at Castle Mountain and Saskatchewan Crossing in

Banff, but prices are much more expensive here.

➡ There are no gas stations within Glacier National Park itself.

➡ Most car-rental companies provide breakdown cover as part of the rental package.

➡ If you're driving your own vehicle, it's worth joining one of the major breakdown agencies to avoid getting stranded or paying a fortune for a tow.

Road Conditions

Most of the main roads are well maintained, although minor roads to trailheads and mountains are often steep, narrow and winding, making them nasty driving for RVs.

➡ Some roads (such as the Smith-Dorrien/Spray Trail Rd from Canmore into Kananaskis) are unsealed, so take extra care when driving on them.

➡ Ice and snow are frequent hazards in winter, so be prepared if you're driving during the colder months.

➡ Accidents involving trains and automobiles are one of the major causes of animal fatalities in the mountain parks. Wildlife can appear suddenly, and bolt across the road when scared, so slow down and be alert.

➡ Some road passes (such as the Highwood Pass in Kananaskis and Logan Pass on Going-to-the-Sun Rd in Glacier) are closed in winter due to snow.

➡ For up-to-date road conditions and closure information check out http://home.nps.gov/applications/glac/roadstatus/roadstatus.cfm for Glacier, www.pc.gc.ca/en/pn-np/ab/banff/visit/parkbus/routes-roads for Banff, and www.pc.gc.ca/

en/pn-np/ab/jasper/visit/routessaisonnieres-seasonalroad for Jasper.

Driving in Winter

Driving around in winter in any of the parks can be dangerous, but especially so in the Canadian parks, which are blanketed by snow and ice for well over six months of the year. Whiteouts are not uncommon and several roads (including the Icefields Pkwy) are closed during mid-winter or periods of heavy snow – check ahead with the parks offices and keep abreast of local news and traffic bulletins. The iconic Going-to-the-Sun Rd in Glacier is plowed in winter only between the West Glacier entrance at Apgar and Lake McDonald Lodge.

In Banff and Jasper, it's legally required that you have snow tires or carry chains on all roads in winter except the main Trans-Canada Hwy 1 (obviously it's also worth knowing how to fit them). Car-rental agencies should provide these if you're renting from them in winter, although you might be charged extra.

Winter travelers should also carry a small emergency supply kit, including antifreeze, blankets, water, flashlight, snow shovel, matches and emergency food supplies. A cell phone can come in handy if you need to phone for an emergency tow, though bear in mind that service gets very spotty in parts of the Rockies. Top up antifreeze, transmission, brake and windshield-washer fluids.

Be especially careful of invisible patches of ice on the road, especially once the temperature drops at night. Use your gears rather than

your brakes to slow down (look for the 'L' or 'Low' gear if you're driving an automatic). Slamming on your brakes will only increase your chances of skidding.

Road Rules

In Canada and the US, driving is on the right. You are legally required to wear a seatbelt at all times, and headlights must be turned on when visibility is restricted to 150m (500ft) or less. Motorcyclists are required to wear helmets and drive with headlights on.

One rule that often confuses overseas drivers is that it's legal to turn right on a stoplight (as long as there is no traffic coming from the left). At four-way stop junctions, drivers should pause and allow the first vehicle that stopped to pull away first.

Hitchhiking

Hitching is never entirely safe in any country, and we don't recommend it. Travelers who decide to hitch should understand that they are taking a small but potentially serious risk. That said, thumbing a lift is an option in the mountain parks, although you might find you're waiting on the highway for quite a while before anyone stops.

As always, take the usual precautions: hitch with a friend if possible and avoid hitching in remote areas after dark.

At trailheads you can sometimes hook up with other returning hikers who have their own transport. A smile and a positive attitude go a long way. Many hostels in Banff and Jasper also have ride boards where you can seek a lift.

Behind the Scenes

SEND US YOUR FEEDBACK

We love to hear from travelers – your comments keep us on our toes and help make our books better. Our well-traveled team reads every word on what you loved or loathed about this book. Although we cannot reply individually to your submissions, we always guarantee that your feedback goes straight to the appropriate authors, in time for the next edition. Each person who sends us information is thanked in the next edition – the most useful submissions are rewarded with a selection of digital PDF chapters.

Visit **lonelyplanet.com/contact** to submit your updates and suggestions or to ask for help. Our award-winning website also features inspirational travel stories, news and discussions.

Note: We may edit, reproduce and incorporate your comments in Lonely Planet products such as guidebooks, websites and digital products, so let us know if you don't want your comments reproduced or your name acknowledged. For a copy of our privacy policy visit lonelyplanet.com/privacy.

WRITER THANKS

Gregor Clark

Heartfelt thanks to all of the kind Albertans and fellow travelers who shared their love and knowledge of Banff and Jasper – especially Karina Birch, Kate Williams, Ken Wood, Paul Krywicki, Erin Wilkinson, Ed and Vanessa, Shauna and Lindsay. Thanks also to the family and friends who helped me explore Banff and Jasper's trails: Chloe, Sophie, Wes and Ted, that means you! Couldn't have asked for a more delightful research crew.

Michael Grosberg

Many thanks to all those who shared their experiences, knowledge and deep passion for Glacier, Whitefish and Waterton including Brian Schott, Greg Fortin, Riley Polumbus, Rhonda Fitzgerald, Chris Schustrom, Cricket Butler, BJ Elzinga, Marc Ducharme, Michelle Gaudet, Kimmy Walt, Angel Esperanueva and Monica Jungster. And to Carly, Rosie, Willa and Boone for keeping in touch while in the wilderness.

Craig McLachlan

A hearty thanks to all those who helped out on the road, but most of all, to my exceptionally beautiful wife, Yuriko, who maintained semi-control of my craft beer intake.

ACKNOWLEDGEMENTS

Climate map data adapted from Peel MC, Finlayson BL & McMahon TA (2007) 'Updated World Map of the Köppen-Geiger Climate Classification', *Hydrology and Earth System Sciences*, 11, 1633–44.

Cover photograph: Moraine Lake at sunrise, Banff National Park, Matteo Colombo/AWL Images ©

THIS BOOK

This 5th edition of Lonely Planet's *Banff, Jasper & Glacier National Parks* guidebook was curated by Gregor Clark, and researched and written by Gregor, Michael Grosberg and Craig McLachlan. The previous edition was written by Michael and Brendan Sainsbury and the 3rd edition by Brendan and Oliver Berry. This guidebook was produced by the following:

Destination Editor
Ben Buckner

Senior Product Editors
Grace Dobell, Martine Power, Saralinda Turner

Regional Senior Cartographer Corey Hutchison

Product Editor Katie Connolly

Book Designer Fergal Condon

Assisting Editors Victoria Harrison, Lou McGregor, Christopher Pitts, Maja Vatrić, Simon Williamson

Cartographer David Connolly

Cover Researcher
Naomi Parker

Thanks to April Arnatt, Andrea Cadieux, Hannah Cartmel, Javier Chan, Samuel Mason, Joan Ng, Martin Pratt, Vicky Smith, Stephanie Yates

Index

Map Legend

Sights
- Beach
- Bird Sanctuary
- Buddhist
- Castle/Palace
- Christian
- Confucian
- Hindu
- Islamic
- Jain
- Jewish
- Monument
- Museum/Gallery/Historic Building
- Ruin
- Shinto
- Sikh
- Taoist
- Winery/Vineyard
- Zoo/Wildlife Sanctuary
- Other Sight

Activities, Courses & Tours
- Bodysurfing
- Diving
- Canoeing/Kayaking
- Course/Tour
- Sento Hot Baths/Onsen
- Skiing
- Snorkeling
- Surfing
- Swimming/Pool
- Walking
- Windsurfing
- Other Activity

Sleeping
- Sleeping
- Camping
- Hut/Shelter

Eating
- Eating

Drinking & Nightlife
- Drinking & Nightlife
- Cafe

Entertainment
- Entertainment

Shopping
- Shopping

Information
- Bank
- Embassy/Consulate
- Hospital/Medical
- Internet
- Police
- Post Office
- Telephone
- Toilet
- Tourist Information
- Other Information

Geographic
- Beach
- Gate
- Hut/Shelter
- Lighthouse
- Lookout
- Mountain/Volcano
- Oasis
- Park
- Pass
- Picnic Area
- Waterfall

Population
- Capital (National)
- Capital (State/Province)
- City/Large Town
- Town/Village

Transport
- Airport
- BART station
- Border crossing
- Boston T station
- Bus
- Cable car/Funicular
- Cycling
- Ferry
- Metro/Muni station
- Monorail
- Parking
- Petrol station
- Subway/SkyTrain station
- Taxi
- Train station/Railway
- Tram
- Underground station
- Other Transport

Routes
- Tollway
- Freeway
- Primary
- Secondary
- Tertiary
- Lane
- Unsealed road
- Road under construction
- Plaza/Mall
- Steps
- Tunnel
- Pedestrian overpass
- Walking Tour
- Walking Tour detour
- Path/Walking Trail

Boundaries
- International
- State/Province
- Disputed
- Regional/Suburb
- Marine Park
- Cliff
- Wall

Hydrography
- River, Creek
- Intermittent River
- Canal
- Water
- Dry/Salt/Intermittent Lake
- Reef

Areas
- Airport/Runway
- Beach/Desert
- Cemetery (Christian)
- Cemetery (Other)
- Glacier
- Mudflat
- Park/Forest
- Sight (Building)
- Sportsground
- Swamp/Mangrove

Note: Not all symbols displayed above appear on the maps in this book

OUR STORY

A beat-up old car, a few dollars in the pocket and a sense of adventure. In 1972 that's all Tony and Maureen Wheeler needed for the trip of a lifetime – across Europe and Asia overland to Australia. It took several months, and at the end – broke but inspired – they sat at their kitchen table writing and stapling together their first travel guide, *Across Asia on the Cheap*. Within a week they'd sold 1500 copies. Lonely Planet was born.

Today, Lonely Planet has offices in Franklin, London, Melbourne, Oakland, Dublin, Beijing and Delhi, with more than 600 staff and writers. We share Tony's belief that 'a great guidebook should do three things: inform, educate and amuse'.

OUR WRITERS

Gregor Clark

Banff National Park, Jasper National Park, Waterton Lakes National Park Gregor is a US-based writer whose love of foreign languages and curiosity about what's around the next bend have taken him to dozens of countries on five continents. Chronic wanderlust has also led him to visit all 50 states and most Canadian provinces on countless road trips through his native North America. Since 2000, Gregor has regularly contributed to Lonely Planet guides, with a focus on Europe and the Americas. Titles include *Italy, France, Brazil, Costa Rica, Argentina, Portugal, Switzerland, Mexico, Montréal & Québec City, France's Best Trips, New England's Best Trips*, cycling guides to Italy and California and coffee-table pictorials such as *Food Trails*, the *USA Book* and the *Lonely Planet Guide to the Middle of Nowhere*. Gregor was born in New York City. He has lived in California, France, Spain and Italy prior to settling with his wife and two daughters in his current home state of Vermont. Gregor also wrote the Plan Your Trip, Understand and Survival Guide chapters.

Michael Grosberg

Glacier National Park Michael has worked on over 50 Lonely Planet guidebooks. Other international work has included development on Rota in the western Pacific; investigating and writing about political violence and training newly elected government representatives in South Africa; and teaching in Quito, Ecuador. He has received a Masters in Comparative Literature and has taught literature and writing as an adjunct professor.

Craig McLachlan

Golden, Kootenay National Park, Yoho National Park Craig has covered destinations all over the globe for Lonely Planet for two decades. Based in Queenstown, New Zealand for half the year, he runs an outdoor activities company and a sake brewery, then moonlights overseas for the other half, leading tours and writing for Lonely Planet. Craig has completed a number of adventures in Japan and his books are available on Amazon. Describing himself as a 'freelance anything', Craig has an MBA from the University of Hawai'i and is also a Japanese interpreter, pilot, hiking guide, tour leader, karate instructor, marriage celebrant and budding novelist. Check out www.craigmclachlan.com.

Published by Lonely Planet Global Limited
CRN 554153
5th edition – Apr 2020
ISBN 978 1 78657 592 0
© Lonely Planet 2020   Photographs © as indicated 2020
10 9 8 7 6 5 4 3 2 1
Printed in China